Social Foundations of Education

Third Edition

RICHARD D. VAN SCOTTER
Colorado Springs, Colorado

JOHN D. HAAS
RICHARD J. KRAFT
JAMES C. SCHOTT
Boulder, Colorado

Prentice Hall, Englewood Cliffs, New Jersey 07632

Library of Congress Cataloging-in-Publication Data

Social foundations of education / Richard D. Van Scotter ... [et al.].
  -- 3rd ed.
      p.   cm.
  Includes bibliographical references.
  ISBN 0-13-816992-6
  1. Educational sociology. 2. Educational sociology--United
States. 3. Education--Social aspects. 4. Education--Social
aspects--United States. 5. Education--Philosophy.   I. Van Scotter,
Richard D.
LC189.S6684 1991
370.19--dc20   90-35476
                                                          CIP

Previously published under the title
Foundations of Education: Social Perspectives.

Editorial/production supervision: Mary McDonald
Interior design: Karen Buck
Cover design: Wanda Lubelska Design
Manufacturing buyer: Robert Anderson

 © 1991, 1985, 1979 by Prentice-Hall, Inc.
A Division of Simon & Schuster
Englewood Cliffs, New Jersey 07632

Printed in the United States of America

10 9 8 7 6 5 4 3 2 1

ISBN 0-13-816992-6

Prentice-Hall International (UK) Limited, *London*
Prentice-Hall of Australia Pty. Limited, *Sydney*
Prentice-Hall Canada Inc., *Toronto*
Prentice-Hall Hispanoamericana, S.A., *Mexico*
Prentice-Hall of India Private Limited, *New Delhi*
Prentice-Hall of Japan, Inc., *Tokyo*
Simon & Schuster Asia Pte. Ltd., *Singapore*
Editora Prentice-Hall do Brasil, Ltda., *Rio de Janeiro*

Contents

Preface   ix

About the Authors   xiii

PART I   Life in Classrooms and Schools

1. **The Professional Teacher**   1

   Is Teaching a Profession?   1
   The Art of Teaching   3
   Behind the Classroom Door   10
   Professional Organizations for Teachers   12
   The Legal Rights of Teachers   15
   The Legal Rights of Students   17
   Case Study: Intellectual Freedom   19
   Thought Questions   20
   Practical Activities   21
   Bibliography   22

2. **Contemporary Issues Facing Educators**   24

   The School as a Crucible   24
   The Need for Hard Heads and Soft Hearts   27
   The Conflict in Education   30
   Knowledge Worth Knowing   41
   School Reform in Focus   48
   Public Schools at the Precipice   54
   Case Study: Remaking the Curriculum   57
   Thought Questions   58
   Practical Activities   58
   Bibliography   59

PART II   Values in Education

3. **Philosophies of Education**   61

   Philosophy Matters   61
   Relationship of Philosophy to Education   63
   What Is Philosophy?   65
   Idealism, Realism, and Pragmatism   69
   Philosophies of Education   71
   Existentialism   77
   A Personal Philosophy of Education   79
   Case Study: Education in the Stone Age   81
   Thought Questions   81
   Practical Activities   82
   Bibliography   82

4. **Values in Society and School**   84

   The American Creed   85
   Values in the Schools   87
   Moral Education   94
   Values in Conflict   96
   Case Study: School Holidays   101
   Thought Questions   102
   Practical Activities   102
   Bibliography   104

PART III   School and Society

5. **Sociological Perspectives**   105

   The Nature of a Society   105
   Relationship of Society, Education, and Schools   106
   Socialization, Education, and Schools   106
   The Social Functions of Schools   108
   Influences on Children and Adolescents   113
   Multiple Domains of Education   119
   Configurations of Learning   120
   Education and Social Change   122
   A Marxist Perspective   122
   Case Study: Reporting Student Achievement   125
   Thought Questions   125
   Practical Activities   126
   Bibliography   127

6. **The Structure and Politics of Education   129**

A Definition of Politics   130
Educational and Political Linkages   131
Political Influences on Education   131
Educational Influences on Politics   135
The Structure of Schooling   137
The Federal Government and Education   140
State Governments and Education   142
The Local District   144
Battlegrounds in Educational Politics   146
Case Study: Changing School Organization   149
Case Study: Academic Freedom   150
Thought Questions   150
Practical Activities   151
Bibliography   152

7. **Economics of Education   153**

The Economic System and Education in America   156
People as Producers   163
Some Discrepant Findings   168
The Human Side of Global Competitiveness   171
Quality of Educational Opportunity: A Special Problem in Financing
    Schools   172
School Finance Reform   178
Reducing the Burden on Schools   182
Case Study: Equalization of Educational Opportunity   182
Thought Questions   183
Practical Activities   184
Bibliography   184

PART IV Education in a Pluralistic Society

8. **Race, Equality, Ethnicity, and Education   186**

Ethnicity   187
Historical Overview   188
Melting Pot: Assimilation and Acculturation   194
Prejudice   195
The Schools   199
Cultural Pluralism   209
Case Study: The Newly Integrated School System   210
Thought Questions   210
Practical Activities   211
Bibliography   212

9. Gender and Education   213

Socialization and Gender Identity   213
Sex Discrimination, Sex Stereotyping, Sex Bias, Sexism   215
History of Patriarchy   217
Sex Discrimination in Schools and the Law   218
Schools and Sex Role Socialization   220
Women in Higher Education   226
Case Study: The Nonsexist Classroom   229
Thought Questions   230
Practical Activities   230
Bibliography   231

10. Alternative Schooling   233

A Perspective on Alternative Schools   234
Open Schools   239
Magnet Schools: A Pedagogical Alternative   242
Decentralization: A Political Alternative   243
Educational Vouchers: An Economic Alternative   244
Public Schools of Choice   245
Evaluation of Alternatives   246
Clarifying the Rationale   249
Home Study   250
The Future of Alternatives   251
Case Study: Alternative Schools   252
Thought Questions   252
Practical Activities   253
Bibliography   254

PART V   Historical and Global Dimensions

11. The History of American Education   256

Education of the Young in Colonial America   257
In Quest of a Nation of Literate and Educated Citizens   259
Extending Universal Schooling Upward and Outward   265
The Progressive Mood in Education   268
The Illusion of Educational Reform   271
A Mirror for Society   273
A Return to Traditional Values   276
Prospects for Institutionalized Pluralism   278

Case Study: Home Schooling   279
Thought Questions   280
Practical Activities   281
Bibliography   282

12. **Education from an International Perspective   284**

Dimensions of the Problem   284
Education and Economic Development   285
Political and Anthropological Models   287
Comparing the Incomparable   290
Educational Models   291
A Critique of World Education   302
The Interdependence of People and Nations   303
Case Study: Equity and Excellence   304
Thought Questions   304
Practical Activities   305
Bibliography   306

13. **Futures: Societal and Educational   307**

Orientations to the Future   308
Three Types of Futurists   308
Educational Futures   322
Three Perspectives on Educational Futures   322
Case Study: A Problem in Space Travel   337
Thought Questions   338
Practical Activities   339
Bibliography   341

Index   343

Preface

Social Foundations of Education is intended for undergraduate students who are prepared for a serious examination of educational ideas, concepts, and issues, or for graduate students beginning their study in education. For students who are social science majors, *Social Foundations* should be helpful in relating the threads of information and knowledge they have acquired in these subjects. For the student who has little preparation in this area, the text will serve as an introduction to the subject. This book also will be informative to students who are not planning on a teaching career but want a foundation and framework for understanding educational issues.

END-OF-CHAPTER RESOURCES

As an introductory textbook, *Social Foundations* addresses several problems in education. In order to go beyond the traditional classroom treatment of these issues, we have concluded each chapter with *Practical Activities* and a *Case Study*. Each end-of-chapter section also contains *Thought Questions* and a *Bibliography*. The Practical Activities and Case Studies add an innovative and reportorial dimension to this book that we believe is important in the preparation of future teachers.

Judging from the testimony of our students, the Case Studies and Practical Activities are among the most valuable parts of the courses we teach. Professors who have used earlier editions of this text also indicate that these are useful, even intriguing, teaching resources. The Case Studies can be used in class either at the beginning of an area of study, at the end of the area, or with each chapter. They also serve as a change of pace for both students and professors. We recommend them for short, two-to-three-page typewritten analyses.

The Case Studies don't take students into schools and the community, but they do help bring the reality of issues into college classrooms. The Practical Activities, however, are designed to engage students in educational matters outside the college campus. Students will observe public school classrooms, interview teachers and administrators, talk with students, teach short lessons, poll parents, conduct community studies, and have other eye-opening, educational experiences.

School personnel welcome the involvement of prospective teachers, often commenting that they, too, learn much from the encounters.

The Thought Questions and Bibliographies can inspire sound thinking on issues and topics developed in a chapter. Answers to Thought Questions are not likely to be found directly in a chapter; rather, teachers and students examine the questions by applying their personal experiences to information in the book and other sources.

CHAPTER CONTENT

This third edition of *Social Foundations* is divided into five sections: I—Life in Classrooms and Schools, II—Values in Education, III—School and Society, IV—Education in a Pluralistic Society, and V—Historical and Global Dimensions. In each chapter we have attempted to present the fundamental ideas and understandings related to the topic. In addition, many chapters include a position on the subject or central issue. These positions represent our perspective on the topic, which is a nice way of saying that our points of view are evident throughout the text.

We believe that schools today are part of a web of institutions and organizations in our society that for the most part preserve the status quo and protect those in power. Most proposals to restructure schools, as appealing as some are, don't address this fundamental effect. We do believe the function of schools in our society needs to be more clearly understood and the purpose of schools more narrowly focused. We take the schools as they are—bureaucratic, traditional, rule oriented, evaluative—and look for slippage in the system. We believe there is room in school systems and individual schools to bring about significant changes in curriculum, administrative organization, student rights, and teachers' professionalism, among other areas.

Every chapter in this third edition has been revised to reflect the changing conditions in American education, characterized by heated debate, during this closing era of the twentieth century. A few chapters have been extensively revised. Chapter 2, for example, was completely rewritten to examine the reform agendas of the 1980s and 1990s, and to offer what we intend to be an insightful synthesis. Likewise, we expanded Chapter 13 to provide a framework to understand the future of education as America prepares to enter a new century.

PART I—LIFE IN CLASSROOMS AND SCHOOLS

In Part I we present an overview of the teaching profession (Chapter 1) and the issues faced by educators (Chapter 2). This section describes the roles, responsibilities, and lives of teachers. It also examines the impact of educational reform and recommends ways that teachers and schools can more effectively serve the educational needs of this nation.

PART II—VALUES IN EDUCATION

Part II studies crucial values in American society and education. Philosophies of education and emerging ideologies are surveyed (Chapter 3), and the role of moral issues, religious and secular, in education is examined (Chapter 4).

PART III—SCHOOL AND SOCIETY

This section focuses on the relationship of social science to the foundations of education: sociology and anthropology (Chapter 5), political science (Chapter 6), and economics (Chapter 7). This treatment represents a synthesis of ideas and concepts from various disciplines and studies their relationship to the field of education.

PART IV—EDUCATION IN A PLURALISTIC SOCIETY

In Part IV we examine crucial issues in American society and education, specifically those related to race and ethnicity (Chapter 8) and sexism (Chapter 9). Chapter 10 deals with alternatives in and to public education.

PART V—HISTORICAL AND GLOBAL DIMENSIONS

We conclude *Social Foundations* with three chapters on past and present perspectives of education in an international setting. Chapter 11 discusses the history of schooling in America and suggests future patterns of learning. Chapter 12 examines education in other countries, assessing the effects of schooling in these nations and the impact of American education. Chapter 13 views the future in terms of the effect on human lives and the shapes that schooling and education are likely to take.

About the Authors

All four authors began their education careers as secondary-school teachers in the social studies. Each specializes in and has taught in some area of social foundations and social studies education.

Richard Van Scotter was an economics teacher at Homewood-Flossmoor (Illinois) high school and a professor at Grinnell College. He is active in economics education, is the author of a high-school text on the subject, and currently serves as director of education for Junior Achievement's national office. He holds degrees from Beloit College (BA), the University of Wisconsin (MA), and the University of Colorado (PhD).

John Haas earned his bachelor's degree at Hope College, taught social studies in Michigan, and completed his PhD at the University of Michigan. After joining the University of Colorado's faculty, he directed its Experienced Teacher Fellowship Program and various summer institutes for teachers. He also writes and speaks extensively on future studies in education.

Richard Kraft is an expert on international education and has served as consultant to the education departments of Nicaragua, Ecuador, and Portugal. He has also traveled extensively in China and Africa. He received his bachelor's degree from Wheaton College and his PhD from Michigan State University. Like John Haas, he teaches at the University of Colorado.

James Schott earned his BA, MA, and PhD at the University of Colorado. He spent nine years as a secondary-school social studies teacher and later taught at the University of Wisconsin-Whitewater. He is an authority on alternative schools and is founder and director of the Boulder Community School. He also served as director of education for the Colorado Historical Society and is currently a senior staff associate at the Social Science Education Consortium in Boulder.

1

The Professional Teacher

Sometime between 6 and 8 A.M. each weekday morning about 970,000 public school teachers arrive at school. If they are late, it is rare. One of the hallmarks of the American school is that it starts and stops on time. Visit any high school and you are struck not just by the emphasis placed on punctuality, but by the way time dominates. Clocks are everywhere. Bells announce the beginning and end of each segment of the day.[1]

Teachers may start out "fighting the system," but it is much easier, ultimately, to settle down into conventional ways of teaching. And one tends to look more "normal" by doing so. The cards are stacked against innovation.[2]

The role of teacher in American culture is usually ambiguous, sometimes ridiculed, and generally misunderstood. Teachers earn somewhat below-average salaries for intensive hours of work, under conflicting and often impossible sets of expectations, in a milieu that often tends to infantilize them as well as their clients. Teachers are expected to adhere to codes, to possess impeccable credentials, and to practice to perfection the art and science of their craft.

In a nation of over 240 million people, education (teachers, students, and others) is the primary activity of some 65 million Americans, of whom almost 3.2 million persons are employed as classroom teachers and an additional 300,000 are working as superintendents, principals, supervisors, and other instructional staff members.

IS TEACHING A PROFESSION?

Everyone seems to be knowledgeable concerning life in schools, what teachers do, and what teaching is. Because teaching is so visible and lacks the mystery that surrounds other professions, people believe that virtually anyone can teach. This is

---

[1]Ernest L. Boyer, *High School: A Report on Secondary Education in America*, The Carnegie Foundation for the Advancement of Teaching (New York: Harper & Row, Publishers, Inc., 1983), p. 155.

[2]John I. Goodlad, *A Place Called School: Prospects for the Future* (New York: McGraw-Hill Book Company, Inc., 1984), p. 237.

an unfortunate fact because it discourages society from considering teaching a profession and because it tends to weaken efforts to articulate an art and science of teaching. Teaching usually is perceived as somewhere between a mere occupational group and a true profession.

> Do you remember the fine old story about two bricklayers? They were asked, "What are you doing?" One replied, "I am laying bricks." The other said, "I am building a cathedral." The first man is a tradesman, the second has the soul of an artist or professional. The difference is in the meaning of the activity. It is not in how expertly or skillfully the bricklayers daub mortar onto each brick; it is not in how much information they have about the job; it is not in their loyalty to the boss; it is not in their familiarity with other constructions. It is in how they savor and feel about what they are doing, in their sensing of relationships between their work and that of others, in their appreciation of potentialities, in their sense of form, in their need for and enjoyment of significance, in their identification of self with civilized aspirations, in their whole outlook on life.[3]

In the preceding quotation Herbert Thelen suggests that when a group of workers consider themselves a profession, they possess a number of rather vague attitudes toward their work and toward life. A more precise definition of a profession is provided by Myron Lieberman, even though he admits there is no authoritative definition and that his is a synthesis of characteristics derived from the analysis of several traditionally acknowledged professions. Lieberman claims that eight criteria define a kind of work and its practitioners as a profession.

1. A unique, definite, and essential social service is performed by the members of the group.
2. There is an emphasis on intellectual skills in the performance of the service.
3. A long period of specialized training is required of all members.
4. The group is allowed, by the society in which it exists, a broad range of autonomy for individual members and for the total group.
5. The practitioners accept extensive responsibility for judgments and behaviors performed within the scope of their special competence.
6. There is an emphasis on the service performed (rather than the economic rewards) as the basis for organization and for judging quality *within* the group.
7. Practitioners are members of a comprehensive, self-governing, and self-regulating organization.
8. A code of ethics has been formally adopted by the organization's membership, and has been clarified and interpreted at ambiguous points by concrete cases.[4]

We conclude, as do Lieberman and others, that the claim of teachers to professional status is at present only marginally warranted and that this will

[3]Herbert A. Thelen, "Professional Anyone?" in *New Perspectives on Teacher Education,* ed. Donald J. McCarthy (San Francisco: Jossey-Bass, Inc., Publishers, 1973), p. 198.
[4]Myron Lieberman, *Education as a Profession* (Englewood Cliffs, N.J.: Prentice-Hall, Inc., 1956), pp. 2–6.

probably be the case as long as we can foresee. Bureaucratization continues to force school administrators into a managerial mode and ethic and teachers into an employee/laborer role and ethic. This then reinforces teachers' fears of being treated as mere replaceable parts in a mechanical system and drives them to seek collective security in unions and unionlike organizations. Some educators resist this tendency to equate public education with the corporation model, but the trend seems unavoidable.

THE ART OF TEACHING

One who chooses the occupation *and* role of teacher, with or without credentials or portfolio, in schools and classrooms or not, appointed and paid or not, has decided to intervene with purpose in the lives of one or more human beings. These intentional acts of purposeful intervention are referred to collectively as teaching. Although a myriad of cultural, social, economic, political, psychological, organizational, historical, spatial, and environmental influences impinge pervasively on the work of teachers, we still insist that the essence of teaching is the exercise of whatever margin of freedom remains after all the external forces have exacted their toll. For us, to teach is to make decisions in an arena where the freedom to choose is severely restricted but is present in precious measure.

What it is that learners are expected to learn—the intended outcomes—is always problematical, modifiable, subject to grave risks, and constantly emerging—before, during, and after the teaching intervention—in the lives of both those who teach and those who are taught. Also, passively or actively, teacher and student are always interacting. Both are seeking satisfaction and, ideally, an even exchange of "worldly goods"; both are recipients.

Finally, a teacher imposes many of his or her values on others. To try to change another person, in whatever direction, for whatever purpose, is to assume a moral obligation.

Essential to the process of teaching, then, are (1) purposeful interventions in others' lives, (2) the exercise of a modest margin of freedom, (3) decision making in generally unpredictable contexts, (4) an interaction benefiting all participants, and

TABLE 1-1 The American Public School Teacher

The average age of a public school teacher is 42 (up from 36 in 1976).
Nine percent of all teachers are nonwhite.
Sixty-nine percent of the teaching corps are female.
Seventy-five percent of teachers are married.
Teachers are not working for the money, but to use their minds and to help children and youth.
Almost all teachers are members of a union (NEA or AFT).
Eighty percent have five or more years of higher education.
Thirty-seven percent have been teaching between 15 and 24 years.
The average salary is $25,000 per nine-month school year.

Source: C. Emily Feistritzer, *Profile of Teachers in the U.S.* (Washington, D.C.: National Center for Education Information, 1986).

(5) a moral undertaking. What, then, is required of the effective teacher? We have answered this question from our own perspective, based on many years of public school teaching and, in colleges and universities, of teaching teachers to teach.

Making Oneself a Teacher

The person who chooses to teach undertakes a lifelong process of learning how to teach. The more one teaches and learns, the more one becomes aware of how complex relationships are between teacher and student and between teaching and learning. The search for the most effective balance never stops.

Teaching involves the freedom to make decisions within the limits of particular situations. The effective use of this freedom depends on knowing the available options and their probable consequences and on a willingness to risk the results of a choice.

The classroom requires that teachers possess knowledge or skill in at least eight special areas: (1) characteristics and developmental cycles of children and adolescents; (2) ways in which people learn; (3) structure of concepts, generalizations, modes of inquiry, and models for integrating knowledge and also specialized knowledge in various academic disciplines; (4) methods of teaching; (5) cognitive, affective, and psychomotor learning objectives; (6) values and attitudes conducive to learning and to satisfying human relationships; (7) skills of communication, conflict management and reduction, human relations, and decision making; and (8) skill in integrating these seven categories with one another.

orchestra-
leader

As an interpersonal art, teaching has certain analogies to the work of the surgeon, the baseball umpire, and the potter. The surgeon learns diagnosis, surgical procedures, and pre- and postoperative care, partly from reading, listening, and observing, but mainly from working with an experienced, expert surgeon and from independent and supervised practice. Excellence in a surgeon presupposes precision, neatness, simplicity, good timing, elegance in performance, *and* the success of the surgery in terms of the patient. Some judgments of excellence are made by the surgeon's peers, some by the surgeon's patients, and all by the surgeon personally.

Baseball umpires generally are former players, as children and adolescents and often as semiprofessional or professional baseball players. The transition from player to umpire is seldom smooth and always involves "beginning over again" or "starting at the bottom." The skills of an umpire include conflict management under pressure; total recall of formal and informal rules; and most important, the ability to make judgments accurately, quickly, and assertively.

The potter begins by selecting the malleable clay, which is kneaded and pressed onto the potter's wheel and then centered as the wheel turns. Centering is "the bringing of the clay into a spinning, unwobbling pivot, which will then be free to take innumerable shapes as potter and clay press against each other—the firm, tender, sensitive pressure which yields as much as it asserts. It is like a handclasp between two living hands, receiving the greeting at the very moment they give it."[5]

[5]Mary Caroline Richards, *Centering* (Middletown, Conn.: Wesleyan University Press, 1964), p. 9.

It's a mystical experience, the satisfying feeling of having found center. As the union of hands and clay mold and change each other, they both sense when harmony prevails, when both are centered.

> A pot should this, and a pot should that—I have little patience with these prescriptions. I cannot escape paradox when I look deep into things, in the crafts as well as in poetry, in metaphysics or in physics. . . . We can't fake craft. It lies in the act. The strains we have put in the clay break open in the fire. We do not have the craft or craftsmanship, if we do not speak to the light that lives within the early materials, including men themselves.[6]

In teaching, also, this is the case: When teacher and student are centered, they both will sense and feel it—a too rare rapturous experience.

Who or What Is a Good Teacher?

Who is a good teacher? Can such a person be defined or described? Jean Grambs represents the majority viewpoint when she explains that competence is whatever people think it is. A principal's perception of the good teacher is likely to be different from a parent's perception, or a student's, or even a teacher's; and one parent will differ with another, just as will students or teachers. As she explains, "Teachers see good teachers as those who are like themselves—whatever that may be."[7] Proponents of free schools, open schools, Montessori schools, or basics schools may have a clearer conception than the general public of what good teaching is, but they certainly can't agree among their disparate groups.

In a recent Gallup poll, the qualities respondents named most often as characterizing the ideal teacher in order of mention were:

> Ability to communicate, to understand, to relate.
> Patience.
> Ability to discipline, to be firm and fair.
> High moral character.
> Friendliness, good personality, sense of humor.
> Dedication to teaching profession, enthusiasm.
> Ability to inspire, motivate students.
> Intelligence.
> Caring about students.[8]

As *Phi Delta Kappan* magazine (where the survey was reported) concluded, Americans want as a teacher "a model of perfection—someone who is understand-

[6]Ibid., pp. 11–12.

[7]Jean Dresden Grambs, *Schools, Scholars, and Society* (Englewood Cliffs, N.J.: Prentice-Hall, Inc., 1978), pp. 162–64.

[8]George H. Gallup, "The 15th Annual Gallup Poll of the Public's Attitudes Toward the Public Schools," *Phi Delta Kappan*, 65 no. 1 (Sept. 1983), p. 44. Each year *Phi Delta Kappan* reports the findings of the annual Gallup survey, which is informative reading for schoolteachers.

ing, patient, friendly, intelligent, and who has a sense of humor and high moral character." Low on the list is the ability to inspire and motivate students. Conspicuously absent are enthusiasm for the subject being taught and critical thinking skills.

Good teachers have an assortment of talents; some are superb speakers, others excellent discussion leaders, and others skillful classroom organizers. From another perspective, the competent teacher may be subject oriented, inquiry oriented, or people oriented.

Important as teachers' personalities may be, despite a half century of research, little is known for certain about what personalities are most appropriate for teaching. The study by David Ryans, however, is classic. Ryans found that effective teachers tend to be extremely generous in appraising the efforts of others, possess strong literary and artistic interests, participate in social groups, prefer nondirective classroom procedures, and employ student-centered methods. He went somewhat further in identifying three major criteria of teachers' behavior—democratic-autocratic, organized-disorganized, and stimulating-dull—that distinguish the effective from the ineffective teacher. As reported in Ryans's study, the behaviors associated with these three criteria were:

Pattern X_o—warm, understanding, friendly *versus* aloof, restricted.
Pattern Y_o—responsible, businesslike, systematic *versus* evading, unplanned, slipshod.
Pattern Z_o—stimulating, imaginative *versus* dull, routine.[9]

The Practice of Teaching

Philip Jackson, as described in *Life in Classrooms,* interviewed teachers identified as outstanding by their administrators and supervisors. From these interviews emerged four themes that describe the effective teacher. The first, *immediacy,* Jackson described as a sensitive awareness of the present situation or the "here and now." These teachers are spontaneous, particularly in responding to students' needs. The second theme, *informality,* is characterized by a lack of undue routine and an emphasis on freedom of movement and thought for students. A third theme, *autonomy,* indicates a dislike both of a prescribed, inflexible curriculum and of administration invasion of the classroom for teacher evaluation (even though these teachers presumably had the most to gain and least to lose from such evaluation). The final theme, *individuality,* highlights the good teacher's ability to be keenly aware of an individual student's progress even though confronted with an entire class.[10]

Seymour Sarason adds that from his experiences these teachers exist in very small numbers, and he poses several other important questions. How many average teachers could become significantly better with the proper training and support? Are these people a special breed, born to be top-notch teachers, or did they acquire these characteristics? Would the outstanding teacher in a suburban school also be

[9]David G. Ryans, *Characteristics of Teachers, Their Description, Comparison and Appraisal* (Washington, D.C.: American Council on Education, 1960), chap. 4.
[10]Philip W. Jackson, *Life in Classrooms* (New York: Holt, Rinehart & Winston, 1968), pp. 119–43.

considered so in an inner-city or rural school? (The same can be asked of good teachers in the other two settings.) Sarason emphatically comments that based on his observations, "characteristics of individuals are always, to some extent, a reflection of the setting in which these characteristics are manifested."[11] In the right place with sufficient support, there would be many more excellent teachers.

A Model of the Model Teacher

The good teacher can use various teaching styles and is defined differently by different people. We offer one model for identifying and developing the "desirable" teacher.

STUDENTS SPEAK OUT ON TEACHERS

"Discipline is one of the biggest problems. Most teachers are much too lenient. Part of it is the parents though. I see so many kids whose parents just say, 'He's in school and you're supposed to take care of him.'" *15-year-old sophomore, Indiana*

"Most teachers don't give enough homework, and what they do give is poor quality. There's too much busywork: Go home and answer stupid questions out of books instead of sit and write something thoughtful." *17-year-old senior, Ohio*

"My favorite teacher discusses things thoroughly; he lets the kids ask questions; he knows his subject well; he knows a lot about other subjects also; he's very helpful and he's got a sense of humor." *16-year-old senior, New York*

"An English teacher I had this year is going for her doctorate, and her own search for knowledge comes across in her teaching. Her class works a lot harder than another class where the teacher has taught the same thing year after year." *18-year-old senior, New Jersey*

"Teachers are not really fair in the way they grade. I think grades are inflated a lot. A high percentage of students at my school are on the honor roll. Teachers don't like to fail kids." *18-year-old senior, Massachusetts*

"The teachers I really liked inspired me and made me think because of their dedication and love of what they did. At least half of what I learn is through homework—figuring things out for myself—and I sometimes feel this school does not assign enough." *16-year-old sophomore, California*

"A lot of students have their minds on television. In middle-class homes, television is a constant companion. It's like clothing—it's never off. Commercial television breaks down the mental processes. It encourages apathy." *19-year-old senior, Los Angeles*

"I love my calculus teacher. Every day when we walk into class, there's a problem on the board. We try the problem; we go over it and that reinforces what you've learned." *17-year-old senior, Los Angeles*

"A teacher needs to provide discussion and explanation of the subject other than that offered by the book, particularly in history and the social sciences." *16-year-old junior, Georgia*

Source: "When Students Grade Their Teachers," *U.S. News & World Report*, 88, no. 17 (Apr. 28, 1980), pp. 71–72.

[11]Seymour B. Sarason, *The Culture of the School and the Problem of Change* (Boston: Allyn & Bacon, Inc., 1971), pp. 170–71.

This model borrows selectively from psychological and clinical theories of personality and development. Psychologists have constructed and empirically tested various models of personality development. These include Carl Rogers's "Stasis Process Continuum" (explaining how healthy individuals, that is, "fully functioning" people, have progressed from a mental state of relative rigidity to "flowingness")[12] and Abraham Maslow's "self-actualization" theory (describing the healthy or self-actualizing person as one who has satisfied the basic needs for safety, belonging, love, and respect, and is free to explore his or her capacities and talents).[13]

The traits outlined in the six clusters that follow represent a synthesis of the findings of several theorists and our personal experiences in classrooms. These clusters represent the personal needs, cognitive perspective, and emotional disposition that teachers bring to the classroom. Our model is sequential, with an inner logic, and with each successive stage building on the preceding one. Despite the possible negative aspects of some clusters, there are positive qualities to all; each has an appropriate place in the classroom. Nevertheless, we believe that the sequence from cluster 1 to cluster 6 is hierarchical: Each successive cluster is potentially more educative.

Cluster-1 teachers prefer teacher-directed learning and can be described as *authority centered.* They have internalized the traditional institutional norms of the school and are prepared to fill roles that reinforce those norms. They believe that basic skills and essential knowledge should be taught before other curriculum subjects can be considered. The classrooms of these teachers are extraordinarily disciplined environments; exactness, punctuality, orderliness, and predictability are highly valued. These teachers approve of punitive measures and use testing and grading for both evaluative and disciplinary reasons. In addition, they demand respect for and are deferential to status and authority.

Cluster-1 teachers may be remembered by their students either favorably or unfavorably. Their classroom precision, clarity, and discipline, along with their personal candor, can be impressive. Students often feel that these teachers have given them substantive and very valuable learning. However, students may conclude that learning was greatly inhibited by the authoritarian posture or lack of spontaneity, divergence, and freedom.

Cluster-2 teachers are *guardian centered,* though they resemble the authority-centered teacher. They tend to be traditional teachers with a respect for well-behaved classes, prescribed curriculum, and the accepted norms of school and society. They also prefer teacher-directed classes, in which students assume a receptive learning role, and have little tolerance for exploratory learning. Their curriculum is designed around basic skills and established content.

[12]Carl R. Rogers, *On Becoming a Person* (Boston: Houghton Mifflin Company, 1961). Another important source particularly applicable to the teacher is Carl R. Rogers, *Freedom to Learn* (Columbus, Ohio: Charles E. Merrill Publishing Company, 1969).

[13]Abraham H. Maslow, *Motivation and Personality,* 2nd ed. (New York: Harper & Row, Publishers, Inc., 1970); and Abraham H. Maslow, *Toward a Psychology of Being,* 2nd ed. (New York: Van Nostrand Reinhold Company, 1968).

Cluster-2 teachers, however, are mild mannered, virtuous, and considerate. They tend to be protective of children's welfare and to display a concern for learning. This concern is not necessarily in response to individual students' needs but rather to the socially prescribed behavior that students ought to acquire.

Cluster-3 teachers are tradition oriented, but in an intellectual and academic fashion. They are accepting of school norms, supportive of traditional curriculum and methods, and intellectually skeptical of modern or nontraditional curricula as well as many extracurricular activities. These teachers proudly fulfill the role of a dispenser of wisdom, truth, and knowledge and are essentially *content centered.*

Cluster-3 teachers prefer rational processes emphasizing reflection and analysis. Noticeably absent is the ability or willingness to evoke intuitive leaps, hunches, or imagination, divergent thought patterns, and feelings, and to deal with student-initiated concerns. Although their thinking is more differentiated and integrated than that of cluster-1 and cluster-2 representatives, they are likely to rely on traditional academic sources of authority.

Cluster-4 teachers exhibit interest in individual students' needs; still, they are best described as *self centered.* They are eager to deal with the interests of students, often creating imaginatively arranged and displayed classrooms. Like their cluster-3 counterparts, they tend to be more abstract, less dogmatic, and less evaluative than representatives of the first two clusters. Unlike cluster-3 teachers, they practice more "progressive" teaching strategies.

Their behavior is usually empathetic and responsive, resulting from a desire for interpersonal harmony and mutual dependency. The cluster-4 teacher is skilled at orchestrating and controlling the classroom environment by means of social engineering and interpersonal manipulation. Outwardly, what appears to be an informal, student-centered classroom is likely to be under the subtle control of the teacher. This teacher fits very closely to the conceptual personality of O. J. Harvey's system-3 individual.[14] As Harvey found, this teacher's classroom techniques are often in conflict with the exploratory, autonomous needs of students and are apt to result in disharmony and rejection. Only with those students who require the same interpersonal dependency and reinforcement is a harmonious symbiosis achieved.

Cluster-5 teachers are essentially *task centered*; they are ambitious, efficient, and productive classroom managers. Duty in this cluster is defined in terms of contractual obligations or mutually agreeable ground rules, and education is expected to be carried out in an expedient, rational way. More than representatives of previous clusters, the cluster-5 teacher is flexible, tolerant of ambiguity, and can withstand uncertainty, largely because the process is within his or her control.

Cluster-5 teachers are the "most likely to succeed." They tend to be the most respected members of the public school faculties, though they may be envied, despised, or both because of their ambition, productiveness, and determined leadership. They also tend to advance to more powerful positions, such as depart-

[14]Several articles by Harvey and his associates describe his belief systems. Among these we suggest O. J. Harvey, "Belief and Behaviors: Some Implications for Education," *The Science Teacher,* 37, no. 9 (Dec. 1970).

TABLE 1-2 Teacher Behavior Clusters

CLASSROOM ORIENTATION	PERSONALITY DESCRIPTORS
1. Authority centered	rule oriented, disciplined, authoritarian, traditional, strong willed, conforming to institutional norms
2. Guardian centered	rule oriented, mild mannered, orderly, virtuous, low ambiguity threshold, conforming to prescribed social roles
3. Content centered	tradition oriented, scholarly, academic, analytic, conforming to accepted educational norms
4. Self centered	approval oriented, progressive, creative, dependent, manipulative, needing strong interdependent relations
5. Task centered	job oriented, analytical, resourceful, achieving, pragmatic, productive, emphasizing contractual relations
6. Goal centered	individual oriented, democratic, imaginative, independent, autonomous, integrative, rational, expressive, guided by internal standards

ment heads, district staff members, principals, superintendents, presidents of educational associations, leaders in teacher unions, state department of education officers, and members of university faculties. These educators have a deep respect for logic, empirical evidence, expertise, cooperation, and organizational planning.

Cluster-6 teachers can be called *goal centered* in the sense that they are motivated by ideals, conscience, and universal principles such as individual freedom, justice, and human dignity. These teachers are willing to act on such principles despite unfavorable odds and personal risk, and in other ways will pursue their goals in a persistent, open, and tactful manner. Like cluster-5 teachers, they are abstract, flexible, democratic, innovative, self-secure, and able to understand the viewpoints of others. They are also productive by almost any definition, but particularly in view of Erich Fromm's idea of spontaneous (in contrast to compulsive) and creative work. Unlike cluster-5 individuals, they are more committed to personal ideals and more clearly recognize the inseparability of emotions and intellect in learning. Cluster-6 teachers tend to use many informational sources in devising their teaching approaches, though the final product is distinctly original. More than any other teachers, they have a set of internal standards independent of external criteria, sometimes coinciding with social norms and sometimes not.

Cluster-6 exemplifies an intellectually and emotionally integrated person. This functioning is variously described as abstract and integrative, committed to idealization, appealing to universal principles, self-actualizing (Maslow), fully functioning (Rogers), open, expressive, introspective, conscientious, and so on.

BEHIND THE CLASSROOM DOOR

In the late 1960s John Goodlad and his colleagues conducted a study of the administrative and curricular reforms from the so-called education decade (1957–67). Among other things, Goodlad found that teachers are very much alone in their work. Principals, for the most part, remain in their offices offering little pedagogical or moral support, and fellow teachers stay in their respective class-rooms. Teachers, Goodlad explains, feel isolated in their classrooms without support from someone who knows about their work, is sympathetic to it, and wants to help.[15]

During the 1970s and then the 1980s, teachers increasingly confronted other problems: overflowing classes, disruptive students, vandalism and violence, deteriorating school buildings, inadequate salaries, demanding parents, and declining public respect. "The joy of teaching," as Willard McQuire said in addressing a convention of the National Education Association, "is being replaced by fear, insecurity, anxiety and, ultimately, teacher dropouts." *Teacher burnout,* a familiar term to describe the physical and emotional stress afflicting many teachers, is a condition all teachers must confront at some time.

Contrary to public opinion, teaching is not a soft job. The working day and year are shorter than in most other occupations, but the time spent in the classroom can be very intense. The stress of teaching is not unlike that of a surgeon or trial lawyer at work. The job has become more difficult in modern society as teachers face students who are exposed to spectacular media (television, films, videos, popular magazines), loud and sensational music, drugs, and sex. Many students lack the discipline to listen, interact, and study.

[Teaching is much like a love affair; it does not run smoothly. There are highs and lows, good years and bad, good classes and bad. Facing adversity is inevitable, but burning out is not. The first step in dealing with fatigue and sagging morale is to seek change] Don't accept the status quo. Many avenues to rejuvenation exist.

> Try new learning approaches: group work, student reports, independent study, contracts, simulations and games, and field study outside the classroom.
>
> Hold students responsible for understanding a concept, theory, reading, experiment, or procedure, and have them present it to other students.
>
> Change texts, or discard the text and use other materials.
>
> Expand your outside reading from fiction to contemporary issues, and enliven your subject with anecdotes and messages from the literature.
>
> Propose to your department chairperson or principal that the school send you to a state or national education conference. See what other teachers are doing, bring a report to fellow teachers, and try the new ideas.
>
> Write an article for a local newspaper on an educational issue or topic of personal interest, and work with the editor, if necessary, to sharpen it for publication. Many teachers have become newspaper columnists.
>
> Work out an exchange program with another school at home or abroad.
>
> Apply for a sabbatical or leave of absence, and work with a private business.

In another major study some twenty years after his earlier research, Goodlad found that the "circumstances of teaching" had changed little. Teachers were

---

[15]John I. Goodlad and M. Frances Klein, *Behind the Classroom Door* (Worthington, Ohio: Charles A. Jones Publishing Company, 1970), pp. 12–19, 94–99.

isolated in their efforts to enrich classroom learning and gain little from staff development, inservice classes, and college courses. When confronted with the daily demands of class management, most sacrifice innovative practices for more controlling traditional approaches.[16]

Teaching can be a lonely profession, but teachers have much to learn from each other. Compare ideas with respected teachers, visit their classrooms, and try some of their techniques with your classes.

PROFESSIONAL ORGANIZATIONS FOR TEACHERS

A teacher is eligible to become a member of several professional organizations. An array of national, state, and local organizations compete with each other for members. Further, each of the national organizations has an affiliated state group, and some even have local affiliates.

The two most powerful teachers' professional organizations are the American Federation of Teachers (AFT) and the National Education Association (NEA). Both groups have made great strides in the past two decades in achieving economic gains for American teachers. They became effective agents in collective bargaining sessions with local school boards, and they used their political power to influence state and federal politics. But so far these organizations have been unable to do much about giving teachers control of their working conditions or control of the curriculum, or, perhaps most significantly, control over who enters the profession, who is retained after a probationary period, and who is expelled for incompetency.

Organizations of educators appear to provide their members one or several, but seldom all, of the following benefits:

1. The political leverage of a pressure group, and sometimes of a full- or part-time lobbyist.
2. The group solidarity of a union, committed to the dual tools of collective bargaining and the threat or reality of withholding services, and employing expert contract negotiators.
3. Publications, such as scholarly-theoretical and practical-trendy yearbooks, journals, bulletins, and newsletters.
4. The collegiality of local, state, and national conferences, workshops, and meetings.
5. Preferred-buyer status for purchasing insurance, professional books, and even appliances and automobiles.
6. A reserve fund to employ legal counsel for members in cases involving academic freedom, illegal strikes, and other education-related suits.
7. Free or inexpensive professional consultation to school districts, usually from the national level to a state unit or from the state level to a local unit.

Only the AFT and the NEA, and their respective affiliates, offer all seven benefits, in varying degrees.

[16]Goodlad, *A Place Called School,* pp. 186–93.

The Battle for Control of the Profession

Since about 1960 teachers' organizations have become militant, outspoken, and politically active, especially the two prominent national professional unions — the AFT and the NEA. At first the more militant but smaller group, the AFT, pushed teachers toward unionization, whereas the more conservative NEA deplored such an outrageous departure from the tenets of professionalism. As the AFT began to make inroads into NEA membership, however, the NEA changed its political stance and began to support collective bargaining, bargaining-agent elections in school districts, imposition of statewide or nationwide sanctions on school districts opposing or violating negotiated contracts, and even strikes (euphemistically termed withdrawal or withholding of services). Even after 1967, when the NEA accepted in principle and practice the procedures and strategies of the trade union movement, it continued to claim to be a "professional association." We consider, however, that both the NEA and the AFT are unions *and* professional organizations.

FIGURE 1-1   Estimated Supply of New Teacher Graduates and Estimated Total Demand for Additional Teachers

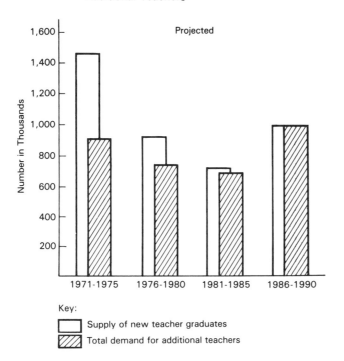

Key:

☐ Supply of new teacher graduates

▨ Total demand for additional teachers

Source: The Conditions of Education, 1983 (Washington, D.C.: National Center for Educational Statistics, 1983), p. 183.

The state-level education associations are probably the strongest link in the NEA's national-state-local chain. In particular, as political pressure groups, the NEA's state education association affiliates have been highly successful in influencing state legislatures and state boards and departments of education. It's at this level that teachers have won significant victories and exerted crucial leverage. The victories include, among others, the passage of tenure and collective-bargaining acts; the leverage has been used to increase the public schools' appropriations and to endorse and supply campaign funds for gubernatorial and state legislature candidates.

The most heated competition between the AFT and NEA, especially in large urban and suburban school districts, occurs at the local level. What is at stake are dues-paying members and the right (determined by special elections) to become the *exclusive* bargaining agent for *all* of a district's teachers, regardless of organization membership.

The AFT is the younger and smaller of the national teachers' organizations. From its inception, the AFT at all levels has been an integral part of the American labor union movement and a member affiliate of the American Federation of Labor and Congress of Industrial Organizations (AFL/CIO).

The AFT has had its greatest successes in urban school districts and in states where organized labor in general has had its greatest impact. Although only about one-fourth the size of the NEA, the AFT membership tends to concentrate in large and moderate-sized cities, where internal unity, combined with solidarity with the rest of the AFL/CIO unions, has yielded pioneering gains in negotiated contracts. In addition to its organizing efforts and its fight for state and federal legislation to recognize the rights of teachers to negotiate, bargain collectively, and strike (which are now also NEA goals), the AFT seeks to strengthen state tenure laws, to eliminate classroom overcrowding by lowering pupil-teacher ratios, to eliminate excessive class interruptions, to guarantee by law free and unencumbered lunch periods for teachers, to improve teachers' pensions and fringe benefits (for example, paid hospitalization and medical insurance), and to achieve as many as possible of these improvements as parts of legislation or negotiated contracts without the use of the last resort—a strike.

During the 1960s there was furious competition between the AFT and the NEA for members and in the bargaining-agent elections. The most visible signs of this conflict were in school districts in the larger cities such as New York and Detroit. Actual strikes, rather than mere threats, began to occur. By 1968 it was clear that the union movement had been successfully expanded to include America's teachers, and that the relative successes of the union strategies employed by the AFT had led to the conversion of the NEA to a union. In fact, by the early 1970s two to four times more strikes were called by NEA affiliates than by AFT locals.

Also, by 1968 it was becoming obvious that the goals, policies, and practices of the two unions were rapidly converging and that merger in the long run was probably inevitable. Just as the paths to convergence were paved with bitterness

TABLE 1-3   Principal Reasons Selected by All Teachers for Deciding to Become a Teacher, 1971–1981 (percent)

REASON	1971	1976	1981
1	2	3	4
Desire to work with young people	71.8	71.4	69.6
Interest in subject-matter field	34.5	38.3	44.1
Value or significance of education in society	37.1	38.3	44.1
Influence of a teacher in elementary or secondary school	17.9	20.6	25.4
Long summer vacation	14.4	19.1	21.5
Influence of family	29.5	18.4	21.5
Job security	16.2	17.4	20.6
Never really considered anything else	17.4	17.4	20.3
Opportunity for a lifetime of self-growth	21.4	17.4	13.1

Source: Education Week, Mar. 10, 1982.

and hostility, however, so the roads to merger thus far have been cluttered with obstacles. Today, the NEA–AFT rivalry continues unabated, possibly awaiting a more favorable climate and more conciliatory leaders.

THE LEGAL RIGHTS OF TEACHERS

As citizens of the United States, both teachers and students have legal rights. Their rights as citizens are enumerated in the U.S. Constitution (especially in the Bill of Rights) and in the state constitutions. As citizens *and* as teachers, they have the rights and responsibilities specified in federal and state statutory law; in school district policies and regulations; and in local, state, and federal case law.

In the same way that parents emphasize their children's responsibilities rather than their rights, school boards, school administrators, parents of students, and other citizens have tended to emphasize teachers' responsibilities and to limit their rights. Ironically, teachers tend to treat their charges similarly.

For all teachers to be able to enjoy their civil and professional rights, some, really only a few, must test these rights in practice or in legal cases in order to establish precedents. In fact, well-publicized cases make visible to all parties some specific aspect of a teacher's rights. In a court case, both the decision itself and its "educative" value are essential to the continuous defining of teachers' rights.

A considerable body of case law relates to teachers' civil rights. These cases cover a broad range of controversy involving teachers' actions both as teachers and as citizens. Louis Fischer and David Schimmel have provided a succinct set of conclusions regarding teachers' civil rights. These are presented here, under the topical headings used by these authors.[17]

[17]Louis Fischer and David Schimmel, *The Civil Rights of Teachers* (New York: Harper & Row, Publishers, Inc., 1973), pp. 146-61.

Freedom of Expression

Twentieth-century court decisions have tended to remove restrictions on teachers' freedom to speak out on controversial issues, both in school and away from school. A distinction is still drawn, however, between in-school expression (somewhat restricted) and out-of-school expression (very few restrictions). In general, when teachers are not at work, they enjoy the same First Amendment guarantees as any private citizen. While in school, the teacher is protected by the concept of academic freedom, *but within limits.* The limits are determined by the extent to which statements, methods, or materials "can be shown [to be] irrelevant to her [or his] teaching objective, inappropriate to the age and maturity of . . . students, or disruptive of school discipline."

The Teacher as a Person

No longer are teachers expected to "be paragons of virtue twenty-four hours a day." A teacher is autonomous in his or her values, concept of morality, leisure activities, and personal appearance. In general, "the rights of teachers to pursue a normal life consistent with others in the community receives legal protection." Here again there are exceptions, such as a teacher's immoral conduct with students or the general crime of contributing to the delinquency of a minor.

Loyalty and Freedom

This topic deals with cases that are focused on "loyalty oaths for teachers, membership in controversial organizations, [teachers'] political activities, and membership in teacher organizations." Except for "overly broad or vague" oaths, the courts have upheld the swearing to and signing of loyalty oaths, to state and/or nation, as a condition of public school employment. Other than in the case where a teacher subscribes to the *illegal* goals of an organization, there can be no restrictions on teachers' rights to join any organization. With respect to teachers' political activities, "the judicial trend will probably reflect the recent holding that a teacher can be barred from political activity only if it materially and substantially interferes with the operation of the school." Although in some states strikes and other coercive measures may be illegal, "the right of teachers to organize and to bargain collectively is clearly established."

Arbitrary Action, Discrimination, and Fair Procedures

As agents of a state, school board members and administrators are delegated the power to make decisions for schools under their jurisdiction. This is discretionary power, which can be abused, and sometimes is, especially in policies and actions affecting teachers and students. If the abuse involves the "arbitrary, unreasonable, or discriminatory" use of discretionary power, the courts will find these decisions and actions to be illegal. If discrimination is involved, it is typically by race, sex, religion, or nationality.

Teachers are also protected by state tenure laws, which allow dismissal or disciplinary action only under rare circumstances, and then only when fair procedures have been scrupulously followed. The only resort for untenured, probationary teachers (usually teachers employed one, two, or three years in a given district), however, are the conditions expressly stipulated in their one-year contracts. Their employment may be terminated at the end of any school year without notification of cause and without a hearing.

The preceding generalizations are valid but are not guarantees that practice in every instance will conform to them. Further, the courts, in honoring the concept of separation of powers at the state and federal levels, will refuse to hear cases involving purely educational decisions. Their rule is "Educational matters are for educators to decide."

THE LEGAL RIGHTS OF STUDENTS

Students, like teachers, historically have been exhorted ceaselessly to meet their responsibilities but are seldom informed of their rights. This section on student rights is included in a chapter about the teacher as professional because we believe that, along with parents, teachers should be the chief advocates and defenders of children and youth, and also that schools should be places where the young do not have to pay too dearly for their mistakes. Further, a primary responsibility of teachers is the care and nurture of students.

As with teachers' rights, students' rights are most clearly defined and affirmed in case law dealing with complaints brought against teachers and school officials by students, their parents, or their legal guardians. In order to avoid the lengthy explanation of numerous precedent-setting court cases, we again rely on the work of Schimmel and Fischer to summarize the relevant case law regarding students' civil rights.[18]

Freedom of Speech

For students as for teachers, a distinction exists between freedom of expression *in* school and *away from* school. "As a general rule, students who are *away from school* have the same freedom to speak as anyone else. The *Tinker* case established that their right to speak *inside* the schools is also constitutionally protected." Only if the actual speech or symbolic statement (for example, wearing armbands as a form of social protest) disrupts school operations may school officials curtail students' freedom of speech *in school*.

[18]David Schimmel and Louis Fischer, *The Civil Rights of Students* (New York: Harper & Row, Publishers, Inc., 1975), pp. 264–84.

Freedom of the Press

For this topic, again the *Tinker* case is applicable. The courts will tolerate "restrictions only to prevent substantial or material interference with school activities or the rights of others." The burden of proof for the potential disruptiveness of an article or issue of a paper is on school officials. Also, the courts have been ambivalent on the issue of "prior restraint," which is a form of press censorship prior to publication and distribution of a document. Further, student publications must refrain from the use of obscenity, especially because their readership is mainly composed of minors.

Freedom of Association

This right has been considered by the courts as an *implied* constitutional freedom. The courts have considered it to guarantee within *reasonably* prescribed limits public school students' rights "to organize and use school facilities . . . [and] to protest and demonstrate." Case law, however, has upheld state statutes that prohibit minors (but not "adults") from forming or joining such organizations as fraternities, sororities, and secret clubs. The courts have held "that schools may bar all outside speakers," but that if speakers are allowed to speak in the schools of a district, school officials may not permit only those with whom they agree or are sympathetic with to come in and exclude all others.

Freedom of Religion

The First Amendment to the Constitution prohibits the official establishment of any religion by the nation or any state. This prohibition has been interpreted by the Supreme Court to mean that a "wall of separation" must be maintained between church and state. In education, this interpretation has come to mean that religion should be kept separate from public education. The two exceptions have been to permit students "released time" to receive religious instruction and to allow teachers, usually in social studies classes, to teach *about* world religions.

The Supreme Court declared in 1962 that Bible reading and prayers are unconstitutional in the public schools, and also made it clear that such activities are illegal, whether required or optional. This applies only to public schools.

A significant case involving Amish children successfully challenged Wisconsin's compulsory attendance laws, but the decision emphasized the uniqueness of the Amish community and the inability to separate religious and secular aspects of the Amish way of life.

Personal Appearance

Students' personal appearance is a school issue, particularly with respect to standards of grooming and clothing. Although most applicable court cases have held that personal grooming is a private matter, some have upheld various school rules concerning hair lengths and styles. Concerning choice of clothing, "most courts hold there is no such constitutional right" for students. Because dress codes apply only during school hours, courts have upheld the legality of these codes when they are "reasonable and related to educational goals."

Due Process

Although "today courts generally hold that students have a right to due process before serious punishment, such as expulsion or long-term suspension, can be imposed," court decisions have upheld corporal punishment *in loco parentis.*

The Family Educational Rights and Privacy Act of 1974 has contributed significantly to the civil rights of students and their parents. This act is designed to counter the abuses of unfair or exploitative uses of data collected by schools about individual students and their families. Specifically, it provides that persons who are subjects of data systems must be informed of such systems and the data on them as individuals; that they must be assured the data are used only for the purposes intended when they were collected; that students or their parents or guardians must be able to see the records and be able to correct them; and that they must be assured that the persons responsible for data or record systems take reasonable precautions to prevent misuse of data and personal information. Another provision ensures that the schools neither disclose information about their students nor permit inspection of students' records without permission from the student or the student's parents or guardian.

●——————————————————————————————————————●

Case Study: Intellectual Freedom

You have assigned a book to your class that you realize may be controversial. You know it is regarded as a good piece of literature, fits in well with the course and age group, and is currently being used by other public schools in the country. Class discussions have been very spirited but thoughtful and mature. The students appear to be learning more from their study of this work than they would be from most other books.

As a precaution you informed your principal that you have chosen this book, gave her your reasons, and left a copy for her review. It is now a couple of weeks later, and the principal asks you to withdraw the book from your reading list, explaining that she has received pressure from a group of parents. A school board member has also suggested that the principal look into the matter. A few students in your class indicated that some of the material was upsetting to them, but they were hesitant to claim that as a whole the book didn't have sound educational value.

What should you do? When a teacher's values conflict with those of some members of the community, whose should prevail? Should parents, students, and the community have any say in curricular matters? If so, how much?

Thought Questions

1. What do you consider the essential criteria for deciding whether teaching is or isn't a profession? Examine Lieberman's eight criteria and decide if you would include or exclude each one on your own list of criteria.
2. Evaluate each of the following aspects of a teacher-preparation program for its potential usefulness for the practicing classroom teacher:

    Knowledge of the characteristics of children and adolescents and their developmental cycles.

    Knowledge of theories about and kinds of human learning.

    Knowledge of the structure of knowledge—its concepts, generalizations, and modes of inquiry; specialized knowledge in given academic disciplines.

    Ability to use the technical skills of teaching.

    Knowledge of the scope of possible educational objectives in the cognitive, affective, and psychomotor domains.

    Acceptance of values and attitudes that enhance learning and lead to mutually satisfying human relationships.

    Mastery of the skills of communication, conflict management and reduction, human relations, and decision making.

    Extensive practice in the art of effectively integrating these seven items.

3. In what respects is teaching *both* an art and a science?
4. To what extent do teachers enjoy the same legal rights as all other citizens of the United States?
5. To what extent should students, as students and minors, enjoy the same legal rights as all other citizens of the United States? As a public school teacher, what rights will you accord to the students in your classes? State the rights in the form of a Students' Bill of Rights.
6. Having considered the roles that teachers play both in school and in life, what characteristics do you have that would make you particularly suited to be a teacher? What qualities in your personality might interfere with your effectiveness as a teacher? What personal needs do you have that fit in well with elementary, junior high, or senior high school teaching? Which of your needs would a teaching career tend to satisfy?
7. After reading the authors' views of the "good" teacher, what words would you use to describe such a teacher? What characteristics or abilities do you ascribe to those teachers whom you judged as "good"? How do these characteristics match with Ryans's X_o, Y_o, and Z_o pattern? How do they match with Jackson's themes of immediacy, informality, autonomy, and individuality? To what extent do you feel you possess the qualities that Ryans and Jackson describe?
8. Where do you fit among the six teacher clusters outlined in the chapter? Are you neatly in one cluster, or are your traits spread over several clusters? What are some characteristics of your teaching personality? Would you prefer to change any of these? If so, what characteristics would you like to have? Do most teachers fit essentially into one cluster, or are they a mixture of several?

Practical Activities

1. Arrange to observe a teacher's classroom for several periods, preferably over a few days. Observe both teaching (large-group instruction, small-group discussion, individual work) and nonteaching functions (clerical, counseling, custodial, and policing tasks) with which the teacher is involved. Figure out how much time is spent on teaching and on nonteaching activities. Discuss the teacher's apparent attitude toward these functions. Ask the teacher about the importance of nonteaching functions, the time spent on them, and the effect on a person's teaching. Write up the results of your findings.

2. Interview two public school teachers: one in the first, second, or third year of teaching, and one with ten or more years of experience. Plan an interview that includes asking how interesting and exciting is teaching at this point in their careers; what are the rewarding and unrewarding aspects of the work; what are the difficult and taxing aspects of teaching; how does each person's attitude toward teaching compare with what it was five or ten years ago (or what do they think it will be in five or ten years); how long do they plan to stay in teaching, and why. Add other pertinent questions. Interpret, compare, and contrast the two views represented.

3. Assign yourself to a group of students for a day, and follow them from class to class, study hall, recess, lunch, and the like. If necessary, explain that you are doing an informal study for a class at the college and would like them to act as they normally do. To guide your study, develop several observation questions, including how much intellectual activity they engage in; how involved and interested or bored and inattentive they are; how crowds, noise, delays, and intrusions appear to affect them; how much time they spend alone or in groups, silent or talking, active or inactive, expressive or inexpressive; when they seem the happiest and most mentally alert.

4. Attend a teachers' meeting in a local public elementary, junior high, or senior high school. What issues were discussed? What were the major concerns of the teachers? Who ran the meeting? What was the superintendent's or principal's role? Describe the relationship between the principal and teachers or among the administrators and teachers. What percentage of the teachers were present at the meeting? How many took an active part in the meeting? What conclusions and generalizations can you draw?

5. Arrange to serve as a teacher's assistant for a couple of hours a day for a week. Help the teacher in any appropriate capacity—instructional, clerical, or other. In writing your assessment of the nature of the teacher's work, consider these questions: How "professional" were the various tasks? What does the teacher need to spend more time doing, and what ought to take less time?

6. Conduct a survey of employed public school teachers to determine which of the following aspects of preservice teacher-education programs they think should receive the highest priority. Have them rank items, giving a 1 to the highest ranked priority and continuing through a 5 for the lowest priority item.

   Mastery of subject matter.
   Competence in using a variety of teaching methods and materials.

Effective use of human relations skills, including classroom management and control.

Understanding the nature, development, and concerns of children and adolescents.

Understanding the theories and principles of human learning.

7. Locate a copy of a student handbook from a school in a nearby school district. Analyze it in regard to students' rights and responsibilities and write up your findings.

Bibliography

BOYER, ERNEST L., *High School: A Report on Secondary Education in America.* New York: Harper & Row, Publishers, Inc., 1983.

BRENTON, MYRON, *What's Happened to Teacher?* New York: Coward, McCann & Geoghegan, Inc., 1970.

CURWIN, RICHARD L., and BARBARA SCHNEIDER FUHRMANN, *Discovering Your Teaching Self: Humanistic Approaches to Effective Teaching.* Englewood Cliffs, N.J.: Prentice-Hall, Inc., 1975.

FISCHER, LOUIS, and DAVID SCHIMMEL, *The Rights of Students and Teachers: Resolving Conflicts in the School Community.* New York: Harper & Row, Publishers, Inc., 1982.

FISCHER, LOUIS, DAVID SCHIMMEL, and CYNTHIA KELLY, *Teachers and the Law.* New York: Longman, Inc., 1981.

FISHMAN, STERLING, ANDREAS M. KAZAMIAS, and HERBERT M. KLIEBARD, *Teacher, Student and Society.* Boston: Little, Brown & Company, 1974.

GOOD, THOMAS L., BRUCE J. BIDDLE, and JERE E. BROPHY, *Teachers Make a Difference.* New York: Holt, Rinehart & Winston, 1975.

GOODLAD, JOHN I., *A Place Called School: Prospects for the Future.* New York: McGraw-Hill Book Company, Inc., 1984.

GOODLAD, JOHN I., and M. FRANCES KLEIN, *Behind the Classroom Door.* Worthington, Ohio: Charles A. Jones Publishing Company, 1970.

GRAMBS, JEAN DRESDEN, *Schools, Scholars, and Society.* Englewood Cliffs, N.J.: Prentice-Hall, Inc., 1978.

GREENBERG, HERBERT M., *Teaching with Feeling.* New York: Macmillan, 1969.

HARMIN, MERRILL, and TOM GREGORY, *Teaching is . . . .* Chicago: Science Research Associates, Inc., 1974.

JACKSON, PHILIP W., *Life in Classrooms.* New York: Holt, Rinehart & Winston, 1968.

JOYCE, BRUCE, and MARSHA WEIL, *Models of Teaching,* 2nd ed. Englewood Cliffs, N.J.: Prentice-Hall, Inc., 1980.

LIEBERMAN, MYRON, *Education as a Profession.* Englewood Cliffs, N.J.: Prentice-Hall, Inc., 1956.

———, *The Future of Public Education.* Chicago: The University of Chicago Press, 1960.

MILLER, JOHN P., *Humanizing the Classroom: Models of Teaching in Affective Education.* New York: Praeger Publishers, Inc., 1976.

PROEFRIEDT, WILLIAM A., *The Teacher You Choose to Be.* New York: Holt, Rinehart & Winston, 1975.

RATHS, LOUIS E., *Teaching for Learning.* Columbus, Ohio: Charles E. Merrill Publishing Company, 1969.

RICHEY, ROBERT W., *Preparing for a Career in Education.* New York: McGraw-Hill Book Company, Inc., 1974.

SEABERG, DOROTHY I., *The Four Faces of Teaching.* Pacific Palisades, Calif.: Goodyear Publishing Company, Inc., 1974.

2

Contemporary Issues Facing Educators

Today's high school is called upon to provide the services and transmit the values we used to expect from the community and the home and the church. And if they fail anywhere along the line, they are condemned.

What do Americans want high schools to accomplish? Quite simply, we want it all.[1]

I readily concede that here and there I am probably hard to read, and I am likely to become harder as the illiteracy of the public increases. It is never an easy task to take the mental measure of your readers. There are things people should know if they are to read books at all, and out of respect for them, or to save appearances, one is apt to assume more familiarity on their part with the history of the twentieth century than is objectively justified.[2]

Outcry over the quality of public schools is hardly new. The history of American education reads as a stream of reform movements. Liberal critics tend to claim that schools must respond more to the needs of individual students and a changing world. In contrast, conservatives want to emphasize discipline, basic learning, and traditional values. Intermittent turmoil and persistent change should come as no surprise. For most of the twentieth century, schools have been charged with educating all children and carrying out many of society's goals.

THE SCHOOL AS A CRUCIBLE

As social problems surface, Americans often turn to schools for solutions. This is particularly true in times of major crises, or what are perceived as such.

When the cold war heated up in the 1950s and the Soviet Union launched

[1] Ernest L. Boyer, *High School: A Report on Secondary Education in America*, The Carnegie Foundation for the Advancement of Teaching (New York: Harper & Row, Publishers, Inc., 1983), p. 57.

[2] Saul Bellow, foreword to Allan Bloom, *The Closing of the American Mind: How Higher Education Has Failed Democracy and Impoverished the Souls of Today's Students* (New York: Simon & Schuster, 1987), p. 15.

Sputnik into space, leaders called for more rigor in the school curriculum. The public, politicians, and business leaders saw a direct connection between the nation's lagging military technology and power and the quality of mathematics and science in the schools.

In the 1980s, America's primary concern shifted to economic productivity and its ability to compete in the international trade arena with Japan. The conventional view held that a direct link existed between students' learning basic skills and knowledge and the nation's economic capability. In response, business interest in schooling intensified during the 1980s.

The drive to educate everyone led to some unintended effects — providing more and more of the children's education. America has attempted to prepare each person for a life as a producer, consumer, worker, parent, and citizen. Understandably, the results have fallen short of the goals.

Schooling and Education

The goals society has set for schools remain out of reach for several reasons. First, society confuses education and schooling and places the whole burden of education on schools. As historian Henry Steele Commager points out, the responsibility for educating citizens, since the days of ancient Greece, belonged with every institution in a society: the family, church, business, and community. Today, these institutions include the press, labor unions, political groups, sports, medicine, law enforcement, the media, and community organizations. Few of these institutions, however, include education as one of their functions.[3]

The family and church, once pillars of society, no longer function as the primary source of moral guidance for most people. Other institutions, whether they produce goods, services, information, or entertainment, are essentially self-serving. In a society dedicated to free enterprise and the profit motive, public service creates a fundamental conflict. In simpler times, before the corporate landscape dominated our economic society, incidental education played a central part. Education today has fallen entirely on the schools, both a shortsighted and impossible assignment.

In our modern, postindustrial culture, children, like adults, receive much of their education from movies, video, radio, advertising, popular magazines, and particularly television. As Neil Postman points out, television constitutes the major educational enterprise undertaken in the United States, which is why he calls it the "First Curriculum, school is the second."[4] In this sense, much learning is incidental today. The problem is that too much of it is miseducative.

In an educative society, the efforts of schools, television and other media, and institutions would be coordinated. School can effectively play only a part in the

[3]Henry Steele Commager, *The People and Their Schools*, Fastback 79 (Bloomington, Ind.: Phi Delta Kappa Educational Foundation, 1976), pp. 28–33.
[4]Neil Postman, *Teaching as a Conserving Activity* (New York: Dell Publishing Company, Inc., 1979), p. 50.

overall educational picture. Other agencies are needed to complement and supplement its role.

The Eclectic Agenda

The task of schools is made more difficult, if not impossible, because they have been assigned or have assumed responsibilities that belong to other agencies — mainly because these agencies perform them poorly, if at all. Schools teach a host of vocational-technical skills as well as teach about driving, health, drugs, alcohol, sex, AIDS, nutrition, values, family life, careers, entrepreneurship, the law, and more.

Why, for example, don't police departments and insurance companies assume the function of driver's education? They have much to gain from good driving and should be able to instruct more effectively. Where are the medical community and food industry when it comes to teaching health-related topics? Where are business and industry when it comes to teaching job-related skills? Computer technology, for example, could be taught in virtually any community today by experts from business in the communications and information industry. How involved are the media in school journalism and theater? These potential agencies of education serve those who can afford to pay for their services.

Home economics, far from teaching traditional housekeeping, is a catchall for teaching about health, nutrition, sex, drugs, personal conflict, and social relations. Not long ago these were responsibilities of the family.

There are other areas. Physical education and participatory sports are vital for developing children, but in American schools they take a backseat to entertainment provided by interscholastic football, basketball, and other spectator sports. A more sensible model would be community-supported teams for many sports at various levels of competency, coached by adults in the community.

Conflicting Values

Values bombard young people from many sources — television, magazines, music, corporations, religious groups, as well as churches and families. Schools are only one more voice in the dark. Many observers correctly argue that promiscuous drug use and sex are essentially moral dilemmas. Some critics, however, add that schools have been stripped of any moral dimension to deal with problems of adolescents by social and educational activists who have driven prayer from the classroom and religion from textbooks while promoting value-free curricula.

Contrary to this popular view, schools have sufficient moral authority to teach values that are valid in a democratic society and other universal principles that have helped guide human conduct for centuries. These include principles established in the Constitution, rational thinking, and ultimately the appeal of human dignity. Such values may or may not coincide with religious beliefs, but holding a certain religious belief is not a condition of moral authority.

Moral or ethical values, in fact, are taught through the study of history, government, economics, literature, and the sciences. Indeed, schools can "teach about" religion, as the Supreme Court has made clear; they just cannot promote religion in any form. A primary reason for the founding of our nation was to ensure religious freedom, and the courts wisely prohibit public schools from undermining this civil right.

The problem is not that schools have become value free, but that they are expected to teach values that society subscribes to but does not consistently practice. In trying to do so, teachers often appear foolish, idealistic, or romantic. In the early days of American schooling, as Commager reminds us, the beliefs of society were by and large harmonious with the lives people led. A growing child saw cultural values displayed daily in the home, workshop, and community. Schools served merely to reinforce the dominant morality displayed throughout society. Statesmen such as Thomas Jefferson and James Madison were seen as genuinely in pursuit of the public welfare. By contrast, many public figures today appear corrupt, incompetent, or opportunistic.

Society requires schools to teach the Bill of Rights and respect for law but elects to office people who will ignore the Constitution when convenient. The work ethic and craftsmanship are espoused, but society showcases those who lead extravagant lives regardless of how their affluence was obtained. Children are taught the virtues of honesty, fairness, and cooperation, but our economic system often rewards those who are cunning. Children are told to "say no to drugs" but can obtain nicotine from vending machines and consume caffeinated soda while their parents unwind with scotch and soda. Schools are encouraged to teach that the United States is a peace-loving nation, while the military establishment and weapons development are generously funded. Schools are asked to foster sportsmanship, but society rewards and reveres the winner.

These lessons are not lost on the young. Unfortunately, many either accept the contradictions and hypocrisy or come away feeling negative and cynical.

THE NEED FOR HARD HEADS AND SOFT HEARTS

Educational reform for most of the twentieth century can be likened to a swinging pendulum. Prior to this century, the history of education in America followed a relatively steady course that gradually made schools accessible to more and more children. The efforts of such political and educational giants as William Penn and Benjamin Franklin during the colonial period, Thomas Jefferson in the early days of the Republic, and later Horace Mann defined the aims and shape of American schooling. Although the progress of common schooling advanced the goal of *equity*, the elite of society consistently supported schools—both private and public—that focused on *excellence*. Until the 1900s, these twin goals served separate needs that seldom were in conflict.

For a full half century from 1890 until 1940, the number of 14–17-year-olds attending high school virtually doubled every decade. In 1900 approximately 10 percent of the high-school-age population was in school; by 1930 this figure had reached 50 percent and by 1960 nearly 90 percent, when it began to level off. During the early decades of the twentieth century, the progressive reform movement added a new dimension to America's persistent search for a way to educate its diverse population. In a stable agrarian society, *traditional* education, with its teacher-centered emphasis on subject matter that supplemented learning in the central culture, was appropriate. John Dewey, who spearheaded the *progressive* movement, and others saw that an increasingly industrial and urban society, characterized by sprawling cities, mass immigration, ethnic ghettos, and factory labor, needed a new education. For the growing number of children from diverse backgrounds, who would have to cope with a complex social and economic environment, progressive education emphasized applying knowledge to the "real world" and "learning by doing."

William Burt Lauderdale points out that representatives of the two dominant philosophies influencing education were not blind to the merits of each other's aims. Those who supported the western European tradition of classical education wanted to serve the "common people" as well as the academically elite and economically powerful. In turn, the progressives were not out to corrupt classical studies by advocating a broader, more practical education. The genius of American education, he adds, resides in the ability of both positions "to assimilate varied purposes . . . and open opportunities for a wider audience of American youth."[5] No one exemplified this understanding more than John Dewey, who went to great lengths to integrate subject matter with the learner's experiences.

Nevertheless, it is not surprising that as the mass of educational reform increased during the first half of the twentieth century, it began to resemble a swinging pendulum. The common school, designed to meet the needs of virtually all students through the secondary years, had become reality. Heretofore, the two traditions in educational reform were at least compatible, if not unified. One, based on the quest for equity, opened opportunities to varied constituents of an immigrant nation and addressed the school curriculum to the needs of the whole child in an industrialized society. The other, based on the pursuit of academic excellence, championed education for literacy that is rooted in the knowledge accumulated through centuries of Western civilization.

By the 1930s, and particularly the forties, traditionalists became alarmed at what they perceived as a severely listing "educational ship" dangerously weighted in favor of student interests and nonacademic subjects. The assault was led by essentialists William Bagley, Arthur Bestor, Mortimer Smith, Hyman Rickover, and Max Rafferty. During the 1950s, critics such as Robert Hutchins and James Conant offered balanced proposals to guide the school curriculum. But the barriers were erected, with most educational reformers choosing sides in this dualistic environment.

---

[5]William Burt Lauderdale, *Educational Reform: The Forgotten Half*, Fastback 252 (Bloomington, Ind.: Phi Delta Kappa Educational Foundation, 1987), p. 20.

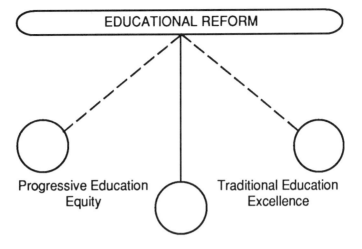

FIGURE 2-1

During much of the 1900s, reform in American education has been jerked from side to side rather than guided down a rational path. Proponents of the two reform traditions today appear to wear blinders that provide them but a narrow view of what makes for an appropriate education. On the one hand, modern traditionalists, in their pursuit of high standards, achievement, literacy, and accountability, display justifiably *hard heads* when they demand that schools offer a solid academic curriculum. Unfortunately, many traditionalists have equally *hard hearts* when they neglect to consider the strides public education has made in opening school doors to a wide range of students from different ethnic backgrounds, intellectual abilities, and socioeconomic levels. Progress toward standards of excellence is painfully slow when schools and teachers work with *all* children, not just the academically talented. Still, schools do neglect serving some students when they frame policies and curricula that treat all students as if they were equal in their ability to handle academics and freedom. Also, they fail to challenge many when they don't demand competency.

On the other hand, progressive educators have had both the good sense and the compassion to display *soft hearts* in opening educational opportunities to disadvantaged students while helping to craft curricula that address the interests and needs of all students. Despite the pitfalls sometimes encountered, these efforts adapt the educational legacy of Jefferson, Mann, and Dewey to modern times. Unfortunately, in their compassion, some advocates in this tradition display *soft heads* when they act as if *what* students learn is unimportant so long as they enjoy the experience.

A commitment to both equity and academic excellence is by no means mutually exclusive. Yet spokespersons tend to favor one goal at the expense of the other. The point is that national leadership is needed to show the way towards educational policy that integrates excellence and equity—an educational policy that is both hardheaded and softhearted. As with the two ideals of democracy— liberty and equality—these goals often conflict, with no easy answers to the dilemma.[6]

THE CONFLICT IN EDUCATION

The dichotomy between those who advocate equity and those who demand excellence is vividly illustrated by two recent benchmark events in American education: the passing of the Elementary and Secondary Education Act (ESEA) in 1965 and the publication of *A Nation at Risk: The Imperative for Educational Reform* in 1983. As Lauderdale writes, "These two events—occurring less than two decades apart—symbolically represent the polarity of views on what should be the national priorities for education."[7]

Era of Softness

The ESEA was a significant departure in educational policy and a major effort to serve the underprivileged. The five parts of ESEA (which substantially increased federal spending for schooling) provided funds to help school districts develop libraries, purchase instructional materials, set up reading programs, conduct research, and train teachers to work with children who came from culturally different and economically deprived environments.

This act came at a time of keen interest in the quality of elementary and secondary school education. To start, university scholars in the physical sciences, history and social sciences, mathematics, and English took a hand in reshaping the school curricula to convey the underlying structure of learning and the science of teaching. As Jerome Bruner wrote in *The Process of Education* (1960), "Any subject can be taught effectively in some intellectually honest form to any child at any stage of development."[8] Discovery learning was the underlying theme of these "new math," "new science," and "new social studies" curricula. A few projects, such as "Man: A Course of Study," which Bruner directed, cut across disciplines.

Another group of romantic and radical critics were taking aim at schools for failing to teach the underprivileged and understand the emotional needs of middle-

[6]I'm indebted to economist Alan Blinder for the metaphoric use of *heads* and *hearts* that he insightfully applied to economic policy and its twin pillars, efficiency and equity, in *Hard Heads, Soft Hearts: Tough-Minded Economics for a Just Society* (Menlo Park, Calif.: Addison-Wesley Publishing Company, Inc., 1987).

[7]Lauderdale, *Educational Reform*, p. 24.

[8]Jerome Bruner, *The Process of Education* (New York: Random House, 1960), p. 33.

class students while breaking the spirits of nearly all youngsters. Authors such as John Holt, *How Children Fail* (1964), Paul Goodman, *Compulsory Mis-education* (1964), Jonathan Kozol, *Death at an Early Age* (1967), and Herbert Kohl, *36 Children* (1967) were just a few who defined this spirit and message. It was also a period when some reformers were calling for "alternative schools"—usually "free school" alternatives to the prevailing "order and control" of the conventional school. A few scholars, most notably Ivan Illich, *Deschooling Society,* and Everett Reimer, *School Is Dead,* both written in 1971, said that people will be genuinely educated only when formal schooling is eliminated and education is designed around convivial and incidental learning.

In arguably the most important work of the period, Charles Silberman, *Crisis in the Classroom: The Remaking of American Education* (1970) explained that it was time educational reformers understood the teachings of John Dewey and took them seriously. Many progressive educators earlier in the century were preoccupied with child-centered curricula and school environments at the expense of intellectual content. In reacting to the softness and vulgarities of "life-adjustment" curricula in particular, Silberman explained, reformers from the academic community made the same mistake, except that they opted for the other side of the dichotomy. He asserted that if educational reform is to be purposeful and to succeed, it needs to address what methods of instruction and classroom organization are effective as well as what subject matter is worth knowing.[9]

Desegregation.   One way public schools addressed the cultural demands for equity was through extensive school desegregation in the 1970s; another was through the so-called mainstreaming of handicapped children. Perhaps the most historic landmark in American education is the U.S. Supreme Court's *Brown v. Board of Education* (1954), which struck down the separate-but-equal doctrine that had justified segregated schools. Change was not immediate. Most communities did not favor integrating blacks and other minorities with the dominant Caucasian school population, so schools found ways to avoid desegregation orders. This ended in 1971, when the Supreme Court in *Swann v. Charlotte-Mecklenburg Board of Education* directed district courts to set down specific ways schools were to desegregate. The results were sweeping and striking, particularly in the South. By 1980 only about one out of every four black students attended nearly all-minority schools; two decades earlier the vast majority attended such schools.

The disruptive effects of this transformation on schools were significant: redistricting and busing students led to violence and strong measures to control it, disintegration of school spirit, white flight to suburban and private schools, and teacher resignations. Segregated schools were the result of housing patterns based on socioeconomic factors and an underlying racism in communities; but because they were unable to affect the root causes of this inequality, courts placed the burden of redress on schools. Not surprisingly, the strains of integration took their

[9]Charles E. Silberman, *Crisis in the Classroom: The Remaking of American Education* (New York: Random House, 1970), pp. 179–83.

toll on both the culture of schools and the quality of the curriculum. Any reform proposal that expects to have credibility must acknowledge the responsibility and burden this places on schools.

Mainstreaming.   The Education for All Handicapped Children Act of 1975 (Public Law 94-142) has been hailed as the Bill of Rights for handicapped children and their parents. The law requires that all handicapped children, depending on how severe the handicap, be placed in whatever school setting is the "least restrictive" and comes closest to the climate of the "regular classroom." The effect is that virtually all handicapped students are mainstreamed, or instructed in the same class with everyone else. Schools also are required to provide programs individually tailored for the handicapped, though in *Board of Education of the Hendrick Hudson Central School District* v. *Rowley* (1982) the U.S. Supreme Court said the intent of P.L. 94-142 was "more to open the door of public education . . . than to guarantee any particular level of education once inside."

In some classrooms mainstreaming has been a significant help to the handicapped without distracting other students — even benefiting the nonhandicapped. In other classrooms, however, it has put tremendous strain on the teacher. Some students need a great deal of attention and disrupt the class to get it. On balance, including the handicapped student in the mainstream classroom has improved education by advancing the goal of equity. Any reform proposal demanding excellence, however, must consider the constraints of this responsibility.

In the wake of events in the larger society and efforts to provide opportunities for low-ability, handicapped, and non-English speaking students, schools attempted to accommodate all students. As David Cohen points out in *The Shopping Mall High School* (1985), they did this in three broad ways: by increasing the number of courses offered, thereby fragmenting the curriculum; by de-emphasizing academic work and increasing remedial courses; and by relaxing course standards and requirements. "This flexibility," Cohen remarks, "is in one sense deplorable because students have been shortchanged. But in another it is admirable, because the schools have faced so many demands from so many quarters, and have tried to respond helpfully and in a certain sense humanely — even though they do not have the resources to do the many jobs they have embraced or have been assigned."[10] In the process, more than a few educators and schools lost sight of a primary purpose of schooling — to ensure that all students come away with the basic skills and knowledge to prepare them to be capable citizens and workers in society.

Era of Hardness

The swing to the essentials of learning in the 1940s and 1950s was a response to excesses of progressive educators in the preceding decade. Critics, such as historian Arthur Bestor and Hyman Rickover, albeit hardheaded and hardhearted,

[10]Arthur G. Powell, Eleanor Farrar, and David K. Cohen, *The Shopping Mall High School: Winners and Losers in the Educational Marketplace* (Boston: Houghton Mifflin Company, 1985), pp. 295–97.

were justified in throwing the spotlight on weaknesses in child-centered methods, permissive attitudes, and "life-adjustment" education. Many of those "progressive" educators, with whom John Dewey disagreed sharply, were guilty of carrying a soft head atop that soft heart.

Less than two decades after the ESEA, the *A Nation At Risk* report from the National Commission on Excellence in Education revived the spirit of the 1950s and again set off a lively discussion on the potentially fatal shortcomings of public schools. The commission loaded its message with inflammatory passages such as,

> If an unfriendly foreign power had attempted to impose on America the mediocre educational performance that exists today, we might well have viewed it as an act of war. As it stands, we have allowed this to happen ourselves. We have squandered the gains in student achievement made in the wake of the Sputnik challenge.... We have, in effect, been committing an act of unthinking, unilateral educational disarmament.[11]

The commission "fired a salvo of ammunition" to support its claim: American students fare poorly on international comparisons of achievement; 40 percent of the minority youth are functionally illiterate; average achievement of high school students on standardized tests is lower than when Sputnik was launched a generation earlier; gifted students are not performing to their ability; average SAT scores fell between 1963 and 1980; achievement scores in science by 17-year-olds have declined since 1969. The list goes on and concludes by citing the need for business and the military to increase spending on costly remedial education in reading, writing, spelling, and computation.

Lost in the tough talk of the *A Nation at Risk* report was its awareness of the environmental context. The commission writes,

> It is important, of course, to recognize that the *average citizen* today is better educated and more knowledgeable than the average citizen of a generation ago—more literate, and exposed to more mathematics, literature, and science. The positive impact of this fact on the well-being of our country and the lives of our people cannot be overstated. Nevertheless, the average graduate of our schools and colleges today is not as well-educated as the average graduate of 25 or 35 years ago, when a much smaller proportion of our population completed high school and college. The negative impact of this fact likewise cannot be overstated.[12]

Of more importance, the report makes a pitch for creating a "Learning Society"—one in which "educational opportunities extend beyond schools and colleges into homes, workplaces; into libraries, art galleries, museums, and science centers; indeed, into every place where the individual can develop and mature in work and life." This is a genuine plea for lifelong learning that not only contributes to a person's career goals but also to the general quality of life.[13]

---

[11]*A Nation at Risk: The Imperative For Educational Reform*, A Report to the Nation and the Secretary of Education, U.S. Department of Education, by the National Commission on Excellence in Education (Washington, D.C.: U.S. Government Printing Office, 1983), p. 5.

[12]Ibid., p. 11.

[13]Ibid., pp. 13–14.

Back to the basics.   The *A Nation at Risk* report came on the heels of the "back-to-basics" movement in the latter part of the 1970s. "Back-to-basics" was a bumper-sticker phrase that had more political than pedagogical significance. The tack taken in back-to-basics had at least two serious flaws: It didn't really teach reading or math, and it ignored other learning.

Reading, writing, and arithmetic are not self-contained skills like wallpapering and tennis. They are cognitive skills that are inseparable from subject matter and content. Remedial programs are little more than drills when isolated from purposeful literature and real issues. English teachers, for example, are obliged to spend valuable time gearing students for tests at the expense of other learning. Reading is most effectively taught in the context of academic subjects, including not only literature but history, social studies, and science. Reading, or any intellectual skill, does not exist in a vacuum.

Experienced teachers know how to raise students' test scores, if that's what "carrot and stick" incentives demand. Timing and drill are everything if you're not concerned about depth of understanding and retention.

Despite rising test scores in recent years, research by the National Association for Educational Progress (NAEP) indicates that high school graduates do not possess the reasoning power needed to function as citizens and workers in an "information society." Fewer than half can draw inferences from written material; only one-fifth can write persuasive essays; and only one-third can solve math problems requiring several steps.

Students do not develop intellectual qualities — the ability to think rationally and logically, do problem-solving tasks, evaluate issues, and use different modes of inquiry — because that is not what is taught in most classrooms. One of John Goodlad's salient conclusions in *A Place Called School* is that the curriculum is dominated by "the persistent and repetitive attention to basic facts and skills." The schools, he adds, are failing to develop intellectual qualities: "the ability to think rationally, the ability to use, evaluate, and accumulate knowledge, a desire for learning."[14]

It's not surprising that *critical thinking* is one of the latest buzzwords in education reform circles. Emphasis on the basics today has nothing to do with returning anywhere; rather, it demands a leap forward to the fundamentals of higher-order thinking.

Essentialism revisited.   More than anything, back-to-basics signaled a return to traditional values and was but a stepping-stone to the stronger swing to conservative educational thought in the 1980s. Several other assessments and reports followed *A Nation at Risk* and reinforced its message: E. D. Hirsch's *Cultural Literacy: What Every American Needs to Know* (1987) with Diane Ravitch and Chester Finn's *What Do Our 17-Year-Olds Know?* (1987) fall into this vector of the reform continuum. When they advocate a return to academic studies and essential

---

[14]John I. Goodlad, *A Place Called School: Prospects for the Future* (New York: McGraw-Hill Book Company, Inc., 1984), p. 236.

SUBJECT	1st YEAR	2nd YEAR	3rd YEAR	4th YEAR
ENGLISH	Introduction to Literature	American Literature	British Literature	Introduction to World Literature
SOCIAL STUDIES	Western Civilization	American History	Prin. of American Democracy / American Democracy & the World	
MATH	Three years required from among the following: Algebra I, Plane & Solid Geometry, Algebra II & Trigonometry, Statistics & Probability (1 sem.), Pre-Calculus (1 sem.), and Calculus AB or BC			
SCIENCE	Three years required from among the following: Astronomy/Geology, Biology, Chemistry, and Physics or Principles of Technology			
FOREIGN LANGUAGE	Two years required in a single foreign language from among offerings determined by local jurisdictions		**ELECTIVES**	
PHYSICAL EDUCATION/ HEALTH	Physical Education/ Health 9	Physical Education/ Health 10		
FINE ARTS	Art History — — — Music History			

FIGURE 2-2   James Madison High School: A Four-Year Plan

knowledge, these reformers represent an extension of the essentialist position of a generation earlier.

The similarity between the reform literature of the 1980s and that of the 1940s and 1950s is uncanny: The earlier essentialists' works include Idding Bell's *Crisis in Education* (1949), Arthur Bestor's *Educational Wastelands* (1953), Albert Lynd's *Quackery in the Public Schools* (1953), and Mortimer Smith's *The Diminished Mind* (1953).

Perhaps the most vocal critic of all was President Reagan's Secretary of Education William Bennett, who conveyed a similar theme in his many public speeches and reports: The quality of American schools is deteriorating while the basic competency and knowledge of students are eroding. At the midpoint of this movement, Bennett recommended a course of study that emphasizes history, literature, and the humanities. During the high school years, students in the English curriculum would study literature, including American, British, and world, for four years. Social studies would consist of three required years of history, including Western civilization, U.S. history, and principles of American and world democracy. Both the science and mathematics curricula would require three years of study restricted to "academic" as opposed to "applied" offerings. And all students would be required to take two years of a foreign language.[15] Bennett's *James Madison High School* (1987) curriculum (Figure 2-2) forms a bridge to the classical dimension of traditional education.

An essentialist program represents one view of the traditional agenda; perennialism is the other. In the 1940s and 1950s, Robert Hutchins, then president of the University of Chicago, was its primary spokesperson. The message of Allan Bloom's best seller *The Closing of the American Mind* (1987), although not aimed at precollegiate schooling, is couched in the perennialist's tradition. In his book, Bloom, a professor of philosophy and political science at the University of Chicago, uses eloquence, humor, and sarcasm to plea for a return to the classics. He simply wants to restore the humanities to what he regards as their rightful position in the liberal arts curriculum. As the subtitle of his book reveals, "higher education has failed democracy and impoverished the souls of today's students." The answer to this malaise, according to Bloom, is as basic and perennial as Western thought and the "Great Books"—a liberal arts curriculum based on reading classic texts as their authors intended them to be read, letting these works dictate the big questions to discuss.[16]

The perennialist, or classical, tradition has been related to elementary and secondary education through the work of Mortimer Adler, architect of the Paideia Proposal. Adler is chairman of the Paideia Project, made up of university scholars and public school administrators who generated ideas for this project. Given its name from the Greek word meaning "the upbringing of a child," this position is built on the ideas of Robert Hutchins, Adler's former colleague at the University of Chicago, and other classical scholars who share this pedagogical position. Hutchins captured the essence of the position when he wrote that since "democracy makes everyone a ruler, and a liberal education is the education that rulers need, then every citizen should have a liberal education."[17]

The Paideia Proposal is based on several assumptions about learning; a main one is that all children are educable, regardless of background or ability. It follows from this that tracking students is inherently unequal, and schooling should be a one-track system. To provide quality education for all students, schools must eliminate specialized courses and electives. The central feature of the Paideia plan is twelve years of the same course of study for all children, beginning at age 4. The three columns illustrated in Figure 2-3 are integrated and rise in complexity and difficulty throughout the years of schooling. As Adler explains, the Paideia curriculum uses three teaching styles to achieve the three educational goals: *lecturing*, to transfer fundamental knowledge; *coaching*, to teach basic intellectual skills; and *Socratic questioning*, to enlarge understanding.[18]

[15]William J. Bennett, *James Madison High School: A Curriculum for American Students* (Washington, D.C.: U.S. Department of Education, 1987), pp. 9–12.

[16]Allan Bloom, *The Closing of the American Mind: How Higher Education Has Failed Democracy and Impoverished the Souls of Today's Students* (New York: Simon & Schuster, Inc., 1987), p. 344.

[17]Robert M. Hutchins, *The Conflict in Education in a Democratic Society* (New York: Harper & Row Publishers, Inc., 1953), p. 84.

[18]Mortimer J. Adler, *The Paideia Proposal: An Educational Manifesto* (New York: Macmillan, 1982), pp. 21–32.

	COLUMN ONE	COLUMN TWO	COLUMN THREE
Goals	ACQUISITION OF ORGANIZED KNOWLEDGE	DEVELOPMENT OF INTELLECTUAL SKILLS — SKILLS OF LEARNING	ENLARGED UNDERSTANDING OF IDEAS AND VALUES
	by means of	by means of	by means of
Means	DIDACTIC INSTRUCTION LECTURES AND RESPONSES TEXTBOOKS AND OTHER AIDS	COACHING, EXERCISES AND SUPERVISED PRACTICE	MAIEUTIC OR SOCRATIC QUESTIONING AND ACTIVE PARTICIPATION
	in three areas of subject matter	in the operations of	in the
Areas Operations and Activites	LANGUAGE, LITERATURE AND THE FINE ARTS MATHEMATICS AND NATURAL SCIENCE HISTORY GEOGRAPHY AND SOCIAL STUDIES	READING, WRITING, SPEAKING, AND LISTENING CALCULATING, PROBLEM-SOLVING, OBSERVING, MEASURING ESTIMATING EXERCISING CRITICAL JUDGEMENT	DISCUSSION OF BOOKS (NOT TEXTBOOKS) AND OTHER WORKS OF ART AND INVOLVEMENT IN ARTISTIC ACTIVITIES e.g. MUSIC, DRAMA, VISUAL ARTS

FIGURE 2-3   Paideia Course of Study for All

Note: The three columns do not correspond to separate courses, nor is one kind of teaching and learning necessarily confined to any one class. *Source:* Reprinted with permission of MacMillan Publishing Company from *The Paideia Proposal: An Educational Manifesto* by Mortimer J. Adler. Copyright © 1982 by the Institute for Philosophical Research.

Adler's position is that "all genuine learning is active, not passive. It involves the use of the mind, not just the memory. It is a process of discovery, in which the student is the main agent, not the teacher." Adler, an admirer of John Dewey's work, takes care to clarify Dewey's oft-quoted maxim that genuine "learning is by doing."

> What John Dewey had in mind was not exclusively physical doing or even social doing—engagement in practical projects of one kind or another. The most important kind of doing, so far as learning is concerned, is intellectual or mental doing. In other words, one can learn to read or write well only by reading and writing. . . . To learn how to do any of these things well, one must not only engage in doing them, but one must be guided in doing them by someone more expert in doing them than oneself.[19]

The goal of the Paideia Proposal is admirable, but lacking dramatic changes in the training and support given teachers who work with a wide range of children, it also appears utopian. Nevertheless, Adler is on firm ground when he explains

[19]Ibid., p. 50.

that an overarching goal of schooling is to create "lifelong learners" who have the ability to learn on their own. To accomplish this, learning must be challenging, meaningful, and enjoyable.

> There is little joy in most of the learning they are now compelled to do. Too much of it is make-believe, in which neither teacher nor pupil can take a lively interest. Without some joy in learning—a joy that arises from hard work well done and from the participation of one's mind in a common task—basic schooling cannot initiate the young into the life of learning, let alone give them the skill and incentive to engage in it further. Only the student whose mind has been engaged in thinking for itself is an active participant in the learning process that is essential to basic schooling.[20]

The Delicate Balance

It may come as a revelation that the objectives of a hardheaded schooling can be combined with those of the softhearted. That we can have schools with high standards of academic achievement while meeting the comprehensive needs of the wide variety of students is not only feasible but imperative. Such a synthesis, in fact, has been available throughout most of this century. Today, blueprints for this education exist in several works:

> The Carnegie Council on Adolescent Development set forth plans to reconstruct and revitalize middle-grade schools in its 1989 report "Turning Points: Preparing American Youth for the 21st Century."
>
> Earlier, The Carnegie Foundation, in *High School: A Report on Secondary Education in America* (1984), written by the Foundation's president Ernest Boyer, constructed a plan to overhaul the high school curriculum.
>
> In his book *A Place Called School: Prospects for the Future* (1985), John Goodlad proposes to refashion both elementary and secondary school programs. Goodlad's work, based on an extensive study of schools across America, is being implemented, albeit piecemeal, through the Network for Education Renewal that he directs.

Unfortunately, simplistic and sensational measures in education policy tend to gain public support. Responses to the *A Nation at Risk* report and other reform reports of the 1980s testify to this. Recommendations have led to more academic requirements—more credits required for graduation and more required courses, especially in science, mathematics, history, and English. Ironically, this has encouraged more students to drop out of school—a result that comes as no surprise to keen observers of the connection between school and society. As Cohen points out, "A large fraction of students now in high school seem quite immune to such requirements. These students are educationally purposeless," and with justifiable reason.[21]

Students, like most adults, Cohen explains, do not regard academics as the

---

[20]Ibid., p. 52.
[21]Powell et al., *The Shopping Mall High School*, p. 303.

primary purpose of schools. For most students, staying in school serves to keep them off the streets, delays entry into a crowded labor market, permits them to socialize with friends, and is a convenient place to teach many life skills, such as driving a car and avoiding the hazards of sexual contact. Students know that, armed only with a high school diploma, most available jobs will be on assembly lines, in supermarkets, with fast-food restaurants, and at shopping malls—those that require minimal skills and knowledge.

Students who plan to attend college to avoid this fate also know that being admitted to most colleges requires modest academic achievement.

As the opening quotation from Ernest Boyer suggests, the major impediment to a coherent, effective school curriculum is the demand for schools to "do it all." In 1953, Arthur Bestor warned, "The idea that the school must undertake to meet every need that some other agency is failing to meet, regardless of the suitability of the schoolroom to the task, is a preposterous delusion that in the end can wreck the educational system.[22]

In *High School,* Boyer outlined a core curriculum that weaves together an academic and practical course of study grounded in genuine "learning by doing," for students from diverse backgrounds and abilities. Figure 2-4 shows how this four-year high school program is structured.[23]

The *First Priority* in the curriculum is *language*—oral and written. Mastery of the English language is a prerequisite to all other learning in school and is developed throughout the core curriculum. Although all areas of the language curriculum are important, writing, which may be the most difficult to master, is the most critical. "Clear writing," Boyer explains, "leads to clear thinking; clear thinking is the basis for clear writing. Perhaps more than any other form of communication, writing holds us responsible for our words and ultimately makes us more thoughtful human beings."[24]

The *Second Priority* in the Carnegie proposal is a *core of common learning* made up of several components:

Cultural Literacy—including the study of literature, the arts, and a foreign language.

The Perspective of History—highlighting themes in U.S. history, Western civilization, and non-Western studies.

Civics—emphasizing the traditions of democratic thought, structures of our government, law, social and global issues.

Science—introducing all students to the processes of discovery in the biological and physical sciences.

The Study of Mathematics—developing the ability to solve practical problems, structure them systematically, and find appropriate solutions.

[22]Arthur Eugene Bestor, *Educational Wastelands: The Retreat from Learning in Our Public Schools* (Urbana: University of Illinois Press, 1953), p. 75.

[23]Boyer, *High School,* p. 137.

[24]Ibid., pp. 85–90.

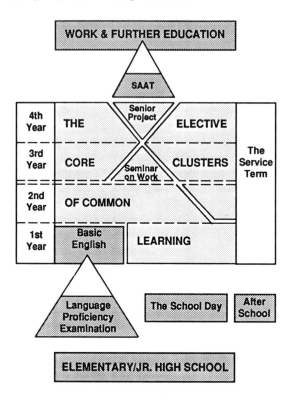

FIGURE 2-4   Carnegie High School Curriculum

From: High School: A Report on Secondary Education in America, edited by Ernest L. Boyer.
Copyright © 1983 by the Carnegie Foundation for the Advancement of Teaching. Reprinted by
permission of Harper & Row, Publishers, Inc.

> The Impact of Technology—including the history of man's use of tools, how science
> and technology have been joined, and the ethical and social issues technology has
> raised.
>
> Health—focusing on the functions and changes in the human body and lifetime
> fitness.[25]

To help young people make the transition from school to the world of work
or higher education, students could take courses during the last two years of
schooling from an *elective cluster* in which they explore career options or do further
study in selected academic subjects.[26]

All students also would take a *seminar on work* that examines how attitudes
toward work have changed over the years, how they differ from one culture to
another, and how changes in the economy affect careers and job opportunities.
The Carnegie Commission's curriculum is topped off with a *senior independent
project* that focuses on a significant contemporary issue drawing on various fields

[25]Ibid., pp. 94–113.
[26]Ibid., pp. 128–30.

of study that have made up the student's program. To enrich students' understanding of the adult world they are entering and impress on them the value of social and civic obligations, Boyer would establish a "new Carnegie unit" on service to the community.[27]

This type of curriculum, when properly implemented, combines academic, vocational, and cultural understandings appropriate for a postindustrial age. It also has the potential to reveal the richness of literature and history, science and technology. In the hands of skilled teachers, it can help students apply knowledge to the lives they lead in our society, and it can help them develop the desire and capacity to learn for themselves as well as to judge what is worth learning. Ultimately, this curriculum, as Silberman points out, promises to "prepare people not just to earn a living but to live a life—a creative, humane, and sensitive life." In other words, it is designed to meet the requirements of *excellence* and *equity*.

Will a framework such as this capture the attention of all students? The distractions and temptations of our consumption- and entertainment-oriented culture are many, and conditions in the vast corporate world or in higher education are not likely to change significantly. Business executives decry the "shoddy products" turned out by schools, but mostly companies need people with steady work habits and modest intellectual skills. The skills needed, however, are more than those required in the past, and they are required of more workers. A few colleges and universities maintain high academic standards, but the salient goal for most is to fill classrooms and dormitories.

As pointed out in *The Shopping Mall High School,* there are ways to cope with potential dropouts and those who languish in secondary schools. These include a national youth service for high-school-age youth and those not yet ready for the intensity of demanding college studies; lifetime educational entitlements for people to return to high school at any time; lowering the school-leaving age and eliminating twelfth grade. Given the elusiveness of effecting change in business, higher education, and other institutions, schools are an easy target for reform. Nevertheless, if students are to be prepared for the modern world, reformers will need to create a configuration of learning.

KNOWLEDGE WORTH KNOWING

One work that shaped public opinion in the 1980s was E. D. Hirsch's *Cultural Literacy*. Although it affected the national mood, it's not likely to have much effect on school curriculum. The irony in the proposals of Hirsch and others, who make the case for teaching more content through didactic strategies, is that this is what has existed for years.

Functional (to be distinguished from cultural) literacy has only recently been a topic of major concern in the United States. Jeanne Chall, director of the Reading Laboratory at Harvard University, estimates that 27 million adults are incapable of reading even the simplest texts or street signs. An estimated 45 million Americans are unable to read at an eighth-grade level—the ability required to read

[27]Ibid., pp. 113–16, 209–15.

the local newspaper or articles in digest magazines. Some 72 million, or about half the adult population, have not reached a high school reading level and are incapable of reading technical manuals, novels, and major news magazines. Given these figures, it's not surprising that cultural illiteracy, as Hirsch defines it, is so extensive and likely to number some 100 to 150 million Americans.

Cultural literacy refers to the knowledge that people share about their culture—knowledge that prepares them to read a newspaper with an adequate degree of comprehension. "Cultural literacy," Hirsch explains, "lies above the everyday levels of knowledge that everyone possesses and below the expert level known only to specialists."[28] This is similar to the approach Ravitch and Finn (*What Do Our 17-Year-Olds Know?*) take with history and literature and feel schools are neglecting. Schools may not be teaching, or students learning, knowledge that is critical to sustaining a cohesive, purposeful American culture, but it's not for reasons traditional critics offer.

English and Literature

English/language arts forms the backbone of the school curriculum, especially in the elementary grades. The emphasis throughout the grades is on reading, writing, and grammar, as well as the mechanics of spelling, punctuation, and paragraph development. Some speaking and listening skills also are included in this area. Literature weaves a consistent thread through the elementary, junior high, and senior high school curriculum. High school courses generally are a combination of mechanics with some literature, courses with only literature, and courses in grammar and composition. These are themes that have been constant over the decades.

Ravitch and Finn focus on literature and history because these two core areas, they say, have been shortchanged in the curriculum. Literature has had to give way increasingly to general language arts skills across the grade levels. The social sciences, including government, economics, sociology, psychology, and global studies, also have been an intrusion. The reform movement of the 1980s, they point out, led to state after state passing requirements to strengthen the sciences, mathematics, and basic skills. Although these areas deserve emphasis, little attention was given to literature and history. It's difficult to make the case, they add, that these subjects help keep us abreast of technological developments or strengthen the national economy. But the well-being of a nation does not depend on technology or material wealth alone. An understanding of literature and the humanities, they correctly argue, is critical to the cohesiveness and morality of a society.[29]

The overarching impediment to more literature in the school curriculum

[28]E. D. Hirsch, *Cultural Literacy: What Every American Needs to Know* (Boston: Houghton Mifflin Company, 1987), p. 19.

[29]Diane Ravitch and Chester E. Finn, Jr., *What Do Our 17-Year-Olds Know? A Report on the First National Assessment of History and Literature* (New York: Harper & Row, Publishers, Inc., 1987), pp. 5–8.

does not lie, however, with the place allotted for science, math, and the social sciences. Rather, the lack of time devoted to any academic subject is rooted in the schools' acquiring more general education responsibilities that ought to be shared with the larger community. The problems with student literacy and achievement run deeper still.

Literature is and has been a main staple of the English curriculum. It probably is more difficult to teach than language skills, because it is less interesting to many young people today who are stimulated by popular culture. Teachers have an immensely difficult time holding students' interest in literature, history, government, or anything that is conceptual and reflective; the most successful often prevail by imitating television and other forms of entertainment. The job of teachers, however, would be less trying if students came to school more predisposed to academics. Nowhere do Ravitch, Finn, and Hirsch address the strategic role families play in preparing young people for school, something that most observers emphasize. As Terrell Bell explains, "Even the best of schools cannot compensate for failure in the home. And failure in the home is at the root of the decline in student achievement."[30] Families who turn off the television and read to children in preschool, who encourage them to read during the school years, and who themselves are role models for learning set the stage for effective school curricula.

The argument that schools value what Hirsch refers to as "educational formalism" also doesn't square with reality. He means by this that teachers are obsessed with the processes or skills of learning at the expense of academic content. Ravitch and Finn, for example, say, "There is a tendency in the education profession to believe that *what* children learn is unimportant compared to *how* they learn . . . that content is in fact irrelevant, so long as the proper skills are developed and exercised.[31] But as school researchers have learned, classrooms remain overwhelmingly content centered and teacher dominated. Goodlad relates that in the English/language arts program his team saw "a heavy emphasis on mechanics in the topics covered by teachers, textbooks stressing these topics, and workbooks, worksheets, and quizzes emphasizing short answers and the recall of specific information."[32] In this pattern, which applies across the curriculum, teachers attempt to convey large bodies of inert information to passive students who are periodically tested on their ability to recall facts. The critics view of what ought to be in the curriculum consists largely of what is there.

History and the Social Studies

The situation in the social studies is similar to that in English but with the added burden of being a lower priority, particularly in the elementary grades. As a result, the civic literacy, historical understandings, and critical-thinking skills of

[30]Terrell H. Bell, "On the Need for National Leadership to Make American Education Work," *Phi Delta Kappan*, 70, no. 1 (Sept. 1988), pp. 8–9.
[31]Ravitch and Finn, *What Do Our 17-Year-Olds Know?* pp. 111–12.
[32]Goodlad, *A Place Called School*, p. 207.

students are weak. Many Americans are uneasy with fundamental democratic principles embedded in the Constitution and Bill of Rights, which leads to an impatience with efforts to ensure civil liberties and an intolerance towards an investigative, probing press. As Paul Gagnon, who headed the Bradley Commission on History in Schools, remarked, "We should stop pretending we are educating citizens when we really are not." The lessons of history, government, and economics for the prospective citizen are interrelated.

The attack on the social studies from traditional critics who argue that history, like literature, is neglected by schools and systematically devalued by educators is peculiar. United States history has always been a mainstay of the social studies, typically taught for a full year in grades 5, 8, and 11. Likewise, world history holds a significant position across the curriculum and is frequently required for graduation from high school. In addition, much history is included in courses such as government, geography, world cultures, and economics. If more history is to be required, the public must be willing to eliminate some of the "nonessential" curriculum. Yet teaching more history won't advance the cause of citizenship education if we continue to use didactic methods and rely on history texts overloaded with facts.

Very few social studies teachers want less history in the curriculum, and most recognize that it serves as a flagship to guide related studies. Economics teachers, for example, realize that for students to understand the banking system they need to know its historical antecedents. That other courses are laced with history serves to enhance both students' interest in and understanding of the subject. Jan Tucker, a leading social studies educator, explains that the argument for history, nevertheless, must be based upon something more than "history is good and we need more of it." History is much more than facts—names, dates, places, and events. As he adds, "The fundamental questions about the teaching of history are analytic and qualitative. . . . How can we deal with conflicting historical interpretations of events? How can history assist us to examine unexamined assumptions and to make 'puzzles of facts'? How can history make us more critically aware of the human condition and our own society?"[33]

Civic education, Gagnon explains, is inherently difficult "because it asks people to accept the burdens of living with tentative answers, with unfinished and often dangerous business." Democracies cherish both liberty and equality, two ideals that inevitably clash, he adds, "yet each is indispensable to the preservation of a bearable level of the other." And there is no tidy recipe for just the right blend in any given situation.[34]

Central to the conflict between traditional and progressive reformers is the relation between facts and concepts. Ravitch and Finn remark that some in the social studies field believe that concepts matter more than facts. Perhaps "some"

[33]Jan L. Tucker, "History in Our Classrooms," *The Social Studies Professional*, 91 (Mar./Apr. 1988), p. 2.
[34]Paul Gagnon, "Why Study History?" *The Atlantic*, 262, no. 5 (Nov. 1988), p. 44.

do, but, in fact, a majority of social studies educators strongly support Ravitch and Finn's statement that "a knowledge of disconnected facts that are joined, related, or explained by no concepts is obviously without significance; we learn particular facts in order to grasp ideas and develop generalizations. At best, concepts explain the facts of given situations, while facts provide examples with which to illustrate or test concepts."[35] Indeed, concepts are the framework upon which facts hang; in turn, facts are the building blocks that learners use to construct concepts, generalizations, and fresh insights. The false dichotomy between facts and concepts that Ravitch and Finn warn of never was perpetrated—at least not by the villains in their scenario.

Unfortunately, as with English and literature, the social sciences, particularly history, fall prey to an emphasis on the disparate and trivial. As Goodlad observes, topics in the social studies appear to be of great human interest. "But something strange seems to have happened to them on the way to the classroom. The topics of study become removed from their intrinsically human character, reduced to the dates and places readers will recall memorizing for tests."[36] Ironically, it is works such as Ravitch and Finn's assessment of history and literature and Hirsch's test of cultural literacy that perpetuate the pursuit of disconnected names, dates, titles, events, and authors. In their emphasis on facts, they make the heroic assumption that somehow learners will grasp the "big picture" underlying historical, moral, and philosophical themes.

Quite the opposite approach is necessary if history is to have any relevance for civic education. Historical study, the Bradley Commission reports, should "focus on broad significant themes and questions" such as "the story of American democracy," "the gathering of diverse groups of people," and "the economic transformation of America from the pre-industrial society of the colonies into the contemporary technological, post-industrial society." Along with selecting major themes, it is imperative to teach for depth of understanding rather than merely imparting shallow knowledge.[37]

Other dimensions of citizenship education. Most calls for curriculum reform make little mention of economics, government, and international studies. Yet a central function of public schools in our democratic society is to foster enlightened citizens who participate in our political economic system—a system that is increasingly taking on a global dimension. A citizen is unable to participate intelligently in our political system without an understanding of world events and foreign policy. Likewise, those who lack basic knowledge of international economics know little about economic events that affect their lives daily.

Schools cannot fulfill a primary mission if students are allowed choices in these essential areas of the social studies—to choose to study or not study geography, international relations, and our political and economic systems.

[35]Ravitch and Finn, *What Do Our 17-Year-Olds Know?* pp. 15–16.
[36]Goodlad, *A Place Called School*, p. 212.
[37]Gagnon, "Why Study History?" p. 45.

The sorry state of economic literacy, for example, prompted Alan Blinder to describe a "Murphy's Law of Economics" in public policy making that reads,

> Economists have the least influence on policy where they know the most and are most agreed; they have the most influence on policy where they know the least and disagree most vehemently.[38]

Most people's views on economic issues are based on public opinion and an identification with a special interest group. A sound understanding of fundamental economic concepts, however, often runs counter to conventional wisdom. For example, protectionism is popular among voters and politicians, though economists are nearly unanimous in agreeing that tariffs and quotas on imported goods reduce general economic welfare.

If we are to repeal "Murphy's Law," Americans' understanding of economics must go beyond the level of T-shirt and bumper-sticker slogans that admonish us to "Buy American" or "Cut Taxes, Not Jobs." Requiring students to take more economics, government, or international relations is only a start. Schools need to teach these subjects in a way that relates fundamental concepts to the daily decisions of consumers, voters, businesses, and government. Said differently, teachers must be prepared to integrate the theoretical with the practical.

In contrast, geography, like history, has been identified as a neglected area in the social studies, mostly by geography educators. And the alarm has fallen on sympathetic ears. Today America even observes "National Geography Awareness Week," something afforded few subjects.

On the surface, attention has focused on students' lack of geographic knowledge—to identify major rivers and mountain ranges, to locate countries, to name state capitals, and the like. Beyond this, geographic literacy is critical to understanding such larger issues as production of food supplies, location of industries, growth of urban areas, distribution of resources and wealth, environmental change, and global conflict. Geography, like history, serves as a framework, or resource, to understand economics, political science, and other subjects. The stance many geography advocates take, however, is to "move aside other subjects and make room for geography in the curriculum." However, geography, more than any other subject, deserves to be integrated in the social studies.

Mathematics and Science

Elementary school students receive on the average one hour of science instruction per week and four hours of mathematics. The time and resources allocated to science instruction are about the same as for the social studies. Mathematics is a centerpiece of instruction from the primary grades through high school. The mathematics curriculum in the elementary school is almost entirely

[38]Alan S. Blinder, *Hard Heads, Soft Hearts: Tough-Minded Economics for a Just Society* (Menlo Park, Calif.: Addison-Wesley Publishing Company, Inc., 1987), p. 1.

basic skills: numeration, addition, subtraction, division, multiplication, fractions, decimals, percentages, geometric shapes and measurements. At the secondary level, the math curriculum is very consistent from school to school: informal tracking directs "basic" and "regular" students into courses ranging from remedial skills to elementary algebra and geometry. The college-bound advance to higher levels of algebra, trigonometry, calculus, and computer science.

In the sciences, the tracking is more explicit, with courses titled "Applied" Physical Science or Biology clearly distinguishable from "Academic" Physical Science or Biology. The sciences, as with mathematics (calculus), English, history, government, and economics, also have courses designated for "honors" and "advanced placement" (the latter are those in which students can earn college credit).

The goals and objectives of science courses often highlight thinking skills consistent with the scientific process. Despite this and class periods devoted to laboratory exercises, students are involved in little discovery or inquiry learning. Again, textbooks dominate while students complete worksheets that elicit mostly recall information and are directed through experiments to predetermined conclusions.

Criticism leveled by the National Academy of Sciences at the biology curriculum also holds for chemistry and physics. Textbooks, it says, attempt to cover too many topics and in a fashion that is too abstract for most students. Biology texts today that often number over a thousand pages are, by and large, beautifully illustrated dictionaries. In the words of Bruce Alberts of the Academy, the biology curriculum presents topics as a series of "factlets."[39] Scientific knowledge has virtually exploded in recent decades, especially in biology, and the scientific community has not made the effort to decide what should be taught and how. As a result, students have little understanding of science and are unable to relate it to their lives.

The mathematics curriculum in particular tends to be out of date and dull. Drill in basic functions and the drudgery of paper-and-pencil solutions to square roots, quadratic equations, and logarithms still prevail. Math classes make little use of calculators and computers—the equipment that mathematicians and scientists use. Didactic methods are encouraged by administrators and the general public, who tend to equate learning with the quantity of homework and tests. As Goodlad reports, mathematics is perceived as "a body of fixed facts and skills to be acquired, not as a tool for developing a particular kind of intellectual power in the student."[40]

Innovative teachers, who provide academic rigor while fostering fascination with a subject, do so, unfortunately, without much support from university scientists. Improving and developing school curricula is a low priority among professors and researchers on the cutting edge of science. This is a far cry from the heyday of support from the National Science Foundation and the U.S. Office of Education in the 1960s, when many university scientists in mathematics, physics, biology, chemistry, and geology created innovative school curricula.

[39]Reported in *Education Week*, 8, no. 7 (Oct. 19, 1988), p. 5.
[40]Goodlad, *A Place Called School*, p. 209.

SCHOOL REFORM IN FOCUS

Much of the educational reform during the 1980s from the top down—from state legislatures and departments of education. Instead of working with principals and teachers to renew school learning environments, reformers focused on regulations. They erected more and higher hurdles for students to scale, including an increase in academic courses required for graduation. And students as early as first grade are being assigned letter grades from A to F. Although this served to stimulate some students, it further demoralized many it was intended to help—those "at risk." As a result, the number of dropouts increased.

Teachers also have been less than enthusiastic about the national school reform movement. When the Carnegie Foundation for the Advancement of Teaching interviewed over 13,500 teachers in 1988, 70 percent said the reforms (since the 1983 A *Nation at Risk* report) deserved no more than a C rating, and 20 percent gave them a failing grade. Half of the teachers surveyed said morale within the profession had declined in the last five years. A majority pointed out that political interference, state regulations, and bureaucratic paperwork had increased. On a positive note, teachers said that "goals at their schools are more clearly defined" than they were five years earlier; "student achievement has gone up in . . . math, reading, and writing"; and instructional materials, including textbooks, have improved.[41]

Despite gains, many teachers are disenchanted with the reforms because they have not been involved. This approach to reform sent a clear signal that teachers were part of the problem, not the solution. Boyer pointed out in the introduction to the report that "teachers have remained dispirited, confronted with working conditions that have left them more responsible, but less empowered." As most educators realize, educational excellence cannot be legislated, but must be patiently nurtured within the school and classroom.

Reformers tend to respond to some critics of schooling and misread the public. Most parents and students are basically pleased with schools because the shopping-mall environment serves a variety of purposes. Schools in the past several decades have increased the scope of the curriculum and made numerous accommodations and compromises. Measures to enhance excellence will be made at the expense of equity unless the needs of a diverse student population and service-oriented economy are realized. Reformers who ignore this fact of life in schools and expect intellectualism to flourish will only bang their hard heads against the classroom wall.

Nevertheless, schools are responsible to their primary mission: teaching the core curriculum, however defined. The Carnegie Report, as described, defines it broadly to fit the demands of modern postindustrial society. Within this core, a primary block of time could be reserved exclusively for the academic subjects: English language and literature; mathematics and the physical sciences; history,

[41]*Report Card on School Reform: The Teachers Speak* (Princeton, N.J.: The Carnegie Foundation for the Advancement of Teaching, 1988), pp. 1-11.

government, economics, geography, and world studies; and foreign languages. This block should be in the heart of the school day, from 8:00 A.M. to approximately noon so as not to be violated by work-study programs, extracurricular activities, and other student interests. The career-oriented offerings and elective clusters would fall after or outside this primary block of time. As a general rule, each student would be expected to do about two hours of homework daily. This arrangement places core subjects at the center of the school day, emphasizes academics as the primary function of schools, and allows adequate time for other educational offerings.

Beyond the learning imparted through the core curriculum, schools also must provide students with ways of sorting out the blizzard of informational stimuli that they face in daily life. Neil Postman recommends that they serve as a "thermostatic" device—to provide balance in the culture. Schools should be a countervailing force to the persuasions and biases of the culture.[42]

The dominant curriculum of the present society, Postman points out, is the information environment shaped by television, telecommunications, and computers. This environment stresses images—the visual, concrete, specific, and immediate, and nonparaphrasable. This television curriculum consists of picture stories that are distinct and analogous to what is represented. According to the thermostatic view, the school curriculum should stress television's counterpart— words that are conceptual, abstract, symbolic, and translatable.[43]

Essentials for the Twenty-First Century

The impediment to stating clearly a mandate for all schools lies in the political structure of education. The U.S. Constitution gives states the overall responsibility for education. Consequently, any federal government or national task force recommendations must be interpreted and enacted by states and local school districts. Federal laws, funds, and persuasion at times do effect changes in state educational policy, but Goodlad has found no clear aims for education and schooling.

His major conclusion after examining state guides to education is that the area is a "conceptual swamp." The time is long past due, he says, for "the 50 states to articulate as basic policy a commitment to a broad array of educational goals . . . that have emerged in this country over more than three hundred years."[44]

In his report on secondary education in America (*High School*), Ernest Boyer set forth *four essential goals* that with minor adjustments could also serve elementary and middle schools.

> First, according to Boyer, "schooling should help students develop the capacity to think critically and communicate effectively through a mastery of language."
> Second, "it should help all students learn about themselves, the human heritage, and the interdependent world curriculum."

[42]Postman, *Teaching as a Conserving Activity*, pp. 19–24.
[43]Ibid., pp. 52–56.
[44]Goodlad, *A Place Called School*, pp. 48–50.

Third, Boyer would have high schools "prepare all students for work and further education through a program of electives that develop individual aptitudes and interests."

Fourth, schools "should help all students fulfill their social and civic obligations through school and community service."[45]

John Goodlad also proposed a set of comprehensive goals that define the role of schools in the larger educational context. Goodlad's extensive research and policy recommendations, which complement Boyer's work, provide a clear guide for schools as they wade through the quagmire of educational reform proposals of recent years.

The goals for schooling that Goodlad outlines encompass four areas:

Academic goals—including mastery of basic skills and intellectual development;

Vocational goals—emphasizing skills related to careers and attitudes toward work;

Social, Civic, and Cultural goals—developing interpersonal understandings, citizenship participation, and values characteristic of the common culture;

Personal goals—focusing on emotional and physical well-being, creativity and aesthetic expression, and self-realization.[46]

Unlike some reform ideas that have surfaced during the 1980s, Boyer's and Goodlad's proposals are rooted in an understanding of the historical function of schools in American society. Reform ideas that focus exclusively on the basics; or on history, literature, math, and science; or on classical studies define the role of schools too narrowly. On the other hand, educational policy must guard against assuming a too ambitious role for schools, as cautioned.

Although these goals would provide young people with the knowledge, skills, and attitudes that it is reasonable to expect of schools, they leave a strategic role for other agencies to complete the whole education of students.

Coalition of essential schools. Ted Sizer, former Harvard dean and Phillips Academy headmaster who is now at Brown University, is putting into practice ideas consistent with the quest to blend excellence and equity. Through the Coalition of Essential Schools, which he also directs, Sizer's group is helping schools change in fundamental says. Small schools, big schools, even private and parochial schools, he observes, have the basic problem of trying to do too much—a theme that runs throughout this chapter and book.

Sizer's answer is to simplify what schools do and concentrate on the "essentials." One path to simplification is to restructure overloaded and ineffective schools. In the approximately fifty schools the coalition works with, teachers form teams—science, social studies, and humanities teams—in which they can pool their expertise and spend more time with a fewer number of students. A counter-

[45]Boyer, *High School*, pp. 66–67.
[46]Goodlad, *A Place Called School*, pp. 51–56.

part to this focusing is that greater academic demands are placed on students. The theme is one of "student as worker" who is accountable for a high-level intellectual performance.

A second essential to change is simplifying the smorgasbord curriculum of schools and focusing a particular course on critical themes and higher-level thinking. The message is "less is more," and schools must make tough decisions about what is most essential to know; then teach it thoroughly. Sizer calls this the "politics of subtraction." There is no quibbling over what is more important — subject matter or thinking skills, knowledge or critical thinking. One does not truly exist without the other.[47]

Restructuring Schools

Over the past few decades, many courses have been added to the school curriculum, but school time remains relatively constant: 8:00 A.M.–2:30 P.M., Monday through Friday, September through May. As Denis Doyle and David Kearns remind us in *Winning the Brain Race: A Bold Plan to Make Our Schools Competitive* (1988), American schooling is still based on an agrarian calendar that is outdated, irrelevant, and counterproductive in a modern industrial era.

Ironically, a major obstacle to changing the traditional school year is the leisure-time agenda of families. Since the early 1970s, the state of California has encouraged school districts to implement a year-round school calendar. Although it has become more appealing since the *A Nation at Risk* report in 1983, parents have been cool to the concept, explaining that it interferes with family vacations. Teachers, not surprisingly, have been even less receptive than families to the extended school year, especially if their responsibilities and pay would remain constant. If an eleven-month school calendar, for example, meant a comparable increase in pay, they perhaps would support the idea.

If the comprehensive curriculum is to be taught effectively, the school day, week, and year must be expanded. And the schoolhouse will have to be used more efficiently. School buildings across the land, some magnificent structures, sit idle nearly 180 days a year. In the business world, this is "underutilization of capital goods" and a matter of much concern.

In this high-technology world dominated by electronic media and multinational enterprises, the role of schooling has changed. Competency in basic skills (math, reading, and writing) and basic knowledge (literature, history, and science) is only a start. Equally as important as these are critical thinking and problem solving that can be taught across the curriculum. These intellectual abilities apply equally to core subjects, vocational studies, citizenship, and values.

Despite experimenting with flexible scheduling, informal classrooms, and open campuses, the school organization has changed little over the years. Likewise, the curriculum has remained remarkably unchanged. Nevertheless, if you could be

[47]Ron Brandt, "On Changing Secondary Schools: A Conversation with Ted Sizer," *Educational Leadership*, 45, no. 5 (Feb. 1988), pp. 30–36.

TABLE 2-1   Should the School Year Be Lengthened?

THE PUBLIC'S VIEW[48]

In some nations students spend about 25% more time in school than do students in the U.S. Would
You favor or oppose increasing the amount of time that students in this community spend in school?

	NATIONAL TOTALS %	NO CHILDREN IN SCHOOL %	PUBLIC SCHOOL PARENTS %	NONPUBLIC SCHOOL PARENTS %
Favor	48	48	46	54
Oppose	44	43	48	40
Don't know	8	9	6	6

TEACHERS' VIEW[49]

In some nations students attend school as many as 240 days a year, as compared to about 180
days in the U.S. Aside from the question of teacher/staff compensation, how do you feel about
extending the public school year in this community by 30 days, making the school year about 210
days or 10 months long? Do you favor or oppose this idea?

	ALL TEACHERS		U.S. PUBLIC	ELEMENTARY TEACHERS		HIGH SCHOOL TEACHERS	
	1984 %	1989 %	1984 %	1984 %	1989 %	1984 %	1989 %
Favor	28	30	44	27	29	29	31
Oppose	66	63	50	67	64	66	61
No opinion	6	7	6	6	7	5	8

transported in time to the 1940s, you would observe clear differences in schools
and classrooms. Textbooks today are more colorful, richly illustrated, and thicker;
most teachers use forms of positive reinforcement and audiovisual materials to
interest students; and principals are ladened with administrative chores. But the
prevailing school environment has changed little over the years. Secondary schools
operate on fixed schedules of six or seven periods, nearly one hour long with a set
time in between classes—just enough for students to make the next class. And
teaching is centered on lessons from the text, lectures with some discussion led by
the teacher, and emphasis on facts, skills, and drills. As Goodlad's study group
found, teachers and administrators, by and large, are uncomfortable with "hands-
on" activities or "learning by doing," whereas those who plan field trips, community-based projects, workshops, and small conferences encounter logistical hurdles.
In his words, "Teachers may start out 'fighting the system,' but it is easier,
ultimately, to settle down into conventional ways of teaching. And one tends to
look more normal doing so. The cards are stacked against innovation."[50]

[48]Stanley M. Elam and Alec M. Gallup, "The 21st Annual Gallup Poll of the Public's Attitudes
Toward the Public Schools," *Phi Delta Kappan*, 71, no. 1 (Sept. 1989), pp. 48–49.

[49]Stanley M. Elam, "The Second Gallup Phi Delta Kappa Poll of Teachers' Attitudes Toward the
Public Schools," *Phi Delta Kappan*, 70, no. 10 (June 1989), p. 797.

[50]Goodlad, *A Place Called School*, p. 237.

Albert Shanker, president of the American Federation of Teachers (AFT), believes that public schools have a golden opportunity to become much more effective, but that moment won't last long. If governors, businesses, and organizations don't see results from the resources they have begun to provide, that support will be withdrawn and many schools left to wither. Unfortunately, it appears that community leaders underestimate the nature and magnitude of the change required. Providing resources for schools to do their job is only one side of the reform coin; the other is to assume some educational functions that now, to paraphrase Arthur Powell, force schools to become treatment centers and rob them of the energy and incentives to engage in their intellectual agenda, which is their unique chance to reconcile the twin goals of equity and excellence.

But schools, Shanker believes, must seize the initiative if they are to carry out this "intellectual agenda" and survive. He recommends that schools restructure by organizing teaching staffs into teams of six or seven instructors. Each team would be responsible for the learning of a group of about 120 students across subjects throughout the entire elementary years, middle school, or high school grades. This team-group approach could be implemented differently from school to school, but essentially it is "school within a school." A team would be headed by at least one lead or master teacher and include some combination of paraprofessions, student or intern teachers, administrative assistants, and regular teachers. Each team would decide how it is organized to carry out the many tasks that go on in classrooms. There would be no department heads, assistant principals, and guidance counselors; these people would be part of the instructional team. A team would plan and organize instruction, implement the curriculum, advise students, serve as a mentor for new teachers, coach the less competent, and weed out the incompetent.

Learning would take place in small groups, with much cooperative learning and little or no lecturing. Instruction would be based on active learning—problem solving, simulations, interactive computer programs, oral and written reports. Each activity would take as long as needed to accomplish the task, so bells would be eliminated. The intent, needless to say, is for students to become intellectually involved and enjoy school, but they are also responsible for what they learn. Students can no longer sit back and be passive. In Sizer's terms, students are the workers.

One member of each team would serve on a faculty senate to help forge school policy, and another would work on the curriculum committee. In short, with the help of a principal or master planner who oversees the school operations, teaching teams run the school.[51]

In "Turning Points: Preparing American Youth for the 21st Century," the Carnegie Council on Adolescent Development turned its attention to restructuring the nation's middle-grade schools. A major theme of this report is to restructure the enormous middle-grade schools, which exceed a thousand students and reach as high as two thousand in some urban communities, into much smaller "commu-

---

[51]We've taken liberty in elaborating on Mr. Shanker's general proposal that he delivered in a talk on restructuring schools for the Association of Supervision and Curriculum Development (ASCD).

nities of learning." Schools would be formed around teams of teachers and students so that teachers would have the opportunity to work with students as individuals, and students would get to know each other well. Also, each student would have an adult adviser whom he or she could talk to about academic matters and personal problems.[52]

PUBLIC SCHOOLS AT THE PRECIPICE

Schools are essentially political institutions, the chief instrument for reproducing society in a desired image. And they have consistently served this purpose. Not everything society demands of its schools is inspiring or sensible. In this last quarter of the twentieth century, schools are being asked to educate everyone in virtually all aspects of living. Try as hard as schools might to meet this demand, they will be unable to deliver. As a result, public education today is in jeopardy.

Schools, as Postman explains, should not attempt to accomplish goals that other institutions serve. The family, church, medical profession, communications media, and community groups all have specific functions. Schools do not have the time to assume these functions, nor are teachers competent to serve as therapists, psychologists, priests, social workers, or parents. It may be tempting to assume these responsibilities when they are performed inadequately by other institutions, but nothing in the training of teachers prepares them to do what others are supposed to do. The task of teaching the academic curriculum is challenging enough without trying to do everyone's work.[53]

Approximately one hundred years ago, near the turn of century, American schools last underwent fundamental change. This also was a period of restructuring in our society. The changing economic base no longer depended on adolescent labor, but it demanded different workplace skills and attitudes, while mass immigration prompted the need to "Americanize" the many new citizens. City school systems grew rapidly.

Sizer, Shanker, and others sense that now is the time for another fundamental change in the structure of American schooling. The transformation of our economic society and the wave of new immigrant groups from Third World countries begs for a reshaping of school organization and curriculum. Many leaders argue that the United States is in a competitive race for its life. And schools are seen as the fulcrum to the economic and political well-being of our nation.

Discipline and Order

For nearly two decades the Gallup organization has been asking people what they consider the foremost problem facing schools. In nearly all those years, the answer has been "a lack of discipline." Actually, the problem is not insufficient

---

[52]"The American Adolescent; Facing a 'Vortex of New Risks,' " *Education Week*, 8, no. 39 (June 21, 1989), pp. 22–23.

[53]Postman, *Teaching as a Conserving Activity*, pp. 113–15.

discipline in schools, but the undisciplined behavior of some students. Students, teachers, and even administrators are physically attacked in many junior or senior high schools; the problem is particularly acute in urban schools.

School officials have not created the problem, but they are responsible for controlling it. Most antisocial behavior of students originates in the homes and streets, not in schools. Because nearly everyone is required to attend school until the age of sixteen, classrooms contain unruly youngsters with little interest in studies. Even though the root cause of disrespectful, unmotivated, and even violent students lies in the messages of a larger society that values acquisitiveness and gratification more than intellectual effort, schools will have to lead the way.

Unfortunately, some school officials overreact in their zeal to bring order and control to the classroom and surrounding environment. This response has been particularly evident following the more permissive school policies of the 1970s. School officials often suspend students from classes and other activities or expel them from school for behavior that has no relation to their studies or the learning environment of the school. A young person's use, for example, of cigarettes, alcohol, and other drugs off the school grounds is not relevant to school business. Decent adults, whatever their roles, want to discourage this behavior, but it makes little sense to choose ways that contradict the central educational purpose of schools.

A preoccupation with order and control is no less characteristic of schools today than it was in 1970 when Charles Silberman wrote *Crisis in the Classroom*. When managed with an eye toward the greater purpose of education, this quality can provide the structure necessary for productive and enjoyable learning environments. In many schools, however, such a preoccupation leads to oppressive and petty regulations that make them grim and joyless places.[54]

Creating healthy, orderly schools need not be an overwhelming task. Schools need only follow a simple but fair maxim to ensure and maintain this order: *A child's right to an education should be terminated only where that child interferes with the right of other children to have one. Teachers must have the power to dismiss students who disrupt learning in the classroom, and administrators should suspend students who violate the greater school environment.* Such a policy also sends a clear message to students and parents as to school's paramount purpose.

Schools are responsible for providing an engaging learning environment, but educators should not be either jail keepers or entertainers. The fact that many students are not "intellectually motivated" need not alter the central purpose of schooling. As Postman remarks, "the school is not an extension of the street, the movie theater, a rock concert, or a playground, and certainly not an extension of the psychiatric clinic." The school may be the only remaining public situation, he adds, in which traditional rules control group interaction, and it would be a grave mistake to change the rules because some students cannot function within them.[55]

[54]Silberman, *Crisis in the Classroom*, pp. 122–26.
[55]Neil Postman, "Order in the Classroom," *The Atlantic*, 244, no. 3 (Sept. 1979), pp. 35–38.

Where Schools Succeed

The foremost purpose of public education has been to educate every citizen. Only during the twentieth century has this purpose included equal educational opportunity, or equity, as a goal. In the early days, public education attempted to assimilate and control a rapidly growing and diverse population in order to reinforce traditional authority. Still, the finest achievement of the American system has been to give everyone a chance for an education. No amount of criticism should overlook this accomplishment—one that no other nation shares.

In 1950, fewer than 50 percent of all U.S. students graduated from high school; by 1980 there were over 80 percent. Ten percent of the black students graduated from high school in 1950; today the rate is over 75 percent. The number of students graduating from college tripled between 1955 and 1980. More than 90 percent of today's adult population attended public schools. The list goes on.

Providing the opportunity for education, of course, does not ensure that all students will receive it. Some students slip through the "cracks of the schoolhouse walls" and learn far less than what they are capable of, whereas a few graduate functionally illiterate. Silberman's sentiments two decades ago are no less true today: "Public schools are failing dismally in what has always been regarded as one of their primary tasks—in Horace Mann's phrase, to be 'the great equalizer of the conditions of man.' " "Far from being 'the great equalizer,' " he adds, "the schools help perpetuate the differences in condition, or at the very least, do little to reduce them."[56] The greater danger today, however, is that, swept up in the tide of public opinion, people easily forget the accomplishments and basic purpose of public schooling.

"Public education, for all its flaws and shortcomings," writes John Egerton, "is the nearest thing we have to a publicly owned and operated institution devoted to the general welfare." Plans such as the tuition tax credit for families with students in private schools are thinly veiled measures to subsidize the well-to-do and undermine public schooling. Unless government is willing to fund educational vouchers generously, to ensure that schools by choice don't lead to resegregation, or to establish curriculum guidelines for any market-driven school plans, the gains of recent decades, especially for the poor and minorities, will be reversed. It's true that students of poor families and the less educated have not benefited from public education as much as those of the middle class. But if the public school system is allowed to deteriorate, the quality of education for the underclass will sink to the level of inadequate health care, legal services, transportation, insurance, and retirement benefits that they now receive.[57]

Paideia

For all the worthy ideas embedded in Mortimer Adler's *Paideia Proposal* for public schooling, his group did not take the main theme far enough. The Greeks' use of the word *paideia* implied that the child's upbringing or education would

[56]Silberman, *Crisis in the Classroom*, p. 54.
[57]John Egerton, "Can We Save the Schools?" *Progressive*, 46, no. 3 (Mar. 1982), p. 27.

come not just from schools but from all agencies of society. In modern society this includes television, films, mass media, churches and synagogues, law, medicine, social work, business, libraries, museums, and youth organizations. As Silberman explains, these agencies have a major influence on the growing child, but they essentially serve to enculturate, not educate. "The weakness of American education," he writes, "is not that the paideia does not educate, but that it educates to the wrong ends."[58] When properly employed, community agencies extend education; otherwise, they can undermine the value of schooling.

Although society as a whole needs to play an important role in the total education of people, schools are the central academic component. Part of this responsibility is what educators from Cicero to the present have advocated and what Postman labeled the "thermostatic view." Schools must protect the maturing student from the biases of society and ensure against a one-dimensional education and a half-developed personality. The educated among us are able to stand on the edge of culture, always viewing and evaluating in a prospective and objective manner.

Case Study: Remaking the Curriculum

You are department chairperson in a high school that has completely changed the math, science, social studies, and English curricula over the past ten years. Several faculty members, including yourself, have taken sabbaticals or leaves of absence during this period to study at the state university, which is on the cutting edge of school curriculum innovation. You feel a sense of accomplishment regarding the content and methods of the courses in your department. All teachers have textbooks that are modern and up to date, and most use a variety of supplemental materials that help further the inquiry learning skills emphasized in the department.

This past year a group of parents and other citizens organized to analyze the curriculum offered by the core departments at the high school. This research committee examined the texts, other learning materials, and teaching methods of your department and others. They concluded, among other things, that students are not spending enough time on basic computation skills; diagramming English sentences; and learning the facts of history, geography and science. In their report to the school board they specifically criticized the reflective-inquiry approach, the emphasis on contemporary issues, and the use of modern literature in many classes. Although students' achievement scores have not declined in recent years, neither have they increased. Given the resources devoted to curriculum improvement, the committee claimed that your department and others have not advanced education in the district.

You have received a memorandum from the school principal asking you to show evidence that students are better prepared now in the subject areas of your

[58]Silberman, *Crisis in the Classroom*, p. 5.

department than they were five or ten years ago. The principal also wants you to show why an essential curriculum proposed by the committee should not be implemented.

Thought Questions

1. What do the authors mean when they say that many, if not all, institutions in society have an educational role to play? Name several institutions or agencies (for example, the medical community or the media) and explain the educational role they could fulfill.

2. Discuss why and in what ways the public school curriculum has expanded during the past thirty or more years. What broad educational needs has it come to serve? Explain why this expansion is desirable or undesirable.

3. Assuming that a school district is faced with budget constraints, what areas, if any, in the curriculum would you eliminate? Explain why you would drop some areas and why others, or all, would be retained.

4. Consider the four areas set forth in John Goodlad's goals for schooling and explain to what extent each can be and should be developed in your teaching field (e.g., physical science, English, business education, special education).

5. According to the "thermostatic" view of schooling, what should be emphasized in the school curriculum today? Which courses and what type of learning are most important? Would your response be different if you were answering this question in the 1960s? To what extent do schools follow the thermostatic view? Should they be guided by this view or reinforce dominant cultural values?

6. Should sex education be part of the school curriculum? Why or why not? If so, at what grade levels and in what way should it be taught? What role should the community play?

7. How are schools in the area you live restructuring or radically changing? What will the result be, and will it be appropriate for the individual learner? For the larger society?

8. If a school starts from the maxim "a child's right to an education should be terminated only where that child interferes with the right of other children to have one," what policies should it establish toward: drug and alcohol use, language use and abuse, dress codes, and disruptive behavior?

9. Is it possible for public schooling in the United States to achieve both equity and excellence? What policies are needed to accomplish these? If both goals are not simultaneously attainable, which would you emphasize more?

Practical Activities

1. Obtain the curriculum offering of a public or private school in your college or hometown. List the courses and activities that are (a) essential to quality education; (b) those that are important, but not essential, and probably would not be accomplished by agencies outside the schools; (c) those that definitely should not be the

schools' responsibility. Summarize the rationale underlying the development of each list.

2. Take a unit of study from a course that you have taught or will be teaching and list three objectives that demand higher-order knowledge or skills (not basic recall or information items). Develop an evaluation item for each object that could be used to test and measure for accountability purposes.

3. Interview a local school administrator and obtain a statement of the district's or school's accountability procedure. Discuss how the policy is implemented. Analyze and evaluate the effectiveness of the policy in a two- to three-page position paper.

4. Develop a questionnaire to survey the public on the importance of achieving excellence and equity in education. Include items that assess what learning should be emphasized, what knowledge is most worth knowing, and, if necessary, what should be eliminated from the curriculum. Review the questionnaire with your professor before administering it, and write up the results.

5. Ask a public librarian and school media specialist about the library's policy on censorship: What criteria do they use for screening books? What provisions exist for input from public citizens? What procedures are used to ensure that intellectual freedom is respected? Also report on any instances of censorship the librarian has had to confront. Write up your findings.

6. Determine the discipline and dress-code regulations of several schools in your district. Develop a set of guidelines for discipline and dress that you would want to apply to your school and classroom. Reproduce the guidelines and prepare for a discussion with other students. Report on the views expressed in the discussion.

7. Starting from either Ernest Boyer's *High School* core curriculum, Mortimer Adler's *Paideia Proposal,* or William Bennett's *James Madison High School* plan, or a combination of these, design your own comprehensive curriculum. This curriculum can cover K-6, 5-8, 7-12, 9-12, or K-12. Build the design from a set of major goals, and describe the methods of instruction to be used.

Bibliography

ADLER, MORTIMER J., *The Paideia Proposal: An Educational Manifesto.* New York: Macmillan, 1982.

BOYER, ERNEST L., *High School: A Report on Secondary Education in America.* New York: Harper & Row, Publishers, Inc., 1983.

BROUDY, HARRY S., *The Real World of Public Schools.* New York: Harcourt Brace Jovanovich, Inc., 1972.

CHANAN, GABRIEL, and LINDA GILCHRIST, *What School Is For.* New York: Praeger Publishers, Inc., 1974.

GOODLAD, JOHN I., *What Schools Are For.* Bloomington, Ind.: Phi Delta Kappa Educational Foundation, 1979.

_____, *A Place Called School: Prospects for the Future.* New York: McGraw-Hill Book Company, Inc., 1984.

GROSS, BEATRICE and RONALD, eds., *The Great School Debate.* New York: Simon & Schuster, Inc., 1985.

HAMPEL, ROBERT L., *The Last Little Citadel: American High Schools Since 1940.* Boston: Houghton Mifflin Company, 1985.

HIRSCH, E. D., *Cultural Literacy: What Every American Needs to Know.* Boston: Houghton Mifflin Company, 1987.

KEARNS, DAVID T., and DENIS P. DOYLE, *Winning the Brain Race: A Bold Plan to Make Our Schools Competitive.* San Francisco: ICS Press, Institute for Contemporary Studies, 1988.

LAUDERDALE, WILLIAM BURT, *Educational Reform: The Forgotten Half.* Bloomington, Ind.: Phi Delta Kappa Educational Foundation, 1987.

NATIONAL COMMISSION ON EXCELLENCE IN EDUCATION, *A Nation at Risk: The Imperative for Educational Reform.* Washington, D.C.: U.S. Government Printing Office, 1983.

POSTMAN, NEIL, *Teaching as a Conserving Activity.* New York: Dell Publishing Company, Inc., 1979.

POWELL, ARTHUR G., ELEANOR FARRAR, and DAVID K. COHEN, *The Shopping Mall High School: Winners and Losers in the Educational Marketplace.* Boston: Houghton Mifflin Company, 1985.

RAVITCH, DIANE, and CHESTER E. FINN, JR. *What Do Our 17-Year-Olds Know? A Report on the First National Assessment of History and Literature.* New York: Harper & Row, Publishers, Inc., 1987.

SIZER, THEODORE, *Horace's Compromise: The Dilemma of the American High School.* Boston: Houghton Mifflin Company, 1984.

Turning Points: Preparing American Youth for the 21st Century: The Report of the Task Force on Education of Young Adolescents. Washington, D. C.: Carnegie Council on Adolescent Development, 1989.

3

Philosophies of Education

The Rule in philosophy is that no belief, however indispensable to practical life, is to be regarded as true without supporting evidence.[1]

People become educated, as opposed to trained, insofar as they achieve a grasp of critical principles and an ability and passion to choose, organize, and shape their own ideas and living beliefs by means of them.[2]

PHILOSOPHY MATTERS

A five-year-old boy asks his father, "Do birds know they have wings?" A kindergarten child asks her teacher, "How much is infinity?" These are the questions of the philosopher. Why is it that questions such as these come so easily, naturally, and sincerely from children, yet students of education groan with dismay when faced with a course or a chapter on philosophy and education? Perhaps it is the reputation philosophy has for being obtuse, bewildering, impenetrable, or pointless that has finally caught up with older students. Perhaps students have experienced philosophy as a meaningless catalog of names and descriptions that they were required to memorize and reproduce on tests.

However, it may be that teachers and soon-to-be teachers avoid philosophy because it seems irrelevant to their interpretation of the teaching task. If a teacher views the job of teaching primarily as a matter of applying appropriate and effective teaching strategies, then philosophy, which tends to ask difficult questions about the purposes and meaning of education, may seem of little value or interest. The teacher concerned only with questions of *how* to achieve predetermined ends is not likely to look kindly on a discipline that tends to ask difficult *why* questions about both ends and means.

This chapter takes the position that, as a profession, teaching requires its practitioners to be thoughtful and reflective about the enterprise of teaching. Alan

[1]Arnold B. Levison, "The Uses of Philosophy and the Problems of Educators," in *Selected Readings in the Philosophy of Education*, ed. Joe Park (New York: Macmillan, 1969), p. 31.

[2]Richard Paul, "Dialogical Thinking: Critical Thought Essential to the Acquisition of Rational Knowledge and Passions," in *Teaching Thinking Skills: Theory and Practice*, eds. Joan Boykoff Baron and Robert Sternberg (New York: W. H. Freeman & Company, 1986), p. 143.

Tom, in his *Teaching as a Moral Craft,* sees teachers as "self-directed, critical, experimental persons" who must "accept responsibility for the educational constructions we find around us."[3] What Tom means is that a teacher cannot simply abdicate responsibility for the purposes of education while attending only to figuring out the best method for achieving objectives. A trainer is a technician who need not concern him- or herself with the ultimate value or worth of an enterprise. On the other hand, a teacher is concerned not with just training, but with education. In Richard Paul's words,

> [Education is] not a mere piling up of more and more bits and pieces of information. It is a process of deciding for ourselves what we believe. . . . It is a process of autonomously deciding what is and what is not true and false. It calls for self-motivated action on our own mental nature and a participation in the form of our own character. It is a process in which we learn to open our mind, correct and refine it, and enable it to learn rationally, thereby empowering it to analyze, digest, master and rule its own knowledge.[4]

John Dewey, a giant of American educational philosophy, spent his career promoting the idea that education is a matter of *fostering thinking* rather than transmitting knowledge. The Association for Supervision and Curriculum Development (ASCD), in fact, takes the position that the primary concern of education should be the development of rational thinkers.[5] If one accepts Dewey's and Paul's views, then the role of the teacher not only is complex but is involved in making reasoned judgments about matters where there are no right or wrong answers. If you disagree with this statement, you have joined a classical philosophic debate at its most fundamental level. You have taken sides in an old and respected division between those who have viewed education as Dewey and Paul have and those who believe that the role of education is to pass along the accumulated knowledge and wisdom of the culture.

If a major goal of education is to develop thoughtful, reflective students, we must have teachers with similar traits. "It is unreasonable," asserts Matthew Lipman, "to think that a child brought up in irrational institutions will behave rationally."[6] It is also unreasonable to think that a school can be any more rational, thoughtful, or reflective than its teachers. It may be that teachers of the so-called gifted and talented can be successful without, themselves, being gifted or talented, but it is not possible for teachers to teach children to be thoughtful, reflective, clear-thinking people if they do not possess those qualities themselves.

Where do you stand on these issues? Will you be a reflective professional

[3]Alan Tom, *Teaching as a Moral Craft* (New York: Longman, Inc., 1984), pp. 97, 202.

[4]Paul, "Dialogical Thinking," p. 143.

[5]Robert J. Marsano et al., *Dimensions for Thinking: A Framework for Curriculum and Instruction* (Alexandria, Va.: Association for Supervision and Curriculum Development, 1988).

[6]Matthew Lipman, *Philosophy Goes to School* (Philadelphia: Temple University Press, 1988), p. 8.

making judgments based upon self-knowledge? Will you be free to choose your position on matters of curriculum or discipline or purpose, or will your responses simply be automatic, mindless, and predictable products of your own conditioning? Freedom implies not only a lack of imposed restraint in making choices, but the availability of adequate information about the alternatives from which you may choose, the skill to evaluate the choices in a rational way, and the courage to choose in favor of your reasoned, ethical judgment—even in the face of opposition.

To the extent that you believe that your job as an educator is mainly a matter of learning *how* to execute a set of preselected behaviors, you will be a technician who might better choose a job in a more predictable environment than a school full of human beings. To the extent that you do not reflect upon or think critically about your own behavior, beliefs, attitudes, and the enterprise of education, you will be a slave to your personal history and conditioning. As a teacher you will be able to do little more than pass along to the next generation your unchallenged prejudices and unanalyzed attitudes. If you accept that all the decisions about what education is for and why a person should go to school have already been made and are no longer in question or in need of examination, then for you philosophy will be irrelevant. If, on the other hand, you believe that education is a socially constructed phenomenon whose goals and purposes are still open for question, then philosophy has an important role to play in your professional activities.

RELATIONSHIP OF PHILOSOPHY TO EDUCATION

George Kneller, noted American philosopher, in an address before the American Educational Studies Association entitled "The Proper Study of Education," said that education has largely ignored the disciplines that are basic to it. He contends that education's root disciplines are history, philosophy, literature, and some aspects of cultural anthropology, not the social sciences that have for so long dominated education. Those who expect the human sciences such as psychology and sociology to produce a science of education, he added, are bound to be disappointed and misled. Kneller asked his listeners to imagine what a science of education would be like. "It would attempt to formulate laws and theories explaining, predicting, and controlling the educational process."[7] Neither science nor the scientific method will ever be able to resolve educational debates between those who believe there should be prayer in school and those who do not; or between those who believe that school should primarily prepare people for the workplace and those who think school should teach students to become critical thinkers. He observes that, "despite prodigious efforts and enormous expenditures of money,

[7]George Kneller, Keynote address at the annual meeting of the American Educational Studies Association, Milwaukee, Wis., Nov. 3, 1987. Reprinted in AESA *News and Comments*, 14, no. 2, March, 1988, p. 3.

human scientists have produced no universal laws or theories that are either scientific or precise."[8]

Kneller takes the position that philosophy is the discipline most relevant to education because it is concerned with knowledge, ethics, and values. The difficulty of dealing with the problematic nature of teaching and learning has caused many to strive for certainty—certainty in the sense of scientific certainty. Because our educational system focuses on measurable outcomes, we tend to believe that it should be possible to identify those factors that will guarantee consistent outcomes. Alan Tom claims that knowledge derived from a scientific approach to teaching will "be inherently trivial, since it is generated by applying a purely technical perspective to phenomena intimately connected to underlying human purposes."[9]

Philosophy, rather than science, should be the touchstone of education, because philosophy, unlike science, deals with the "wholeness" of existence. Science takes human existence apart and delivers partial images of human beings. It presupposes that its results are objective, that they are not tainted by human intervention. Philosophy, on the other hand, acknowledges that in human matters there is no way to extricate the influence of human choice and perception. Philosophy acknowledges the complexity and contingency of human behavior. Science has attempted to simplify and generalize about matters that are complex and contingent.

Teaching is fundamentally a moral activity requiring teachers to take moral responsibility. Philosopher and educator David Hawkins believes that "the [teacher-learner] relationship, by its very nature, involves an offer of control by one individual over the functioning of another, who in accepting this offer, is tacitly assured that control will not be exploitive but will be used to enhance the competence and extend the independence of the once controlled."[10] Tom expands the moral concerns of teachers beyond the teacher-learner relationship to the ends of education. He points out that when we consider ends, or purposes, in our private lives, we are exercising personal choice. That is, when we consider the kind of life or activity we think best for ourselves, it is a personal consideration that we are free to deal with as we choose. But when we move the moral situations to the public realm of teaching, then we must carefully analyze and select the most desirable ends.[11]

Behind every educational program and most educational decisions, explains Bertrand Russell, lies a set of assumptions about what constitutes a good life, a good person, and good society.[12] "The effective teacher," in Tom's words, "is not necessarily the one who has been programmed with research-based prescriptions

[8]Ibid., p. 4.

[9]Tom, *Teaching,* p. 80.

[10]David Hawkins quoted in Tom, *Teaching,* p. 80.

[11]Tom, *Teaching,* p. 79.

[12]Bertrand Russell, *Education and the Good Life* (New York: Liveright Publishing Corporation, 1970).

for various teaching problems. Instead the effective teacher may be the one who is able to conceive of his teaching in purposeful terms, analyze a particular teaching problem, choose a teaching approach that seems appropriate to the problem, attempt the approach, judge the results in relation to the original purpose, and reconsider either the teaching approach or the original purpose.[13]

However much one may learn about the techniques of teaching, most of what one does as a teacher will be governed by one's beliefs about students, knowledge, school, what is good and bad, and what is right and wrong. This composite of attitudes, values, and beliefs is one's frame of reference—the window through which to view the world; in short, a philosophy. What one sees through this window determines the meaning attributed to events and subsequent reactions. If a frame of reference is distorted or inaccurate, then the conclusions arrived at will be distorted and inaccurate.

Studying philosophy will not guarantee a perfectly clear window for anyone. In fact, some philosophic positions hold that there is no such thing as a clear window. There is, according to some philosophies, no reality independent of our perceptions of it. If one is to use philosophy as a means for seeing more clearly, one must first acquire the disposition and the skill of the philosopher. Second, one must study the philosophical systems that philosophers have spent their lives creating and thinking about.

It is the function of philosophy to challenge thinking: to ask us to examine our assumptions, to clarify our thinking, to back up our claims with evidence, to demand that our thinking be rational. The teacher possessing this philosophical turn of mind will be a reflective professional interested not only in knowing what to do on Monday but in understanding why he or she is doing it. The teacher who understands that an inquiry-based social studies or science program is rooted in the belief that students can discover knowledge, is not tied to any particular activity but has the freedom to respond with appropriate alternatives when a particular activity is not working. Having a desire and a passion to question and understand will help a teacher be able to empower students rather than enslave them.

WHAT IS PHILOSOPHY?

Philosophy, like education, does not lend itself to a simple definition. By describing the characteristics of a philosophic mind, the skills of philosophizing, and different philosophies, however, one can obtain a sense of the intellectual domain occupied by philosophy.

Charles Brauner, in his *Problems in Education and Philosophy*, helps clarify what philosophy is by describing it first as a process, then as a product.[14]

[13]Tom, *Teaching*, p. 72.
[14]Charles Brauner and Herbert W. Burns, *Problems in Education and Philosophy* (Englewood Cliffs, N.J.: Prentice-Hall, Inc., 1965), p. 15.

Doing Philosophy: A Process

Although it is not expected that teachers become philosophers, philosophy must, if it is to be of use to teachers, be something that one does as opposed to something that one simply learns about. Philosophy is primarily an activity and secondarily a subject matter consisting of a definite body of literature.[15] *Doing* philosophy means being reflective about experience. John Dewey defined reflective thought as "active, persistent and careful consideration on any belief or supposed form of knowledge in the light of the grounds that support it and the further conclusions to which it tends."[16] Doing philosophy means that one thinks critically, and a critical thinker is one who takes a position of informed skepticism. One who thinks critically tends to raise and answer questions about the claims, conclusions, beliefs, and definitions, whether they are one's own or others'. Richard Paul defines critical thinking as "fairmindedly interpreting, analyzing or evaluating information, arguments or experiences with a set of reflective attitudes, skills and abilities to guide our thoughts, beliefs and actions."[17]

Philosophers and scholars have developed many schemes for describing and organizing the skills for thinking critically and philosophically. However, unless these skills are combined with a "critical thinking disposition," they are little more than mechanical motions unlikely to produce clarity or wisdom. In general, a critical thinking disposition means that one is willing to challenge and question even the most widely held beliefs and assumptions. Robert Ennis suggests that a person with a critical thinking disposition would do the following:

1. Seek a clear statement of the questions.
2. Seek reasons.
3. Try to be well informed.
4. Use and mention credible sources.
5. Take into account the total situation.
6. Try to remain relevant to the main point.
7. Keep in mind the original or basic concern.
8. Look for an alternative.
9. Be open-minded, which means considering seriously other points of view, reasoning from premises with which one disagrees (suppositional thinking), and withholding judgment.
10. Take a position and change a position when the evidence and reasons are sufficient.
11. Seek as much precision as the subject permits.
12. Deal in an orderly manner with the parts of a complex whole.

[15]Levison, "The Uses of Philosophy and the Problems of Educators," pp. 25–32.

[16]John Dewey quoted in Levison, "The Uses of Philosophy and the Problems of Educators," p. 27.

[17]Debbie Walsh and Richard Paul, *The Goal of Critical Thinking, From Educational Ideal to Educational Reality* (New York: American Federation of Teachers, Educational Issues Department, 1987), p. 8.

13. Use one's critical thinking abilities.
14. Be sensitive to the feelings, level of knowledge, and degrees of sophistication of others.[18]

Carlton Bowyer adds that those who exhibit a philosophic attitude respect other people and their opinions and act as if all "beliefs and commitments are open to continued investigation and freedom of inquiry prevails."[19]

"Doing philosophy" also can be divided into four distinct processes: analytic, evaluative, speculative, and integrative.

Analysis means examining the assumptions and beliefs that lie behind educational decisions and practices. For example, in analyzing, one might question the assumptions upon which ability grouping of students, or tracking, is based. What assumptions about students and learning are implied in deciding to group students by test scores for purposes of instruction?

Evaluation means determining criteria by which to judge actions. For example, the discipline policies and practices of a teacher who believes that little boys are naturally bad will be much different from those of a teacher who believes that children, be they boys or girls, are neither bad nor good but have the capability for both kinds of behavior. Scientific studies do not prove conclusively that either position is correct. Hence, teachers' behaviors will vary depending upon what they have come to believe. The person with a critical frame of mind would be interested in examining the validity, reasonableness, and consequences of both points of view.

Speculation, or the speculative function of philosophy, asks, What if? Why not? In this process the educator combines the analytic and evaluative functions to create alternatives. It is not, as some might think, random, undisciplined activity. In order for speculation to have importance and meaning, it must adhere to standards of rationality, logic, and evidence.

Through *integration,* the process of philosophy becomes a philosophical product. When educators arrive at beliefs through critical analysis and evaluation, these beliefs become a coherent product capable of being applied to a wide range of circumstances and conditions. The results of an integrative process arrived at by philosophers have become important schools of thought.[20]

Philosophy as a Product

If philosophizing is asking questions, then philosophies are the answers. They are the understandings and clarifications that result from systematic inquiry. The products of philosophy are the coherent systems of thought developed by great philosophers who spend their lives grappling with philosophic issues.

[18]Robert H. Ennis, "A Taxonomy of Critical Thinking Dispositions and Abilities," in *Teaching Thinking Skills: Theory and Practice*, eds. Joan Boykoff Baron and Robert Sternberg (W. H. Freeman & Company, 1986), pp. 12–13.

[19]Carlton H. Bowyer, *Philosophical Perspectives for Education* (Glenview, Ill.: Scott, Foresman & Company, 1970), p. 11.

[20]Brauner, *Problems in Education and Philosophy*, pp. 20–21.

One way to describe philosophy is to describe the philosophic issues about which philosophers concern themselves. The terms used to label the subdivisions of the philosophic territory are formidable-sounding words: ontology, axiology, and epistemology. Each philosophy, such as idealism or pragmatism, is a systematic attempt to deal with the topics of these philosophic subdivisions.

Ontology, or metaphysics, attempts to describe or understand what is real, what exists. Metaphysics asks questions such as: Is the universe the result of a rational creation, or is it ultimately meaningless? Is human behavior predetermined, or are humans really free? Science does not address these questions; in fact, science, and people generally, just carry around unconscious assumptions about the nature and origin of existence.

Axiology is that realm of philosophy concerned with values. Questions about right and wrong, good and bad are the domain of axiology. This branch of philosophy is most important to education. Every educational system and all education programs and practices are based upon assumptions, conscious or not, about what makes for a good person and a good society.

A controversy that rages in the schools is the question of whether values are derived from human experience or emanate from some independent source beyond human beings. Matters of morality and ethics are both unavoidable and controversial in American education.

Epistemology, or the study of knowledge, is as equally important to education as axiology. What is knowledge? and How do we know? are essential questions for the philosopher. The five types of knowledge described by George Kneller help to clarify these epistemological questions.

> *Revealed knowledge* is knowledge that some people believe comes from God. Books such as the Bible and the Koran are the worldly expressions of revealed knowledge. If a person believes that God has revealed God's knowledge in these documents, then debates about the meaning of words and passages become critical.
>
> *Intuitive knowledge* comes through human insight and is often associated with the arts. Great writers and artists are believed to have perceived truths about human existence, truths whose verification comes only from insight itself.
>
> *Rational knowledge* is derived from thought alone and is not dependent upon observation. It is abstract in the sense that formal logic and mathematics are abstract. The truth or validity of this knowledge is demonstrable through logic. For example, the principle that if A is larger than B, and B is larger than C, then A is larger than C is a principle that can be demonstrated in the physical world but is not dependent upon the physical world for its validity. This is the realm of thought that much of speculative philosophy deals with.
>
> *Empirical knowledge*, unlike rational knowledge, is completely dependent upon the physical world for its proof. Empirical knowledge is the realm of science. Scientific knowledge is knowledge that is revealed by observation and tested by experiments that can be repeated under identical circumstances.
>
> *Authoritative knowledge* is the information we accept because we believe the source of the knowledge. Knowledge that is created or generated from other sources is often accepted on the basis of the authority from whom we received the knowledge. It

may be possible to prove through observation that Antarctica is in the Southern Hemisphere, but, in practice, we simply accept it because we have been informed by sources we choose to believe.[21]

These systematic responses to the perennial human questions about existence, reality, and beauty provide a means for comparing one's thoughts and practices with clearly articulated thoughts of others. This process may be helpful in clarifying one's own thinking.

IDEALISM, REALISM, AND PRAGMATISM

In the Western philosophical tradition, two positions have historically vied for predominance: *idealism* and *realism*. A third, younger tradition, and distinct minority position, is *pragmatism*. Each of these three philosophies is a relatively complete system; that is, each makes claims within the realms of ontology, epistemology, and axiology.

Among the three traditional philosophical positions, idealism traces its heritage from Plato and the theologies of Judeo-Christian religions; realism from Aristotle, Thomas Aquinas, and various forms of naturalism; and pragmatism from Charles S. Peirce, William James, John Dewey, and the emergence of modern science.

Idealism

Advocates of idealism postulate a world of mind and ideas, of microcosm *and* macrocosm (for example, minds of men *and* Mind of God), of forms and shadows of forms. To the idealist, the human mind creates what it knows, and those creations are ideas. Only ideas enter consciousness; only the mind is capable of creativity, cognition, and volition. In turn, only humans (or gods) create ideas of truth, goodness, and beauty.

In the tradition of idealism, an Absolute Mind (or God or pantheon of gods) created reality, knows all, continues to create, and regulates the world. The truth of an idea can be determined by the degree to which it corresponds to or is in coherence with a body of knowledge already in existence—revealed literature, "great" books, wisdom of the past, the process of formal deductive logic. Values are manifest in concrete forms and discrete behaviors; value is "merely" human, never adequate and always imperfect; justice is temporal. On the other hand, Values, Value, and Justice (ideal types, underlying forms) are infinite and eternal conceptions, never totally understood or achieved by humankind. Yet, human behavior is purposive (volitional); it does not merely react to stimuli. Free will exists, though motivation for its exercise is internal, emanating from the individual's quest for value.

[21]George F. Kneller, *Introduction to the Philosophy of Education* (New York: John Wiley & Sons, Inc., 1964), pp. 8–12.

Realism

Proponents of realism postulate a world of things, of material existence, of "real" concrete objects, or "commonsense" reality. The realist "sees" an external world (including himself or herself) that exists independent of mind. This external world is created and determined by matter (what exists) and process (evolution). To the realist, humankind *can* know the real nature of this world independent of a priori conceptions of Mind. Both human mind and external object exist separately though at times in interaction (for example, person-to-person interaction).

A proposition can be said to be true if it is agreed that it corresponds to scientifically validated knowledge, which is to say it is observable and its *qualities* are independently (of the observer) verifiable. Anything that exists possesses quantity and quality. Idea and reality are the same; thus everything is knowable. Nature possesses discoverable plan, order, structure, and law. The world, the natural order, is permanent, though evolving, and can be predicted and controlled. Value inheres in the laws of nature; beauty inheres in the elegance of nature and its laws; goodness is harmony with natural law. Realism is dependent on the ways of both formal/deductive and scientific/inductive logic.

Realism is an umbrella term under which are clustered several separate schools of thought. For example, although all realists assert belief in the reality of matter, of the physical material world, they disagree about the origin of this world, which exists separate from and independent of the observer. For the religious realist, both matter and spirit are created by God, and spirit is the more significant mode of being or existing. The classical realist, on the other hand, sees no need for divine intervention as an explanation for the origin of the universe and extols the rational mind over material existence. Both these schools of thought harbor several variants. A type of religious realism, for example, is scholasticism or Thomism (after Thomas Aquinas), which is one of the philosophies of the Roman Catholic Church. An example of a type of classical realism is natural or scientific realism, which grew out of the early scientific movement, specifically the work of Francis Bacon.

Today, two prominent realist schools of thought are neo-realism and neo-Thomism. Neo-realism is the attempt to apply the rigor and methodologies of modern science and mathematics to philosophical problems, as in the writings of Bertrand Russell and Alfred North Whitehead. The neo-Thomists accept the duality of matter and spirit as articulated by Aquinas but add a second duality of faith and reason (and, for some, intuition and revelation are added to faith and reason) as sources of knowledge, operating in harmony.

Pragmatism

Pragmatism had its birth in the American nation—in the mid-nineteenth century with Peirce and in the late nineteenth and early twentieth centuries with James and Dewey. It grew out of the emergence of science and the scientific method, but especially out of the works of Charles Darwin. Later, in the twentieth century, the work of Albert Einstein provided additional ammunition for pragma-

TABLE 3-1 Synopsis of Idealism, Realism, and Pragmatism

	REALITY	KNOWLEDGE	VALUE	LOGIC
Idealism	Reality is Mind and Form.	Knowledge is the idea, vis-à-vis the idea.	Value is the reflection of and imitation of the Ideal Mind and Idea.	Formal/ Deductive
Realism	Reality is things, objects, matter.	Knowledge is the correspondence of ideas to observable facts.	Value is the emulation of Nature and Natural Law.	Formal/ Deductive and Scientific/ Inductive
Pragmatism	Reality is human experience.	Knowledge is the consequences of an idea that can be acted on.	Value is derived from experience. Valuing yields criteria that can be used to evaluate experience.	Scientific/ Inductive and Formal/ Deductive

tists. Thus, from the scientific method, Darwinian evolution, and Einstein's theories of general and specific relativity came pragmatism's emphasis on process and relativism.

To the pragmatist, ideas have consequences; the meaning of a proposition is in its consequences. If an idea were acted on, the consequences of that action would define (attribute meaning to) the idea. Thus, a "meaningful" idea is one that can be tested, can be acted on, can be tried out in practice. To Peirce, consequences are amenable to experimental verification, which is to say they are grounded in human experience. To the extent one cannot experience God or love, these "ideas" have no consequences, are untestable, and lack meaning. To the extend Mind (or mind) has no location or physiology (structure or function), it does not exist; on the other hand, brain and cognitive and affective processes do exist. In the axiological realm, pragmatists allow the existence of ethical and esthetic ideas to the extent that such ideas affect human behavior. Here such concepts as cultural relativism, ethical relativism, and artistic relativism have meaning for pragmatists.

Pragmatism is a philosophy of action—of actors who act on the world. Its focus is the realm of epistemology, with some axiological claims, and little concern for ontology. The process of humankind's interactions and the propositions derived from these interactions are at the heart of pragmatism.

PHILOSOPHIES OF EDUCATION

Although *aspects* of educational philosophy can be derived from each of the traditions of idealism, realism, and pragmatism, another approach provides a coherent pattern of four educational philosophies: essentialism, perennialism, progressivism, and reconstructionism.

Each of these four philosophies of education has roots in one or more of the three philosophical traditions of idealism, realism, and pragmatism. For example, pragmatism spawned both progressivism and reconstructionism; aspects of both idealism and realism can be found in essentialism; and perennialism evolved primarily out of idealism.

The choice of developing these educational philosophies is made partly because these four positions derive from questions of both an educational and philosophical nature, rather than from primarily philosophical interests, and partly because of the relationships of these philosophies of education to American educational history.

A philosophy of education probes topics peculiar to education. Not only are claims concerning the nature of knowledge necessary but also judgments and justifications for what knowledge is of most worth. Further, educational philosophy seeks meanings for those global concepts that define the educational process: learning, teaching methods, curriculum, and others. Because the process of education occurs in particular social contexts, educational philosophy also overlaps social, political, and economic philosophy. For example, John Dewey found it necessary to speculate on the relationships of school and society, of child (student) and curriculum, and of democracy and education, as well as on other relationships peculiar to education. Finally, a particularly important topic in educational philosophy has been the aims or goals of education, both in terms of individual growth or self-realization and in terms of the relationships between educational goals and those of society.

Essentialism

As the dominant educational philosophy in American education, essentialism possesses constant currency and appeal, especially for those who are the leaders in society and in education. Being a conservative position, essentialism attracts adherents who believe in conserving the best of the traditions of a particular society (for example, the United States) and civilization (for example, Western) and in promoting intellectual growth of the individual. Essentialists agree on these *primary* purposes of education. They disagree, however, as to what, if any, *secondary* purposes should be served by education. Some argue that education should simply deal with transmission of the cultural heritage and intellectual training. Others would affirm the priority of these two goals but allow for such secondary goals as physical health, emotional health, vocational competency, and avocational pursuits.

To the essentialist, the core of the curriculum must be the "essentials." In the elementary school, the essentials are reading, speaking, writing, spelling, and arithmetic, and later the introduction of history, geography (and perhaps a few other social sciences, but always as separate subjects or disciplines), physical and biological science, and foreign languages (usually Spanish, Latin, French, or German). In the secondary school, the essentials of the elementary school are more specialized and more rigorous. For example, arithmetic becomes mathematics (algebra, geometry, trigonometry, calculus); physical science becomes physics, chemistry, biology, and geology. Less essential are art, music, vocational subjects, and physical education. All forms of extracurricular activities such as clubs, athletics, band, or chorus are tolerated but given low priority.

Throughout the curriculum, essentialists demand that values be taught, and the values are to be those of a particular reference group; namely, the social and cultural values of the dominant class in the society, of the political and intellectual leaders (both dead and alive) of the nation. To teach the traditions of the society one must also teach the traditional values of the society.

Essentialists regard teaching as the transmission of essential knowledge, skills, and values. The teacher is the agent of society whose primary task is to ensure continuity. The teacher is also the model: of intellectual competency, of knowledgeability in the cultural heritage, and of the traditional social values. The teacher (and the school) should reflect the best of what was and is the society.

Perennialism

Also in the conservative tradition, yet opposed to much of essentialism, stands perennialism. The perennialists abhor much in the modern world, such as the results of the industrial revolution, the scientific revolution, the secularization and proletarianization of values, and the technological and electronic revolutions.

As a philosophy of education, perennialism is an assertion of the primacy of the past, especially of that past represented by the "great" writers and their works. Perennialism is a plea for permanencies, for the unchanging nature of the universe, human nature, truth, knowledge, virtue, and beauty. The desirable is what is perennial. As Robert Hutchins remarked,

> The function of man as man is the same in every age and in every society, since it results from his nature as man. The aim of the educational system is the same in every age and in every society where such a system can exist: it is to improve man as man.[22]

For perennialists, the answers to all educational questions flow from the answer to one question: What is human nature? To the perennialist, human nature is constant. Humankind's most distinctive characteristic is the ability to reason; the ideal, adult human being is perfectly rational (or at least pursues the rule of reason in all human affairs). Only the human species can comprehend the physical and spiritual constancies of existence. All humanity has the same potential to realize perfection in personal and social achievement. From this conception of human nature flows the perennialist philosophy of education.

If human nature is always and everywhere the same, education must be the same for all, always and everywhere. The goal of education is constant, absolute,

[22]Robert M. Hutchins, *The Conflict in Education in a Democratic Society* (New York: Harper & Row, Publishers, Inc., 1953), p. 68.

and universal—to develop the rational person. This is not to say that ethical dimensions are ignored; on the contrary, rationality is a broad concept that includes the application of the process of reasoning to *all* domains of human affairs.

To the perennialist, teaching is an art—the art of stimulating and directing the development of the individual's inherent powers to think rationally, powers possessed by all humans. Teaching is primarily exhortation, Socratic discourse, and oral exposition.

The perennialist curriculum is derived from ancient Greek and Latin conceptions of a liberal education, of the liberal arts represented in the medieval trivium and quadrivium. The trivium is composed of grammar, rhetoric, and dialectic; the quadrivium consists of arithmetic, geometry, astronomy, and music. From these seven liberal arts flow the perennialist emphasis on language and mathematics, on arts as opposed to sciences. Also, because these arts were firmly established early in the history of Western civilization, the perennialist considers them as permanent, perennially fixed. The liberal arts (that is, literary and mathematical arts) are represented in the great books, which have become confirmed as "great" by having stood the tests of time (immortality) and significance (the choices of the literati and intelligentsia in successive eras). They are "contemporary" for any age. Among the "great books" are the works of Plato, Aristotle, Marcus Aurelius, St. Augustine, St. Thomas Aquinas, Copernicus, Galileo, Erasmus, Shakespeare, and so on. Obviously, if one is to read these writers in the languages in which they wrote, Latin and Greek must be studied by all students.

The classical education advocated by perennialists appeals to only a minority of American citizens, but these are frequently the intellectual leaders of the society who are able to articulate and make visible the perennialist position. Although perennialism is a conservative philosophy of education, its chief target is the other conservative philosophy, essentialism.

Progressivism

The peculiarly American philosophy of pragmatism gave birth to the two educational philosophies of progressivism and reconstructionism. The progressive philosophy of education emerged in late nineteenth-century America and reached its peak of influence in the 1920s and 1930s. Reconstructionism had numerous intellectual and sociological roots, but its lineage is most readily traced to progressivism. Reconstructionists formed a faction of the progressive education movement during the 1930s.

As a protest to essentialism, progressivism is spurred by dissatisfaction: that American democracy has become perverted from its enabling ideology; that American schools have become oppressive to children and youth. Progressivism is the educational manifestation of the liberal, humanitarian reform movement that sought to combat the political and economic evils of industrial society. Progressives pursued reform and change in both educational *and* social affairs.

In his most comprehensive work, *Democracy and Education*, John Dewey argued that democracy is not merely a political form but also a total way of social living, and that the greatest strength of a democratic way of life lies in democratic education. To Dewey, democracy and education are key interactive elements: The democratic society is an educative model to its citizens; democratic education flows naturally, organically, from a democratic society. Progress in a democratic society is change; in a Hegelian sense, progress is represented by new syntheses that emerge from the resolutions of conflicts between theses and antitheses. Progress for the individual is growth, becoming, maturation. At any point, enjoyable and effective personal or social living is at stake, is being risked in the crucible of intra- and interpersonal interaction and conflict. Democratic society and democratic education are participatory and emergent, not preparatory and absolute. Living *is* learning; education (like democracy) *is* living, *is* a way of life.

To learn is to change. Given interest, curiosity, or a disturbing situation, the human organism is impelled to action. To act is to experience and experiment, to bring intelligence to bear, to direct goal-oriented behavior, to solve problems, and to make decisions. Action leads to relief of the disturbance (or to a new motivation to act), to a reconstruction of experience, to new truths (or to new dilemmas and paradoxes), to conclusions that call forth commitments to act on the conclusions. The cycle goes on, as it were, forever.

It is the individual who learns, alone or in groups, but always in the interactive mode, in interaction with the environment, with other persons, or with oneself. One of the ways in which human evolution operates is through individual differences resulting in human variability in groups, cultures, and societies. To cultivate human variability is to value human dignity and to ensure the survival of the species.

The progressive philosophy leads to education as an end in itself. Education is a way, a process to discover ends. Learning is the reconstruction of personal and social experience, and an individual's experience is the infrastructure for learning. Respect for individual differences is the starting point for planning instruction. Democratic group living is the preferred mode in classrooms and schools. The application of intelligence to problems and projects is the basis for determining the curriculum. Individual freedom, within the constraints of the democratic social contract, is a goal for all members (students, teachers, administrators, and others) of the school community.

Reconstructionism

During the Great Depression of the 1930s, when the "progressive education" (progressivism) movement was at its height of popularity, many Americans, and especially a significant minority of progressive educators, became disillusioned with American society and impatient with the pace of reform in both education and society. A "radical caucus" of progressives argued that progressivism was in need of redirection: to place less emphasis on child-centered (individualistic) education and more emphasis on society-centered (social reform) education; less interest in the growth of the person and more interest in the reform of society. This splinter group of progressives became the founders and advocates of reconstructionism (also called *social reconstructionism*).

As a spinoff of progressivism, the reconstructionists adhered to the philosophy of pragmatism and the principles of progressivism but extended these positions to include the explicit reform of society as a major goal of education. Reconstructionists believe that an image of the ideal society should be the basis for determining educational programs; schools should seek to educate future citizens for a society of the future, a society that is "becoming" rather than one that currently exists. This challenge was presented by George S. Counts at the 1932 national convention of the Progressive Education Association in a speech entitled "Dare the School Build a New Social Order?" Counts had the audacity to suggest that the educational institution of a society might *lead* the society in the quest to realize its values and ideals. For Counts, the schools could become the social reform institution, the agent of change, of a society. In the rhetoric of a "romantic," he wrote,

> The weakness of Progressive Education thus lies in the fact that it has elaborated no theory of social welfare, unless it be that of anarchy or extreme individualism. . . . If Progressive Education is to be genuinely progressive, it must . . . face squarely and courageously every social issue, come to grips with life in all its stark reality, establish an organic relation with the community, develop a realistic and comprehensive theory of welfare, fashion a compelling and challenging vision of human destiny, and become less frightened than it is today at the bogeys of *imposition* and *indoctrination*.[23]

Another reconstructionist, Theodore Brameld, has observed that reconstructionism is a crisis philosophy, appropriate for a culture or a society in crisis, which is the essence of a democratic society. Little wonder, then, that reconstructionism has had its greatest appeal in the America of the 1930s and 1960s, the two periods in twentieth-century American history when disillusionment became the prevailing ethos.

Not only is reconstructionism an educational philosophy; it also harbors the strategies of sociopolitical action and the collectivization of teachers' power, both as means to promote social reform. For the reconstructionist, analysis and conclusion are insufficient; they must lead to commitment and action, by both teachers and students.

In education, the reconstructionists advocate the commitment of teachers (and students) to the creation of a new, progressive, reconstructed view of society. The emerging, "becoming" society must be democratic, based on communalism rather than individualism. The school must model this new society, for it is the young who will bring the new society to fruition. Cooperative endeavors must replace individualistic and competitive striving. Group living and action will replace individualistic leadership and achievement as the motivating forces of the future.

---

[23]George S. Counts, *Dare the School Build a New Social Order?* (New York: The John Day Company, 1932), pp. 7–8.

TABLE 3-2 Synopsis of Four Philosophies of Education

ESSENTIALISM	PERENNIALISM
1. Preserving the "best" of the cultural traditions of a particular society and civilization.	1. Enhancing and promoting the superiority of the past and the permanency of the "classics."
2. Promoting the intellectual growth of the individual.	2. Believing that human nature is constant, its most distinctive trait being the ability to reason.
3. Providing a curriculum composed of "essentials": subjects with intellectual substance and basic skills.	3. Promoting the development of the rational person.
4. Explicit teaching of values: those traditional values prized by the dominant class.	4. Teaching, an art that helps students use their inherent power to think rationally, by exhortation, explication, Socratic discourse, and oral exposition.
5. Teaching, the most effective and efficient transmission of "essentials."	5. Centering the curriculum on the seven liberal arts and the "great books" of human history.
PROGRESSIVISM	RECONSTRUCTIONISM
1. Believing that education is growth and development, the continuous reconstruction of experience, a living/learning process rather than a preparation for later adult life.	1. Education leading society to realize its values through goals and programs of social betterment.
2. Believing that democratic social living includes democratic education, being both participatory and emergent.	2. Schools becoming the agents of change and social reform.
3. Learning active and leading to change in behavior.	3. Basing curriculum on an image of the ideal society.
4. Curriculum emerging from the needs of students and of society and involving the application of intelligence to human problems.	4. Learning active and leading to involvement in programs of social reform through citizens' political action.
5. Teaching the guiding of inquiry.	5. School, teacher, and students modeling the new, more perfect, democratic society.

EXISTENTIALISM

The four philosophies of education—essentialism, perennialism, progressivism, and reconstructionism—command the stage in debates on educational issues. There is, however, another philosophical position that has enjoyed some appeal in the past four decades and that has some implications for education. The philosophy of existentialism is of European origin and only became popular in the period just prior to, during, and after World War II. It is a highly individualistic philosophy, heavily dependent on subjective factors—intuition, introspection, emotional commitment, and the feeling of aloneness. As such, its educational implications are for the teacher and student *as individuals.*

Perhaps the greatest appeal of existentialism is to those who see little else but meaninglessness and absurdity, cruelty, and horror in modern living; to those who feel oppressed by the institutions created by industrial, technological societies; and to those who feel anonymity and the loss of freedom.

If the dilemma of Western civilization is between analysis and commitment, between reason and passion, the existentialist asserts the primacy of commitment and passion. One's existence—the dangers, the risks, the choices—precedes one's essence—the models, theories, and concepts of human nature.

The individual human being is born, enters existence, grows, becomes aware of his or her existence, aloneness, and mortality. A person becomes what he or she decides to become; a person is free to choose his or her essence—in spite of or even in defiance of hereditary and environmental influences. One acts, asserts person-hood; or one becomes *merely* the product of external forces, which amounts to the loss (or abdication) of freedom. Existentialists proclaim the individual as the exemplary philosopher, a person willing to choose freely, when all else seems to overwhelm.

Though these roots of existentialism are to be found in the nineteenth century, in the writings of Sören Kierkegaard, Friedrich Nietzsche, and Fyodor Dostoevsky, existentialism did not gain widespread appeal until World War II. Leading contemporary existentialists were Albert Camus, Jean-Paul Sartre, Martin Heidegger, and Maurice Merleau-Ponty. Because it lends itself to all forms of literary expression, existentialism seems to pervade the writings of Franz Kafka, Edward Albee, Harold Pinter, Kurt Vonnegut, Jr., Samuel Beckett, William Bur-roughs, John Barth, Rainer Maria Rilke, Joan Didion, Saul Bellow, and Joseph Heller. The most articulate and literate American educator to espouse existential-ism is Maxine Greene.

As one might expect, the individual human experience is the primary unit of explanation for the existentialist. One *is* alone—apart from the physical universe, and for the most part, apart from other human beings. Living is a passionate confrontation with the dangers of and threats to existence, especially freedom and death.

Reality is defined by the individual, "becoming" human being, who must contend with things and others. A human may create things and goods, but primarily a human creates himself or herself. A person is free to choose to become what he or she will. And to be free is to choose, to act, and to be responsible for one's acts. Freedom is an awesome and dreadful potential: for good or evil, to oneself or to others.

To the existentialist, what we know are the events and phenomena perceived in consciousness. What is perceived directly we ascribe meaning to, creating, as it were, our own separate universes—sometimes "hells," sometimes "heavens," usu-ally both.

Clearly, it is virtually impossible to have schools or educational systems based on existentialism. What *is* possible is the individual existentialist teacher or student, a person who passionately opposes the forces that deny the individual his or her freedom. The existentialist teacher prizes his or her freedom and respects the freedom of others, of students, other teachers, and administrators. Further, the existentialist teacher expects students to accept the consequences, results, and outcomes of all their actions. Mutual respect for mutual growth characterizes the existential interaction. But human growth and interpersonal interaction always combine joy and tragedy, hope and despair.

The subjects of the existential curriculum are unspecified, although any subject can be, at the right moment, the tool, the vehicle, to engage the individual in his or her striving to "become." The educational methods appropriate to existentialism are dialogue, reflective inquiry, and individual introspection.

It should be apparent that existentialism has limited application as an educational philosophy. This is true only because education as a concept has been interpreted in all Western societies as necessitating some form of schooling. Schooling involves an institutionalized socialization process that requires group instruction and bureaucratic organization. Schooling is a process that proscribes freedom and mirrors those social conditions and forces that the existentialist opposes. Yet if the individual existentialist can exert his or her will regardless of deterministic forces, the will can survive even in the crucible of the school.

A PERSONAL PHILOSOPHY OF EDUCATION

It is doubtful if any person or teacher ever lives by or teaches by a carefully thought out, systematic philosophical position. Nevertheless, the search for meaning goes on, by each person and by each teacher.

In the pursuit of meaning by persons-as-teachers, the interaction of all facets of life is focused on the behaviors called teaching. In those arenas where teaching (and learning) as interpersonal interaction occurs, the person-as-teacher needs some moorings, some beliefs he or she can rely on, a harmony of purposes. Though these may change with experience, a set of assertions concerning education is a useful beginning.

The following schema of questions about education, a beginning in the search for meaning in educational philosophy, is designed to stimulate reflection by the person-as-teacher.

Questions for a Philosophy of Education

    I. Questions of Reality and Humanness.
        A. What is the nature of "reality?"
            1. What is "universe?"
            2. What are the ecological relationships in physical and biological existence?
        B. What is the nature of "humanness?"
            1. What are the characteristics of the human species?
            2. What are the aspects of relatedness and aloneness of humankind?

II. Questions of Knowing and the Known.
    A. What is the nature of "knowledge?"
       1. What is "truth," "knowledge," "the known?"
       2. How do human beings validate (prove) knowledge?
       3. What are the sources of knowledge?
    B. What are the ways of "human knowing?"
       1. What are the cognitive processes?
       2. What are the affective processes?
    C. What knowledge is most worth knowing?
       1. Is science or humanities most worthwhile?
       2. Is self-knowledge or publicly verifiable knowledge most worthwhile?
       3. Are products or processes of knowledge most worth knowing?
    D. What are the meanings of global (abstract at high level) educational concepts such as
       1. "democracy"
       2. "freedom"
       3. "human dignity"
III. Questions of Value.
    A. What is the nature of "values?"
       1. Are values transient, permanent, relative, absolute?
       2. Are values solely human creations, mystical creations, inherent in the physical universe?
    B. What values are manifest in the process of education?
       1. What are the values of the society in which the educational institution exists?
       The values of the human species?
       The values of Western civilization?
       The values of the particular nation-state?
       The values of the local community?
       2. What are the values underlying the goals of education?
       The goals of education in a society?
       The goals of education in a school district?
       The goals of education in a school?
       The goals of education for a person-as-teacher?
       3. What are the values underlying the selection of (and omission of) curricular content? What subjects should be included in the curriculum? What content (knowledge, skills, and attitudes) should be included in a particular course?

Clearly, a teacher needs to know far more than has been presented in this chapter in order to respond adequately, thoughtfully, and honestly to each of the questions posed in the preceding outline. Throughout a person's teaching career, however, it might be helpful periodically to ask oneself these questions, to compare current responses to earlier responses, and to compare one's positions with those of one's colleagues. In fact, it is usually only after several years of teaching experience that teachers recognize the need for and helpfulness of educational philosophy. It is then that the complexity and profundity of the educational process become evident, and it is then also that justifying and conceptualizing this process becomes a helpful tool.

Case Study: Education in the Stone Age[24]

    A million years ago, a concerned and dedicated reformer turned his attention to the problems of survival of his tribe: How were the tribal ways of life to be passed on to the young?

    Inno the Younger asked himself, "What are the skills we members of the Ugo tribe need to know in order to survive?" He reflected, analyzed, synthesized, and finally concluded there were three survival skills: (1) catching fish with bare hands in the river; (2) capturing and killing small, deerlike animals with clubs and rocks; and (3) driving away the feared saber-toothed tigers with fire.

    So Inno created the first curriculum, composed of three subjects. Soon all the young of the tribe (ages five through ten) were studying the three skills of the tribe's new "Education for Survival." Schools were set up and conducted, first by the river, in the forest, and by the campsites, and later only in a grove near the campsite. Thus, education became schooling. The curriculum was standardized, and the young were segregated from the rest of the tribe in order to receive instruction. Inno the Younger had become the first of the great educators of the Ugos, and when he died, his loincloth was hung on a tree limb in the educational grove.

    As long as the conditions and ways of life of the Ugos remained unchanged, the curriculum of Inno had a direct relationship to reality and ensured tribal survival. But one day, one of the Ugos surveyed the entire area for hundreds of miles around the tribe's home and discovered, to her amazement and to the amazement of the entire tribe, that there were no more saber-toothed tigers. The tigers had either changed habitats or become extinct.

    What educational philosophy did Inno seem to prefer? What would you expect to happen to the third subject in Inno's curriculum, "Driving away saber-toothed tigers with fire," after the disappearance of saber-toothed tigers? Today, what is a "Curriculum of Survival"?

Thought Questions

1. From your own experience as a student in the American educational system, which philosophical position would you say is the most prevalent: essentialism, perennialism, progressivism, or reconstructionism? Supply as much evidence as you can to support your decision.

2. As a newly employed first-year teacher in a public school, which philosophical position is most appealing to you? Give your reasons for your choice.

3. As a teacher, you will be intervening in the lives of children and youth. As a form of self-examination, try to probe your deepest motives in order to answer for yourself, "Why do I want to teach?"

---

[24]Adapted from Harold Benjamin, *The Saber-Tooth Curriculum* (New York: McGraw-Hill Book Company, Inc., 1939).

4. Teachers must devise some form of "economy of knowledge," because it is impossible to teach everything that is known. For you as a teacher in a public school, what is it that everyone needs to know? What knowledge is of most worth?

5. Probably the most radical philosophical position is that of reconstructionism. Why has this position seldom been a viable philosophy for public education in the United States? In what situations or historical eras would one expect reconstructionism to become popular and win adherents?

6. One form of realism is Thomism (or neo-Thomism). In what ways is this philosophy appropriate or inappropriate as a basis for public education in the United States?

Practical Activities

1. Obtain a copy of the goals for your school or for a local school district and discuss them in terms of one or more of the educational philosophies presented in this chapter.

2. Using the Questions for a Philosophy of Education as a basis, attempt to state your philosophical assertions regarding education.

3. Visit a local elementary or secondary school. Talk to an administrator and two or three teachers about the general, overall goals they have for education at the school. See if you can determine which philosophy of education seems to prevail.

4. From your knowledge of existentialism as a philosophy applied to education, describe what you imagine might be "A Day in the Life of an Existentialist Teacher."

5. Ask a practicing teacher to indicate for you how what he or she does in the classroom is related to a more general philosophy of education. Ask for three or four philosophical principles on which this teacher bases his or her teaching.

6. Many school districts use application forms that ask the applicant to state his or her philosophy of education in about four hundred words. As succinctly as possible, what would you write on this form?

Bibliography

ADLER, MORTIMER J., *The Paideia Proposal: An Educational Manifesto.* New York: Macmillan, 1982.

BRAMELD, THEODORE B., *Patterns of Educational Philosophy.* New York: Holt, Rinehart & Winston, 1971.

BRUBACHER, JOHN S., *Modern Philosophies of Education,* 4th ed. New York: McGraw-Hill Book Company, Inc., 1969.

COUNTS, GEORGE S., *Dare the School Build a New Social Order?* New York: The John Day Company, 1932.

DEWEY, JOHN, *Democracy and Education.* New York: Macmillan, 1916.

————, *Experience and Education.* New York: Macmillan, 1939.

FRANKENA, WILLIAM K., *Three Historical Philosophies of Education.* Chicago: Scott, Foresman & Company, 1965.

GREENE, MAXINE, *Teacher as Stranger*. Belmont, Calif.: Wadsworth Publishing Company, Inc., 1973.

HAKES, J. EDWARD, ed., *An Introduction to Evangelical Christian Education*. Chicago: Moody Press, 1971.

HUTCHINS, ROBERT M., *The Conflict in Education in a Democratic Society*. New York: Harper & Row, Publishers, Inc., 1953.

ILLICH, IVAN, *Deschooling Society*. New York: Harper & Row, Publishers, Inc., 1971.

KNELLER, GEORGE F., *Introduction to the Philosophy of Education*, 4th ed. New York: Macmillan, 1974.

MORRIS, VAN CLEVE, and YOUNG PAI, *Existentialism in Education: What It Means*. New York: Harper & Row, Publishers, Inc., 1966.

_____, *Philosophy and the American School*, 2nd ed. Boston: Houghton Mifflin Company, 1976.

O'NEILL, WILLIAM F., *Educational Ideologies: Contemporary Expressions of Educational Philosophy*. Santa Monica, Calif.: Goodyear Publishing Company, Inc., 1981.

OZMAN, HOWARD A., and SAMUEL M. CRAVER, *Philosophical Foundations of Education*, 2nd ed. Columbus, Ohio: Charles E. Merrill Publishing Company, 1981.

PETERS, RICHARD S., *Ethics and Education*. Chicago: Scott, Foresman & Company, 1967.

PRATTE, RICHARD, *Ideology and Education*. New York: David McKay Company, Inc., 1977.

SARAP, MADAN, *Marxism and Education*. London: Routledge & Kegan Paul, 1978.

SHIMAHARA, NOBUO, ed., *Educational Reconstruction: Promise and Challenge*. Columbus, Ohio: Charles E. Merrill Publishing Company, 1973.

SOLTIS, JONAS F., *An Introduction to the Analysis of Educational Concepts*, 2nd ed. Reading, Mass.: Addison-Wesley Publishing Company, Inc., 1977.

WHITEHEAD, ALFRED N., *The Aims of Education and Other Essays*. New York: Macmillan, 1929.

WINGO, MAX, *The Philosophy of American Education*. Boston: D.C. Heath & Company, 1965.

4

Values in Society and School

A great and continuing purpose of education has been the development of moral and spiritual values. To fulfill this purpose, society calls upon all its institutions.[1]

The unity of a culture depends on the existence of a shared set of values that its citizens believe in. A system of values is the infrastructure that supports and gives coherence to all of a society's institutions. In each society this values base is relatively stable, though at crucial times it enters a state of flux when new emergent values challenge traditional values. At such times, the resulting conflict and strife within a society usually lead to a modification or new synthesis, or to an almost totally new infrastructure and, therefore, to a new society born of revolution.

It is highly likely that in the modern world social values are in constant turmoil, either bubbling just beneath the surface of daily events or boiling over in the debates over ubiquitous social issues. Constant tension seems to exist in every society between traditional values and emerging values, creating perturbations in the infrastructure that normally result in a new set of values. Clearly, such is the case in the United States today.

The American Republic was born of revolution, yet its ideology was an importation from the shores of western Europe and the islands of Great Britain. American values derived from five related (and on occasion contradictory) traditions: (1) the Protestant ethic, (2) the Puritan temper, (3) bourgeois capitalism, (4) republican democracy, and (5) Western philosophy. Like one of the five-pointed stars in the flag of the new American nation, these five value clusters were merged into a new ideology.

[1]Educational Policies Commission of the National Education Association, *Moral and Spiritual Values in the Public Schools* (Washington, D.C.: Education Policies Commission, National Education Association of the United States and the Association of School Administrators, 1951).

THE AMERICAN CREED

At the heart of the American ideology are the *Protestant ethic* and the *Puritan temper*, two codes that emphasized work, sobriety, frugality, sexual restraint, and a forbidding attitude toward life. These complementary concepts contributed to what Gunnar Myrdal has called "the American Creed": the values of self-denial or endurance of distress; deferred gratification; sexual restraint and chastity; frugality and thrift; industriousness; self-control, temperance, and moderation; order and punctuality; humility and charity; and the survival of the fittest as derived from the Calvinist idea of predestination, or "the elect of God."

As Max Weber argued so persuasively, there is an intimate relationship between the Protestant ethic and the practice of bourgeois capitalism. The values in each tradition are mutually supportive: the successful entrepreneur is easily justified and confirmed by appeal to such values as resolution, frugality, industry, order, punctuality, striving, and especially to the concept of "the elect of God," those who might be viewed as preordained to "success."[2]

The values inherent in *bourgeois capitalism* are the profit motive, competitiveness, scarcity as a function of unlimited demand with limited supply, a free-market economy, contrived demand through advertising and "forced" obsolescence, social class distinctions based on wealth and possessions, materialism, acquisitiveness, conspicuous consumption, meritocratic hiring and promotion, and the priority of private property ownership rights.

In addition to Protestant, Puritan, and capitalistic values, the American Creed also comprises *democratic value orientations*. These are enhancement of human dignity, rational consent of the governed, rule of the majority, guarantees of individual and minority rights and of due process, the quality of freedom or liberty or independence, and the search for equality and equity in conjoint living.

Finally, the ideology of United States society contains a number of values that have pervaded the development of Western civilization and are embedded in *Western philosophy* and science. These value positions are rationality, empiricism and experimentation, humanism, dualistic analysis, and various forms of reductionism, especially the quantification of phenomena.

The American Creed, then, is a composite ideology that gradually coalesced during the seventeenth and eighteenth centuries and has endured with some modification for the past two hundred years. Even though the structure of American society has changed in the past two centuries, the ideological infrastructure has remained intact.

Daniel Yankelovich has found that some traditional norms still command overwhelming assent.[3] These state that people:

---

[2]Max Weber, *The Protestant Ethic and the Spirit of Capitalism* (London: G. Allen & Unwin, 1930).

[3]Daniel Yankelovich, *New Rules* (New York: Random House, 1981), pp. xviii, 5.

1. Would still have children if they had to do it over again (90 percent).
2. Feel that the use of hard drugs is morally wrong (87 percent).
3. Feel it's up to parents to educate teenagers about birth control (84 percent).
4. Feel mate swapping is morally wrong (81 percent).
5. Disapprove of married women having affairs (79 percent).
6. Disapprove of married men having affairs (76 percent).
7. Agree that a woman should put her husband and children ahead of her career (77 percent).
8. Want their children to be better off and more successful than they are (74 percent).

On the other hand, there are also "major changes in the norms guiding American life."[4] Some of these are:

1. Whereas over 70 percent of respondents in 1938 "disapproved of a married woman earning money if she has a husband capable of supporting her," by 1978 this was down to about 25 percent.
2. No longer is a family with four or more children considered ideal (1945); in 1980 the ideal was two children.
3. In 1957, a woman who remained unmarried must have been sick, neurotic, or immoral (80 percent), but by 1978 the percent had decreased to 25.
4. In 1937, only 25 percent of those polled would vote for a qualified woman nominee for president, but by 1980 the percent was almost 80.
5. About 85 percent of subjects in 1967 condemned premarital sex as morally wrong, whereas in 1979 less than 40 percent thought so.
6. In 1979, 75 percent of those polled agreed that it was morally acceptable to be single and have children.
7. Over 60 percent approved of interracial marriages in 1977.
8. About 75 percent of working women in 1976 would go on working even if they didn't have to.

Yankelovich further observes that "perhaps the sharpest shift in American attitudes has been a steady erosion of trust in government and other institutions, falling from a peak of trust and confidence in the late fifties to a trough of mistrust in the early eighties." For example, he reports the following survey research findings from a University of Michigan study in which "the changes move only in one direction—from trust to mistrust":[5]

1. "The people running the government in Washington are smart people who know what they are doing"—from 69 percent to 29 percent.
2. "You can trust the government to do what is right most or all of the time"—from 56 percent to 29 percent.

[4]Ibid., pp. 93–96.
[5]Ibid., p. 185.

3. "The government is run for the benefit of all, rather than for a few big interests"—from 72 percent to 35 percent.
4. "Public officials care what people like me think"—from 71 percent to 33 percent.
5. "The government wastes a lot of the money we pay in taxes"—from 42 percent to 77 percent.

What has happened in the past two or three decades? Yankelovich believes that "doubts have now set in, and Americans now believe that the old giving/getting compact needlessly restricts the individual while advancing the power of large institutions—government and business particularly—who use the power to enhance their own interests at the expense of the public."[6]

As self-fulfillment begins to replace the ethic of self-denial, however, a void is created in the social realm. Excessive self-indulgence destroys all commitment to community, leaving no social ethic. "Any viable social ethic has real work to do: it binds the individual to the society; it synchronizes society's goals with those of each person; it holds society together and keeps it from degenerating into a chaos of competing interests."[7] Yankelovich thinks a new ethic is emerging in embryonic form out of "two kinds of commitments: closer and deeper personal relationships, and the switch from certain instrumental values to sacred/expressive ones."[8]

If out of crisis comes change, then a crucial question is, Are we presently in the midst of a crisis? Many futurists, though by no means a majority, argue that we are now in a crisis. Values often change in crises. In dealing with values shifts, a common practice is to present value rubrics in two parallel columns, with the list on the left referring to *traditional* values—those from which *emergent* values, the list on the right, are shifting away. The list on the left may be titled "Traditional" or merely "From," whereas the parallel list on the right may be headed "Emergent" or "To." Table 4-1 represents the author's view of current values shifts in American society.

VALUES IN THE SCHOOLS

Traditionally, public schools and the family have been responsible for passing on the fundamental values of our society. As the family began to abrogate its role in the transmission of values, the schools took on more of the responsibility. As a consequence, the schools have become battlegrounds for value conflicts that originate in the larger society. In this century, legislators and the courts as well as educators and school boards have decided which values the schools should attempt to transmit to the younger generation.

Although some citizens and even some educators argue that the schools should be value free, most national, state, and local educational policy makers

[6]Ibid., p. 231.
[7]Ibid., p. 246.
[8]Ibid., p. 250.

TABLE 4-1   Values Shifts

FROM (TRADITIONAL VALUES)	TO (EMERGENT VALUES)
1. Self-denial, endurance of stress, and deferred gratification	1. Pursuit of immediate pleasures or hedonism
2. Sexual taboos and constraints	2. Sexual permissiveness or openness
3. Self-control, belief that hard work yields success, striving to achieve	3. Self-actualization and self-expressiveness, acceptance and expression of feelings, self-realization
4. "Survival of the fittest"	4. "Survival of the wisest," the individual's survival entwined with species, global survival
5. Progress equated with growth, promotion of increased consumption and number of consumers	5. Limits to growth, search for ecological balances, stress on qualitative aspects of progress
6. Competitiveness—a win-lose, either-or attitude	6. Cooperation, conflict resolution and reduction, win-win attitude
7. Materialism, acquisitiveness and conspicuous consumption	7. Focus on essentials, greater desire for quality and durability of goods
8. Social class distinction based primarily on wealth	8. Greater concern for equality and equity; class distinctions based on multiple criteria (de-emphasis on accumulated wealth), which will tend to blur class lines
9. Preoccupation with private property ownership rights	9. Increasing pressures to ensure basic human rights—nationally and globally, greater concern for "the commons" that are shared collectively (e.g., water, parks, air, neighborhoods)
10. Government by isolated elected officials in state and national capitals	10. Government by association, involvement, and participation of the entire citizenry; increased pressures from interest groups
11. Nationalism, exclusive national sovereignties as loci of loyalties, independence of nation-states	11. World-order models, transnational economic grouping as bases for regional political grouping (e.g., European Common Market), regional and world federalisms, interdependence of nations
12. Freedom or liberty or independence, individualism	12. Mutuality of concern, cooperative processes, greater attention to interpersonal relations and quality of conjoint living
13. Nationalism, empiricism, scientism, dualistic analysis, reductionism, and quantification	13. Renewed reliance on faith and feeling, practice of meditative modes, global humanism, blending of Taoist and Buddhist worldviews with those of Judeo-Christian tradition, abandoning the search for value-free knowledge, greater trust in all human ways of knowing

consider that values need to be a part of school curricula—both as part of the formal curriculum and at the heart of the "hidden curriculum." As long as values are in the school, in the curriculum, and in the classroom, there will be public controversy as to which set of values should be emphasized. The debates about values are policy issues that sooner or later are decided by school boards, legislators, educators, and on occasion by the courts.

Historical Background

At the time that the U.S. Constitution was framed, a situation existed in the thirteen colonies wherein "schools taught the doctrines of the dominant religion. In most northern schools, Congregational Calvinism was the church established by the colonial legislatures; in southern colonies the orthodox Anglican beliefs of the Church of England were taught in schools."[9]

It was against this background that James Madison said, in a speech to the Virginia Convention in 1788, "Freedom of religion arises from the multiplicity of sects, which pervades America, and which is the best and only security for religious liberty in any society." It was Madison's sentiment that guided Jefferson and others in writing the First Amendment to the Constitution.

> Congress shall make no law respecting an establishment of religion, or prohibiting the free exercise thereof; or abridging the freedom of speech, or of the press; or the right of the people peaceably to assemble, and to petition the Government for a redress of grievances.

When this amendment is read in conjunction with the Fourteenth Amendment, it prohibits all levels of government from abridging the freedoms guaranteed therein. The amendment contains three clauses that have been applied to schools and moral values.

The first two clauses require government, and hence public schools, which are governmental entities, to walk a narrow path between the constitutional protection of the people's right to the religion of their choice or no religion at all (free exercise clause) on the one side, and the protection from government-imposed religious practices (establishment clause) on the other. In other words, schools are required by these two provisions to take a position of neutrality — neither to promote religious beliefs or exercises nor to prohibit them.

Free Speech and Moral Values

In general, the courts have found that free expression may not be abridged unless there is some justifiable reason to do so. For example, it is acceptable to prohibit persons from falsely shouting "fire."

The Supreme Court also expanded the concept of speech to include symbolic nonverbal displays such as black armbands [*Tinker* v. *Des Moines School District*, 393 U.S. 503, 508 (1969)]. In this same case the Court determined that public schools were subject to the same restrictions as other government agents and that there must be an overriding justification before the right of students to free speech could be suppressed.

The other side of this issue was debated in a 1943 case in which the West Virginia State Board of Education made the daily salute to the flag a condition of

---

[9]R. Freeman Butts, "Search for Freedom: The Story of American Education," *NEA Journal*, 49 (Mar. 1960), p. 35.

attendance. The Court outlawed the practice on the basis of the free expression clause, saying that a compulsory flag salute "compels a belief and attitude of mind" and that to do so without there being a "clear and present danger" was to compel students to say what they did not believe.

The test the courts developed to determine whether a person's free expression has been unlawfully abridged is twofold: unlawful *intent* and unlawful *impact*. Thus, a school policy that is not intended to restrict expression will usually be valid, but it must go no further in limiting expression than is necessary.

Excusal

One remedy that schools have available with an otherwise unconstitutional policy, such as a flag salute, is to allow those who object to be excused from the practice. This condition could also be applied to courses such as sex education, which, although lawfully acceptable practices, may be objected to by a minority of the community.

Free expression is also the issue in cases involving a school's attempt to censor or ban objectionable or obscene material from the curriculum, student newspapers, or school libraries. Although the courts have handled each of these categories somewhat differently, they have all required that an acceptable policy or a lawful exclusion contain a precise definition of obscenity, and the courts have generally found "feelings about good taste" insufficient reason for censoring free expression. It is important to note that in *Zykan* v. *Warsaw Community School Corporation* [631, F.2d 1300, 1304–05 (7th Cir. 1980)] the Supreme Court recognized that "academic freedom at the secondary level . . . is bounded . . . by the level of [students'] intellectual development," suggesting that there may be reason for allowing school boards to be more flexible in their interpretation of a minor student's freedom of expression than they would in the case of adults.

Establishment Clause

As noted earlier, the religion clauses of the First Amendment are two-edged. The establishment clause prohibits the government from setting up an official church, whereas the "free exercise clause prohibits government from interfering in the individual's religious choices." Court decisions over the years have fleshed out the meanings and applications of the two clauses.

In 1947, the Supreme Court detailed the meaning and intent of the establishment clause in their decision in *Everson* v. *Board of Education*:

> The "establishment of religion" clause of the First Amendment means at least this: Neither a state nor the Federal Government can set up a church. Neither can it pass laws which aid one religion, all religions, or prefer one religion over another. Neither can force nor influence a person to go or to remain away from church against his will or force him to profess a belief or disbelief in any religion. No person can be punished for entertaining or professing religious beliefs or disbeliefs, for church attendance or

non-attendance. No tax in any amount, large or small, can be levied to support any religious activities or institutions, whatever they may be called, or whatever form they may adopt to teach or practice religion. Neither a state nor the federal government can, openly or secretly, participate in the affairs of any religious organizations or groups and *vice versa*. In the words of Jefferson, the clause against establishment of religion by law was intended to erect a "wall of separation between church and state." [330 U.S. 1, 15–16 (1947)]

Prayer in school. Reciting a prayer in school has been and in some places continues to be a common practice in spite of the 1947 Everson case and another Supreme Court ruling declaring school prayer to be inconsistent with the establishment clause [*Engle* v. *Vitale,* 370 U.S. 42 (1962)]. A year later in a separate case [*School District of Abington Township* v. *Schempp,* 374, U.S. 203 (1963)], the ruling was extended to include a prohibition against a required Bible reading. Since 1963, the courts have consistently struck down any form of state-regulated prayer, including voluntary prayer. However, the courts have allowed periods of silence for meditation, secular thoughts, or prayer.

From the text of the school-prayer decisions, two tests or criteria were established which have, in conjunction with a third test developed in 1970, become a three-part test in establishment clause cases. The test asks three fundamental questions:

Does the law as practiced have a secular intent?
Does the law as practiced have a secular effect which neither advances nor inhibits religion?
Does the law avoid fostering "excessive government entanglement with religion?" [*Lemon* v. *Kuntzman,* 403 U.S. 602, (1971)].

In addition to school prayer and Bible readings, a number of other school practices, such as posting the Ten Commandments and presenting Christmas songs, also have been tested with the three-part test.

The courts have allowed the use of religious material in schools if it can be demonstrated that the purpose for its use is clearly academic and secular and that the effect of its use does not have a religiously sectarian effect or promote entanglement with religion. For example, it is acceptable for portions of religious literature, such as the Bible, to become a part of a literature course or even a social studies course in which the Bible or Koran is used to study concepts of law.

Free Exercise Clause

The free exercise cases have usually involved two issues: whether or not there has been an infringement of a person's right to the free exercise of his or her religion, and if there has been an infringement, whether or not the infringement was justified.

There have been two categories of free exercise cases in schools. In the first category are those occasions when someone has contended that some aspect of the school program encroaches on his or her religious beliefs or practices. When the courts have found that the school practice that is offensive is otherwise lawful, they have remedied the situation by allowing the practice to continue but allowing the offended person to be excused from participation. For example, a federal court in Illinois excused students who were members of the United Pentecostal Church from a physical education requirement on the grounds that their religion found the athletic clothing to be too immodest for coeducational activity. In another case in 1972, students of the Amish religion were excused from compulsory attendance in public schools on the grounds that such attendance interfered with the practices of their religion [*Wisconsin* v. *Yoder,* 406 U.S. 205 (1972)].

The second category involves cases in which it has been claimed that school policies or school officials have hindered the rights of persons to participate in a religious activity within the school.

Although the First Amendment has been interpreted to mean that one may not be compelled to espouse any creed or participate in any religious practice and that the freedom to hold any belief or opinion is nearly absolute, it is possible under some circumstances to restrict some acts even when these acts are in accord with one's beliefs [*Braunfeld* v. *Brow,* 366 U.S. 599, 603 (1961)]. For example, the government has forbidden men to have more than one wife, although the prohibition has been contrary to some religious orthodoxy.

The free exercise clause and the establishment clause have conflicted with one another when the former has been used as a defense for voluntary school prayer. To date, the courts have continued to say that their prohibition of school prayers that are organized and administered by the school is not an infringement of an individual's right to pray. The courts countered that under their ruling, anyone may pray in an independent and private way in school.

In 1981, a new twist on the free exercise clause developed when a group of high school students brought suit against a school district because their prayer group was denied the use of a school classroom to conduct a voluntary prayer meeting before school began. The courts found in favor of the school district on the basis that permission would have created an unwarranted entanglement of religion in school. However, in 1981, the courts upheld the right of a religious group to meet on a college campus on the grounds that a college campus was an open forum and could not be selective without being hostile to religion.

Religious use of school facilities has become an issue that many school policy makers must face. To date, the courts have leaned in the direction of disallowing all those uses that seem to fail any part of the three-part test—intent, result, and entanglement—but allowing religious groups to use facilities within the same conditions that apply to other organizations.

Religious Celebrations and Observances

Yet unresolved are the constitutional issues inherent in school celebrations of religious holidays and the performance of religious music in public schools. Most schools handle the issue by accommodating the dominant religious values of the community. However, it would appear that only one religious observance, representing only one religious tradition, in a school during the year would be challengeable under the three-part test of the establishment clause.

State and Federal Aid to Religious Schools

The Court has never squarely decided the constitutionality of state or federal aid to religious schools. However, as part of the landmark *Everson* case in 1947, the Court said, "No tax in any amount, large or small, can be levied to support any religious activities or institutions, whatever they may be called, or whatever form they may adapt to teach or practice religion" [*Everson v. Board of Education*, 330 U.S. 1, 15–16 (1947)].

Everson did not result in an absolute prohibition of money to religious institutions. The line the courts have attempted to draw is based on the concept that tax money may go to a religious school for secular purposes when there are sufficient assurances that the secular intent can be guaranteed. This rule allows tax dollars for secular textbooks and disallows tax dollars for salaries of teachers of secular subjects because "unlike a book a teacher cannot be inspected to determine his or her personal beliefs and subjective acceptance of the limitation imposed by the First Amendment" [*Lemon v. Kurtzman* (1971)].

Proposed Constitutional Amendments

Because prayer in schools has been disallowed on the basis of the Constitution, proponents of prayer in schools have proposed constitutional amendments. In 1982, Senator Strom Thurmond proposed an amendment which said, "Nothing in this constitution shall be construed to prohibit individual or group prayer in public schools or other public institutions. No person shall be required by the United States or by any state to participate in prayer."[10] This and other proposals like it attempt to reinstate school prayers by taking the issue out of the realm of federal litigation and leaving the matter strictly in the hands of state legislators and state courts.

There are many church and religious representatives who support the Supreme Court's school-prayer decisions and oppose efforts to change the constitution. *Liberty* magazine in 1981, a "publication of the Religious Liberty Association of America and the Seventh Day Adventist Church,"[11] devoted their November-December issue to a discussion of the danger to religion of allowing official school prayers. The magazine editor also notes in an article regarding the proposed "voluntary school prayer act," which seeks "to restore the right of voluntary prayer in public schools and to promote the separation of powers," that the "leadership of virtually every major Christian denomination" is opposed to "such acts."[12]

[10]Education Commission of the States, "Policy Perspectives: Issues in Law and Education," no. 12 (Fall 1982), Mimeographed, p. 5.

[11]"*Engle v. Vitale*: The Supreme Court's Decision on Prayer," *Liberty*, 76, no. 6 (Nov./Dec. 1981).

[12]Education Commission of the States, p. 6.

MORAL EDUCATION

Character formation is one of schooling's oldest traditional tasks. Max Lerner believes that schools have retreated from the task of inculcating moral values and left the field entirely to other institutions, such as churches, families, friends, peers, and the mass media.[13] One reason schools have abandoned the task of building character or teaching the young how to be good people, Lerner states, is that most values have been labeled parochial or partisan by those who oppose teaching them in schools. The result is that schools that claim to teach values have become targets for charges of indoctrination from individuals and groups whose values differ from those being taught.

One response of the schools has been to withdraw public and open support for teaching a set of values. But schools continue to communicate values through the curriculum, through teachers' biases, and through administrative policies governing behavior and discipline. These unstated values have come to be known in the education literature as the "hidden curriculum": the values and standards that are not stated but that are a powerful part of every child's school experience.

For a school to advocate and teach a particular set of values effectively and without controversy requires a community consensus supporting those values. Without a consensus, the school that dares to state that it is teaching a particular set of values is open to charges of indoctrination. Max Lerner has aptly described the school-community symbiosis in saying that public education can be a cohesive force in the community when there is clarity and consensus about "means and ends," and it can be a dissolving force when that clarity is missing.[14]

The internal cultural, social, and political conflict that took place in the 1960s and 1970s damaged the consensus on an "American creed" that had existed at an earlier time and had survived two world wars and a depression

The civil rights movements of those decades promoted the rights of racial and cultural minorities and women, seeing them as victims of a white, middle-class, male value structure. It became clear that many of the victimized groups shared neither the "American dream" nor the "American creed." Freedom was a rallying point for many groups who were either disenfranchised or disillusioned with American culture and saw an American creed as a tool of those in power to subjugate and control those who were not in power.

Finally, the Vietnam war revealed the extent to which there was a lack of consensus about American foreign policy and a growing mistrust of the federal government. These events and the revelations about dishonesty in government that emerged from the Watergate hearings, and the publications of the tapes and activities of President Richard Nixon, either caused or revealed a lack of the consensus on which many of our institutions, including schools, depend for their effectiveness.

---

[13]Max Lerner, *Values in Education* (Bloomington, Ind.: Phi Delta Kappa Educational Foundation, 1976), pp. 1–12.

[14]Ibid., p. 12.

Teachers and other school officials could no longer assume that their standards of behavior and morality could be imposed on the young people in their charge. Schools were vulnerable to being called "racist," "sexist," or "middle class." In the extreme case, they risked being taken to court for interfering in the rights of students if they imposed rules of behavior, dress, conduct, or language. The connection between a tacit assumption of agreement on an American creed and these symbols of freedom created an atmosphere of conflict between individuals and the institutions that upheld the values implicit in the creed.

Educators, fearing charges of indoctrination if they taught specific values, were quick to adopt some form of values clarification or analysis, moral reasoning, or values awareness, all of which claimed to teach people how to make value decisions rather than teaching specific values. More often than not, the particular brand of values education presented a conceptual scheme that explained the valuing process and a systematic way to go about analyzing a problem and making value judgments.

Although the variations in values or moral education differ from one another in important ways, they all share the underlying assumption that indoctrination can be avoided by teaching a process of thinking rather than a set of principles to live by.

Character Education

The rise of *character education* (sometimes referred to as "moral literacy") reflected the mood of the United States in the 1980s. The intent of groups that promote character education is to develop moral strength and attitudes through teaching traditional American values. In fact, the National School Boards Association identified the following values as crucial to "a democratic and humane society":

Altruism	Loyalty
Compassion	Obedience
Courage	Punctuality
Courtesy	Respect for Authority
Generosity	Responsibility
Honesty	Self-discipline
Industriousness	Self-respect
Integrity	Tolerance

Although character education has significant popular appeal and no doubt helps some youngsters who lack the inner strength and direction to cope with pressures of modern society, it is vulnerable to criticism. As civil rights and civil libertarian groups are quick to point out, in the wrong hands it risks serving as a Trojan horse to usher religious values into the school. Short of this, various exercises border on indoctrination and an invasion of privacy. From another perspective, educators, sensitive to many other demands placed on the school, question how yet another program can be crammed into an already crowded school day.

Character education earmarks values that are indigenous to a democratic society and moral literacy, but it omits equally important, and sometimes conflicting, values. Values such as *independence, equity, social justice, disobedience,* and *intolerance* are also part of the American tradition. Acting on these values will likely conflict with the more conventional values on the character-education agenda. Then again, values such as honesty and respect for authority, industriousness and punctuality, or loyalty and self-respect also may conflict. We would certainly not argue that conflict is inappropriate in values education, or any part of a genuinely educational curriculum. To the contrary, conflict is a necessary ingredient in the struggle to understand history, science, economics, and public policy—in short, to act as a responsible citizen. Any curriculum that purports to deal with a subject as sensitive and complex as values must be prepared to confront conflict. Any program, however, whose goal is to instill a set of prescribed values is ill prepared to deal with the subject in an intellectually honest fashion.

VALUES IN CONFLICT

In the public schools, the values issues of the society are bubbling just under the surface of daily routines or occasionally bursting through into school, classroom, school board meetings, and ultimately into the media. The specific issues are usually manifestations of general value disputes that have existed in American society for decades or even centuries.

One source of conflict is inherent in the two general goals of public education: *Individual* and *societal.* The claim is made that the public schools should serve both the individual and the society, both self-realization and social adjustment if not betterment. This issue might be termed the "I/We Dilemma"—how to develop personal potential and at the same time promote "We, the people," or social cohesiveness.

Another source of conflict derives from the values in various *secular* and *religious* ideologies when these are present in the same classroom, in the same school, or in the same community. And in a pluralistic society loosely tied together by values borrowed from many disparate sources, it is almost impossible to avoid the presence of competing ideologies, although some groups such as the Amish succeed surprisingly well. Also, given modern media, it is not even necessary for opposing groups to be in close physical proximity to each other.

A final source of conflict that emerges in the schools is that between *local* particularistic values and those of the *larger society* represented by the modern industrial or postindustrial nation-state. Thus, the Supreme Court has found it necessary to protect students from certain local norms such as proscribed hairstyles or denying school attendance to pregnant females.

To see how these sources of value conflict emerge in the public school arena, we'll examine three contemporary disputes: (1) secular humanism: religious or societal value system? (2) creationism v. evolutionism, and (3) nationalism v. globalism.

Secular Humanism

Humanism is not a singular concept. There are many different brands of humanists ranging from the religious to the secular. The various humanist positions include any number of the following concepts: positivism, the scientific method, evolution, democracy, capitalism, liberalism, welfare stateism, arms limitation, environmental conservation, and sexual freedom.[15] However varied their specific beliefs, the core of humanist thought generally includes a rejection of the supernatural, including all deities, and a faith that man can improve the world. Although the concerns of most humanists are clearly secular rather than religious, most humanists do not call themselves *secular humanist.*

The term *secular humanist* has been popularized not by humanists but by fundamentalist religious writers, many of whom identify themselves with the "new right" or the "Moral Majority." According to Ben Brodinsky, the "new Right is using Secular Humanism as an all-inclusive enemy."[16] At the root of the fundamentalists' attacks on humanism is a legal argument that they hope will give them a lever for gaining the legal sanction to include religious material in schools, including school prayer and the creationist view of the beginning of the world.

Their technique is to claim that secular humanism is a religion just like Christianity or any other religion. They then claim that the educational establishment is controlled by secular humanists and that secular humanism as a creed is actively taught in schools. The courts have given them some support. In a 1961 Supreme Court case, *Torcaso* v. *Watkins,* which involved a conscientious objector's religious views, the Court named secular humanism as a religion along with Buddhism and Taoism. The fundamentalists are pointing to this definition and saying that because the laws do not allow Christian religious teachings, the law should not allow secular humanist teaching.

What appears to be at issue is how different citizens see the direction of historical forces in Western civilization and in the American experience. Two trends are particularly pertinent: (1) from clergy-dominated societies to secular, citizen-controlled societies; and (2) from faith based on reason to naturalism and the scientific method.

In ancient Egypt, the pharaoh was considered to be half-human and half-god. Only male descendants of the pharaonic family could succeed to the throne, and all others in the kingdom were the subjects of the pharaoh. Such obedient subjects considered it an honor to dedicate themselves and generations of their families to the laborious tasks of building tombs for their pharaohs. These tombs are the greater and lesser pyramids of Egypt. Since that time there has been a slow evolution of placing curbs and constraints on absolute monarchs, a movement toward limited monarchy and later to constitutional democratic republics. One might call this historical progression one of movement from subject to citizen. A

---

[15]Herbert Wray, "Fundamentalism vs. Humanism," *Humanities Report,* 3, no. 9 (Sept. 1981), pp. 4–8.

[16]Ben Brodinsky, "The New Right: The Movement and Its Impact," *Phi Delta Kappan,* 64, no. 2 (Oct. 1982), p. 90.

part of the same progression is the transition from control of government by the clergy to one of control by secular authorities, by presidents, prime ministers, parliaments, and congresses—from clerical to secular.

The second trend is one that can be traced at least from the times of Plato and Aristotle in ancient Greece. At the same time that the Christian religion was evolving throughout the eastern Mediterranean region, there was also another system of thought emerging. The Greeks were among the first to explore and promote the principles of science as a form of reliable knowledge separate from religion. Over the ensuing centuries, a faith in science as method began to challenge the religious faith in revealed literature. Gradually, naturalism and the scientific method became preferred approaches in the search for knowledge, though not without fierce opposition from religion. The antagonism between these seemingly opposed ways of knowing has continued to the present.

The modern curriculum in America's public schools reflects the best current state of knowledge derived from the academic disciplines, a literature based on science, mathematics, and reason, cumulative and changing in nature, and secular rather than religious. Those who consider revealed literature to be superior to science, mathematics, and reason fear for their belief systems and attempt to stifle all supposed challenges. One way of curtailing the teaching of knowledge based on the academic disciplines is to characterize such knowledge as no more than another form of religion. Because the teaching of any single form of religion by an agency of the state constitutes an establishment of religion, such teaching is prohibited by the First Amendment to the U.S. Constitution. Thus, aggregating all knowledge in school subjects under the rubric "Secular Humanism" and having that body of knowledge declared a "religion" would have the effect of making all bodies of knowledge, however derived, religions. This would in turn preclude the public schools from having any curriculum or teaching anything. Such absurdity derives from the inability of certain sects and organizations in America today to harmonize reason and dogma, science and religion, and is a contemporary manifestation, albeit in aberrant form, of the historical trends from clerical to secular and from faith to reason and science.

Creationism v. Evolutionism

Those who read revealed literature as unchanging, literal truth (even if contaminated by dozens of translations), often claim the status of knowledge for their beliefs. In the case of the Book of Genesis in the Bible, much heat has been generated over the centuries concerning the accuracy of the account of the origin of the universe in this document. Some hold that the English-language version of Genesis is literal truth and advocate the teaching of this account in the schools. This position is called "creationism," after the notion that a supreme being acted to bring the universe into existence: a creator created the world.

The modern curriculum in the public schools follows scientific thought on this matter, teaching that the ultimate origin of the universe is not now known, but that since the original "Big Bang," the universe, the solar system, the earth, and all biological organisms have been evolving or changing; this position is referred to as "evolutionism." The crux of the matter seems to be that the Judeo-Christian tradition calls for purpose in the universe and agency (i.e., a creator) in its origin, whereas the scientific tradition takes a more pragmatic approach whereby the frontiers of knowledge are constantly changing and agency resides in matter and its laws.

Instruction about origins (i.e., of the universe, of the solar system, of earth, of plant and animal life on earth, and of most significance, of the human species) has been a perennial issue in public education. This is a "natural" educational issue in that in Western culture there has always been tension and conflict between two powerful traditions: science and naturalism on the one hand and the revealed literature of Judaism and Christianity on the other. The issue has been further confounded in the past few decades because no longer is it seen as "Faith" versus "Science/Reason," but now is stated as "Scientific Creationism" opposed to "Evolutionary Science." Both camps now claim the cloak of scientific respectability.

Scientific creationists today want their view presented as a version of science in science classes and courses. Their claim is that there is "some scientific justification" that (1) the earth is only ten thousand years old, (2) the flood of Noah's time shaped the modern features of the planet, (3) stars and life were created in six days, (4) plants and animals were created in essentially their present form, (5) fossils are products of the Great Flood. They demand that this position be juxtaposed to that of evolutionary science.

The courts seem to be of two minds with respect to this dispute. If a creationist view is presented in the public schools as the product of religious literature and teachings, it has been declared illegal on the basis of the separation clause in the First Amendment to the Constitution. If this view is presented as a product of legitimate science (an arguable claim that is hotly debated), then case law can be found that either permits or disallows such teaching.

Nationalism v. Globalism

Since the founding of the American Republic, there has been ambivalence among citizens over foreign policy. Should the United States avoid entanglement or seek involvement with other nations? To what extent should one be involved in the affairs of the nations of the Americas or of Europe or of the world community? Consequently, U.S. foreign policy has vacillated between the extremes of continental isolation and worldwide bilateral and multilateral treaties and trade pacts. The American people seem to desire friendship with other countries but never at the expense of sovereignty—a contradictory and impossible goal.

In public education, and especially in the social studies curriculum, the issue erupts over ways in which schools and teachers should deal with international relations. For example, how should a teacher present the events surrounding the refusal of the Congress of the United States to ratify the charter of the League of Nations after World War I? Is this an example of isolationism, of a reluctance to participate in an international forum, of a paranoia emerging from a fear of relinquishing some small degree of national autonomy? Is teaching about the United Nations, its successes and failures, a violation of American patriotism? Is any mention of international relations, other than nice-to-know curiosities about the "peculiar" ways of other peoples, a form of treason? Are issues in the global domain to be considered taboo in the public school classroom?

A global perspective of necessity challenges various forms of nationalism, including the definition of citizenship. In the "Introduction to Teachers" portion of *World Citizen Curriculum,* for example, the authors state: "Citizenship refers to the choices and actions through which individuals link themselves to the affairs of the groups of which they are members. Since every person born on the planet Earth automatically becomes a member of the world community group, 'world citizenship' is the initial and lifelong membership we all inherit. . . . In the same way that we have a unique relationship with our family, our community and our nation, we also have a unique relationship with the whole world system."[17]

Some ardent "national sovereignty" advocates would also oppose such activities as "What if?" if the statements offered to students were any of the following:

> What if all national borders were removed, so that people could move, live, and work wherever they choose?
>
> What if all individuals of voting age voted by electronic referendum on global and local issues that affected them?
>
> What if less-developed nations put an embargo on the shipment of oil and raw materials to the developed nations?

In a Colorado newspaper, a controversy over a planned global-education curriculum yielded the following excerpt from a letter to the editor:

> I believe that the citizens of this community have been deceived as to the true nature and purpose of Global Education. It is not merely a new course or class that is to be taught. It is a definite political/religious philosophy. The advocates of Global Education are seeking to integrate this philosophy into the entire educational structure of our schools. If adopted, Globalism would permeate everything that is taught here, K–12.
>
> If the true intent of Globalism is merely to expose students to other cultures, why do we need it? We already have history, geography, and foreign language classes. Why then do we need Globalism? As I see it, the real reason for bringing in Globalism is (1) to remove control of curriculum from the local level and place it in the hands of the professional education elite; (2) to develop a society of mindless, fearful, uncritical, pacifistic puppets who will blindly follow the "enlightened masters" the global activists seek to enthrone; and (3) to destroy the principles and values that have made this the greatest nation history has ever known. . . .
>
> Globalism is not merely Un-American, it is openly Anti-American. It portrays the United States as the source of all the world's problems, and Globalists interpret history from this perspective.[18]

[17]Center for Teaching International Relations, *World Citizen Curriculum* (Denver, Colo.: University of Denver, 1986), p. 1.
[18]Scott E. Churnock, "Comments On Globalism," *Colorado Weekly News,* Bennett, Colo., April 17, 1986, p. 2.

Global education is not solely the target in towns and cities; it also comes in for criticism from the U.S. Department of Education, at least from the Region VIII Representative of the Secretary. In a paper prepared for this official, the author, Gregg Cunningham, writes:

> In conclusion, most globalist curricular materials contain none of the crude anti-American polemics that characterized "New Left" denunciations of the 1960s. They have matured into a subtle and sophisticated series of Socratically delivered doctrinal bromides that no longer assail the core beliefs and assumptions of our American heritage. They seek, instead, to ridicule our value system by suggesting that we relinquish our economic and political preeminence in the interest of some shadowy "global justice."
>
> Their worldview is utopian and pacifistic. They are also redistributionists [of the wealth of the rich nations to the poor nations]. Although they decry doctrinaire absolutes, they paradoxically strive to replace conventional morality—based on Judeo-Christian principles—with an eclectic, mystical ethos of their own concoction. . . .
>
> When heat is applied to their curriculum, it distills into a hard left policy agenda. Their self-avowed objective is radical political change, and they intend to achieve it by turning students into activists.[19]

The commitment and loyalty of citizens to their nation cannot be merely a matter of indoctrination if it is to have any durability throughout the adult years. The issues too briefly discussed above are but three of the many societal disputes that often and regularly erupt in American public education and in American public school classrooms. The wisdom of the past two hundred years cautions that we should not proscribe acceptable curricular issues and topics, even on the basis that the learner is not an adult citizen. To curtail the freedom to raise issues is to risk later indifference and cynicism. A durable patriotism grows from openness and freedom in the public arena—even in the public school classroom.

●━━●

Case Study: School Holidays

It will be a quiet and short school board meeting, the superintendent thought as he perused the agenda, because the only major item was the approval of next year's school year calendar. Discussion of this item had just begun when a parent rose and moved that Yom Kippur and Rosh Hashanah, two Jewish holidays, be added to the list of school holidays. These two holidays were to be observed on September 20 and September 29, both regularly scheduled school attendance days. There was considerable vocal support for the motion among a dozen or so parents in attendance at the meeting.

As discussion of the motion continued, several complaints surfaced that the board was not too sensitive to several other non-Christian religions, namely,

[19]Gregg L. Cunningham, "Blowing the Whistle on 'Global Education'" (Denver, Colo.: Region VIII, U.S. Department of Education, 1986, Mimeographed), p. 21.

Seventh Day Adventists, Mormons, and Muslims, all of whom were represented in the student body of the school district. It was pointed out that about 15 percent of the students were from non-Christian families and almost 10 percent from Jewish families. Further, a few parents were angered by the behavior of two coaches of varsity sports, who, it was claimed, were quite intolerant of players who refused to practice or play on their religious holidays.

At this point, the school board president sought the guidance of the superintendent of schools for her recommendation on the matter. What policy position(s) would you suggest to the board for their consideration? Where do you stand on this issue?

Thought Questions

1. Is there a set of common values ("ties that bind") that constitute an American Creed? Is this creed secular or religious or a combination of the two? What might be four or five core values in such a creed? How might such value "pushes" for unity still allow for diversity?
2. What policies should a local board of education adopt in regard to the teaching of values in the public schools under its jurisdiction?
3. The United States Supreme Court, in deciding various cases concerning conflict between church and state, has declared that a "wall of separation" needs to be maintained between the two without creating hostility toward any particular religion. In the practices of the public schools, how does this church/state issue erupt?
4. Where do you stand on the three value conflicts raised in the chapter: (1) secular humanism, (2) creationism v. evolutionism, and (3) nationalism v. globalism?
5. Using your own experience in school as the basis, what values did your teachers attempt to inculcate in you and your classmates? Were any of these values clearly religious values?
6. Some groups have argued that the public schools should not become involved at all in the teaching or even examination of values, but that these concerns should be left to the discretion of families. Do you agree or disagree with this position?
7. Defend or refute the claim of "values shifts" as described in Table 4-1.
8. Are any subjects taught in the public school curriculum "value free"? Defend your position.
9. When local values conflict with national values, how should local officials and teachers deal with the issue?
10. Attempt to list the sources from which your present values derived.

Practical Activities

1. Attend a local school board meeting. Note the composition of the board as to age, gender, race, ethnicity, socioeconomic class, educational level. What values come

up in the discussion of agenda items? Who else is in attendance? What is their special interest in the meeting? What values do they appear to evince?

2. Visit a school and try to determine which values are being taught (explicitly or implicitly). How are the values presented? How do the students react to the teaching of values? Can you determine the values students already possess, values that they have learned in social institutions (including the family) other than the schools?

3. The following is a list of potential emerging American values. Most of them have been written about in books and magazines in the past twenty years. Which ones do you think are emerging, soon to become dominant, values? Check those you think will become dominant values in the future. If you think some values not listed are also emerging, write them on lines 11 and 12.

_____ 1. Pursuit of immediate pleasures.
_____ 2. Sexual permissiveness and openness.
_____ 3. Acceptance and expression of feelings and emotions.
_____ 4. Limits to growth and search for balanced stability.
_____ 5. More cooperation and less competitiveness.
_____ 6. More concern for quality of life rather than for acquiring material possessions.
_____ 7. More internationalism and less nationalism.
_____ 8. More protection of nature rather than mastery of nature.
_____ 9. Greater political participation (beyond voting).
_____ 10. Work as self-fulfillment rather than hard and arduous labor.
_____ 11. _____
_____ 12. _____

4. The values listed below might be considered basic, traditional American values (though the list is far from complete). In your experience, which ones seem to be still dominant in your community, state, and nation? Which ones seem to be declining in importance?

A dominant value is one that for generations and/or centuries has traditionally been followed by the vast majority of members of a society. Dominant values are usually taken for granted; that is, people follow them without thinking about them. A declining value, on the other hand, is a traditional value that recently (in the past few decades) has been challenged; fewer and fewer people are adhering to it.

For those values you feel are still dominant, place a + on the blank line in front of the value. For those you feel are now declining, place a − on the blank line. If you think a crucial value has been left off the list, write it on line 16. Other values can be added on lines 17 and 18.

_____ 1. Self-denial and the ability to endure distress.
_____ 2. Deferred gratification, or the willingness to wait patiently for the rewards of work and action.
_____ 3. Sexual taboos and constraints on sexual practices.

_____ 4. Striving, working hard (hard work yields success).

_____ 5. Punctuality (time is money), being "on time."

_____ 6. Self-control, reining in emotions, "staying cool."

_____ 7. Volunteering (charity for the good of society).

_____ 8. Profit motive (the desire to profit from work and/or investment).

_____ 9. Acquisitiveness, or the desire for material possessions.

_____ 10. Upward social mobility (the desire to improve one's socioeconomic status).

_____ 11. Human dignity, worth of the individual, personal rights.

_____ 12. Consent of the governed and majority rule.

_____ 13. Equality and equity.

_____ 14. Patriotic loyalty.

_____ 15. Territoriality, or protection of national sovereignty.

_____ 16. _____

_____ 17. _____

_____ 18. _____

Bibliography

BUTTS, R. FREEMAN, *The Revival of Civic Learning.* Bloomington, Ind.: Phi Delta Kappa Educational Foundation, 1980.

CAHN, STEVEN M., *Education and the Democratic Ideal.* Chicago: Nelson-Hall Publishers, 1979.

DEWEY, JOHN, *Moral Principles in Education.* Boston: Houghton Mifflin Company, 1909.

_____, *A Common Faith.* New Haven, Conn.: Yale University Press, 1934.

FERGUSON, MARILYN, *The Aquarian Conspiracy.* New York: J. P. Tarcher, 1981.

GALLUP, GEORGE, JR., *Adventures in Immortality.* New York: McGraw-Hill Book Company, Inc., 1982.

LERNER, MAX, *Values in Education.* Bloomington, Ind.: Phi Delta Kappa Educational Foundation, 1976.

LINES, PATRICIA M., *Religious and Moral Values in Public Schools: A Constitutional Analysis.* Denver, Colo.: Education Commission of the States, 1982.

MITCHELL, ARNOLD, *The Nine American Lifestyles.* New York: Macmillan, 1983.

ROSZAK, THEODORE, *Person/Planet.* New York: Doubleday & Company, Inc., 1978.

YANKELOVICH, DANIEL, *New Rules.* New York: Random House, 1981.

5

Sociological Perspectives

We have come to know that every individual lives, from one generation to the next, in some society; that he lives out a biography, and that he lives it out within some historical sequence. By the fact of his living he contributes, however minutely, to the shaping of this society and to the course of its history, even as he is made by society and by its historical push and shove.[1]

Society can survive only if there exists among its members a sufficient degree of homogeneity; education perpetuates and reinforces this homogeneity by fixing in the child, from the beginning, the essential similarities that collective life demands.[2]

People are schooled to accept a society. They are educated to create or re-create one.[3]

THE NATURE OF A SOCIETY

A relatively large, cohesive group of people possessing a common culture is termed a *society*. By this definition, every nation is a society, but also every tribe and ethnic or racial group within a nation (or sometimes within two or more nations, such as the Basques in Spain and France) is a society. As a matter of logical convenience, however, such groups in the United States today as blacks, Mexican-Americans, and Native American tribes are classified as subcultures.

The primary goal of every society, and to a greater or lesser extent of each subculture within a society, is to survive. Secondary goals concern the quality of life, the degree of health, stability and change, and justice desired by the society. In order to continue to exist, a society must meet at least these six survival requirements:[4]

1. The population has to be reproduced or the group will die out.
2. The population also has to be reproduced culturally and socially; its children must

[1]C. Wright Mills, *The Sociological Imagination* (New York: Oxford University Press, 1959), p. 6.
[2]Emile Durkheim, *Education and Sociology* (New York: The Free Press, 1956), p. 70.
[3]Everett Reimer, *School is Dead* (Garden City, N.Y.: Doubleday & Company, Inc., 1972), p. 121.
[4]Melvin M. Tumin, *Patterns of Society: Identities, Roles, Resources* (Boston: Little, Brown & Company, 1973), p. 272.

be educated and trained in the values and skills needed to function as adequate adults.

3. Goods and services have to be produced and distributed.
4. Order must be maintained both internally and externally.
5. The population must be maintained at a reasonable level of physical and mental health.
6. The society's members must see enough meaning and purpose in life to be motivated to perform their various tasks.

These survival tasks are carried out by social institutions: "the family, the educational system, the economy, the polity, the health and welfare system, and the religious or moral system." Each of these social institutions "is a major area of organized social activity required for social continuity."[5]

RELATIONSHIP OF SOCIETY, EDUCATION, AND SCHOOLS

Clearly, then, education is one of the social institutions charged with cultural and social reproduction, that is, with the education of children and youth for individual and social survival. To state that education is a social institution, however, is not to equate education with schools and schooling. During the Golden Age in ancient Greece, Pericles asserted that Athens served as an education to the world, that the entire way of life in Athenian society was a model educational environment to its citizens as well as to outside observers and visitors to the city-state.

The culture of Athens was educative, but Athens also had schools such as Plato's academy. The point here is that the education of a person is only partly the result of schooling and mainly the result of other educative agencies (and individuals) such as the family, the community, and the communications media. School or schooling is only one influence, one "teacher" among several that form the social institution of education.

Each of the six social institutions — family, education, polity, economy, health/welfare system, and religious/moral system — is to some extent an educative agent. Although each of these institutions influences the cognitive and affective "maps" of all members of a society, their greatest impact is on the society's younger members — children and youth. Sociologists refer to this pervasive process of initiation and conditioning as socialization.

SOCIALIZATION, EDUCATION, AND SCHOOLS

Socialization is a process of teaching and learning, where the family, the culture, the society, the community, and the other social institutions combine to be the "teacher," and where all members of the society are the "learners." In this context,

[5]Ibid., p. 171.

each individual societal member is both a teacher and a learner: a "teacher" when in the role of group member, and a "learner" when, as an individual, others influence one's behaviors. A person, then, is both a part of the "we" and a separate, unique "I." Audrey Schwartz describes socialization this way:

> Socialization . . . produces social patterns in that it provides both a body of expectations and ways to meet them that are more or less shared by other members of a social group. . . . From the point of view of individuals, socialization helps them to cope with the demands of their social groups by giving them the capacity to meet these demands. From the point of view of a group, socialization contributes to its stability and continued existence by transmitting established behavior and value patterns to its members.[6]

Education, however, is more than merely external impositions, implicit or explicit, of a social institution on the individual members of a society. It is also the process of self-development initiated by the individual. Education involves both the demands of socialization, of societal membership, of community, *and* the drives for individuality, for personal growth, for self-actualization, and for self-realization. In addition, education is both process and product. It is societal and individual efforts as well as the outcomes of those efforts.

One social agency created to enhance the processes of socialization *and* education is the school. In one form or another, schools exist in almost every society on earth. In some societies, the school is only a secondary agency of socialization, with the family, religion, and community as the primary socializing agencies. In other societies, especially those of western Europe, Japan, and North America, the school has become the primary agency of socialization. In the United States, the school emerged as the primary educative agency only during the past two centuries. Before the nineteenth century, American society relied more heavily on the family and the church.[7]

As agents of society, schools perform a number of socialization functions, the kinds being dependent on the nature of the society. For today's schools in almost all nations, Everett Reimer identifies four social functions: (1) custodial care, (2) social-role selection, (3) indoctrination, and (4) education.[8] From a different vantage point, Kenneth Boulding describes five outcomes or products of the schooling industry: (1) knowledge, (2) skills, (3) custodial care, (4) certification, and (5) community activity.[9] Of Reimer's four functions and Boulding's five outcomes, three from these two lists concern what is commonly regarded as *education*. Reimer uses the term *education*, whereas Boulding employs the two words *knowledge* and *skills*. Both writers include *custodial care* as a function or product of schooling. It appears that Boulding's term *certification* would be subsumed as a part of Reimer's broader

[6]Audrey James Schwartz, *The Schools and Socialization* (New York: Harper & Row, Publishers, Inc., 1975), p. 2.

[7]Lawrence A. Cremin, *Public Education* (New York: Basic Books, Inc., Publishers, 1976), p. 37.

[8]Reimer, *School Is Dead*, p. 13.

[9]Kenneth Boulding, "The Schooling Industry as a Possibly Pathological Section of the American Economy," *Review of Educational Research*, 42, no. 1 (Winter 1972), pp. 129–43.

concept of *social-role selection*. Reimer's term *indoctrination* and Boulding's use of *community activity* seem to be distinct and mutually exclusive concepts.

THE SOCIAL FUNCTIONS OF SCHOOLS

Those socialization functions performed by schools include at least the five alluded to previously: (1) education (including not only knowledge and skills but also attitudes, values, and sensibilities), (2) social-role selection (including not only the highly visible act of certification but also the more subtle forms of sorting and selecting), (3) indoctrination, (4) custodial care, and (5) community activity.

Although education is a form of socialization that today is performed primarily by schools, education is also a function of other agencies affecting children and youth *and* of the individual's own actions directed toward self-development. Such groups as the family, peers, church, mass media, and youth-serving organizations all play roles in the education of the young. In or out of schools, the individual child or adolescent is an agent in his or her own education.

The Function of Education

As a social function of schools, education comprises knowledge, skills, attitudes, values, and sensibilities. Most of these types of learning are in the category of what is termed *general education*, as distinguished from *specialized education*. In this context, *general education* refers to learning needed to function effectively as a citizen and member of a particular society, which in the United States includes several modes of communication (reading, writing, speaking, computing); several modes of thinking (problem solving, scientific method); the values of human dignity and the rational consent of the governed, coupled with materialism and capitalist economics; the attitudes of competitiveness, individualism, and elitism, coupled with egalitarianism, communalism, and cooperativeness; and many other cognitive and affective attributes.

By *specialized education* we mean the variety of optional "elective" activities that schools provide to cater to individuals' interests, leisure choices, occupational tendencies, and desires for continuing education. Thus, social studies is a subject in the domain of general education, although for some students it is also a subject of individual interest (for purposes of leisure, occupation, or college admission) and therefore falls into the domain of specialized education. Although home economics and industrial arts generally are considered general education, for some students these areas are specialized education, usually for purposes of occupational preference.

All school subjects can be both general and specialized education, though it is common for some subjects to be thought of as primarily general education (English or mathematics) and other subjects as primarily specialized education (building-construction trades, cosmetology, advanced placement courses). At the elementary school level, almost all education is general education, whereas there are increasing specialized educational options as students enter middle schools, junior high schools, high schools, and colleges.

It should be obvious that as a social function of schools, education (both general and specialized) is what most persons would consider the major reason for the existence of schools in the United States. It will become increasingly clear, however, that other social functions of schools interfere with the function of education, especially that aspect of education referred to as *individual self-development* or *self-realization.*

The Function of Social-Role Selection

The schools in the United States engage in numerous activities that are carried on ostensibly to complement the educational function but that, in effect, perform a different socialization function—that of social-role selection. Sociologists use the concepts of *role* and *status* to describe the social positions held by the individual members of a social group.

> While closely related, the terms *status* and *role* have somewhat different meanings: status properly signifies a social position without reference to the behavior it entails; role, on the other hand, refers to the dynamic aspects of status, to the behavioral expectations that all persons who hold similar social positions are expected to meet.... A role, then, is a collection of *prescribed, proscribed,* and *permitted* behaviors associated with a social position or status.[10]

Although the term *student* refers to a status, the expected behaviors of someone holding the status of student comprise the role of a student. Thus, *student* is a term that denotes both a status and a role.

Each of us holds, simultaneously, many social statuses and roles. Over time we drop certain age-specific statuses and roles and acquire new ones. Also, over time we desire, pursue, and sometimes achieve new, valued, and rewarding statuses and roles, usually in the realm of occupations. Unfortunately, or fortunately, depending on one's sense of justice and preference for a particular social ideology, every society possesses a differential reward system with respect to occupational statuses. As David Goslin observes, "Although the number and variety of positions to be filled varies from society to society, it has thus far been true in every society that the available positions have carried with them unequal responsibilities for and demands upon their occupants."[11] Even more important, "the world has not yet seen a society in which the occupants of all positions were accorded equal rewards or status. As a result there is competition among the members of the society . . . for those positions receiving the greatest rewards and carrying with them the greatest responsibility and prestige."[12]

[10]Schwartz, *The Schools,* pp. 9–10.

[11]David A. Goslin, *The School in Contemporary Society* (Glenview, Ill.: Scott, Foresman & Company, 1965), p. 8.

[12]Ibid.

Groupings of statuses can be identified within any society by clustering those statuses that possess relatively similar (1) qualifications for membership, (2) level of responsibility, (3) supply and demand ratio, (4) degree of prestige, (5) types and levels of rewards, (6) level of difficulty or risk, and (7) degree of desirability. Such status or social-role groupings are usually termed *social classes,* and these are invariably weighted, scaled, and stratified in a hierarchical pattern. Robert Havighurst and Bernice Neugarten describe the nature of social class stratification this way: "All human societies that we know about exhibit social inequality: that is, inequality in power, prestige, and material goods." Then, quoting David Riesman: "Everywhere and in every epoch there has existed some form of stratification with those at the top holding more privilege, power, and enjoying greater rewards than those at the bottom."[13]

As a basis for describing the characteristics of each social class and for ranking social classes, Joseph Kahl used the following seven dimensions:[14]

1. Prestige
2. Occupation
3. Possessions, or wealth, or income
4. Social interaction (that is, patterns of differential social contacts; people stick with their own kind)
5. Class consciousness (that is, awareness of belonging to a class, such as working class or middle class)
6. Value orientations
7. Power, or control

For some persons, and especially for children and youth, their positions on the continuum of each of these dimensions are mainly the result of *ascribed* or inherited characteristics, that is, of having been born into families that are in particular social classes. For other persons, and especially for those in complex, industrialized, and technologically "advanced" societies, their positions are more the result of *acquired* characteristics, of ability and achievement.

There are a number of ways to stratify social classes. For our general needs, we will use the five-level category system Kahl favors for describing cities in the United States. The five classes are upper, upper middle, lower middle, working, and lower. An average American city would have a distribution of its population by these five classes that approximates the following:[15]

Upper class	1%
Upper-middle class	9
Lower-middle class	40
Working class	40
Lower class	10
Total	100%

[13]Robert J. Havighurst and Bernice L. Neugarten, *Society and Education,* 4th ed. (Boston: Allyn & Bacon, Inc., 1975), p. 7.

[14]Ibid., p. 20.

[15]Joseph A. Kahl, *The American Class Structure* (New York: Holt, Rinehart & Winston, 1959), pp. 184–220.

A person's social position and social class membership are determined by both ascribed (inherited) and acquired (achieved) statuses or characteristics. For example, a person who is black and female, who is a first-born child in a family of four children, whose family belongs to a Methodist church and is classified as lower-middle class, possesses these statuses and social class position as a result of ascribed, or inherited, characteristics. If this woman, during her adult life, becomes wife and mother, completes a Ph.D. in economics, works her way up to being president of a large banking institution, and, together with her husband, achieves social mobility into the upper class, these new statuses and social class would be the results of acquired, or achieved, characteristics. In U.S. society, ascribed and acquired statuses combine to determine social position and class. Although American values stress acquired characteristics as preferred criteria for determining social position and class, ascribed statuses still weigh heavily in the allocation of social positions.

The schools of America play a part in this determination of social position. It is the school in modern, complex, industrial, technological societies that, on the one hand, reinforces the individual's ascribed statuses and, on the other hand, provides arenas and activities for the individual to perform and achieve acquired characteristics. Teachers and other school personnel subtly reward students' behaviors that they consider acceptable and desirable. The school tests and certifies (by diplomas, degrees, and transcripts of letter grades); the school promotes and graduates; it rewards and punishes; and it sorts students along continua or in either-or categories for its many curricular and extracurricular activities. Goslin describes the part the school plays in social status selection:

> With the rise of mass education the school functions as an integral part of the process of status allocation in four ways: (1) by providing a context in which the individual can demonstrate his abilities, (2) by channeling individuals into paths that lead in the direction of different occupations or classes of occupations, (3) by providing the particular skills needed to fulfill the requirements of various positions, and finally (4) by transferring to the individual the differential prestige of the school itself.[16]

Also describing the school's role in status allocation, Reimer is more critical of this function than most other observers, chiefly because he views it as seriously undermining the more important function of schools—education. He calls this status-allocation function "the sorting of the young into the social slots they will occupy in adult life," and for Reimer the "aspect of job selection in school is wasteful and often personally disastrous. . . . The major part of job selection is not a matter of personal choice at all, but a matter of survival in the school system. . . . Age at dropout determines whether boys and girls will be paid for their bodies, hands, or brains, and also how much they will be paid. This in turn will largely determine where they can live, with whom they can associate, and the rest of their style of life."[17]

[16]Goslin, *The School,* p. 9.
[17]Reimer, *School Is Dead,* p. 17.

The Function of Transmission of Social Values

Closely related to the school's function of status and class selection is the socialization function of indoctrination, as Reimer calls it, or the transmission of social values. Of course, the school is not the only social institution charged with the transmission of cultural and social values. In fact, all social institutions transmit these values in the normal course of their activities. The schools transmit and reinforce social values, both overtly and explicitly as well as covertly and implicitly. For example, through simulated economic activities, such as "playing store" in the primary grades, schools teach the value of free enterprise capitalism. This is overt and explicit socialization to a particular societal value. But schools also transmit values in less obvious, implicit ways, such as through the organizational structure of a school itself, which is hierarchical in nature, mirroring the hierarchical structure of virtually all organizations in contemporary, industrial societies.

The Function of Custodial Care

The fourth function of schools is also one that interferes with and diverts attention from the function of education. This is the child-care or custodial-care function, sometimes referred to pejoratively as *baby-sitting* or *keeping the kids off the streets.* Goslin calls this "the role of the school in providing mothers with relief from the task of taking care of their children during a significant part of the day, which in turn makes possible the addition of large numbers of married women to the labor force."[18] Schools in the United States today, at all levels from prekindergarten through the college years, provide extensive and progressively more expensive custodial care. Reimer and others have pointed out that "packaging custody" has the consequence of extending "childhood from age twelve to twenty-five...."[19] Reimer claims that "child care is the most tangible service schools provide, and since parents are naturally concerned about the quality of such care, this function has a priority claim on school resources. Other functions must compete for what is left after prevailing local standards of safety, comfort, and convenience have been met."[20]

The Function of Community Activity

The fifth and final social function is that of community activity, by which we mean those activities initiated by the school that serve as a focus for the entire community and therefore serve as vehicles for the enhancement of social cohesiveness. This function includes such highly visible activities as athletic contests (mainly football and basketball), drama performances, musical events, and special

[18]Goslin, *The School,* p. 11.
[19]Reimer, *School Is Dead,* p. 15.
[20]Ibid., p. 14.

ceremonies such as commencements and pageants; and such less visible activities as recreation clubs and leagues (chess, skiing, basketball, softball) and various self-improvement, vocational, or avocational adult education courses (painting, car repair, macrame, "Great Books," photography). The point here is that schools are often community oriented and thus become community centers that foster identification with a community. The school's community activities serve to engender a sense of community in those who participate.

INFLUENCES ON CHILDREN AND ADOLESCENTS

There are many influences on the lives of children and youth, among which the most important and potent are the family, the peer group, and the school, with the media, and especially television and the recording industry, vying with the other three. Because children and youth also hold the status and role of student, these same influences have an impact on students' performance and behavior in school. Thus, a duality of influence exists, where family, peer group, school, and media (and others such as churches) all affect children and youth *both* as individuals and as students. It is the latter impact that is of greater concern to us in education, although the impact of schooling on the lives of individuals *after leaving school* is also of interest.

The Influence of Family

From birth onward, the baby and then the child become progressively more and more humanized, primarily as a result of social interaction and social learning. "The family, as the major socializing agency in the society, acts to teach the child the culture and subculture."[21] As the family socializes and humanizes the child for participation in the arenas and activities of sociocultural life, one of the institutions for which the child is prepared is the school.

There is too much diversity among families in the United States to identify one pattern of preparing the child to participate in school life. One factor that accounts for differences in family attitudes toward schooling is that of social class. This is to say that the family not only "educates" the child to the values, norms, and mores of the social class to which the family belongs; it also "educates" the child to the entire social structure, which includes all social classes, and also to the possibilities and ways of social class mobility, both upward and downward. Although there may be upward and downward social mobility of many individuals from each of the social classes, nearly all families support, and "educate" their children to support, the total social class structure of the society. When the children of all social classes enter the public schools, it is then that the differences of family social class backgrounds come into sharp contrast.

[21]Havighurst and Neugarten, *Society*, p. 134.

Because schools have come to play an ever-increasing role in the lives of all children and youth, often to the age of twenty-five, families of all social classes prepare their children, in different ways to be sure, to cope with twelve or more years of school attendance. As Havighurst and Neugarten have observed, "different families create environments that influence children's intellectual growth and educational motivation in different ways."[22] Some of the factors that vary from one family environment to another and that appear to affect children's educational progress are (1) language spoken in the home; (2) educational reading materials present in the home; (3) quality and amount of family talk; (4) methods and consistency in disciplining younger family members; (5) quality and amount of family engagement with community activities, family visits to local attractions, and extended family travel; and (6) parents' attitudes toward learning and schooling. As might be expected, many of these factors also correlate significantly with the social class status of the family, and often also with its racial and ethnic background.

The Influence of Peer Groups

Besides belonging to families, children and adolescents also belong to peer groups, to age-similar, status-similar, role-similar groups. These groups are many and varied, but one child or youth will be a member of only a few groups at a time. Some of the kinds of peer groups to which children may belong are neighborhood play groups, friendship groups and cliques in school, clubs, street gangs, Scouts, athletic teams, student governments, student newspapers and yearbooks, cheerleaders, religious classes and clubs, dating groups, and the many group tags students use to refer to other students such as "jocks," "heads," "geeks," and "cowboys."

Like families, peer groups exert influence on individual members, and many peer group influences affect the school performance of members. This is especially true for adolescents in middle, junior high, and senior high school, but it is also true to a lesser degree for children in elementary schools. As the influence of the family wanes and becomes less monopolistic over time, the influence of peer groups increases as individuals move from childhood to adolescence to adulthood. From mid- to late teens, peer-group influence is most pervasive.

As one agency of socialization, the peer group "teaches" children and youth many coping skills, especially those that may or may not be helpful in the social settings of schools. "The peer group teaches children their sex roles, building upon, but changing and elaborating the earlier teaching of the family."[23] Other functions of peer groups are to suggest aspects and modes of social mobility, to provide models of new social roles, and to assist in the process of becoming independent from adults. "Further, peer groups provide a social arena away from adults where members can work out new social identities."[24]

[22]Ibid., p. 145.
[23]Ibid., p. 163.
[24]Schwartz, *The Schools*, p. 151.

Parents and teachers are well aware of the impact peer groups have on children and youth as students in the schools. "Pupils, more than other people in the school, experience conflict between formal school expectations and the informal expectations of their peers."[25] Peer groups that are the outcasts at school tend to drop out of school at the earliest possible time and to influence new members to do the same. On the other hand, a peer group in which planning to attend college is a norm tends to attract and reinforce members who are "college material." "More commonly, though, the child's peer culture tends to be oriented away from the educational process in the direction of leisure time activities, recreation, and fun."[26] Although peer groups can and do function to enhance academic achievement and positive attitudes toward school, they more commonly promote non- and even anti-educational goals and attitudes.

The Influence of School

Not only do the family and peer group influence students, but also the climate, structure, and organization of the school and classroom affect students' attitudes and behaviors. This type of influence is mainly implicit in the ways schools and classrooms are organized and conducted; it is thus often referred to as "the hidden curriculum," in order to distinguish this form of "teaching" from the more generally recognized curriculum of teaching the subjects (science, mathematics, and social studies). Robert Dreeben contends "that what children learn derives as much from the nature of their experiences in the school setting as from what they are taught."[27]

What students experience in schools, separate from the explicit, educational, curricular experiences, are (1) a social class bias reflected by the values and norms schools promote, (2) a bureaucratized institution, and (3) a set of imposed goals designed to change students' behaviors. Although there are other components of the schools' hidden curriculum, these three appear to have the greatest impact on students as individuals.

The social class bias in schools is that of the middle class. With some exceptions, elected school board members tend to come from the upper-middle class (most) and the lower-middle class. For school administrators (superintendents and principals), a preponderance is from the middle classes, whereas teachers mainly come from the middle and working classes. This distribution of those in control of schools and classrooms leads to the conclusion that "the orientation of the American school is predominantly that of the middle class," which in turn means that school personnel will tend to place "strong emphasis upon the character traits of punctuality, honesty, and responsibility. Respect for property is stressed. There is a premium upon sexual modesty and decorum. While both

[25]Ibid., p. 153.
[26]Goslin, *The School*, p. 33.
[27]Robert Dreeben, "The Contribution of Schooling to the Learning of Norms," *Harvard Educational Review*, 37, no. 2 (Spring 1967), p. 211.

competitiveness and cooperation are valued to varying degrees, there is always stress upon mastery and achievement."[28]

In a broader view, Dreeben claims that in schools in the United States students learn, among other things, four crucial social norms, which on closer inspection are also middle-class values. These norms are (1) independence, (2) achievement, (3) universalism, and (4) specificity.[29]

By *independence* Dreeben means "that individuals accept the obligations . . . to act by themselves (unless collaborative effort is called for) and accept personal responsibility and accountability for their conduct and its consequences." By achievement he means that students are obliged "to perform tasks actively and master the environment according to standards of excellence." Finally, for universalism and specificity, Dreeben means that "students must acknowledge the right of others to treat them [students] as members of categories often based on a few discrete characteristics rather than on the full constellation of [characteristics] representing the whole person."[30]

These definitions of independence, achievement, universalism, and specificity take on fuller meanings in the contexts of specific school and classroom activities. For example, students learn the norm-value of independence as they are required by teachers and other school personnel to do their homework assignments on their own; to take both teacher-made and standardized achievement tests as individuals; to avoid, in most cases, cooperative tasks with other students; to avoid cheating; to be graded (letter grades such as A, B, C, D, and F) as individuals; to be individually responsible for personal possessions such as notebooks, writing paper, pencils, and articles of clothing; and to be responsible for school property such as textbooks, desks, library books, and lockers. Even though teachers and principals mouth the goals of cooperation and working with others, "judging the product according to collective standards, however, is another question. . . . In the last analysis it is the individual assessment that counts."[31]

Schools "teach" *achievement* by encouraging, and even commanding, students to succeed in doing school tasks, to always do their best, to master certain skills, to compete with other students, to take all tests and assignments very seriously, and in general to accept and strive to excel on the many standards set up by schools. Achievement standards are evident in every activity teachers evaluate: homework assignments, quizzes, test, number of absences, times tardy, physical prowess (number of push-ups or number of baskets made), and extent of oral participation in discussions. For each task, a student receives a symbolic reward or punishment, an A or an F, a plus or a minus—some type of indicator of success or failure. These indicators in the aggregate determine whether a student has earned promotion to the next grade level or graduation from a middle, junior high, or senior high school. To learn achievement is to learn to cope with success and failure as perceived and determined by others.

[28]Havighurst and Neugarten, *Society*, p. 139.
[29]Dreeben, "The Contribution," p. 215.
[30]Ibid., p. 216.
[31]Ibid., pp. 224–225.

Through the contrasting norms of universalism and specificity, students learn to accept the school's practices of categorization. In school, a student's complex individuality is mostly denied as a result of the treatment of individuals as members of categories, but categorization has its positive aspects, "especially when contrasted to nepotism, favoritism, and arbitrariness." The distinction between universalism and specificity hinges on "whether individuals are treated as members of categories [universalism] or as special cases [specificity]."[32] As a member of a family, a child is usually treated with specificity, whereas in school the treatment he or she receives is most frequently based on universalism. For example, a child in a family may be fed at a time (later or earlier) and in a location (perhaps other than the kitchen or dining room) different from other family members, but in school this child may be required to get in line to be served at a time and place that is the same for all students in a particular classroom, in a particular grade level, or in a particular school.

Universalism is fostered in schools by such procedures and activities as group instruction (30:1 pupil-teacher ratios), grouping of students by grade levels that approximate like-age groupings, annual (and "automatic" in elementary schools) promotions, sex-segregated lavatories and locker rooms, tracking (often based on career interest and academic ability) in secondary schools, getting in line ("no cutting-in") for a variety of activities like lunch and assemblies, and raising hands and remaining in seats in individual classrooms.

The norm of *specificity* is promoted in schools by special-case treatments of students, such as when an individual is singled out for a special honor because of an outstanding performance in one or more curricular or extracurricular areas. Such commendations may take the form of a varsity letter or a certificate of honor or merely a verbal compliment. Although favoritism by teachers for certain students is frowned on ("teacher's pet"), teachers do single out students for compliments or reprimands based on classroom behavior. Specificity is also learned from the friendships that develop in classes, corridors, and lunchrooms; on teams; in clubs, bands, and orchestras; among cheerleaders; and between student and student, student and teacher, and student and coach, director, or sponsor. In these instances, students are treated not as merely representative of all students but also as special students possessing specific, individual characteristics.

The Influence of Media

"Television technology produces neuro-physiological responses in the people who watch it. It may create illness, it certainly produces confusion and submission to external imagery. Taken together, the effects amount to conditioning for autocratic control."[33] This claim exemplifies the heated controversy that has surrounded the medium of television since the beginning of its widespread use in

---

[32]Ibid., p. 228.

[33]Jerry Mander, *Four Arguments for the Elimination of Television* (New York: William Morrow & Company, Inc., 1978), p. 155.

the late 1940s. Probably no other technology has generated as much debate over its effects on children, youth, and adults as has television.

With over 300 million television sets in the United States today, television has become a ubiquitous, mass communications medium that directly influences the lives of school-age children and adolescents. During the thirteen years of public schooling (kindergarten through twelfth grade), a typical student will view at home more than 15,000 hours of television, including 675,000 commercials (about 1,000 per week). During these same thirteen years, the same typical young person, Neil Postman writes, "will be in the presence of a school curriculum 2,340 days, which comes to about 11,500 hours." Is it any wonder that Postman refers to television (both programs and commercials) as "The First Curriculum?" By using this term, he means to emphasize two points: (1) that both schools and television *are* curricula; a curriculum being "a specially constructed information system whose purpose, *in its totality,* is to influence, teach, train, or cultivate the mind and character of our youth"; and (2) that television is a more pervasive and more powerful "curriculum" than the school. Furthermore, although both school and television represent curriculums, television uses psychosocial means of coercing attention (attendance), whereas schools must resort to the force of law to compel attendance.[34]

What, then, are the major influences, the effects, of television on the lives of school children and youth? As Postman sees it, the curriculum of television is attention centered, nonpunitive, affect centered, present centered, image centered, narration centered, moralistic, nonanalytical, nonhierarchical, authoritarian, contemptuous of authority, continuous in time, isolating in space, discontinuous in content, and immediately and intrinsically gratifying—almost all of which are opposites to characteristics of today's public schools.[35]

Jerry Mander, an avowed opponent of television, argues that it conditions autocratic control, is addictive for prolonged users, encourages passivity and physical inactivity, possesses hypnotic qualities, represses the stimulation it arouses, promotes postviewing hyperactive responses, isolates viewers (precluding social intercourse), forbids relaxation, and provides simplistic models of coping behaviors.[36] Television, of course, presents numerous models—some negative, some positive; but one model of primary concern to parents, teachers, and others is the use of violence in all arenas of human interaction.

In a ten-year study by Leonard Eron of 875 children, he found a direct, positive relation "between TV viewing by small boys and aggressive behavior," but the same did not hold for girls. Another study, of 1,565 London teenage boys, concluded that "long exposure to television noticeably increased the degree to which they engaged in serious acts of violence."[37] A seminal study conducted over twenty years ago generalized,

[34]Neil Postman, *Teaching as a Conserving Activity* (New York: Dell Publishing Company, Inc., 1979), pp. 49–51.

[35]Ibid., pp. 69–70.

[36]Mander, *Four Arguments,* pp. 156, 163–69, 195, 208–15, 253–54.

[37]"Learning to Live with TV," *Time,* May 28, 1979, p. 49–50.

For *some* children under *some* conditions, some television is harmful. For *other* children under the same conditions, or for the same children under *other* conditions, it may be beneficial. For *most* children, under *most* conditions, *most* television is probably neither particularly harmful nor particularly beneficial."[38]

Network television is a commercial enterprise, almost entirely dependent on advertisers for its financial support. One study has summarized "the evidence regarding the effects of television advertising on children":

1. a large number of children eight years of age and younger do not understand the self-interested, entrepreneurial motives behind commercials,
2. children learn the brand names of products advertised on children's programming and consume large quantities of sugar-coated, fast-, and other food products advertised to attract them,
3. children make numerous requests of their parents for advertised products . . . ,
4. exposure of children to commercials for over-the-counter drugs is slightly associated with greater consumption of such products.[39]

In general, what television ads teach is the primacy of consumption, which is also partially true for the actual programs.

MULTIPLE DOMAINS OF EDUCATION

Because of the societal values of freedom, equality, human dignity, and rational consent of the governed; because of the pervasive preference for a democratic way of life; and finally, because education is at once a public and a private concern, a nationwide and a local community interest, there exist in American society perpetual disagreements and conflicts over the goals and methods, the ends and means, of public education. Even this state of affairs itself is cause for dispute, because some people consider perpetual conflict as dysfunctional, whereas others regard it as a sign of health in a democratic society. Regardless, what is clear is that there is an intimate relationship between a society in pursuit of democracy and the process of education in that society.

Not only is there conflict over ends and means within the public schools, but also there is conflict within and between other domains in "public education": the family, religious institutions, the workplace and marketplace, libraries, radio, television, museums, day-care centers, Scout troops, and so on.[40] That is, there are domains of education *other than* public schools. Lawrence Cremin notes that John Dewey and other progressive reformers tended "to focus so exclusively on the

[38]George Comstock, "Television Entertainment: Taking It Seriously," *Character*, 1, no. 12 (Oct. 1980), p. 1.

[39]Ibid., p. 2.

[40]The analysis here and throughout the remainder of this section draws heavily on Cremin, *Public Education.*

potentialities of the school as a level of societal improvement and reform as to ignore the possibilities of *other educative institutions* [emphasis added]."[41] This overemphasis on schooling tends to obscure the educational agendas and significance of other societal agencies. Although Dewey viewed education as a broad, pervasive concept, he split it into *intentional* and *incidental* types. In this duality, education in schools is considered *intentional*, whereas education elsewhere—in the family or neighborhood or marketplace—is *incidental*. This bifurcation tends both to obscure the educational role played by educative agents such as the family and the media and to relegate the educational influences of nonschool agencies to an unplanned, haphazard, capricious, and unintentional category. It is misleading in contemporary American society to consider powerful social influences like families and media either as having only *incidental* effects on the learning of children and adolescents or as having no explicit educational goals for the sons and daughters or listeners and viewers whom they influence.

Cremin quotes Charles Silberman, who argues,

> If our concern is with *education* . . . we cannot restrict our attention to schools, for education is not synonymous with schooling. Children—and adults—learn outside school as well as—perhaps more than—in school. To say this is not to denigrate the importance of schools; it is to give proper weight to all the other educating forces in American society: the family and the community; the armed forces; corporate training programs; libraries, museums, churches, Boy Scout troops, 4-H clubs.[42]

Further, Silberman expands the concept of "teacher" or "educator" to include not only school, college, and university instructors but also parents, community leaders, media directors and journalists, sponsors and leaders of community organizations (for example, Boy Scouts, Girl Scouts, and Junior Achievement), religious educators (pastors, priests, rabbis, and church school teachers), lawyers, doctors and dentists, business and corporate executives and trainers, textbook writers and publishers, military leaders and instructors, and others who *intentionally* and as part of their roles or occupations teach others. United States society, then, contains numerous educative agencies and educators, all of which have curricula that have been as intentionally planned as those of the public schools. Public education, conceived broadly as the education of the American public, includes many educative agencies, only one of which is the public school system.

CONFIGURATIONS OF LEARNING

The "multiplicity of institutions" interact with one another at a particular time and place, a cluster Cremin calls a "configuration of education." For example, a student in a particular community, in a particular class, of a particular elementary school, from a particular family that holds membership in a particular church, with a

[41]Cremin, *Public Education*, p. 3.
[42]Ibid., pp. 11–12.

particular set of radio-listening and television-viewing habits, will be influenced, that is, *educated*, at that age and in that locale by a configuration of educative agencies. He or she will be educated by family, by local community, by school, by peers, by religion, and by media, all within the milieu and ethos of the larger national culture and society, which itself forms a part of the interdependent, global network of cultures and societies.

In the world, in a society, in a community, and even in a family, seldom, if ever, are all parties or all educative agencies in harmony concerning either the goals of public education or the education of a single citizen. Cremin theorizes that the interacting institutions may have "complementary or contradictory, conso-nant or dissonant" relationships. For example, the parents of a high school student may want their son or daughter to be accounted for by the school until he or she returns home. The school's administrators, teachers, and most other parents, however, favor the concept of the "open campus" high school, where students are required to be at and in school only when they have scheduled classes. In this situation, the educative agencies of the school and *most* families are *complementary* and *consonant* in their relations concerning the open campus concept and the value of allowing adolescents some freedom in the use of their time. Between the school and some parents, however, the relationship concerning the open campus and freedom for youth is *contradictory* and *dissonant*.

> Or, to take another example, family and school may share a mutual concern for the child's intellectual development [a complementary and consonant relationship], but the teacher may be more demanding at the same time as the parent is more sustaining [a contradictory and dissonant relationship, but perhaps a healthy tension.][43]

An obvious illustration of contradictory and dissonant relations among educative agencies in a configuration of education is the differing emphases on particular modes of communication by television (visual and oral), the family (oral), and the school (written and oral). Note, however, that all three agencies, to some degree, employ oral communication, which makes their relationship also somewhat com-plementary and consonant.

In the U.S. educational system, conflict among educative institutions and configurations of education is the rule rather than the exception because of at least two crucial factors: the pluralist nature of American society and the decentralized, parent-option nature of the American school system. As a nation composed of many Native American and many immigrant groups from other nations in Africa, Asia, Europe, Latin America, Canada, and Mexico, the United States is a conglom-erate of diverse racial, ethnic, and religious subcultures tenuously held together by a national language, territorial sovereignty, an economic system combining capital-ism and the welfare state, a political system based on constitutional and representa-tive democracy, and a collection of social values that form a hierarchical value structure but is *without* a single, pinnacle value to which all others are subordinate. For such a society, conflict is indigenous to its way of life.

[43]Ibid., pp. 31–32.

EDUCATION AND SOCIAL CHANGE

At the height of the Great Depression in 1932, George S. Counts asked the conventioneers attending the annual convention of the Progressive Education Association, "Dare the school build a new social order?" At that time, most institutions in the United States were under siege and were considered incapable of countering the human devastation wrought by economic collapse. It is curious that at this moment an American educational leader should call for the schools to lead the way toward social reform, toward the reconstruction of society. It is indeed curious because, as a social institution, the schools in all modern, industrial, technological societies typically play a conserving, conservative, perpetuation-of-the-status-quo role. How realistic was Counts or anyone else who looks to the schools as a vehicle for social change?

Some educational historians and most educational polemicists assert that American schools have changed or can change the social order, but such claims do not square with the facts. Perhaps the soundest argument that the schools can bring about social change has to do with the Americanization of European and Asian immigrant groups. It is argued that the schools were primarily responsible for acculturating these racial and/or ethnic groups to the language and ways of their newly adopted country. This may have been the case with some earlier waves of immigration during the nineteenth and early twentieth centuries, but the schools have not had success in acculturating the later immigrant groups such as the Puerto Ricans, nor the "original" natives of North America, nor the very early settlers like the Mexican-Americans, and certainly not black Americans. In short, the American school system never created a melting pot and never achieved *E. Pluribus Unum.*

Since about 1960, public policies and funds have been focused on the schools as agencies for the conduct of "wars" on racism (and racial isolation), poverty, cultural "deprivation," environmental degradation, sexism, and depletion of natural resources, among others. Unfortunately, such pervasive ills of a society cannot be cured by a single institution. It might even be considered deceptive and devious of the leaders of a society to expect the public schools alone to undertake basic social reforms.

If a society includes many educative institutions, its public schools being only one of them, and if these multiple agencies form various clusters or configurations of education whose interaction may be complementary and consonant or contradictory and dissonant, then social change can be best expedited when the educative institutions and configurations act and interact in near harmony of purposes. To rely exclusively on any one of them for social reform is to deny or ignore the complex, interactive, multifaceted nature of social change.

A MARXIST PERSPECTIVE

It is unfortunate that many Americans view Karl Marx (1818–1883) as solely the utopian Communist whose writings have been the ideological underpinning for the USSR since its founding in the revolution of 1917. Although this myopia is understandable in light of the cold war, it obscures the intellectual contributions of Marx in the fields of philosophy, political economy, history, and sociology. Robert Heilbroner and Lester Thurow go so far as to aver that "in the gallery of the world's great thinkers, where Marx unquestionably belongs, his proper place is with historians rather than economists. Most appropriately, his statue would be centrally placed, overlooking many corridors of thought—sociological analysis, philosophic inquiry, and of course, economics."[44]

In the past decade or so a new sociology of education has emerged that owes much of its analysis and theory to the works of Marx. Because these new theorists are neither doctrinaire Communists nor ideological purists, they are often labeled *neo-Marxists*. Further, they are more concerned with critical theory, dialectical methods, and selected concepts (for example, alienation) than they are with historical determinism or social utopias.

Marx's great opus is *Capital*, a penetrating analysis of the workings of capitalist societies, of the emergence of bourgeois capitalism in Europe out of the breakdown of feudalism, and of the contradictions inherent in capitalist economic systems that point to their demise. It's natural, therefore, that neo-Marxist educational sociologists would focus their attention on education and schooling in capitalist societies, especially those in Europe and North America. The major goal of the neo-Marxists appears to be the liberation of the individual—student and teacher—from the alienating influences of the societal institutions in capitalist nations. To attain this goal requires the individual to examine the assumptions and values that undergird a capitalist society, see the contradictions that inevitably emerge in the historical evolution of capitalist societies, and then take personal and collective action to bring about liberation and to hasten the unfolding of a new society. This, of course, is an oversimplification of *consciousness raising, base and superstructure, class conflict, struggle,* and other terms Marx used to explicate his theories.

A Marxist perspective on public education in the United States would probably probe several interrelated propositions. First, there would be an attempt to reveal that the social class structure of the nation derives from the economic system (capitalism) that has evolved historically to its present form. Next there would be the observation that those who control and guide the economy—the dominant class—have a vested interest in maintaining the system and their privileged position in it. In other words, the dominant class, the people in power, desire to perpetuate the status quo. Because all societal institutions take their form from the economic system, each institution is subservient to those who control the economy.

Third, there would be the proposition that the dominant class will be perpetuated in power if succeeding generations approximate the present class structure of the society. That is, all social institutions—economy, government, family, religion, schools—will strive for social and cultural reproduction. Two caveats are necessary at this point: (1) No conspiracy by the power elite is implied here; it is in

[44]Robert Heilbroner and Lester Thurow, *Economics Explained* (Englewood Cliffs, N.J.: Prentice-Hall, Inc., 1982), p. 29.

the nature of capitalism that existing arrangements be continued from generation to generation. (2) Neither capital (dominant class) nor labor (subservient class) is passive in the face of what seems to be economic determinism. By acting in their respective best interests, the two classes of necessity (under capitalism) come into conflict. The resulting class warfare is inevitable in the evolution of capitalism.

Fourth, there is the claim that as an agent of the state (of the dominant class), the public schools cannot avoid their tasks of reproducing the status quo and of controlling, or at best ameliorating, class conflict. Yet these tasks are never explicitly acknowledged. Rather they are obscured (the "hidden curriculum") behind the ostensible goals of general education, that is, of a liberal education for all citizens that would prepare them to think for themselves. Education of this type might indeed be liberating, but the neo-Marxists argue that it is quite impossible to achieve and is merely an illusion perpetuated by the rhetoric of school administrators and school boards.

Finally, there is the proposition that one cannot achieve liberation and freedom until one strips illusion from all the social practices that capitalist society takes for granted or regards as "natural." This critical process is called *demystification,* and it is usually followed by the recognition that conflict between competing ideas and between social classes is the normal state of affairs in a capitalist nation. From this awareness should come a desire to act, to raise the inevitable class conflict to the level of daily living, and to acknowledge the necessity for constant vigil and struggle.

In drastically simplified form, these then are the main arguments pursued by neo-Marxist sociologists for education. There are other "contradictions" and concepts delineated and defined by these scholars. For example, alienation is considered one of the chief pathologies caused by a capitalist system. The "alienation of labour" occurs because, Marx concluded,

> the work is *external* to the worker, that it is not a part of his nature, that consequently he does not fulfill himself in his work but denies himself, has a feeling of misery, not of well-being, does not develop freely a physical and mental energy, but is physically exhausted and mentally debased. The worker therefore feels himself at home only during his leisure, whereas at work he feels homeless. His work is not voluntary but imposed, *forced labour.* It is not the satisfaction of a need, but only a *means* for satisfying other needs. Its alien character is clearly shown by the fact that as soon as there is no physical or other compulsion it is avoided like the plague. Finally, the alienated character of work for the worker appears in the fact that it is not his work but work for someone else, that in work he does not belong to himself but to another person.[45]

This is clearly the plight of the industrial factory worker, and the modern Marxist educational sociologist would say that it is also the condition of the student-as-worker and the teacher-as-worker in today's factorylike public schools.

[45]T. B. Bottomore and Maximilien Rubel, eds., *Karl Marx* (London: Penguin Books, Ltd., 1961), pp. 177–78.

The neo-Marxist perspective on public education serves several useful purposes, among which are its critical stance, its analysis of justifications for and claims made by the public school, its explanation of how and why educational change occurs or fails to occur, and its insistence that public school conflicts be located within the realm of political economy.

Case Study: Reporting Student Achievement

You are a sixth-grade teacher of English in a middle school (grades 6, 7, and 8) where there are two ways of reporting the pupils' progress to parents: (1) a report card containing letter grades for each subject and (2) a narrative description of a student's strengths and weaknesses. Both reports also serve as the basis for conferences with parents willing to come to the school.

There are 150 students in your five sections, or classes, of English. For the first quarter (nine weeks), your report card grades are distributed as follows:

A = 10
B = 20
C = 30
D = 70
F = 20

Justify this distribution, *not* in terms of individual achievement, but rather in terms of the *social function* of schools. Also, justify to a parent the grade of D for his or her daughter. For both justifications, you will need to assume many specifics of classroom behavior and performance.

Thought Questions

1. What are some desirable goals in the two domains of *general education* and *specialized education*?
2. Explain the quotation "People are schooled to accept a society. They are educated to create or re-create one."
3. How do the school's social functions of role selection, indoctrination, custodial care, and community activity interfere with, and often preclude, the school's function of education?
4. Explain the statement "Every social institution is to some extent an educative agency."
5. List several ways in which the schools teach each of the following values-norms:

independence	universalism
achievement	specificity

6. How do the curricula of the school and of television differ?
7. How does a neo-Marxist sociology of education differ from the traditional variety?
8. To what extent do you think schools can bring about social change in a society?

Practical Activities

1. Devise a questionnaire that assesses community satisfaction or dissatisfaction with the schools.
2. Attend a school board meeting and make an informal survey of who is in attendance and who is on the board of education. Deal with factors such as age, sex, race, apparent social class, and apparent educational level. Describe any school-community issues that were discussed.
3. Get or make your own map of a school district; then color-code the ethnic, religious, and socioeconomic group boundaries. Indicate the data source for your map (school records, census data, and so on). Make sure your finished product is a *map*, not a sketchy diagram.
4. Visit an elementary or secondary school classroom and observe and record examples of the "teaching" (usually implicit rather than explicit) of

   independence
   achievement
   universalism
   specificity

5. Interview a number of local "educators" other than those connected with schools, and try to determine what they "teach" children and adolescents. The following is a suggested list:

   local government officials
   newspaper journalists and editors
   radio announcers or program directors
   Scout troop leaders
   4-H Club leaders
   church officials and teachers
   Junior Achievement staff
   business and corporation leaders
   several parents
   public librarians
   museum curators
   television journalists and program directors
   community recreation officials

6. Interview school personnel who are responsible for extracurricular activities and

try to ascertain what educational goals are achieved there. Also, try to determine to what extent such activities contribute to the function of community activity.

7. Try to document a local example of a case in which a configuration of educative agencies have contradictory, dissonant relationships. You may wish to select a single student and chart the effects of family, local television, and so forth.

Bibliography

ADLER, RICHARD P., GERALD S. LESSER, LAURENE KRASNY, THOMAS S. ROBERTSON, JOHN R. ROSSITER, and SCOTT WARD, *The Effects of Television Advertising on Children.* Lexington, Mass.: Lexington Books, 1980.

BOOCOCK, SARANE SPENCE, *Sociology of Education.* Boston: Houghton Mifflin Company, 1980.

BOWLES, SAMUEL, and HERBERT GINTIS, *Schooling in Capitalist America.* New York: Basic Books, Inc., Publishers, 1976.

BROOKOVER, WILBUR B., and EDSEL L. ERICKSON, *Sociology of Education.* Homewood, Ill.: The Dorsey Press, 1975.

CALLAHAN, RAYMOND C., *Education and the Cult of Efficiency.* Chicago: University of Chicago Press, 1962.

CHESLER, MARK A., and WILLIAM M. CAVE, *A Sociology of Education.* New York: Macmillan, 1981.

COMSTOCK, GEORGE, STEVEN CHAFFEE, NATHAN KATZMAN, MAXWELL MCCOMBS, and DONALD ROBERTS, *Television and Human Behavior.* New York: Columbia University Press, 1978.

CREMIN, LAWRENCE A., *Public Education.* New York: Basic Books, Inc., Publishers, 1976.

DEWEY, JOHN, *The Child and the Curriculum/The School and Society.* Chicago: University of Chicago Press, 1902.

DREEBEN, ROBERT, *On What Is Learned in School.* Reading, Mass.: Addison-Wesley Publishing Company, Inc., 1968.

DURKHEIM, EMILE, *Education and Sociology.* New York: The Free Press, 1956.

ERIKSON, ERIK H., *Identity: Youth and Crisis.* New York: W. W. Norton & Company, Inc., 1968.

FRIEDENBERG, EDGAR Z., *Coming of Age in America.* New York: Vintage-Random House, Inc., 1970.

GOSLIN, DAVID, *The School in Contemporary Society.* Glenview, Ill.: Scott, Foresman & Company, 1965.

HAVIGHURST, ROBERT J., and DANIEL LEVINE, *Society and Education,* 5th ed. Boston: Allyn & Bacon, Inc., 1979.

HUNT, MAURICE, *Foundations of Education.* New York: Holt, Rinehart & Winston, 1975.

KNELLER, GEORGE, *Foundations of Education,* 3rd ed. New York: John Wiley & Sons, Inc., 1981.

MANDER, JERRY, *Four Arguments for the Elimination of Television.* New York: William Morrow & Company, Inc., 1978.

MARX, KARL, *Capital.* New York: Modern Library, 1932.

ORNSTEIN, ALLAN C., *Education and Social Inquiry.* Itasca, Ill.: F. E. Peacock, 1978.

POSTMAN, NEIL, *Teaching as a Conserving Activity.* New York: Dell Publishing Company, Inc., 1979.

PRICHARD, KEITH W., and THOMAS H. BUXTON,   *Concepts and Theories in Sociology of Education.* Lincoln, Neb.: Professional Educators Publications, 1973.

SARASON, SEYMOUR B.,   *The Culture of the School and the Problem of Change,* 2nd ed. Boston: Allyn & Bacon, Inc., 1982.

SARUP, MADAN,   *Marxism and Education.* London: Routledge & Kegan Paul, 1978.

SCHLECTY, PHILLIP C.,   *Teaching and Social Behavior.* Boston: Allyn & Bacon, Inc., 1976.

SCHWARTZ, AUDREY JAMES,   *The Schools and Socialization.* New York: Harper & Row, Publishers, Inc., 1975.

SCIMECCA, JOSEPH A.,   *Education and Society.* New York: Holt, Rinehart & Winston, 1980.

WALLER, WILLARD,   *The Sociology of Teaching.* New York: John Wiley & Sons, Inc., 1932.

6

The Structure and Politics of Education

By mutual but unspoken and long-standing agreement, American citizens and scholars have contended that the world of education is and should be separate from the world of politics.[1]

Education represents . . . both a struggle for meaning and a struggle over power relations. . . . Education is that terrain where power and politics are given a fundamental expression.[2]

These quotations indicate the two competing positions on the relationship of education and politics in the late twentieth century. Given the ideological battles being fought in the Communist countries and throughout much of the Third World, many in the United States would hope to maintain the apolitical rhetoric that currently surrounds discussion of education in our country. On the other hand, many scholars and educational critics point to the growing educational and economic "underclass" in American society, and suggest that it is duplicitous to ignore or deny the role that the educational system plays in the distribution of power and resources. As Nicholas A. Masters argues,

> It is obvious that any social institution that performs such a significant role is not going to be allowed to roam freely within the political structure. Groups and individuals which possess the resources of power and influence exert, or will exert when they feel the occasion demands, tremendous efforts to shape and mold the system to their

---

[1]Frederick M. Wirt and Michael W. Kirst, *Schools in Conflict* (Berkeley, Calif.: McCutchan Publishing Corporation, 1982), p. 2.

[2]Henry Giroux, quoted in Paulo Freire, *The Politics of Education* (Boston: Bergin & Garvey Publishers, Inc., 1985), p. xiii.

way of thinking and to tailor the curriculum to meet their special technological and scientific needs.[3]

There can be no question that education and politics are symbiotically linked, with each influencing the fate of the other, but it is generally agreed that overt political ideology plays a lesser role in the United States educational system than most others around the world.

A DEFINITION OF POLITICS

Focusing on the structures and functions of government tends to obscure the presence of political activities. *Politics* may be defined as the acquisition and effective use of power—a process involving interplay among the possessors of political resources and influence. The dynamics of the political process occur within the rules and constraints of the system, but also within those arenas where it is considered legitimate to use power to achieve desired policies and programs. Applied to education, the political process displays some of the same characteristics that it does in other political arenas. Educational politics, like all forms of politics, involves the promotion of an individual's or group's interests by use of such resources as power, money, jobs, information, status, and prestige. Control of such resources constitutes potential power, whereas dispensing resources to achieve certain ends constitutes actual power.

Educational Politics

Educational politics is that process by which educational resources are distributed within a society by the legitimate uses of power through governmental actions. In this definition, educational values are such tangibles and intangibles as the hiring of teachers and school administrators, curricular content, qualifications to be a student (for example, minimum age of a child), sources of funds to operate schools and the formulas determining which taxpayers pay what amounts, and the many status and prestige factors that can be awarded to or withheld from students, teachers, and other education personnel (for example, letter grades for students and merit pay for teachers). The verb *distributed* refers to decision-making acts that determine policies, procedures, and programs for a particular school system or school district, or even for a single school or a single teacher's class. By the *legitimate uses of power* is meant the use of legal and ethical means or practices to arrive at educational decisions. Ethical practices are those consistent with the values of a democratic society, such as respect for human dignity and reliance on rational thought and rational consent. Governmental actions in public education are those quasi-legislative and quasi-judicial decisions made by local school boards,

---

[3]Nicholas A. Masters, "The Politics of Public Education," in *Criticism, Conflict, and Change: Readings in American Education,* Emanuel Hurwitz, Jr., and Robert Maidwent, eds. (New York: Dodd, Mead & Company, 1970), p. 175.

school administrators, and in some cases teachers, as well as legislative, judicial, and administrative decisions relating to education made by state and federal officials.

EDUCATIONAL AND POLITICAL LINKAGES

Several recent scholarly works on education and schooling in the United States have used the word *conflict* in their title.[4] As the twentieth century comes to a close, conflict continues to afflict our educational system; in those conflicts, political values and structures determine which values will be dominant in the education of our children. With almost one quarter of our population attending, teaching, or working in our schools, and with expenditures for preschool through higher education of over $200 billion annually, the stakes are extremely high. It is little wonder that schools are a continuing battleground.

Conflict is inevitable in a diverse culture such as the United States today. Throughout the colonial period of our history, and even well into the twentieth century in some parts of our country, schools reflected the homogeneity of the communities in which they were found, which generally led to less overt conflict. Minority children were segregated into their own schools, and parochial systems took care of those of a different religious persuasion. With the vast influxes of Eastern and Southern Europeans, Jews, and Catholics in the early part of this century, the integration of minorities during the 1950s and 1960s, and the urban migration in the past half century, schools became a major center of conflict over culture, religion, and language, not to mention educational and political ideology. The content of the curriculum, information in textbooks, the language of instruction, affirmative action, and equity in funding, all became sources of conflict as power elites sought to maintain control and those outside the system sought to gain their fair share of the educational pie.

Figure 6-1 shows the symbiotic linkages between our political and educational systems,[5] and the following section explains ways in which the two systems interact.

POLITICAL INFLUENCES ON EDUCATION

Schooling is used by individuals and groups to maintain or gain power in American society, and this has often led to conflict. We will deal with only a few of the more obvious and important examples of these power conflicts in the late twentieth century.

[4]Wirt and Kirst, *Schools in Conflict*; Joel Spring, *Conflict of Interests: The Politics of American Education* (New York: Longman, 1988).
[5]R. Murray Thomas, *Politics and Education: Cases from Eleven Nations* (Oxford: Pergamon Press, 1983), pp. 1–30.

FIGURE 6-1   Components of the Educational and Political Systems

Educational System	Political System
Curriculum	Government
Purposes/Philosophy	Federal
Programs of Study	State
Certification	Local
Administration	Legislative Branch
Pedagogical Methods	Executive Branch
Materials	Judicial Branch
Organizational Structure	Parent/Community Groups
Teachers	Religious Groups
Students	Political Parties
Co-curricular Activities	The Mass Media
	Social Class Groups
	Minority/Ethnic Groups
	Businesses/Unions

Political Parties

Although in most countries of the world the educational system is a mechanism to perpetuate political power, the two main political parties in the United States have generally attempted to promote a nonpartisan educational system. As indicated earlier, this does not mean that our educational system is apolitical, but rather that there is an unspoken agreement by the Democrats and Republicans to not attempt to use the schools for partisan political purposes. This does not mean, however, that ideology does not enter our schools. The pledge of allegiance to the flag, the truth and myths of American history, and a host of other formal and nonformal mechanisms are used to promote aspects of the status quo. Whereas a communist political party might attempt to use the schools to eliminate social classes, in the United States, meritocracy, the belief in equality of opportunity, promotes the value that if one works hard enough, anyone can grow up to be president. Although political parties stop short of promoting their own agendas through the schools, they have consistently promoted their underlying ideologies. The redistribution of income from rich districts and states to the poor, decontrol of schooling, back-to-basics vs. progressive schools, elitism vs. egalitarianism in schooling, testing, and affirmative action are examples of how ideology affects what occurs in the schools, while maintaining the appearance of an apolitical and nonpartisan educational system.

Perhaps the most important way in which political parties, particularly through the federal and state executive and legislative branches, affect the educational system is through the allocation of financial resources to the schools. Education is the largest single enterprise in the United States, surpassing in numbers and expenditures even the defense department. With expenditures well in excess of $200 billion dollars, every taxpayer citizen or corporation has a very real stake in where the taxes come from and how they are spent. Whether more progressive taxes, such as the income tax, are used to support schools, or whether more regressive taxes, such as property and sales taxes, are used is generally a political decision made at the state level. The balance between corporate and individual taxes in support of schools is also made by the dominant political parties in each state. Although generalizations are often found to include exceptions, it can be stated that the Republican party has tended to favor the more regressive tax structures and greater taxation of individuals, whereas the Democratic party has tended to favor more progressive taxes and greater taxation of businesses, land, mining, and other corporate entities.

Language

In the late 1980s, "U.S. English," a movement to have the English language declared the official state and national language, gained strength in many parts of the country. Californians voted almost 3–1 in favor of declaring English the official state language, and legislative and popular votes have been taken in many other states. The Soviet Union and China are two other major powers who have had to continue to confront the issue of language politics. On the one hand, both have had continuing pressures to have a national language to promote assimilation, or, as some would argue, the dominance of one linguistic group over all others, while on the other hand, minorities in those countries have sought equal status for their languages through bilingual programs in the schools. Language politics is one of the major issues in all immigrant countries and in those Third World countries made up of more than one linguistic group.

Bilingual education in the United States has been a constant battleground for over a decade. English Only advocates promote English as a Second Language (ESL) programs and the rapid transition of immigrant or other non–English-speaking children into English as rapidly as possible. On the other hand, many Hispanic, Oriental, Native American, and other non–English-speaking or bilingual populations have sought, if not equal status for their languages, at least the right to maintain their native language while mastering English. Charges of racism, ethnocentrism, and xenophobia are hurled by one side, while the other accuses opponents of separatism and lack of patriotism. Language politics in this country has generally been fought in the courts, legislatures, and ballot boxes, and the schools have had to thread their way through the minefields of local, state, and national politics. With literally millions of new immigrants from Asia and Latin America coming to our country in the last decade, language will continue to be a major source of conflict for both education and politics until well into the next century.

Minorities

Ethnic or minority groups seeking power through schooling is a related battleground. In a somewhat meritocratic society such as the United States, access to equal schooling continues to be one of the major ways in which individuals and groups who have traditionally been discriminated against seek to enter the mainstream power structure. In the several decades since *Brown v. The Board of Education* (1954) struck down segregated schooling in the United States, great strides have been made toward providing equal funding and facilities for all children.

Even though the 1980s have seen a rise in minority dropout rates, along with a drop in overall test scores and college attendance, the trend has been toward greater equality among the various races and ethnic groups that make up the country.

Judiciary

The courts continue to be the center for many of the conflicts concerning equality of opportunity. Affirmative action programs to balance gender and ethnic minorities on school and university teaching faculties, busing of children to achieve racial and ethnic balance, admissions quotas to universities and to graduate and professional schools, minority studies programs, and equal funding for poorer schools are but a few of the legal issues still being decided by state and federal courts. As long as there are significant differences in opportunity and quality based on race, gender, ethnicity, and social class, it is safe to predict that the schools will continue to be a legal and legislative battleground.

Religion

In religiously homogeneous societies such as many Middle Eastern and Latin American countries, the schools reflect and perpetuate the religion of the culture. For much of U.S. history, our public schools were primarily Protestant institutions. Some educational historians have even argued that the common schools were founded in the nineteenth century to ensure the dominance of that Protestant culture over the immigrant Roman Catholic culture. Regardless of the validity of that position, the growing religious heterogeneity in our country has added another battlefield in the control of education. Attempts to eliminate parochial schools have failed in the courts. The right of religious parents to educate their children at home has been upheld in most states, and hundreds of cases on the separation of church and state in the school setting have kept the state and federal courts busy for almost a century.

Recent attempts at textbook censorship and suits over secular humanism, the teaching of values, and other issues must be seen not only in their religious light but also as political conflicts in which different groups in our society seek power over their own lives or those of others.

Business and Industry

With the growth in political power and influence of the business and industrial community during the 1980s, and the decline in union power and popularity, schools have come under increasing pressure to meet the high technology demands of the twenty-first century and to "catch up to the Japanese." The business community put increasingly more pressure on the public schools to "do something" about the failure to educate large numbers of minority young people, who are predicted to make up to one-third of the work force in the next century. Solutions included a longer school day and year, emphasis on the basics, greater control of who enters the teaching profession, more testing and tighter accountability, more money for gifted and talented programs, and the decontrol of schooling from state and even local boards of education. Although it is too early to tell which, if any, of the reforms will make a difference, there can be little disagreement that the business and industry power structure is a more powerful actor in the last decade of the twentieth century than perhaps at any other time in our history.

The political system serves many important functions for education and must decide among the various competing interests listed above. In comparatively homogeneous societies this is much easier done than in the United States, which has such a wide array of religious, ethnic, and linguistic groupings. Political bodies such as legislatures and school boards generally decide who will receive what education and how much. In other words, the political system provides the financial and other types of support for the schools, and controls, directly or indirectly, access to the schools.

In a more specific realm, it is the political system that sets the overall philosophy of the educational system and decides what values will be passed on to the next generation. No society structures its educational system to overthrow its political system or undermine its moral values. This is as true of communist as it is of capitalist countries; of totalitarian as of democratic nations. "What you want in the state, you must put into the school." This is not to say that education has not been a major source of unrest and even revolution in countries around the world, but rather that political systems do not plan their own overthrow. In nations with a strong tradition of academic freedom, political controls are generally less obtrusive. Yet in all societies, the curriculum, skills to be taught, teaching materials, tests of competence, certificates, diplomas, and entrance to the teaching profession are under some sort of political control. The latitude permitted teachers and students to propagate differing political, economic, or philosophical positions varies widely from country to country, and even among local school districts in the United States.

EDUCATIONAL INFLUENCES ON POLITICS

The educational system affects the political system of a nation in numerous ways. These ways reflect the totalitarian or democratic traditions of that country, the stability of the political structures, the wealth of the nation, the recency of its revolution, and other historical and cultural factors. Purity of ideology is of much greater concern in a country that has only recently been through its revolution, whereas manpower production and economic skills are perhaps the highest priority in more stable countries or those seeking economic growth.

The Sorting Machine[6]

Whether they admit to it or not, all countries use their schools as sorting and selecting agencies. Even in the United States, with "universal" primary and secondary education, up to one-quarter of all students drop out of secondary schools, and our systems of higher and technical education sort people into the professions, trades, and various economic levels of society. Ethnicity, language, cultural upbringing, economic status, and opportunity all lead to differentiated roles, status, and economic power in our society. Schools of different nations sort young people through nepotism, discrimination, or "meritocracy."

Economic Development

The emphasis upon catching up with the Russians in space during the 1960s has been replaced by catching up with the Japanese in economic development in the 1990s. The schools have become the center of major state and national attention to produce skilled manpower, particularly in the scientific and technical fields, and to overcome, or at least forestall, the "Asian Century." How the schools respond to pressures to produce a "better product" is rapidly reflected in the economic support the political system gives them. At the local level, citizens are more likely to support bond and mill levy elections when they believe that graduates of the schools are capable of becoming contributing members of the society. In turn, legislators are likely to provide greater sums of money from state coffers if the schools and universities are meeting the demands of the economic system.

Citizenship, Socialization, and Legitimation

Countless formal and informal mechanisms are used to ensure that the schools promote the political values of a society. All nations are concerned with how the history of a nation, past and contemporary, is treated in textbooks and other teaching materials. Appropriate behaviors—whether voting in elections, accepting and questioning authority, or being docile before the political powers—are part of the processes to be taught or caught in the school system. Because education is more than formal schooling, the values of citizenship are also taught through co-curricular activities and quasi-patriotic groups such as the Scouts.

In a pluralistic society such as our own, with a tradition of academic freedom, the young also learn countervalues. Even though these values seldom lead to revolution, they pressure the political system to act in keeping with the Constitution and our stated, if not always practiced, values of justice, equal treatment before the law, and equality of opportunity. Flags in classrooms, the pledge of allegiance, heroes of American history, singing the national anthem, memorizing the Gettysburg Address or the Declaration of Independence, and a variety of other means are used to socialize our children and young people into our political system.

[6]Joel Spring, *The Sorting Machine: National Educational Policy Since 1945* (New York: David McKay Company, Inc., 1976).

Political systems change, whether through a coup d'etat by leftists or the military, as in many Third World countries, or through elections in which Republicans replace Democrats or democratic socialists replace conservatives. In each instance, the new political power must legitimate itself with the populace. The formal school system becomes an important component for the political system to implant its ideas and ideology on the young. The informal educational system of the mass media, voluntary agencies, and churches also are used to legitimate the power structure with the total society. Funding new textbooks and research, visits to the schools by political leaders, high-level commissions on school reform, and new sources of funds for one type of education or another are all ways that our government legitimates itself.

Social Control and Change

All societies use the schools for social control. Universal schooling is seen by some observers as a major control factor in keeping the young out of the job market and in a controlled environment where they can learn the values that their elders and the power structure wish them to learn. Societies who lack critics or advocates of social reform, however, can stagnate. If there are no critics to challenge the status quo, it is likely that the economic and political system will become ripe for an eventual revolution. The Soviet Union under Stalin was a society in which social control was dominant. It stagnated under Brezhnev; but under Gorbachev, the political structure has attempted with every means at its disposal, including the schools, to change the values, behaviors, and attitudes of its people.[7] In democratic societies, critics from the schools, newspapers, religious groups, and even within the political system push for change, recognizing that either a stagnating political or economic system can lead to a revolutionary situation.

Education and politics are not synonymous, as some political leaders have suggested, but the two systems, as we've described in this section, are symbiotically linked.

THE STRUCTURE OF SCHOOLING

The educational system in the United States is a complex, public, local-state-federal enterprise, with a private or parochial alternative available at parents' option. Figure 6-2 is a simplified diagram of this system, showing the lines of direct control and indirect influence for the various levels of government and for the public and private or parochial subsystems. The placement of the state educational system in the center of the schematic diagram reflects the fact that public education in the United States is primarily a creation of each state, with most educational responsibilities delegated to local school boards.

The tradition of local control of schools is still alive and strong despite

---

[7]Gerald Howard Read, "Education in the Soviet Union: Has Perestroika Met Its Match?" *Phi Delta Kappan*, 70, no. 8 (Apr. 6, 1989), pp. 606–13.

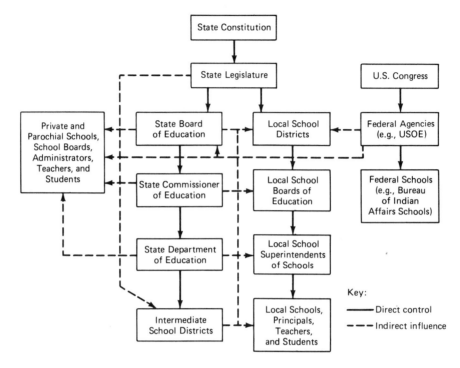

FIGURE 6-2   The Educational System in the United States

massive consolidation, primarily in the 1950s. Today the United States still has over 15,000 school districts. The numbers in each state vary widely, however, with Texas and California each having over a thousand separate districts and Hawaii having just seven districts. Although it is dangerous to predict the future, consolidation for financial and equity reasons likely will continue to diminish the number of districts in most states. Simultaneously, though, most parts of the country are moving to return accountability to the local building level, thus in effect shifting some power from the 15,000 school districts to the over 80,000 individual schools.

Enrollments

Enrollments for the fall of 1988, from kindergarten through higher education, were 58.5 million—down from a high of 60.9 million in 1975 but slowly rising as the "baby boomlet" hits the elementary schools. With the decline in enrollments, the need for teachers decreased throughout the 1970s and 1980s. A large number of the current 3.35 million teachers, however, will retire before the end of the century. As a result, many governmental and private agencies are predicting a teacher shortage in the 1990s.

Perhaps more revealing than the gross numbers of enrollees at each level is the percentage of attendance throughout our educational history. In 1889, only 6.7

percent of 14- to 17-year-olds were enrolled in grades 9 through 12. By 1929, the proportion has risen to 51.4 percent and reached a high of 93.5 percent in 1971. Attendance and graduation rates have fallen over the past decade, particularly among minority young people, causing public policy makers to concentrate a great deal of attention on "at-risk" youth in recent years.

In the early part of the twentieth century, growth was most rapid in secondary education, whereas higher education grew rapidly following World War II. Because the number of women in the job market increased during the past two decades, publicly and privately funded preschool and child care programs are the current areas of major growth. The percentage of 5-year-olds in school rose from 60 percent in 1965 to 86.5 percent in 1985, with figures of 3–5-year-olds rising from 27 percent to over 54 percent. With the large influxes of Asian and Latin American children in recent decades, many states are facing linguistic and cultural challenges. By 1988, all twenty-five of our nation's largest districts had a majority of minorities in their schools. California and Texas had over 50 percent minority children in their elementary schools. Much of the concern, evidenced in movements such as English Only, is in large part the result of the tremendous numbers of legal and illegal immigrants in the past two decades. During the 1980s almost 9 million legal immigrants entered this country, the second largest immigration of this century. The 1970s saw almost 4.5 million legal immigrants, the fourth largest immigration of this century. Preparing the children of these immigrants to participate in the social, economic, and political life of our country is one of the school's greatest challenges of the 1990s.[8]

Levels of School Organization

The pattern of school organization varies throughout the United States. Historical precedent, economic reality, and demographic needs often are more persuasive than the needs of the students. Frequently, an old high school is turned into a junior high school. When student enrollment demands some pattern other than the traditional 6-3-3 or 6-2-4 plan, a middle school is created.

Until 1910, the 8–4 plan, with an eleven-year variant, 7–4, was dominant throughout the United States. This slowly gave way, except in rural areas, to some plan involving a two- or three-year junior high school. There are numerous variations in the current school organizational structure, but in general the middle school is rapidly replacing the traditional junior high school. The trends of the future are 5-3-4, 4-4-4, and other middle-school plans.

Although the growth of junior or community colleges has slowed somewhat in recent years, over 4.6 million citizens attend these institutions. This compares with 7.8 million enrolled in four-year colleges and universities. It is unlikely, and probably undesirable, that we will move toward universal higher education, but in spite of a declining number of high school graduates in the past decade, enrollments in higher education have actually risen.

[8]John B. Kellogg, "Forces for Change," *Phi Delta Kappan*, 70, no. 3 (Nov. 1988), pp. 199–204.

With the need for child care and preschools and the growing complexity of many technical jobs, both early and higher education are likely to grow in coming years, producing a system that might look something like this.

4 years	Colleges/Universities	Ages 19–22 & Adults
(2 years)	Community College	Ages 19–20 & Adults
4 years	High School	Ages 15–18
4 years	Middle	Ages 11–14
8 years	Elementary	Ages 6–10
	Preschool	Ages 3–5

THE FEDERAL GOVERNMENT AND EDUCATION

The federal role in education is a concern that has troubled the American people since the adoption of the Constitution in 1789. Although the Founding Fathers were deeply committed to education, they purposely did not mention it in the federal Constitution. They had a genuine fear of tyrannical control that had existed in their homelands.

Federalism and Constitutional Authority

The concept of federalism, with its division of authority between national and state governments, was set forth in the U.S. Constitution. Relationships between the two levels of government are taken from Articles I, IV, and VI, and the Tenth Amendment. The Tenth Amendment provides: "The powers not delegated to the United States by the Constitution, nor prohibited by it to the States, are reserved to the States respectively, or to the people." Because the Constitution makes no reference to education, the states have been given the basic responsibility for education. The constitutional provisions are subject to constant interpretation and reinterpretation. Strict constructionists have held and continue to hold that powers not expressly provided to the federal government are reserved for the states, and that the increasing encroachment on the part of the federal government into the field of education is a violation of the Constitution.

The most frequently used argument by those in favor of federal involvement in the educational process is the phrase in the Preamble to the Constitution that states that the government of the United States was formed to "promote the general welfare." Further justification for federal involvement is found in the "elastic" clause of Article 1, Section Eight, which states that Congress shall have the power "To make all laws which shall be necessary and proper for carrying into execution the foregoing powers, and all other powers vested by this constitution in the government of the United States." Proponents of federal aid to education argue that this clause gives the federal government constitutional authority to act in accordance with its stated power over taxation, commerce, and other areas provided for in the Constitution.

The debate over federal aid to education has diminished in recent years, but the cry of states' rights can still be heard from many political platforms. The size and depth of federal government involvement in education at all levels make it unlikely that its presence will disappear. Federal aid is a fact of our times and has a long and generally honorable history in the United States. The issue then becomes one of, first, the amount of control the federal government exercises when it distributes funds to the states and, second, the expansion of national power at the expense of the state and local governments. Critics on the political Right believe that any expansion of national power is destructive of individual rights. We must place a high value on individualism and laissez-faire government. These critics say that state and local governments are closer and more responsive to their people. On the other hand, critics on the Left often favor a strengthening of national government in order to provide an adequate education for all children, regardless of race, sex, national origin, state, or region in which they might have been born. These persons argue that an increase in federal power does not necessarily lead to any decrease in the rights of the individual.

Although most people agree that states have the primary jurisdiction over educational matters, the federal government has certain educational functions about which there is little disagreement. Among these are the education of residents of special federal areas (Native Americans on the reservations, the peoples of the territories), the training of people to serve the national government, cooperative educational programs with other countries, scientific research, and the collection and diffusion of information about education. Even before the Constitution was adopted in 1789, the national government found itself involved in educational activities beyond these roles.

Federal Involvement in Education

Pressure for the federal government to be involved in education can come from such grass roots efforts as civil rights and handicapped rights movements. Both groups pressured local and state governments, but only achieved most of their goals when they brought political and judicial pressure to bear at the federal level. The two large teachers' unions, AFT and NEA, convinced the Carter administration to raise the Department of Education to cabinet status. Economic threats from abroad have led the federal government programs that upgrade vocational, scientific, and technical education. Similarly, failure among the poor and minorities to achieve in our schools led to federal initiatives such as Head Start and various programs to help the poor. National commissions on education have also been used by the White House and Congress to promote their educational and political agendas. The *A Nation at Risk* report in 1983 began a wave of local, state, and federal commission reports, whose impact is still being felt.

Historians trace federal involvement in education to the Northwest Ordinance of 1787; the third article of this legislation states that "religion, morality, and knowledge being necessary to good government and the happiness of mankind, schools and the means of education shall be forever encouraged." Taking its cue from the Land Ordinance of 1785, the Northwest Ordinance set aside every sixteenth section of land for the support of education. In addition to the funds raised from the sale of this property, Congress established a policy providing that 5 percent of the proceeds from the sale of federal lands with the various states would revert to the states, provided the states agreed not to tax federal property. Many states used the proceeds from these sales to establish common school funds in the 1830s. The Morrill Acts of 1862 and 1890 provided six million acres of federal lands for the support of sixty-nine land-grant colleges. Since the turn of the century there has been a fairly continuous stream of federal legislation for K–12 and higher education.

The Smith-Lever (1914) and Smith-Doan (1917) Acts focused on agricultural and vocational education respectively. Both acts were motivated by the shortages in our work force during World War I. Additional vocational education acts have provided billions of dollars from the federal government since that time. Preparation for the defense of our country has motivated federal expenditures for the support of military academies and ROTC programs in other institutions of higher education. Sputnik provided the incentive for the National Defense Education Act (1958), which initially focused on science, mathematics, and foreign languages, but later expanded to include a wide array for programs and subject areas. The National Teachers Corps (1966) and the Education Professions Development Act (1967) focused on the education of teachers.

Equality of opportunity has been the goal of a large number of acts starting with the National Youth Conservation Corps, the Civilian Conservation Corps, and the National Youth Administration during the depression of the 1930s, and then a host of programs during the War on Poverty in the 1960s. Grants for poor students to attend college, free and subsidized lunch programs, Head Start, funds for handicapped children, Chapter 1 programs for the education of racial and ethnic minorities, and programs to alleviate discrimination against women have all been federal initiatives during the past thirty years. The most extensive federal involvement in education was with the Elementary and Secondary Education Act (ESEA) in 1965, an act President Johnson considered one of his greatest accomplishments. As a result of this act, billions of dollars of federal funds have been used to help children from low-income families, improve school libraries, establish regional service centers, support research and training in education, and improve and strengthen state departments of education. In the 1980s, federal aid shifted from special-purpose aid to more general-purpose aid, as the Reagan administration attempted to reduce the amount of federal funds going to state and local agencies.

STATE GOVERNMENTS AND EDUCATION

The state government is charged with the responsibility for education, and all state constitutions contain provisions giving them the authority to govern schools. Most states have chosen to delegate much of the constitutional authority to local districts. The operational powers for education come not only from the state constitutions but also from the legislatures and the courts.

State Organization

All the laws, rules, regulations, and judicial opinions affecting education are published in state school codes—documents that have become sizable, owing to the growing complexity of the educational enterprise. State codes deal with the whole range of activities in which schools engage: financial responsibility, accountability laws, certification of teachers, buildings, organization and administration, elections, special programs, school taxes, tenure, and literally hundreds of other laws and judicial opinions affecting the everyday operation of schools throughout the state.

With education again becoming a major state and national issue in the 1980s, governors and legislatures became active participants in the educational reform movement. Educational policy analysts on governors' staffs helped to frame many of the issues. The education committees of the state houses and senates passed legislation on a wide range of topics, including school finance, curriculum, teacher tenure, merit pay, length of school year and school day, student and teacher testing, teacher education, school dropouts, and minority achievement. State departments of education, under the supervision of state boards and the leadership of commissioners or state superintendents of public instruction, were given greater powers in many states to hasten the reform of public schools.

In forty-eight of the fifty states, the state boards of education have been given the responsibility of supervising the elementary and secondary school districts. State boards vary in size from three to twenty-one members and attain office through either partisan or nonpartisan elections or appointment by the governor. Their functions vary but generally consist of appointing a state superintendent or commissioner, passing rules and regulations concerning certification, state aid, special programs for the handicapped, vocational education, and the distribution of federal funds.

State superintendents of education trace back to Gideon Hawley who was appointed New York's chief state officer in 1812. Since that time, some of the most important names in American educational history have been state superintendents; Horace Mann (Massachusetts) and Henry Barnard (Connecticut) are just two in an impressive list. State departments of education enforce the laws, rules, and regulations governing education in the state; distribute the funds allocated by the board, state legislature, and federal government; certify who may teach and administer schools in the state; enforce building, curricular, and other codes; and provide leadership and services to local districts.

The Growing State Role

Numerous educational questions now face the states. Is local control an anachronism in the final decade of the twentieth century, or are we entering a new period of decentralization with site-based management of schools? How can the states continue to support the ever-increasing costs of education? Will the taxpayers vote for bond and mill levy elections without being assured that schools will improve? Will providing greater choice for parents, students, and teachers in selecting their schools bring about the reforms called for by most state and federal commissions?

At the heart of the shift in educational power and decision making is the financial crunch facing the schools. Schooling costs are rising at double the rate of the gross national product, school districts do not have the ability to raise taxes, the public has become disenchanted, and the property tax as the basis for school finance is overloaded. As a result, the states have been forced to take a greater role in school financing.

Court challenges to inequities in school financing, such as *Serrano* in California, *Rodriguez* in Texas, and *Chaill* in New Jersey, have forced many state legislatures to rewrite their school foundation acts to provide more equitable statewide levels of funding. Many states have been forced to move away from the local property tax as the only or major source of school funding and shift to sales or income taxes to support the schools.

With *The Nation at Risk* national report on education and countless state reports during the 1980s, the schools became the number one focus of attention for many governors, legislators, and other state and local politicians. Although new accountability measures were passed in many states and greater equity was sought through new finance acts, excellence has been the major emphasis of that decade. Assessment of teachers and students, minimum competency testing, a renewed interest in the three Rs, tougher graduation standards, mandated curricula, staff-development programs, and an emphasis on effective schools were all used throughout the various states to reach for excellence.

Research literature on effective schools became the basis for countless state actions across the country. The research indicates that such schools are characterized as having strong leadership from the principal, agreement on instructional goals, high teacher expectations of students, a safe and orderly school climate, and assessment instruments that are closely tied to the instructional goals. Some states attempted to mandate reforms; others used incentives to get districts and schools to change, and a recent movement has been for teacher groups to negotiate school reform as part of their contracts.

A major question in the coming years will be regarding the role of the state in promoting educational reform at the district and local level while promoting equality of opportunity for all children. We elaborated on the development of this issue in Chapter 2.

THE LOCAL DISTRICT

Based on the national and state reports of the late 1980s, it appears that site-based management, parent and student choice, parental involvement, teacher empowerment and professionalization will be key to the structural reforms of schools for the rest of this century. This movement contradicts the consolidation movement of the past thirty years and also appears to challenge the emphasis placed upon the state reforms being advocated by governors, legislators, and state boards of education. A critical challenge facing education in the late twentieth century will be how to continue to provide equality of opportunity throughout a state while moving the reform agenda down to the school and preschool level.

The decentralized nature of American schooling is one of its most distinctive features. Although education is a growing federal and state concern, much of the decision-making power still rests at the local level. Some observers would even suggest that the real power exists at the classroom level when a teacher closes his or her door.

Historical Background

Education historians trace the beginnings of local control of education to the Massachusetts Bay Colony, which in 1647 decentralized education to the level of the town or township and mandated that local officials provide for the education of the young. Despite the inability of towns to serve rural areas satisfactorily and the lack of resources in many of the smaller districts, the Massachusetts model of small local districts was adopted throughout many parts of the United States. In the Midwest, West, and Northwest large numbers of rural school districts were formed, and only since the 1950s has consolidation led to larger, more economically viable districts in these parts of the country. In the South, during the colonial period, much of the education was a function of the Church of England, which was organized on a parish, or county, basis. With the adoption of the Constitution and the separation of church and state, the county unit of schooling was maintained and has since been adopted outside the South by Utah and Nevada. In other regions, where it became obvious that small districts could not offer all necessary services, states formed intermediate units called boards of cooperative services.

The Nature of Local Districts

Historically, local communities founded the schools; as a result most power is concentrated at the local level. Receiving their delegated authority from the states rather than from municipal or county government, local school districts often function autonomously from other local governmental bodies. Although school districts possess quasi-corporate powers, the legislature has the power to create, destroy, or reorganize school districts as it sees fit. This legislative supremacy has been well established in the courts, but politicians are wary when it comes to changing what have been traditional prerogatives at the local level. Whereas the local district often encompassed only a one-room school, today "local" districts may enroll hundreds of thousands of students, employ tens of thousands of teachers, and have a budget in excess of one-half billion dollars. These changes have brought pressures recently to decentralize the large, bureaucratic urban school systems.

Groups of lay citizens known as the board of education, school board, school trustees, or some similar name are elected by the public and given legal authority by the legislature to carry out an educational program at the local level. Board members are appointed by the mayor in a few large-city school districts, but most are elected. Terms of office are generally from three to five years, and the size of boards varies from three to as many as fifteen members, seven being considered the ideal number by many experts. Most board members serve without pay, although a few cities pay expenses. Traditionally, boards of education have been dominated by businessmen and professionals, with a large underrepresentation of the poor, minorities, and women. In recent years, gains have been made by these previously underrepresented groups.

Certain functions performed by the local board of education are mandated by state law. The board must adhere to a state school code in such matters as curriculum, finance, building codes, certification, and attendance. If it wishes to go beyond the minimums stated in the laws, it enters the discretionary part of its work. With demands by the public for accountability in the schools and the increasing pressure by many community groups to be included in the decision-making process, the role of school boards has changed. Without question, one of their most important functions is the selection of a superintendent and the approval of the staff of administrators and teachers.

The superintendents of schools are responsible for efficiently managing local education. Superintendents and their staffs are charged with carrying out the instructional program, making personnel decisions, and managing school business affairs. As a result of increasing pressures from teachers' organizations and community groups, as well as tight finances in many districts today, the superintendent's position is one of the most difficult positions in society.

BATTLEGROUNDS IN EDUCATIONAL POLITICS

Although the tensions among individuals and groups seeking to control the schools in American society are present to a greater or lesser degree in all educational decisions, recently five battlegrounds in the contest for control of the schools have received more attention than the others: (1) local school board elections, especially in large and medium-sized cities; (2) court decisions, especially from federal courts and the Supreme Court; (3) votes on legislative bills, especially in Congress and in state legislatures; (4) collective bargaining sessions between teachers' unions and local school boards; and (5) local referenda, especially those required by law to approve bond issues and increases in school taxes. Currently, these are the forums from which decisions emanate on the most highly contested issues in American public education.

Twelve Political Issues in Education

What are those crucial, contemporary, political issues on which educational debate is centered and political power is brought to bear? Even when limited to public education at the elementary and secondary levels, there are today dozens, perhaps even hundreds, of important political issues facing educational decision makers. The decisions taken on these issues will affect the present generation of children and youth as well as one or more future generations. Among these many issues, the following list is representative rather than comprehensive:

1. Because of federal civil rights laws, all public institutions that receive *any* federal funds must institute and implement affirmative action employment policies.

The issue is how to achieve racial, ethnic, and gender representation among school administrators and teachers without violating any applicant's or employee's civil rights, especially the constitutional guarantees of due process and equal protection of the law.

2. Parents, businesspersons, and others have become concerned that high school graduates lack competency in basic skills such as computing, reading, writing, speaking, and knowledge of academic subjects such as history, literature, and science. This has resulted in clarion appeals for going "back-to-basics" and improving cultural literacy.

The issue is one of priorities among educational goals: If skills and certain academics are to receive renewed emphasis, what is to be deemphasized?

3. Citizens lament bureaucracy and unresponsiveness in every governmental unit but especially expect those closest to be the most responsive to their wishes. Local electorates now demand that elected school boards and professionals in the local school bureaucracies be held accountable to the citizenry for what students learn or fail to learn in the schools.

The issue is to determine what learning outcomes are most important and then to decide precisely, considering all the out-of-school influences on students, which ones public school educators can be legitimately held accountable for.

4. Although public schools may not be powerful enough to effect such changes, more and more since the 1960s the nation's leaders, legislators, and general public have placed the burdens of social reform on public education. The schools are expected to eliminate such deep-rooted societal problems as racism, sexism, cultural deprivation, poverty, and other impediments to social and economic equality.

Since the public schools are ill equipped and unprepared to address such monumental tasks, the issue is not only how to approach such problems and what programs offer the most promise but also whether or not the schools are the best agency to attack the problems.

5. Two questions concerning crucial personnel matters have emerged: How to rid the schools of incompetent and insensitive teachers and how to screen new applicants to ensure hiring and retaining outstanding teachers. The practice of tenure is related to both of these questions in that it is difficult to dismiss tenured teachers and it is becoming more difficult and taking longer to attain tenure.

The issue is whether or not states should abolish tenure for public school teachers, or failing this, what changes should be made in the criteria for awarding tenure.

6. In recent years, many administrative decisions made by school administrators or school boards are being challenged in the judicial appeal channels by parents, students, and teachers. The bases of appeal often are claims that either due process or equal protection of the law has been denied the plaintiffs.

The issue is what administrative review procedures are necessary to satisfy constitutional provisions in situations involving alleged violations of policies or rules by students or teachers. Stated differently, the issue is what legitimate rights do students and teachers have as clients and employees of public schools.

7. In 1975, Public Law 94-142 was passed by Congress, providing a "bill of rights" and program-development funds for the education of the nation's almost 8 million handicapped children and adolescents. Over 3 billion dollars in federal funds each year are channeled to state and local education agencies to help support education for the handicapped.

The issue is a complex one, including defining the many categories of handicap, determining how much instruction should occur in regular classrooms and how much in special classrooms, preparing and certifying both regular and special teachers who will be expected to teach the handicapped, and clarifying the civil rights of handicapped students.

8. After more than two decades marked by vigorous merging of contiguous school districts into single, larger districts to expand the curriculum, the trend is now in the opposite direction, especially in large and medium-sized cities. Bigness in education, as in other institutions, has led to cumbersome, impersonal bureaucracies. Secondary schools with 750 to 1,000 students can offer a full range of general and vocational programs, while large junior and senior high schools (1,500 to 3,000 students) often become factorylike, "process" students (and sometimes teachers also), and ignore the desire of parents and community groups. Generally, however, the larger the school district in urban areas, the greater the taxable wealth available for schools.

The issue, then, is how to achieve smaller, more responsive units (school districts, subdistricts, schools) while maintaining tax bases sufficient to support diverse, comprehensive curricula.

9. Most teachers are represented by a collective bargaining agent, usually an affiliate of the National Education Association (NEA) or American Federation of Teachers (AFT), which enters into collective negotiations with the school board (and superintendent) or its paid, professional negotiator. Out of the negotiating sessions comes a contractual agreement signed by both parties.

This employee-employer negotiating process involves several issues: Who represents taxpayers, parents, and students? Should public school teachers have the right to strike? Besides salaries and fringe benefits, what other conditions of employment should be negotiated: number of students per class or per day? number of paid vacation days per year? amount of pay for participation in any "after hours" extracurricular activities? financial support for professional travel? paid sabbatical leaves? special toilet facilities, lounges, and minicafeterias? acceptable forms of disciplining students? grievance procedures? provision of a desk and coat closet for each teacher? number of paraprofessional aides per teacher?

10. As respect for cultural pluralism rose since the late 1960s, public schools have been expected to develop new multiethnic and multicultural curricula, particularly, but not exclusively, for the historically oppressed and neglected racial and ethnic minorities. Ethnic studies that have received the most attention and funds are black, or Afro-American, studies; American Indian, or Native American studies; Mexican-American, Spanish-American, or Chicano studies; and Oriental-Ameri-

can (Japanese, Chinese, Vietnamese, Korean) studies. When a student's language is not English, bilingual education has been added to ethnic education, although some educators and political leaders claim that multiethnic, multicultural, bilingual, or multilingual education is essential for *all* Americans.

The issue here is where to place emphases from region to region, state to state, and community to community; for which groups of students are programs intended; who is to administer and teach these programs; and who pays.

11. Some educators and political authorities argue that equality of educational opportunity is above all else a function of equality of financial support, as measured by average per pupil expenditures for *all* schools in a school district or for *all* school districts in a state. A few even argue for equality among *all* states in the nation.

The issue is how to define "equality of educational opportunity" and determine who—federal government, state government, local school district—is to pay what share of any financial equalization formula.

12. A key political issue, regardless of the kind of election held, is voter qualifications. In educational politics, the question of who is eligible to vote relates primarily to three types of local school elections: elections of school board members, elections to approve selling bonds to raise funds for new facilities, and elections to approve increases in regular school taxes to support operating expenses (mainly salaries of teachers and administrators).

The debate usually focuses on the lower voting-age limit; on who, for *school district* elections (as distinguished from local, state, and federal elections), is a registered voter; and on whether to allow only property owners or both property owners and renters to vote.

● —— ●

Case Study: Changing School Organization

Place yourself in the position of an intermediate or junior high school teacher who has been asked to help organize the new middle school, recently voted in by the board of education. The system will be moving from the current 6-3-3 system of organization to 4-4-4, with a four-year middle school. You have been asked to serve on a committee made up of administrators, teachers, parents, and students.

You have already taught for several years at your current school, and a major shift in organization will no doubt entail many changes in the curriculum, teaching methods, and textbooks. The parents in the community fear that the change will have a negative effect on their boys' athletic opportunities and that the move is really only another of those "radical" ideas by the new superintendent.

What concerns do you feel the teachers have about moving over to the new system? How are you going to facilitate the adjustment of teachers and students to the new school? What can be done about the parents who have decided to oppose the move actively? Deal with changes that have to occur in curriculum, teaching methods, athletics, guidance programs, extracurricular activities, facilities, and any other changes you think should be considered.

Case Study: Academic Freedom

As an experienced junior high school English teacher, you prefer to select your own works of literature for class study rather than relying on a published anthology. One of the books you are using this year is a good, well-known piece of writing by an American winner of the Nobel Prize. The book, however, does contain some profanity, a few explicit sexual scenes, and some references that might be offensive to people of conservative politics or religion.

A few parents of students in your class have called you and your principal, requesting that this book, which you are having all the students read, be eliminated from any and all English courses in your school. After reading the book, your principal asks you to withdraw it from required reading in all your classes.

What will you do? When a teacher's values and professional judgment conflict with the norms of some parents or other community members, who should prevail? In the case described, should it matter if the parents who are making the demands represent a majority? Should community members have *any* say in curricular matters?

Thought Questions

1. What advantages and disadvantages can you see to having three levels of government — federal, state, and local — involved in financing and administrating the schools.
2. What *external* and *internal* forces would you expect to exert pressure on a mandate from the state department of education to revise the criteria for awarding teaching certificates?
3. Of the twelve political issues in education described in this chapter, which three seem to have the highest visibility in your state or region? Explain why you suspect these three issues have become important.
4. Which level of educational governance might have primary responsibility for each of the following decisions? Use *L* for local school district, *S* for state department of education *or* state legislature, and *F* for any kind of federal involvement.

   awards high school diplomas

   purchases classroom textbooks

   requires all schools to offer a state history course

   establishes equalization formulas

   determines minimum number of days of attendance for students

   certifies school administrators

   operates overseas schools for dependents of military personnel

   hires a superintendent

funds Head Start programs

establishes compulsory attendance laws

5. If a foreign visitor asked, "Who runs the schools in the United States?" how would you respond?
6. What are some of the causes of the increase in secondary education since 1890, when only 6.7 percent of 14- to 17-year-olds were enrolled, to the more than 90 percent enrollment today? What are the positive and negative effects of the increase in enrollment?
7. What strengths and weaknesses can you see in a system such as ours, which places much of the power for controlling education at the local level?

Practical Activities

1. Visit a local school district's administrative offices to obtain a copy of the organizational chart and administrative hierarchy. In addition, obtain a copy of the goals and purposes of the district. How compatible are they with the organizational and administrative structure of the district?
2. Attend a state or local school board meeting and note the ethnic, sexual, and socioeconomic makeup of the board and the audience. What can you tell about the superintendent's relationship with the board? Report on what issues were discussed, who raised them, and the board's vote on the issues. Where did the power appear to reside: with the school board, teachers, administrators, parents, or some other group?
3. Find out what early childhood programs operate in your school district and whether they are in publicly or privately run institutions.
4. Attend a teachers' meeting in a local school. (First obtain permission to attend.) What issues were discussed? Who presided at the meeting? How did teachers and administrators participate? Which person or group appeared to have the greatest influence on the decisions? Give your general reaction to the meeting.
5. Attend a "parent-teacher organization" meeting. Who ran it? What issues were discussed? Did the parents seem to have any power in significant educational matters? What was the apparent relationship between the parents and teachers? What was your general reaction?
6. It is usual for Head Start programs (for preschoolers from impoverished families) to be run by not-for-profit organizations outside the public school system. Each separate local Head Start program is governed by an elected governing board. Attend a monthly meeting of a Head Start governing board and report on the educational and political issues raised and discussed.
7. For several months, read your town or city's daily newspaper and clip out all the news articles, editorials, and letters to the editors that touch on matters of educational politics. Next, set up categories into which your clippings can be placed. Then create a scrapbook of these issues. See if you can find items at all political levels: local, state, and national.

Bibliography

ARONOWITZ, STANLEY, and HENRY GIROUX, *Education Under Siege: The Conservative, Liberal and Radical Debate over Schooling.* Boston: Bergin & Garvey Publishers, Inc., 1985.

DOYLE, DENIS, *Excellence in Education: The States Take Charge.* Washington, D.C.: American Enterprise Institute for Public Policy, 1986.

FREIRE, PAULO, *The Politics of Education.* Boston: Bergin & Garvey Publishers, Inc., 1985.

HOLMES GROUP, *Tomorrow's Teachers: A Report of the Holmes Group.* East Lansing, Mich.: Holmes Group, 1986.

HONIG, BILL, *Last Chance for Our Children: How You Can Help Save Our Schools.* Reading, Mass.: Addison-Wesley Publishing Company, Inc., 1985.

KIRST, MICHAEL, *Who Controls Our Schools: American Values in Conflict.* New York: W.H. Freeman & Company, 1984.

KNEZEVICH, STEPHEN J., *Administration of Public Education*, 4th ed. New York: Harper & Row, Publishers, Inc., 1984.

MILLER, ROBERT A., ED., *The Federal Role in Education.* Washington, D.C.: Institute for Educational Leadership, 1981.

NATIONAL CENTER FOR EDUCATION STATISTICS, *Digest of Education Statistics, 1988.* Washington, D.C.: U.S. Government Printing Office, 1988.

NATIONAL COMMISSION ON EXCELLENCE IN EDUCATION, *A Nation at Risk: The Imperative for Educational Reform.* Washington, D.C.: U.S. Government Printing Office, 1983.

NATIONAL GOVERNORS' ASSOCIATION, *Time for Results: The Governors' 1991 Report on Education.* Washington, D.C.: National Governors' Association, 1986.

REBELL, MICHAEL, and ARTHUR BLOCK, *Education Policy Making and the Courts.* Chicago: University of Chicago Press, 1982.

SHORE, IRA, *Culture Wars: School and Society in the Conservative Restoration, 1969–1984.* Boston: Routledge & Kegan Paul, 1986.

SPRING, JOEL, *American Education*, 2nd ed. New York: Longman, Inc., 1982.

———. *The American School: 1642–1985.* New York: Longman, Inc., 1986.

———. *Conflict of Interests: The Politics of American Education.* New York: Longman, Inc., 1988.

WIRT, FREDERICK, and MICHAEL W. KIRST, *Schools in Conflict.* Berkeley, Calif.: McCutchan Publishing Corporation, 1982.

7

Economics of Education

"Invest in yourself," I usually respond. . . . Though it sounds like the name of a warmed-over self-help book, it is literally true; you are your most valuable asset if you are an ordinary American. A strong empirical case can be made for investing in improving your earning power, or even your capacity to enjoy life, and thus receiving a yield at least as high as the rate of return on conventional investments. It is a fact: In cold dollars and cents the average American's wealth in human capital exceeds his wealth in conventional forms (house, car, insurance, and securities).[1]

The economy produces people. The production of commodities may be considered of quite minor importance except as a necessary input into people production. Our critique of the capitalist economy is simple enough: the people production process—in the workplace and in schools—is dominated by the imperatives of profit and domination rather than by human need. The unavoidable necessity of growing up and getting a job in the United States forces us all to become less than we could be: less free, less secure, in short less happy. The U.S. economy is a formally totalitarian system in which the actions of the vast majority (workers) are controlled by a small minority (owners and managers).[2]

American schools are in economic turmoil and have been for the past quarter century. School bond issues often fail, and districts seldom have enough revenue to fund programs adequately. Schools increasingly rely on state money to operate. Despite this, overcrowded classrooms are the rule rather than the exception; in many cities, and not just in the inner city, schools have become more shabby in appearance. Many of today's schools were constructed in the late 1950s and 1960s during a period of school consolidation and increasing enrollments. Now they need extensive repairs, and capital costs (estimated at $25 billion in 1988) are a pressing financial problem.

There are exceptions to this trend. There are districts where construction keeps up with student enrollment and schools are properly maintained. For the

[1]Schlomo Maital, *Minds, Markets, and Money* (New York: Basic Books, Inc., Publishers, 1982), p. 92.

[2]Samuel Bowles and Herbert Gintis, *Schooling in Capitalist America: Educational Reform and the Contradictions of Economic Life* (New York: Basic Books, Inc., Publishers, 1976), pp. 53–54.

most part, these are communities in which family incomes are solid and the industrial base is strong. The American educational landscape, however, is a jigsaw puzzle of over 15,000 school districts — not all with the same funding. Whereas one school has $3,500 a year to spend on each child, the one next door may have $6,500. This, of course, is a direct result of a system based on "local control" of schools, something that is odd to observers from other nations.

Construction of schools has been one step behind the influx of students and the need for more classrooms. Inside the schoolhouse, classrooms, lunchrooms, and faculty lounges appear austere in contrast to the bright, carpeted, attractive surroundings of most private businesses. It is no secret that teachers, even those with doctorate degrees, command considerably lower salaries than physicians, dentists, lawyers, engineers, architects, and other professionals in private industry. The average annual salary of a public school teacher in 1988 was approximately $28,000.[3] This figure was slightly higher for secondary teachers and slightly lower for elementary teachers. Schoolteachers earn less than most corporate managerial, sales, and accounting personnel, who generally have less formal education.

On the other hand, total expenditures for what Kenneth Boulding calls the "schooling industry" amount to a whopping $300 billion annually.[4] This figure is nearly 7 percent of the U.S. Gross National Product (GNP), the federal government's most inclusive measure of productivity during a year.[5] Public schools appear to receive their share of the economic pie.

In 1950 the schooling industry received just 4 percent of a much lower GNP. However, during the quarter-century period from 1950–1975, enrollment in junior and four-year colleges increased significantly as a percentage of the nation's population. Since 1975, schooling's cut of the GNP has slipped from 8 percent to less than 7 percent. The recession years of the late 1970s and early 1980s took their toll on public elementary and secondary school finances. Then federal aid for education was reduced during the 1980s. Allowing for inflation, public school revenues have decreased about 10 percent since 1978.

The hearts of most Americans, if not their pocketbooks, are in the right place. In a recent survey, nearly two-thirds (64 percent) — of those polled said they would be "willing to pay more taxes to help raise the standards of education in the United States."[6] Perhaps in the years ahead, people will follow these words with deeds, but our tax system works against the best intentions of citizens. People have only indirect and little control over how much they are taxed by national and state

[3]*Estimates of School Statistics 1987–88* (Washington, D.C.: National Education Association, 1988).

[4]The schooling industry by this accounting includes the formal institutions of public education: kindergartens, schools, colleges, and vocational-technical centers.

[5]*Digest of Educational Statistics* (Washington, D.C.: National Center for Educational Statistics, U.S. Department of Health, Education, and Welfare, 1988).

[6]Alec M. Gallup and Stanley M. Elam, "The 20th Annual Gallup Poll of the Public's Attitudes Toward the Public Schools," *Phi Delta Kappan*, 70, no. 1 (Sept. 1988), p. 38.

TABLE 7-1   Public Attitudes Toward Financial Support for Public Schools 1983–1988

Would you be willing to pay more taxes to help raise the standards of education in the United States?

	NATIONAL TOTALS %	NO CHILDREN IN SCHOOL %	PUBLIC SCHOOL PARENTS %	NONPUBLIC SCHOOL PARENTS %
Yes	64	61	73	68
No	29	31	23	30
Don't know	7	8	4	2

	1988 %	1983 %
Yes	64	58
No	64	58
Don't know	7	9

Source: Phi Delta Kappa, Inc., "The 20th Annual Gallup Poll of the Public's Attitudes Toward the Public Schools," *Phi Delta Kappan,* 70, no. 1 (Sept. 1988).

governments; in contrast, they can affect local taxes. As Harry Broudy wrote, "Here at last was a foe that the taxpayer could transfix with the stroke of a pencil; here was one wad of money that could not be spent."[7] Despite the persistent debates over the effectiveness of public schools, the financial plight is more a result of the taxpayer's dislike of paying taxes than a dissatisfaction with the schools.

The foregoing should not suggest that too little money necessarily is spent on formal schooling, that funds allocated for public schools could not be spent more efficiently, that waste and excess don't exist, and that perhaps even American students wouldn't be better off with less formal schooling.[8] Yet American schooling is in a puzzling, though hardly amusing, paradoxical state. Our society places much stock in formal education: Education has been called the new state religion in the twentieth century, and the school, according to Ivan Illich, has become the New Church.[9] However, although education, or formal education, is virtually worshipped, we don't support it generously. Schools, like many other social or public institutions, generally suffer from a deprivation that economist John Kenneth Galbraith labeled "private opulence and public squalor."[10]

[7]Harry S. Broudy, *The Real World of the Public Schools* (New York: Harcourt Brace Jovanovich, Inc., 1972), p. 115.

[8]We use the term *schooling* (rather than *education*) deliberately. Schooling is what is done in schools and other places of formal instruction. Education is general learning that occurs in many institutions and elsewhere, more often incidentally than deliberately.

[9]Ivan Illich, *Deschooling Society* (New York: Harper & Row, Publishers, Inc., 1971), pp. 43–46.

[10]John Kenneth Galbraith, *The Affluent Society* (Boston: Houghton Mifflin Company, 1958), p. 257.

THE ECONOMIC SYSTEM AND EDUCATION IN AMERICA

American economic beliefs are rooted in early capitalist thought, the doctrine of laissez-faire capitalism, which the Scottish philosopher Adam Smith eloquently analyzed in the *Wealth of Nations* (1776). Capitalist theory has been revised over time as economic conditions have changed. America, probably because of its adventurous spirit and individualism, clung to the tenets of classical capitalism more than did European nations. Europe also was influenced much more than the United States by socialist thought in politics and economics.

The nature of economic society in the United States betrayed its pure market ideals, particularly during the twentieth century. Small competitive farms, shops, and other businesses gave way to large corporations; big government subsidized some businesses and has been a major producer itself; labor unions grew stronger, affecting production and wages; and price competition withered as business and labor controlled markets. America became a mixed economic system that only remotely resembles the laissez-faire capitalist model. It is a combination of business and government enterprises, of private and social services. Still, primal economic beliefs remain, and people hold distorted views of the U.S economic system. Most telling for the public schools is the myth that when private enterprise spends money, it is its own and is spent for productive purposes; when government, or public enterprises spend, it is a drain on the taxpayer.

Education and the economic system are interrelated, but the relationship is not always clear or benign.

The Conventional Wisdom

In the traditional interpretation of educational history, schooling is viewed as a benefit to a wide range of young people. As schooling became accessible to more people and as the schools expanded or diversified the curriculum, economic opportunities increased.

Schooling expanded substantially, once the quest for the common school became a reality. As educational historian R. Freeman Butts pointed out, by 1870 elementary schooling was beginning to be established, by 1900 the majority of elementary-age children were in school; and by 1960 universal elementary schooling had been won.[11] More remarkable, however, was the march of secondary schools. In 1890 fewer than 7 percent of high school age youth were enrolled in school, but this was to change by geometric leaps. Within ten years, the enrollment had nearly doubled, and by 1920 the figure had more than quadrupled. By 1930 more than 50 percent of the 14- to 17-year-old population were in school, and during the 1960s the total had passed 90 percent.

In the mid–twentieth century, college education also expanded rapidly. By

[11]R. Freeman Butts, "Search for Freedom—The Story of American Education," *NEA Journal,* 49, no. 3 (Mar. 1960), p. 42.

1950 about 30 percent of high school graduates were attending college; by 1970 this figure was over 50 percent. This growth prompted Butts to write that it might not be long before we were back where we were in 1900, with 75 percent of high school graduates bound for college; but in 1900 only 10 percent of the youth were in high school; today 90 percent are.[12] College enrollments have leveled in the past few years, but even if this trend should continue, higher education will have witnessed a tremendous expansion.

It is widely claimed that economic benefits followed the growth of schooling. More schooling, advocates reason, led to a wider range of job opportunities, better jobs, and higher pay, which in turn created higher standards of living and general social mobility. Though educators would agree that schools served some people more effectively than others, most maintain that schools have advanced the education and economic well-being of all their clients. If industry and other businesses also benefited, this was only a natural spin-off of the system, not the primary driving force behind schooling.

Economic development and the growth of schooling have been mutually supportive. In the conventional wisdom, the rewards of more and better educational facilities to business are obvious: Trained and educated individuals are more valuable employees. In turn, industrial development requires more sophisticated education and training.

With the expansion of industrialization and decline of agriculture, young people were less able to find work on family farms or in local shops and crafts. Advances in science and technology created especially tight employment conditions in the agrarian community, where gains in technology were most pronounced. The percentage of workers employed in agriculture declined precipitously with twentieth-century gains in productivity. Industrialization, it was argued, called for better-trained and better-educated people to carry out the tasks required by increasingly sophisticated technology and management. Manufacturers and managers not surprisingly took interest in the school's curricula. Organizations such as the National Association of Manufacturers, the American Federation of Labor, and the Grange actively supported the addition of vocational-technical programs. But "the bread is buttered on both sides"; having access to more schooling, young people found that opportunities for economic advancement in corporate enterprises multiplied. Industry held out the promise of higher pay, shorter work days, in some cases better working conditions, and financial security.

The argument for more schooling inevitably included the requirements of a democratic society. As Butts concluded,

> A society based on steam power, electric power, or nuclear power can be managed and controlled by relatively few people. Technical power leads to political power. To prevent autocratic dictatorial use of political and economic power by a few, everyone must have an education devoted to freedom. There is no other satisfactory way to limit political or economic power.

[12]Ibid., p. 46.

So it became increasingly clear that the opportunity to acquire an expanded and extended education must be made available to all. . . . Equality of opportunity stood alongside freedom as the prime goals of education.[13]

With industrialization came the rise of big labor, first with the American Federation of Labor (AFL) in the late 1800s and later with the Congress of Industrial Organization (CIO) in the 1930s. Labor organizations have been consistent supporters of more resources for education. When schools were attended by a small minority of children, the pupils came almost exclusively from the business and propertied class. The school curriculum often was college preparatory. It served primarily those families whose children were destined for life in politics, professions, and the arts. The goal of the common-school movement was to accommodate children from all socioeconomic backgrounds. In turn, labor recognized the public school as a partner in advancing the academic skills and economic opportunities of working-class families. Although perhaps not as instrumental as other forces, the growth of organized labor benefited the cause of public schooling.

In postindustrial economic society, the liberal and technical areas are critical. High technology demands computer and engineering know-how, multinational corporations are steered by analytical managerial teams, and the now-dominant service sector of the economy is manned by people with strong communications skills.

Economic competitiveness is the "Sputnik of the Eighties—and beyond." When the Soviet Union launched its earth-orbiting satellite in 1957, the United States responded with more than a crash research and development program to launch American satellites into space. Congress also passed the National Defense Education Act to promote the development of science, mathematics, and foreign language programs in schools and colleges. By the 1980s, America was forced to respond to another challenge—major advances in economic technology and productivity made by several countries, particularly Japan. Although business groups and economists recognized that management practices and modern capital goods are strategic ingredients in a dynamic economy, they focused on the quality of education. Researchers found a strong link between the educational level and a nation's ability to compete economically. The extraordinary effectiveness of Japanese schools, they asserted, is a primary reason for Japan's high productivity.[14]

Unlike with Sputnik, however, the federal government did not immediately respond with resources to help schools improve. Instead, federal support for education during the 1980s actually fell to its lowest level in twenty years. Spokespersons from government and private industry tended to tell schools what they should do and to goad states and local districts into improving the schools. Corporations and the business community, understanding their stake in a capable work force, eventually began devoting more resources—money and people—to schools.

Labor, business, and corporate educational programs cost over $50 billion a

---

[13]Ibid., p. 42.

[14]John F. Jennings, "The Sputnik of the Eighties," *Phi Delta Kappan*, 69, no. 2 (Oct. 1987), pp. 104–105.

year. Contracts between industry and education are increasing at all school levels, ranging from adopt-a-school programs to research partnerships between multinationals and major universities. The connection between the quality of education and economic productivity is difficult to assess, but implicit in the investments of industry is the assumption that it pays off.

The Counterview

The unconventional interpretation of the relationship between the individual and our economic society pictures businesses and schools as mutually self-serving. Their goal is to shape learners to accept values compatible with the business ethic, to learn skills useful to economic operations, and to acquire knowledge that is not politically disruptive. In effect, schools function as an intermediary, augmenting and perpetuating the dominant social institutions, particularly the modern corporation.

One proponent for the counterviewpoint, Clarence Karier, stated that the history of American education demonstrates that changes in the means of production result in significant changes in social institutions and life-styles.[15] The growth of large *urban centers* in the last quarter of the nineteenth century and the subsequent development of the *American high school* (an urban school); the decline of the academy (appropriate for a rural setting); the development of *industrial education, manual training,* and *vocational guidance;* as well as the enactment of *child-labor* and *compulsory education laws*—all are historical developments directly or indirectly related to education and traceable to new forms of production. The creation of our mass educational system, Karier adds, followed the shift from handicraft to mass-production enterprises and the adoption of production-line techniques. In turn, the American system of mass education has performed three salient and overlapping functions: training, testing and sorting, and holding.[16]

Training.   The overriding function of *training* has been to help youths meet occupational requirements for an increasingly complex system. Trade classes, woodworking, mechanics, home economics, clerical skills, agricultural instruction, and more recently computer science have been a substantial part of the comprehensive school. During the early part of this century, many corporations operated their own trade classes, physical education programs, literary activities, foreign language training, and even kindergartens. Corporations also saw the economic advantage in having the schools assume this instruction. The National Association of Manufacturers at the turn of the century passed a resolution calling for high schools to teach commercial courses and modern languages. Languages helped employees who would work in the companies' growing foreign markets, partic-

[15]Clarence J. Karier, "Business Values and the Educational State," in *Roots of Crisis: American Education in the Twentieth Century,* eds. Clarence J. Karier, Paul Vilas, and Joel Spring (Chicago: Rand McNally & Company, 1973), pp. 6–8.

[16]Ibid., p. 16.

ularly in South America. Organized business continues to call for work- and life-related courses.

Vocational programs received a boost from the Conant report, *The American High School Today,* published in 1959. James Conant spoke highly of the vocational-technical curriculum of high schools and encouraged their continued support as an important function in preparing many youths for life after high school.[17]

Conant also observed that most "academically talented" students were not carrying adequate course loads in science, mathematics, and a foreign language, and were not sufficiently challenged in their academic program. Given the rapid advances that were being made in science, along with the expanding use of more sophisticated technology in industry, the schools were not maintaining the quality of education that would ensure a talented and trained work force.[18] His recommendations for considerably stronger academic loads in these subjects were based squarely on the personnel needs of industry and the military might of the nation.

The Conant report also recommended that the high school diploma, a fundamentally ornamental document, be supplemented with a durable record of courses a student had completed with the grade received. This record, Conant stated, could be in the form of a card, carried in a wallet. Such a card would prove expedient to future employers when considering an applicant.[19] As educational historian Joel Spring remarked, "Conant wanted all Americans to be card-carrying graduates of the high school."[20]

In *Education and the Rise of the Corporate State,* Spring wrote that the purpose of corporate programs for employees is to foster the kind of worker who later would be called an organization person. He stated, "A socialized and cooperative individual was the type needed both on the assembly line and in the management team...."[21] Because many programs extended corporate control over the social life of the worker, they could be used to increase his or her efficiency. Later, business extended its support to public schooling as a more effective way to achieving the same ends.

Even today, the analogy between school and factory is frequently drawn. Such commonplace characteristics as drab interior settings, bells signifying when to start and stop work, assigned workplaces (desks), rules specifying that students should be in a classroom or study place at all times, the assumption that if they are in the halls or lunchroom they are wasting time, hall permission slips, assemblylike lunchrooms, teacher-established classroom rules, and so on, are conducive to the production of obedient, "good" workers.

Testing and sorting.   Tests became popular during World War I as a method of classifying military personnel. After the war, educational researchers and psy-

[17]James B. Conant, *The American High School Today* (New York: McGraw-Hill Book Company, Inc., 1959), pp. 30–32.

[18]Ibid., pp. 33–36.

[19]Ibid., p. 50.

[20]Joel Spring, *The Sorting Machine: National Educational Policy Since 1945* (New York: David McKay Company, Inc., 1976), p. 48.

[21]Joel Spring, *Education and the Rise of the Corporate State* (Boston: Beacon Press, 1972), p. 32.

chologists applied what had been learned to the expanding school system. With more and more children coming to school from various socioeconomic backgrounds, and with a wider spread in intellectual ability of children, tests were used to measure what children knew, what and how fast they could be expected to learn, and even how they might learn best. The aim of later tests was to increase the response of schools to the individual student—to individualize learning.

Most intelligence tests during the last half century or more reflect the values of middle-class, Protestant, industrial America. For example, in response to the question "What is the difference between work and play?" the Stanford-Binet IQ test tallies as "plus" answers,

> You work to earn money and you play for fun. One is for amusement and the other for a living. Play is a pleasure and work is something you should do, your duty. Work is energy used for doing something useful and play is wasting energy. One's recreation, and one's labor. Play is an enjoyment and work is something you have to do. One is something that most people like to do; the other is a duty. When you're working, you're generally doing what has to be done—when you're playing you're just doing what you feel like. Work you take seriously and play you don't.[22]

At the secondary level, aptitude, achievement, and intelligence tests were used widely to determine what courses students should take and in what track they should be fitted. Conant, in *The American High School Today*, strongly recommended that throughout the high school years students be grouped according to ability in nearly all academic subjects. The lone exception to this was the senior-year social studies course, which, he argued, should be designed to bring together students from disparate backgrounds to help build a democratic community. Tests would be an important device to sort students.[23]

Another major recommendation of the Conant report, central to the testing and sorting function of schools, was a guidance program. Conant believed there should be one full-time counselor for every 250 to 300 students, a vast increase over what had existed. The counselor was to see that students were fitted for appropriate academic and vocational offerings.[24]

Upon graduation, all students were to carry Conant's record card, which was particularly important for those concentrating in vocational studies. This device could be readily used to match high school graduates with needed labor. Conant even suggested that if a particular trade was saturated in a specific geographic area, the schools should cease operating that program.[25]

Holding. Vocational programs also are important for temporarily *holding* young people out of the job market. Colleges perform this function for those who are destined to fill white-collar, managerial positions. In most trades (and even

[22]Lewis M. Terman and Maud A. Merrill, *Stanford-Binet Intelligence Scale* (Boston: Houghton Mifflin Company, 1960), p. 213.

[23]Conant, *The American High School Today*, pp. 49–50.

[24]Ibid., pp. 44–46.

[25]Ibid., pp. 51–52.

professions), youngsters could be more efficiently trained as apprentices on the job, but this would shift a burden and cost to the business community. What schools lack in providing effective training they make up for by regulating the supply of workers who otherwise would flood the job market.

A device that schools and businesses use to maintain this hold on the individual, argue the revisionist critics, is the credentialing or certifying process. Before a person can gain entrance to a particular job, he or she must have earned a high school diploma, a bachelor's degree, or whatever the required credential is. In many cases, studies completed in order to earn the credential have little relation to job experiences that follow. Although this process may serve well to regulate the supply of workers, it tends to produce job dissatisfaction.

Many businesses in our growing service economy have reservations about the holding function of schools. In turn, these businesses often complicate the mission of schools. The needs of growing fast-food, supermarket, auto-service, and retail industries today that depend on unskilled and inexpensive labor—provided in large part by teenagers—intensify the school dropout problem and add to the challenge of educating those who remain in school. Many students leave school at midday to work at what have become more full-time than part-time jobs. This reduces their course of study, distracts them from schoolwork, and eliminates extracurricular activities for many. The mental and physical energy of these students goes mostly into their jobs, which help fuel the low-wage, labor-intensive service economy, which itself depends on the discretionary incomes of these young consumers.

The winners in this struggle for scarce labor resources are industries who benefit from young people as producers and consumers. The losers are businesses who need a more educated or trained work force, some of these same young people who forgo more promising vocations for immediate gratification, and, of course, teachers and school officials who take the heat for failing to educate youngsters adequately.

Revisionist educators argue that school has been an instrument of social control. Those in control are businesspersons, professional groups, school administrators, public instruction bureaucrats, political leaders, and school boards. "The most important feature of the school in the twentieth century," Spring explains, "is its role as the major institution for socialization." Schooling prepares people to accept control by dominant institutions and to depend on professional expertise.[26]

Contrary to the outcry in recent years from business leaders and government officials, schools have done what is expected of them and served the American economic system well. They have provided the first line of training for corporate managers and technicians. At the lower end of the job continuum, the school sorting mechanism creates enough low achievers and dropouts to provide the abundant cheap labor that the economy requires. Overall, the school's hidden curriculum produces young people who will fit into the routine, docile, and cooperative culture of economic institutions. It is true that most schools do not

[26]Spring, *Education*, pp. 149, 152.

encourage creative, autonomous, and inquiring behaviors—qualities that innovators and leaders possess. To do so would undermine the primary cultural mission of schools.

The rules set forth by business leaders are changing, but not too much. Some, such as David Kearns of Xerox and John Scully of Apple, say the factory model that schools have operated within for over a century is obsolete. Just as businesses are abandoning top-down bureaucracies and assembly-line procedures, so must schools—if they are to enhance, not hinder, the productivity and competitiveness of our postindustrial economic system. Businesses no longer want only workers who adapt smoothly; they also need people with sufficient language and quantitative skills to be critical thinkers and problem solvers.

Schools have consistently helped provide a literate work force with basic skills. Business leaders, however, view the changing demographics of the United States and get sweaty palms. They see that an increasing proportion of students in our public schools are coming from the ranks of those who have been on the losing end of schooling and the short end of the job market—the poor, some immigrant groups, and other minorities. And they are blaming the schools for this state of affairs. It's a safe bet that schools will respond, as they have in the past, and come to the aid of our economic system.

Despite changes and accommodations, schools will continue to serve their salient function of socialization. As Spring remarks,

> Dependence upon institutions and expertise represents a form of alienation which goes far beyond anything suggested by Karl Marx in the nineteenth century. . . . The triumph of the school in the twentieth century has resulted in the expansion of this concept of alienation. Technology and state capitalism still make work meaningless to the individual and create a condition of alienation from the product of labor. The school increases this alienation by making alien the very ability of the individual to act or create. In school the ability to act is no longer an individual matter but is turned over to experts who grade, rank, and prescribe. Activity, itself, no longer belongs to the individual but to the institution and its experts. In the nineteenth century man lost the product of his labor; in the twentieth century man lost his will.[27]

PEOPLE AS PRODUCERS

When economists construct models of the economy, the work of people is categorized as *labor*, one of the major factors of production. *Land* (all natural resources) is another factor, but only physical *capital* (plants, machinery, and other equipment) embodies stored productivity. People also are a form of capital—"human capital," as American economist Irving Fisher explained in the early 1900s. Human capital, distinguished from physical capital, consists of knowledge, know-how, and organization.

Individuals and society *invest* in education for at least two purposes: for

[27]Ibid., p. 154.

production to benefit the larger society (that is, in human capital) and for consumption to increase individual living standards. Psychologist Lee Cronbach adds that we also invest in education "as a means of certifying social status."[28] The training of skilled specialists is an investment for production inasmuch as it contributes to general economic growth. This schooling also can contribute to the living standard and social status of individuals. Education for leisure and enjoyment is another dimension to learning as consumption. Education that involves literature, art, music, history, mathematics, physical education, and even economics can be intended for consumption or production, depending on how it is used. Deciding precisely when schooling serves production or consumption (or social status) involves splitting hairs.

Some people question the concept of human capital: Education for human growth, they exclaim, cannot be measured quantitatively. Nevertheless, human capital is a powerfully productive source. Factories, roads, ports, and homes were destroyed during World War II, but Europe and Japan rebuilt more quickly than most people thought possible, in large part, because human know-how was not erased. To state a concept simply and directly: Schooling costs money, is undertaken by individuals to earn money, and adds to economic growth.[29]

Since World War II, the Japanese have what seems to be a "supercharged" form of human capital. Judging from the utterly disproportionate success of Vietnamese students in American schools, they too appear to possess a potent combination of ability and motivation. James Coleman and Thomas Hoffer add a twist to our understanding of human capital and explain that the triumphs of Asian-American students are the result of *social capital*. In a district where texts for school use were purchased by students, school authorities discovered that Asian immigrant families purchased two. The second copy was used by the parents to maximize the help they could offer their child. Even when a parent or student does not have an extraordinary amount of human capital, measured in terms of formal schooling, the social capital available in the family may be extremely high.[30]

The Payoff to Individuals

Figure 7-1, showing the annual incomes earned with various years of schooling, is one method of assessing the investment value of schooling. The data show that additional schooling is associated with higher average incomes. In 1985 the average annual income for men over age twenty-five was $23,853 for high school graduates and $32,822 for college graduates. This relationship between income and years of schooling has persisted through the years, even though the amount of schooling attained by the population has increased. The information in Figure 7-1 does not show this, but individuals with the most education benefit progressively

[28]Lee J. Cronbach, "Five Decades of Public Controversy Over Mental Testing," *American Psychologist*, 30 (1975), pp. 1–13.

[29]Maital, *Minds, Markets, and Money*, p. 91.

[30]James S. Coleman and Thomas Hoffer, *Public and Private High Schools: The Impact of Communities* (New York: Basic Books, Inc., Publishers, 1987), pp. 221–23.

Median annual income,
in thousands of dollars

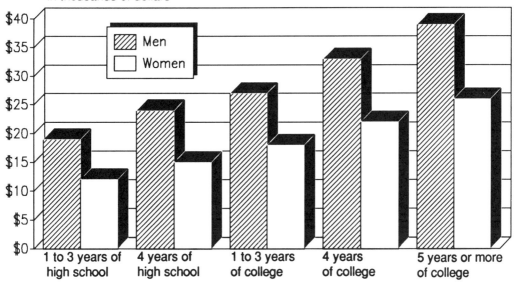

FIGURE 7-1 **Median Annual Income of Full-time Workers 25 Years Old and Over, by Years of School Completed and Sex: 1985**

Source: U.S. Department of Commerce, Bureau of the Census, *Current Population Reports,* Series P-20, "Money Income of Families and Persons in the United States," and Series P-20, No. 154, "Money Income and Poverty Status of Families and Persons in the United States."

more from the number of years on the job. That is, the income differentials, for the same amount of schooling, become wider as the age of the worker increases.

Lifetime earnings of college graduates have been approximately 50 percent greater than those of high school graduates. For example, in 1972 college graduates could expect to earn about $800,000 for a lifetime of work compared with roughly $500,000 for high school graduates. Both groups' earnings have increased over time, doubling every fifteen to twenty years, so the income spread between groups widens over time. As Figure 7-2 illustrates, people with more schooling are less vulnerable to unemployment.

Economists attempt to account for the fact that extended years of schooling delay the individual's income-earning years. As Schlomo Maital points out, the dictum "Time is money" is central to human-capital theory. Acquiring knowledge while earning a college degree is an investment in time.[31] Even using generous discounting procedures, a device to reduce future income to its current equivalent, the contribution of additional schooling to earnings is positive and significant.

It comes as no surprise to college students that schooling costs money. So far we have considered only the monetary returns without any mention of costs.

[31]Maital, *Minds, Markets, and Money,* p. 89.

Another measure of the value of schooling is what economists call the "rate of return on investment in education"; the costs of schooling are needed to arrive at this figure. "Private" costs include (1) tuition and fees paid by individuals; (2) opportunity costs incurred by individuals (namely, income forgone while in school); and (3) incidental school-related costs, like books, supplies, and travel. (Term papers and examination answers purchased on the black market aren't included in this accounting.) Earnings forgone account for more than half the total costs of high school and higher education.

Drawing conclusions from studies on the economic return of an investment is like comparing apples and oranges. Researchers' results depend a great deal on predicting what future earnings will be in different job markets. Studies related to children born in the mid-1940s, and graduating from college in the 1960s, show a 12 to 18 percent "rate of return" on private money for completing college. Because private costs are lower for most high school students, the investment return on completing high school is found to be higher, around 25 percent.

Harvard's Richard Freeman found that the economic return on a college education gradually fell during the 1970s. According to his calculations, the rate of return slipped to between 7 and 8 percent. The earning gap between high school and college graduates also narrowed significantly from about 50 percent to 35 percent. Reasons for the decline in the economic value of college are basic: The

FIGURE 7-2 Unemployment Rates by Educational Attainment

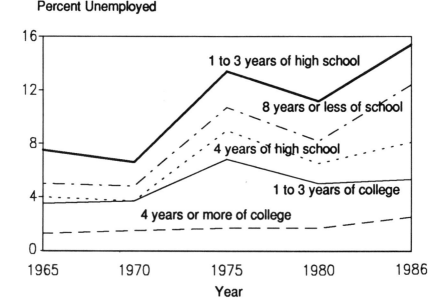

Source: The Condition of Education, 1982 (Washington, D.C.: National Center for Educational Statistics, U.S. Department of Education, 1982), Chart 5.23.

number (supply) of college and university graduates increased considerably during the 1970s, but the demand for these people did not increase at the same pace. A traditional sector of employment for college graduates has been teaching, and public school enrollment declined during that decade. University staffs, the federal bureaucracy, and research and development industries (other major employers for college graduates) have not been expanding enough.

During the 1980s, the economic picture for college graduates began to change. Shortages of teachers in many subjects emerged. Postindustry developments, particularly in high technology, expanded job opportunities, and the service economy grew. (Both draw heavily on people trained in colleges and universities and pay high salaries.) Then job opportunities and wages in the manufacturing economy stagnated, which affected the high school graduate, and the earnings gap reversed direction.

Higher earnings are not the only benefit of a college education and, perhaps, not even the most important. A college education helps enhance a person's depth and breadth in understanding and appreciating aspects of the world—cultural, political, scientific, and artistic. The civic development of American democracy, not to mention global understandings, depends immensely on the liberal education of citizens. H. G. Wells's statement that "history is a race between education and catastrophe" is as pertinent today as when written.

The Payoff to Society

Ultimately, financial gains to an individual are of value to the whole society. Incomes earned are returned to the economy through expenditures for personal consumption, personal savings invested in capital consumption, and personal taxes that end up as public expenditures. The size of the nation's gross national product and income is dependent on these factors. The rate of return on society's investment in schooling is computed in the same manner as for individuals, except that school costs (teachers' salaries, supplies, building maintenance, interest, depreciation on capital) are substituted for individual tuition and fees. Studies indicate that, as should be expected, the return to society runs about 30 to 50 percent less than the return to individuals.[32]

Another way to view the economic value of an investment in schooling is to compute the growth in the economy that might be attributed to it. In the early 1960s, Theodore Schultz and Edward Dennison, using different techniques, came up with similar findings. Schultz calculated the increase in workers' real income in 1957 over 1929, computed the increase in capital investment for education (that is, social costs of schooling), and used various rates of return on the investment in education. From these figures he found what percentage of the increase in earnings per worker could be attributed to schooling. Applying the figures (36 to 70 percent) to the growth of national income, he concluded that "education" ac-

---

[32]Jon T. Innes, Paul B. Jacobson, and Roland J. Pellegrin, *The Economic Returns to Education: A Survey of the Findings* (Eugene: Publication of the Center for the Advanced Study of Educational Administration, University of Oregon, 1965), p. 27, Table 15.

counted for *between 16.6 and 32.2 percent* of this growth in national income (economic growth) from 1929 to 1957.[33]

Dennison chose to compare figures he calculated on the output per laborer due to education with increases in the national income. Adjusting for what he estimated were increases in labor's output (or earnings) arising from factors other than schooling, he found that *23.5 percent* of the growth in the economy from 1930 to 1960 resulted from increased "education" of the labor force.[34]

Nobel laureate Schultz believes that the acquired ability of people—their education, experience, skills, health—are a nation's most important economic resource. This resource, he estimates, is responsible for 80 percent of a nation's income, and the rate of return on education (human capital) exceeds that of physical capital.[35]

A major problem with the economic approach to schooling is that it is based on group (that is, total population) norms and characteristics. Missing are important factors unique to individuals. College graduates earn more than high school graduates, but what would these same people have earned had they only completed high school? It is not likely to be the same as the average high school graduate (or the same as a random individual selected from the population of high school graduates). Individuals who go on to further years of schooling tend to have a variety of personal attributes working in their favor, factors such as intellectual ability, motivation, ambition, imagination, family position in society, and access to economic and educational opportunities. (To his credit, Dennison attempted to account for these "noneducational" factors in his assessment of education and economic growth.) Schooling may not be the only factor in determining future economic returns, though surely it is an important one. As Schultz remarks, America's productive capacity depends more on the quality and drive of the work force than on the technical sophistication of microprocessors and industrial robots.

SOME DISCREPANT FINDINGS

Objectives of schooling, such as knowledge, skills, and custodial care, are difficult to measure (and improve) as economic products. Kenneth Boulding explains that if you compare the dollar cost of the schooling industry as a proportion of the total economy over time with the percentage of children in schools, you get a rough measure of productivity. From 1960 to 1980 schooling expenditures increased from about 5 percent of the GNP to 7 percent, without a commensurate increase in the percentage of children attending school—indicating an increase in the "real price"

[33]Theodore W. Schultz, "Capital Formation by Education," *Journal of Political Economy*, 68, no. 12 (Dec. 1960), pp. 571–83.

[34]Edward F. Dennison, *The Sources of Economic Growth in the United States and the Alternatives Before Us* (New York: Committee for Economic Development, 1962). For a concise summary of both Dennison's and Schultz's findings, see Innes et al., *Economic Returns*, pp. 33–38.

[35]As reported by Marsha Levine, "Public, Private Investments in Schooling," *Education Week*, 1, no. 60 (Nov. 3, 1982), p. 24.

of schooling. During the 1980s, however, relative decreases in spending probably led to an increase in the productivity of schooling. This, of course, is a potentially self-defeating way to make schooling pay off.

Economist Lester Thurow states that schools are a "declining industry" and one of several American institutions responsible for dragging down the nation's productivity. Low productivity is characteristic of service industries in general. Education might not be unique, but economists have difficulty both defining education as a product and increasing its productivity. This helps explain that education is not a consumer good or service as is a house, a car, a piece of furniture, an article of clothing, or even medical care.

The great training robbery. Liberal orthodoxy in the United States is that expenditures on schooling increase productivity as well as educational opportunities. The pervasive slogan throughout the land is "Education pays; stay in school." Sociologist and manpower expert Ivar Berg, in his book with the suggestive title *Education and Jobs: The Great Training Robbery*, takes a skeptical view. Berg does not question either the methodology or the calculations of economists Schultz, Dennison, and others; rather, he makes a simple point that these economists have jumped over the actual variables of productivity and concentrated on incomes earned, a spurious correlate. As another manpower expert, Eli Ginzberg, summarizes in the foreword to Berg's book,

> The critical point is not whether men and women who complete high school or college are able subsequently to earn more than those who don't, but whether their higher earnings are a reflection of better performance as a result of more education or training or of factors other than the diplomas and degrees they have acquired.[36]

Berg's study of the relationship between schooling and employment reveals telling and discrepant findings. To start, he found that additional academic credentials help the worker obtain better-paying jobs; far less clear is how much schooling actually contributes to productivity. He also found that with the passage of time, there is a tendency for more and more people to be in jobs that use less education than they have acquired.[37] Although the data are a little general, they do suggest caution in pursuing "Back to School Drives." The most direct effect of more schooling is likely to be an increase in job dissatisfaction.

In questioning employers, Berg discovered that they continuously raised educational requirements for employment because they believed this would lead to a more ambitious, disciplined, thus productive, work force.[38] Many employers, however, were unaware of the extent to which they had workers with wide differences in education in the same job categories. Employers tend to assume

---

[36]Ivar Berg, *Education and Jobs: The Great Training Robbery* (New York: Praeger Publishers, Inc., 1970), p. xii.

[37]Ibid., pp. 51–60.

[38]Ibid., pp. 70–75.

erroneously that employees in the high-paying job areas are the more educated. In some areas, such as selling insurance or real estate, workers with less education but more experience perform better and earn more. Indeed, the frequency of job turnover is positively related to schooling level.[39] Employers also tend to justify higher schooling demands as a hedge on the future, when workers will be promoted into higher ranks, where the education is needed. Ironically, Berg found that only a small percentage are promoted substantially over time and that the more highly qualified are likely to have departed out of dissatisfaction in search of better jobs.[40]

According to Berg there is little evidence to support the belief that workers with educational credentials are more productive. This, combined with the findings that many workers are underemployed (in jobs requiring less education and skills than they possess) and that there is a lack of demand for workers in many lower job categories, leads to an interesting though perhaps unsettling policy. The solution to unemployment and productivity with certain groups is not to send the dropout back to school or assure that women are educated to their full potential or extend vocational training, but rather to upgrade those underemployed now, fill the open ranks with those suitably qualified, and generally match much more accurately job requirements and workers' competencies.

Educational opportunity.   Christopher Jencks added another twist to the controversy in his study of economic inequality and equal educational opportunity. Jencks and his colleagues at Harvard's Center for Educational Policy Research reassessed much of the data surrounding the interrelation of family background, schooling, and earnings, and came up with convention-shattering findings. There is little evidence, they found, that school reform can substantially reduce the extent of cognitive inequality, as measured by tests of verbal fluency, reading comprehension, or mathematical skill.[41] Inadequate basic cognitive skills, Jencks argued, are the key reason given by reformers to explain why poor children cannot escape poverty. It is believed that without these skills they are unable to obtain well-paying jobs. In turn, educational reform is claimed to be the best mechanism for alleviating this plight of the poor, an assumption Jencks concluded was unfounded. Even if it were true that schools could substantially affect cognitive skills, it is not true, added Jencks, that the economic status of many people would be affected.

The reason some people end up richer than others depends on things other than cognitive skills and schooling.[42] What these things are is not clear, but Jencks and his coresearchers offer some suggestions that by now sound familiar: specialized competencies (unrelated to intellectual abilities), personality, job market

[39]Ibid., pp. 87–101.

[40]Ibid., pp. 76–80, 89–90.

[41]Christopher Jencks, et al., *Inequality: A Reassessment of the Effects of Family and Schooling in America* (New York: Basic Books, Inc., Publishers, 1972), pp. 86–102.

[42]Ibid., pp. 221–25.

TABLE 7-2 Median Family Incomes (1987 Dollars)

1949	$14,868
1959	$21,193
1969	$29,244
1973	$30,820
1979	$30,669
1987	$30,853

Source: U.S. Bureau of the Census, *Current Population Reports,* Series P-60, No. 162, Money Income of Households, Familes, and Persions in the United States: 1987 (Washington D.C.: U.S. Government Printing Office 1989), p. 2.

conditions, weather, availability of natural resources, and luck, for a start.[43] Family background, according to Jencks, and a college degree are the most important factors contributing to economic success.

If the ultimate aim of social policy makers is to eliminate poverty and generally distribute incomes more equally in our economy, then Jencks has some suggestions: Constrain employers to reduce wage disparities among their workers, make taxes more progressive, provide income supplements to the needy, and provide free public services for those who cannot afford adequate services in the private sector. Unless we are willing to invoke such direct socialistic measures, poverty and inequality will remain in our nation.

THE HUMAN SIDE OF GLOBAL COMPETITIVENESS

From the end of World War II to 1973, median family income in the United States grew steadily—in real terms. In 1947 it was less than $15,000 (in 1987 dollars); by 1973 it had risen to over $30,000. After that year, incomes stagnated, as Table 7-2 illustrates.

Wages and salaries of individual workers, explains economist Frank Levy, fared even more poorly than did living standards. Economists measure living standards in terms of income per capita (i.e., income per man, woman, and child). Large numbers of women have entered the labor force since the early 1970s to bolster sagging family incomes and actually increase per capita income. Even though income per worker (earnings) stagnated, there were more workers to support fewer dependents.

Not all workers have been affected equally by stagnating earnings. Since the mid-1970s, two trends have emerged: the growing income gap between high school and college graduates, and the growing inequality among children.

The dilemma of high school educated men begins, explains Levy, with the federal budget deficit. The huge budget deficits occurred in the early 1980s when President Reagan and Congress cut individual and corporate taxes by billions of

[43]Ibid., pp. 226–32.

dollars but would not cut government expenditures correspondingly. Actually, wages had been stagnant since 1973, largely because of slow economic growth and high inflation that beset this period. To offset stagnating wages, workers supported tax cuts (which would put money in their bank accounts) and opposed spending cuts (which would reduce someone's income). As Levy adds, in "this way, wage stagnation helped set the stage for the federal budget deficit."

The budget deficit, in turn, was a major cause of the trade deficit. This deficit, Levy explains, "meant that interest rates had to remain relatively high . . . to attract the necessary funds to buy additional bonds that the government had to issue." The high rates were critical to attracting foreign investors; their need for U.S. currency, in turn, to buy our securities caused a substantial rise in the international value of the dollar. The result was to make our exports very expensive abroad and make foreign imports relatively cheap. Although many consumers of foreign-made stereos, VCRs, and autos benefited, the worker armed only with a high school diploma found that U.S. manufacturing plants were cutting back production and laying off workers, or at least constraining wage increases. Table 7-3 shows the effect on the earning power of young men.

The second trend involves the growing inequality among children. The growth of female-headed households has emerged as a major demographic issue during the past two decades. In 1970, about 10 percent of all children lived in families headed by a single woman; today, over 20 percent are in such families. At the same time, a growing number of children are living in families with two wage earners. "The result," Levy adds, "is more poor children and greater inequality in the incomes of families with children." Between 1973 and 1986, the proportion of children in families with incomes over $50,000 (in 1989 dollars) increased from 16 percent to 21 percent, whereas the proportion of children in families with incomes less than $10,000 also increased from 10 percent to 16 percent. One out of every six children lives in economic poverty—and the numbers are growing.[44]

QUALITY OF EDUCATIONAL OPPORTUNITY: A SPECIAL PROBLEM IN FINANCING SCHOOLS

"The contrast in money available to the school in a wealthy suburb and to the schools in a large city," wrote James Conant several decades ago, "jolts one's notions of the meaning of equality of opportunity."[45] Since Conant made these observations nearly a generation ago, steps have been made to reduce this disparity. The federal government has mounted small-scaled but vigorous efforts to increase educational resources for children of inner cities. State governments also have worked to close the gap in financial resources among communities, but substantial inequities remain.

[44]Frank Levy, "Paying for College: A New Look at Family Income Trends," *The College Board Review*, no. 152 (Summer 1989), pp. 18–21, 32–33.

[45]James B. Conant, *Slums and Suburbs* (New York: McGraw-Hill Book Company, Inc., 1961), p. 10.

TABLE 7-3 The Declining Value of a High School Diploma (1986 Dollars)

	AVERAGE INCOME OF 30-YR.-OLD MAN, 12 YRS. SCHOOL	AVERAGE INCOME OF 30-YR.-OLD MAN, 4 YRS. COLL.	HIGH SCHOOL–COLLEGE INCOME GAP
1973	$24,338	$28,157	16%
1986	$18,257	$27,309	50%

The quest for social and economic equality has been an elusive pursuit of Americans but one ingrained in the ethic of our culture. The public school has been the primary instrument in this search, and "equality of educational opportunity" has been its rallying principle.

In the United States, educational opportunity has taken on a special importance as the handmaiden to economic opportunity. The meaning of equal educational opportunity as historically applied included several elements:

1. Providing a *free* education through a given grade level, which constituted the principal entry point to the labor force.
2. Providing a *common curriculum* for all children, regardless of background.
3. Providing that children from diverse backgrounds attend the *same school.*
4. Providing equality within a given *locality*, since local districts defined the area of tax support and attendance.[46]

The first two criteria in large part have been attained. The third and fourth, however, have been stormy issues in recent years; the last is of special importance for school financing.

Cases in Point

Several court cases illustrate the debate over local school funding and the pursuit of educational equality. *Serrano* v. *Priest* (1971), tried in the California Supreme Court, is a landmark case. This suit and others involving school financing are anchored in the equal protection clause of the Fourteenth Amendment to the U.S. Constitution, which prohibits federal and state governments from discriminating unfairly between classes of people. This clause requires all people to be treated by law in the same manner, unless a case can be made for differential treatment in the best interest of society.

The plaintiffs in *Serrano* alleged that as a result of the public school financing plan in California they were required to pay a higher local property tax rate than residents of other districts in the state to obtain the same or lesser educational opportunities. In examining the state public school financing plans, the court found that over 90 percent of public school funds came from (1) local real property

---

[46]James Coleman, "The Concept of Equality of Educational Opportunity," *Harvard Educational Review,* 38, no. 1 (Winter 1968), p. 11.

taxes and (2) the state school fund. Of these two, the local property tax was the primary source. This tax, they added, was based mainly on the value of private property within a school district; the value per pupil varied widely throughout the state. They also found that the various methods for allocating state school funds to local districts did not offset the disparities created by local financing, and in part, widened the gap between the rich and poor districts.

The court argued that allotting more educational dollars to one district than another, on the basis of local family, commercial, and industrial wealth, is relying on irrelevant and arbitrary factors. It then ruled that the level of spending on children's education must not be a function of wealth, other than that of the state itself. The Supreme Court of California said that the state will have to find an equitable formula.[47]

A U.S. Supreme Court ruling just two years after the *Serrano* decision reversed the momentum toward more equitable financing. In *San Antonio Independent School District* v. *Rodriguez* (1973), the Court held that disparities in school spending among districts do not violate the Fourteenth Amendment's equal protection clause because education is not a "fundamental right" guaranteed by the Constitution. Over a decade later, the Texas Supreme Court, in *Edgewood* v. *Kirby* (1989), negated the *Rodriguez* decision—for Texas at that time.

The Texas Supreme Court found the state's methods of funding schools to be unconstitutional. It cited "glaring disparities" among rich and poor districts in terms of their ability to raise and spend funds for schooling. "Property-poor districts are trapped in a cycle of poverty from which there is no opportunity to free themselves," wrote the Chief Justice. Because of an inadequate tax base, poor districts must tax at significantly higher rates just to meet minimum accreditation requirements. The location of new industry, argued the court, is influenced by tax rates and the quality of schools. Thus, property-poor districts with high tax rates and inferior schools are unable to attract new industry and have little opportunity to improve their tax base.

In a unanimous decision, the justices concluded that school districts must have "substantially equal access to similar revenues per pupil at similar levels of tax effort." They made it clear that the existing system was a "band-aid" approach that must be changed if the state was to meet the Texas constitution's equal rights guarantee to establish, support, and maintain "an efficient system of public free schools" that provided for "a general diffusion of knowledge."[48]

This Texas decision came just a few years after New York State's high court in *Levittown* v. *Nyquist* (1982) said that the disadvantage placed on poor school districts who had to rely heavily on local property taxes did not violate the state or federal constitutions. This court ruled that any attempt to make uniform "educational opportunities" across districts would undermine local control of schools. Education, it explained, is not a fundamental right.

[47]Thomas A. Shannon, "Has the Fourteenth Done It Again?" *Phi Delta Kappan*, 53, no. 8 (Apr. 1972), pp. 466–71.

[48]"School Financing in Texas Declared Unconstitutional," *Education Week*, 9, no. 6 (Oct. 11, 1989), pp. 1, 20.

As matters stand, disparities among school districts within a state to raise school revenue are not protected by the federal Constitution. School finance issues apparently will be decided in state courts based on the provisions of individual state constitutions. In the wake of the 1989 Texas decision, similar lawsuits can be expected to work their way through the courts of other states.

The Financial Picture

The U.S. Constitution makes no mention of federal responsibilities for the education of citizens. This function is delegated to the states, and every state constitution provides for the establishment of a system of public schools. Legisla-

FIGURE 7-3   National Trends in Revenue Sources for Public Elementary and Secondary Education: Selected School Years Ending 1920–1987

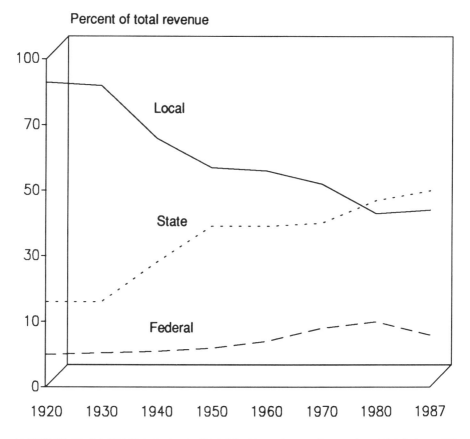

Percent of total revenue

In 1978–79, for the first time revenues for public elementary and secondary schools from state sources exceeded revenues from local sources.

Sources: National Center for Educational Statistics, *Digest of Education Statistics, 1988,* National Education Association, *Estimates of School Statistics, 1986–87.*

tures in all states have the responsibility to provide financing for public education from resources available in the state. And state government, together with local school districts, have been the major sources of revenue. The federal government chips in roughly 6 *percent* of the total school revenue (down from nearly 10 percent in 1980) to support specific programs including handicapped education, bilingual education, gifted and talented programs, vocational education, school lunch programs, and others.

In 1970 local support for public education amounted to about *54 percent* of the total school dollars, and state support the remaining *39 percent*. As a result of the *Serrano* decision in California and others that followed in several states, school finance came to rely less on local property taxes and more on state revenue sources. By 1988 the state's share stood at *50 percent*, and local government funding dropped to *44 percent*.

Local support has reached as high as 89.1 percent (District of Columbia) and as low as 0.1 percent (Hawaii), as shown in Table 7-4. State support in turn has been extended from 89.4 percent (Hawaii) to 6.9 percent (New Hampshire). The federal government's largest contribution has gone to Kentucky (13.3 percent) and the least to Connecticut (3.5 percent).

More important for equality in education are the total resources available and actual expenditures among states and within each state. In 1987 over $160 billion was spent to operate the nation's elementary and secondary schools. The level of support ranged from $8,253 per pupil in Alaska to $2,362 in Mississippi, with the national average standing at $3,752.

By the 1980s the situation had changed: Public school finances were squeezed from several directions. Federal funding under the Reagan administration for such programs as remedial reading and math was cut. Feeling the effects of the prolonged economic slump early in the decade, state educational revenues were tightened. Referenda, such as Proposition 13 in California, which limits property taxes, make it difficult for local governments to pick up the slack. The best hope for raising needed educational dollars while promoting equality lay in tapping state sources.

TABLE 7-4   Revenue Sources 1985–1986 (Selected States)

FEDERAL RECEIPTS		STATE RECEIPTS		LOCAL AND OTHER RECEIPTS	
Kentucky	13.3	Hawaii	89.4	District of Columbia	89.1
New Mexico	12.4	New Mexico	75.4	New Hampshire	88.9
Tennessee	12.3	Washington	74.1	Nebraska	69.3
Oregon	6.6	Maine	50.1	Tennessee	45.2
Nebraska	6.5	Montana	48.0	Texas	45.0
Missouri	6.5	Texas	47.6	Maine	43.7
Wyoming	3.6	Nebraska	24.3	New Mexico	12.2
Connecticut	3.5	New Hampshire	6.9	Hawaii	0.1
National	6.7		49.4		43.9

Source: U.S. Department of Education, National Center for Educational Statistics.

The differences between New York, New Jersey, or Massachusetts and many southern states is significant. Part of this difference is explained by the wealth available in different states. However, a maldistribution of wealth does not account for the total difference in school revenue. Unfortunately, many states that provide lower per-pupil school expenditures are making less effort. These states levy lower tax rates on private property to support schools than do such states as Minnesota, Wisconsin, Iowa, and Oregon.

Federal support to states, which is less than 10 percent of total school revenues, would not offset the differences among states even if more federal grants were based on need. Short of a fundamental change in the financial structure of American schooling, which may take a constitutional amendment, the revenue inequities among states are not likely to be reduced significantly.

As great as the financial difference is among states, it is even greater among school districts within most states. In California, for example, the wealthiest district has fifty times as much local wealth per pupil as the poorest and about triple the total revenue per child (after state and federal grants). In New York, the richest district in per-pupil wealth has approximately fourteen times as much local wealth as the poorest, and the revenue disparity is approximately two to one. In Texas, the richest district is 700 times richer than the poorest; the difference in local revenue is over twice as much.[49]

The Impact of School Resources

So far, this discussion of the equality of educational opportunity has focused on the resources (or inputs) for schooling. But for this approach to be useful, money provided for school buildings, teachers' salaries, books, programs, and the rest must have positive effects on learning. The concept of equality in education, treated as equality in inputs, is based on the assumption that school *inputs* lead to educational *outputs*.

James Coleman, who headed a major survey of equal educational opportunity in the mid-1960s, empirically detected a gap between input and output. Coleman's group carried out their study under a mandate in the Civil Rights Act of 1964. The study pointed out that the meaning of "equal educational opportunity" had undergone modification as a result of the historic *Brown v. The Board of Education* Supreme Court decision in 1954. Here the Court ruled that separate-but-equal school facilities were not enough. Implicit in this argument, Coleman pointed out, was the position that we need to assess the effects of schooling on the student. That is, equal school resources were no guarantee of equal school effectiveness. Unfortunately, this notion was largely overshadowed by the emphasis on the racial aspects of the decision. In Coleman's subsequent review of existing studies and new data, his group came up with interesting, though disturbing, findings.[50]

[49]*Financing the Public Schools: A Search for Equality* (Bloomington, Ind.: Phi Delta Kappa, 1975), pp. 18–21.

[50]Coleman, "Concept of Equality," p. 15.

The Coleman group examined the relation of school inputs to their effects on the academic achievement of black and white students. The order of importance in inputs, both in schools attended by black children and those attended by white children, were facilities and curriculum materials, least important; quality of teachers, next; and educational backgrounds of fellow students, most important. The difference in the availability of these same inputs in those schools was precisely the same: facilities and curriculum materials were the least variant between schools; quality of teachers next; and student backgrounds, the most variant. Said differently, those resources over which the school has the most control are the least important, and vice versa.[51] This is not to say that educational resources have no effect, or even very little effect, on learning, but rather that the effect is remarkably the same for everyone.

We can make sure that schools have equal library, classroom, and playground resources, Coleman and others argue, but this does not mean that the quality of schooling is equal. This finding, however, has been challenged. Herbert Walberg and Sue Rasher found ample evidence, in contrast with Coleman and Jencks, to show that the amount of schooling, the opportunity to learn, and the quality of schools do enhance learning.[52]

Even if the inputs to learning are minor or overshadowed by family and neighborhood factors, this is not justification for maintaining a system of unequal resources. Every schoolchild has a right to an equal share of the state's resources.

SCHOOL FINANCE REFORM

The revenue gap among school districts has been reduced mostly by state funds. Different states use various methods and formulas to share funds with local districts. In principle, the financing systems have the potential of equalizing school revenues among districts, at least in those states that shoulder much of the costs. In practice, however, most plans are not applied vigorously. School financing is very political and often dominates educational issues before state legislatures. Wealthier districts can apply substantial pressure not to reduce the redistribution of funds to schools.

As a result of decisions such as *Serrano v. Priest* in California, many states have adopted new school financing systems. Most of these are a variation of the following two plans.

In *local initiative equalizing,* the amount of school money for a district depends on the local tax effort (the tax rate local citizens are willing to levy) rather then the wealth of a community. Theoretically, richer districts feel the burden of higher tax rates less than poorer districts. Nevertheless, poorer districts often tax themselves as high as or higher than wealthier districts but are unrewarded for the

[51]James S. Coleman et al., *Equality of Educational Opportunity* (Washington, D.C.: U.S. Department of Health, Education, and Welfare, Office of Education, 1966), pp. 20–22.

[52]Herbert J. Walberg and Sue Pinsur Rasher, "The Ways Schooling Makes a Difference," *Phi Delta Kappan,* 58, no. 9 (May 1977), pp. 703–707.

sacrifice. A local-initiative system increases the state aid to districts in proportion to the local units' effort to raise tax revenues.

District power equalizing, in which a state establishes the amount of revenue to be guaranteed local districts for each level of tax effort, is a more radical approach. It reduces the revenue disparity among districts but does not eliminate differences. If a local tax levy raises less than the guaranteed amount for that level of taxation, the state makes up the difference from a fund generated by general taxes. If the local tax produces an excess, this extra revenue goes into the general fund to be redistributed to poorer districts. In effect, the state places a lid on the amount rich districts may spend, a situation that is not popular with wealthy districts, which complain that such a system jeopardizes high-quality programs.

A possible solution is for *states* to assume *full funding* of public schools. All revenues for schooling would be collected by the state and distributed to school districts on an equal per-pupil basis. This is a simple, precise way of eliminating the wide differences in money that exist among schools. It also would cut school financing ties from the regressive and sluggish property tax. Opponents of full-state funding muster several objections, including the argument that it would burden current state tax revenue sources and create even larger state educational bureaucracies.

These plans totally ignore school revenue differences among states. Short of massive federal infusions or full federal funding, which are not likely to occur, a significant inequality will remain. Education, as we pointed out, is a state function; barring a constitutional amendment, it doesn't appear that any federal schemes to reduce inequities substantially would be held constitutional.

Innovations in Response to Crisis

Although state governments' share of revenue for public elementary and secondary schools has gradually increased since about 1970, most school districts struggle to meet their expenses. Schools have cut back programs, or tried to, but families object to this cost cutting. In many communities, booster groups for athletic teams, bands, and other activities raise funds to support these extracurricular programs as a way to help meet burgeoning budgets. In these tight times, states and school districts are resorting to education's version of "creative financing."

Educational foundations.   Battered by Proposition 13, which was passed in the early 1980s, many California school districts have set up tax-exempt foundations, much as charities do, to raise money from citizens. Some school districts have raised funds through community activities, and others have solicited donations to support or retain specific programs. A few large school districts in other parts of the country, such as Dallas and Pittsburgh, also have set up educational foundations to augment tax revenues.

West Virginia was the first state to have a statewide educational foundation to promote a formal partnership between business and public education. The West

Virginia Education Fund is a nonprofit private organization, governed largely by leaders from business and industry, which solicits funds from business and channels the money to education. Several other states also have set up foundations, and the idea is growing.

The lottery luster.   Many state governments during the past decade found what looks, feels, and jingles like the ultimate "money tree"—a lottery. By 1988, twenty-eight states had lotteries (fourteen were started since 1980); eight have earmarked the proceeds of their lotteries for education.[53] Ten other states put the profits into the general fund, which may affect appropriations for education. As we write, most of the remaining state legislatures are debating the lottery, and many also will be in the lottery business within a few years.

A decade or two ago the lottery idea would have been turned down on moral grounds. Or, as economists argue, when you cut through the hoopla, it is little more than a regressive tax that takes from those who can least afford it—lower income families. Others have called it a "tax on the desperate." Acceptance by the public, however, has grown over the years, and state legislatures see it as an easy target for needed funds. How long this will last remains to be seen; the lottery is an "infant business." New lotteries typically start out raising funds at rates higher than predicted, but when the novelty wears off, states find themselves having to spend more and more on advertising to promote new games.

The payoff to education also is suspect. Florida, for example, found that when you extract all costs of operating a lottery—prizes, marketing, and administration—public schools are left money to fund less than seven school days during the year. In California, the lottery accounts for only 3 percent of the total school budget. Lotteries were not intended to pay total costs of education, even when funds were earmarked solely for schools, but often that is not the public's impression. People tend to believe that a lottery supplies a much larger proportion of the education budget than it does and are less inclined to support other local and state funding for education. The jury is still out on the benefit of lotteries to schools, but school officials are nervous. Some educators feel that schools are actually worse off with this questionable innovation.

Private Foundations Get Involved

American businesses are taking a new interest in the quality of public schools. As changes in the postindustrial workplace accelerate, many companies have an increasingly greater need for skilled human capital—workers and managers who possess problem-solving skills and who can adapt to rapidly changing technology. Businesses also recognize that schools are as much a part of a community's infrastructure as are parks, roads, water, and sewage systems. The quality of local schools serves to attract (or discourage) people and companies in moving to a

[53]States that designate lottery money to education are Illinois, Michigan, New Hampshire, New Jersey, New York, Ohio, California, and Florida.

community. Modern vocational training facilities, many businesses now realize, are not good enough in today's economy. A liberal education that emphasizes literacy in math, science, English, and the social studies is more important than job-specific skills.

Communities often must balance the need for school revenues against the use of tax favors to attract businesses. Because public schools depend on local property taxes, they are faced with tough economic choices. Progressive business attitudes, motivated both by self-interest and social concerns that involve the importance of quality education, can lead communities away from the darkness of this ambiguity.

More and higher taxes, however, are not the only answer. The cost of schooling in modern society, in which schools have taken over many education duties that once were shared by the community, has become increasingly expensive. Although contributions to elementary and secondary schools are still less than 10 percent of charitable budgets, they have been increasing in recent years. Large private foundations that traditionally have given to the schools, such as the Carnegie Corporation and the Ford Foundation, are now being joined by others. Foundations established by major corporations, such as ARCO, EXXON, Bell-South, and Matsushita, are providing funds for curriculum development, teacher renewal, and research. In many cases, the funds are tied to programs that demonstrate a link between schooling and economic productivity. At the local level, corporations are participating in "adopt-a-school" programs and supporting efforts to help "at-risk" youngsters.

The heightened interest of many corporate leaders in public education has an added dividend for schools: corporations are speaking out in support of tax hikes. Many see that "reschooling," just as with "reindustrializing," society takes large sums of public expenditures.

Tuition Tax Credit

The parents of students who attend private and parochial schools in Minnesota and Iowa are aided by those states' tuition tax credit law. This includes approximately 10 percent of the school-age population in each state. The amount of the financial aid is small, but there is pressure to increase the assistance.

A federal tuition tax, once advocated by the Reagan Administration, has been debated for several years. Unlike educational vouchers, which redirect public funds from schools to users, the tuition tax credit simply provides relief to families who have tuition expenses at private schools.

Advocates of the tuition tax credit argue that it would reimburse private school families for some of the tax dollars they are obliged to pay in support of public schools and help children of lower- and middle-income families attend schools of their choice. Critics point out that everyone (society and communities as a whole) benefits from public schools and that tax credits for private school tuition are damaging to public school systems.

State aid to parochial and private schools does exist on a large scale. Many states provide a variety of "auxiliary services" for private schools, including grants for textbooks, special education programs, health services, and bus transportation, which have been declared constitutional. Some states, particularly those with large Roman Catholic populations, lend other instructional materials, such as laboratory equipment, and even permit released time for religious instruction in public schools. The constitutionality of a tuition tax credit, however, is uncertain.

REDUCING THE BURDEN ON SCHOOLS

Despite an underlying theme in this chapter—that public schools are relatively underfinanced—the ultimate solution to school financial woes may be to decrease costs by reducing programs and services. All the dollars that can be squeezed from local and state tax bases, plus that supplemented by business, foundations, and the federal government, are not likely to be enough to pay for the education we demand of schools. A cutback in many programs and services will not necessarily diminish the quality of schooling and may enhance it. The economics of education can be paradoxical.

Many responsibilities related to the general education of young people have been heaped on the schools. In addition to teaching language and writing skills, mathematics, science, and other academic knowledge, schools are asked to teach cooking, sewing, auto mechanics, typing, bookkeeping, and driving, as well as information on drugs, alcohol, money, sex, and even firearms. These all may be critical skills or knowledge for survival in our society, but they cost schools millions of dollars annually, and much that is taught distracts from the primary task of schools.

As already argued in other chapters, schools can and should be held accountable for teaching the knowledge and skills of a core curriculum as well as elective courses that help young people take their place in the working world. The other general-survival competencies are more efficiently taught in other agencies of society—in homes, churches, youth groups, community organizations, vocational-technical centers, some magnet programs, and even businesses.

● ── ●

Case Study: Equalization of Educational Opportunity

Your state always has taken pride in its educational systems, but the property tax base varies considerably from one school district to another. Some districts have large manufacturing firms, some are havens for wealthy people who have built expensive homes, and a few are fortunate enough to have oil wells. These districts can raise considerably more money than the majority of districts in small cities with modest tax bases, poor rural areas, or financially pressed urban centers.

Place yourself in the role of a state legislator dealing with the question of equality of educational opportunity. Devise a state school-tax plan that would distribute revenue from wealthy to poor districts. Also consider whether or not you should limit the amount of money that rich districts can spend per pupil, how much poor districts should be forced to raise before they are given aid, and the minimum (and maximum) levels of money per pupil a district should have to support its schools.

Thought Questions

1. Are public schools and other public buildings more austere and generally less attractive than private corporate buildings? What evidence from your observations illustrates this?

2. The cost of schooling in America is now over $200 billion a year and rising. Do you think it is justified that we spend this much on schooling? Is the money we spend on schooling in America wisely spent? What can be done to reduce these high costs?

3. Why are many people refusing to pay any more taxes for schools?

4. How much money should a teacher make at the start of his or her career? After twenty years? Should teachers receive salary increases for acquiring more college credits or advanced degrees? Why is or isn't this system rational? What would be a better system?

5. Why do teachers earn modest incomes when compared with other professionals of equal or less formal schooling? Is this justified? Are economic earnings really an important issue in considering the satisfactions of professional careers?

6. Has education in America provided the individual with otherwise unattainable economic opportunities that enhance one's freedom, or has the individual been accommodated to the needs of big business? What arguments presented in the text are the most convincing? How do these compare with your personal observations?

7. What are you worth in "human capital" terms — in a dollar figure? Is it possible to say with any accuracy? Some people say a price cannot be put on a human life. What do you believe? Do you believe in capitalist theory? Capitalism holds that everything is a commodity with a monetary value. Are there any contradictions in your beliefs?

8. Robert Hutchins remarked that there has been a nasty rumor spreading for several decades to the effect that an individual could become rich by going to college. Not only is this not true, Hutchins believed, but also vocational, technical, professional studies — and economically beneficial training in general — should have no part in education. How would you support Hutchins's statement? Disclaim it? What do you believe concerning this issue?

9. If Coleman, Jencks, and others are correct in their analysis that effects of schooling on cognitive abilities and economic earnings are negligible, how do you explain the large individual and social expenditures on schooling? Is it more reasonable to challenge the Coleman and Jencks theses? What difference does it make, then, if there is an unequal distribution of resources among school districts in the nation?

Practical Activities

1. Attend a school board meeting or public hearing on the school budget for the coming year. Briefly describe the major budget items, the discussion or presentation of the budget, and your reactions.

2. Obtain a map of school districts in your state and list each district's per-pupil expenditure. Color-code your map to illustrate the variations in per-pupil expenditure. If possible, locate and include other related data, such as median family income in each district and tax effort (tax revenue raised for public schools as a percent of personal income in the district). Indicate your data source and discuss your results.

3. Obtain a copy of the current salary schedule for some school district. If possible, select the district where you plan to teach or an area where you would like to teach. Using information about the cost of living, prepare a budget for a family of four and see if you can live within the starting salary.

4. Devise a short questionnaire concerning citizens' reasons for supporting public schools. Areas to survey include major purposes of schools in a community, benefits of public education to society, most and least important areas of the school curriculum, most important areas of a high school economics course (for example, economic theory, consumer economics, business operations), reasons for students to get a college education, and benefits of college to the individual and to the nation. (If you can obtain a large enough sample, separate the responses from high school students and adults.) Tabulate the results and write a summary of your findings.

5. a. Design a semester's course in economics for either a high school or a junior high school. Include the units to be covered, major ideas or topics in each unit, and at least one general objective for each unit.

   b. If you are preparing to be a history, geography, or government teacher, design a major unit on economics as it relates to your subject. Include general objectives, an outline, and potential learning activities to employ.

   c. If you are preparing to be an elementary school teacher, design a plan for including economics in your social studies curriculum. Either select a grade level and develop a detailed plan or present a general scheme for including economics in the kindergarten to sixth-grade curriculum.

Bibliography

Books

BENSON, CHARLES S., *The Economics of Public Education*, 2nd ed. Boston: Houghton Mifflin Company, 1968.

BERG, IVAR, *Education and Jobs: The Great Training Robbery*. New York: Praeger Publishers, Inc., 1970.

BERKE, JOEL S., ALAN K. CAMPBELL, and ROBERT J. GOETTEL, *Financing Equal Educational Opportunity: Alternatives for State Finance*. Berkeley, Calif.: McCutchan Publishing Corporation, 1972.

BOWLES, SAMUEL, and HERBERT GINTIS, *Schooling in Capitalist America: Educational Reform and the Contradictions of Economic Life.* New York: Basic Books, Inc., Publishers, 1976.

COLEMAN, JAMES S., et al., *Equality of Educational Opportunity.* Washington, D.C.: U.S. Department of Health, Education, and Welfare, Office of Education, 1966.

COONS, JOHN, WILLIAM H. CUNE, and STEPHEN D. SUGARMAN, *Private Wealth and Public Education.* Cambridge, Mass.: The Belknap Press of Harvard University, Press, 1970.

FREEMAN, RICHARD B., *The Over-educated American.* New York: Academic Press, 1976.

GALBRAITH, JOHN KENNETH, *The Affluent Society,* 2nd ed. Boston: Houghton Mifflin Company, 1969.

_____, *Economics and the Public Purpose.* Boston: Houghton Mifflin Company, 1973.

GARMS, WALTER I., JAMES W. GUTHERIE, and LAWRENCE C. PIERCE, *School Finance: The Economics and Politics of Public Education.* Englewood Cliffs, N.J.: Prentice-Hall, Inc., 1978.

GREER, COLIN, *The Great School Legend: A Revisionist Interpretation of American Public Education.* New York: The Viking Press, 1972.

HEILBRONER, ROBERT L., *The Making of Economic Society,* 5th ed. Englewood Cliffs, N.J.: Prentice-Hall, Inc., 1975.

JENCKS, CHRISTOPHER, et al., *Inequality: A Reassessment of the Effect of Family and Schooling in America.* New York: Basic Books, Inc., Publishers, 1972.

KNELLER, GEORGE F., *Education and Economic Thought.* New York: John Wiley & Sons, Inc., 1968.

MAITAL, SHLOMO, *Minds, Markets, and Money: Psychological Foundations of Economic Behavior.* New York: Basic Books, Inc., Publishers, 1982.

SPRING, JOEL, *Education and the Rise of the Corporate State.* Boston: Beacon Press, 1972.

_____, *The Sorting Machine: National Educational Policy Since 1945.* New York: David McKay Company, Inc., 1976.

8

Race, Equality,
Ethnicity, and Education

The Goal of the Common School, 1909

Everywhere these people [immigrants] tend to settle in groups or settlements, and to set up here their national manners, customs, and observances. Our task is to break up these groups or settlements, to assimilate and amalgamate these people as part of our American race, and to implant in their children, as far as can be done, the Anglo-Saxon conception of righteousness, law and order, and popular government, and to awaken in them a reverence for our democratic institutions and for those things in our national life which we as a people hold to be of abiding worth.[1]

Diversity

For many decades it was unfashionable to suggest that all people are not the same. It was equally unpopular to insist that we can learn more about a culture from its differences than from its similarities to other cultures, and that the basis of human nature is probably more visible in human diversity than through the relatively few ways in which we are really and fundamentally the same.[2]

Although the culture of the United States has been influenced by its many races, nationalities, and ethnic groups, it has been and continues to be a reflection of the dominant Anglo-Saxon immigrants who by 1800 were the most powerful and influential group. The challenge we face today is to find a way to foster the richness that diversity produces while simultaneously developing a common "American culture" to nourish unity and common purpose. The challenge is to create a workable and just pluralistic society.

The struggle toward justice, equality, and pluralism has been hampered and complicated throughout our history by class and racial prejudices. The history of the United States contains too many episodes in which members of various ethnic

[1]Ellwood P. Cubberley, *Changing Conceptions of Education* (Boston: Houghton Mifflin, 1909), pp. 15–16.
[2]Jamake Highwater, *The Primal Mind* (New York: Harper & Row, Publishers, Inc., 1981), p. 9.

and racial groups have been denied "life, liberty, and happiness" for us to be completely sanguine about finding just solutions quickly.

Throughout our history of abuse and oppression there have been those who have argued and fought for equal treatment for all. With the passage of the Civil Rights Act of 1964 the proponents of equality under the law gained a powerful legal tool for eliminating discrimination in jobs, housing, and schooling.

Public schools have been and continue to be at the very center of the civil rights controversy. Education is considered by many to be the cornerstone for achievement in America. There is a belief that if there is "real" educational equity, it will create equity in the rest of society; that equal educational opportunity will result in equal pay, equal opportunity for jobs, equal housing, and equal treatment in the courts.

ETHNICITY

By the year 2000, one out of every three elementary and secondary school students will be from an ethnic minority family. To continue to refer to these groups as "minorities" is becoming increasingly problematic. Census projections for the year 2000 indicate that the so-called minority students will be in the majority in such states as California and Texas. Minority students already outnumber "white" students in many urban centers. Although "minority" is still a useful concept for some purposes, "ethnicity" is more useful for thinking about the racial and ethnic problems that face the nation and its schools. Although the majority status of the Anglo population of the United States provided the base from which American society became anglicized, race and ethnicity help explain the way various groups have fared in American society. South Africa is an excellent example of a society in which the oppressed ethnic group is not a minority.

James Banks, in his *Multiethnic Education: Theory and Practice*, defines an ethnic group as "an involuntary collectivity of people with a shared feeling of common identity, a sense of peoplehood, and a shared sense of interdependence of fate."[3] The shared feeling results from a common heritage, a common set of values, and a common experience.

The group integrity of such collections of people is maintained by sets of boundaries created by those inside the group and by interactions with other groups. The boundaries of an ethnic group are maintained from the inside by the members of the group and their sense of group identity. However, the interaction of the members of the group with other cultural groups also produces boundaries that are created by the group's perceptions of others.[4]

Banks makes an interesting and powerful distinction between *cultural assimilation* and *structural inclusion* as a way of explaining how it came to be that some

[3]James A. Banks, *Multiethnic Education: Theory and Practice* (Boston: Allyn & Bacon, Inc., 1988), p. 61.
[4]Ibid. (Quoting Wsevold W. Isajiw, "Definitions of Ethnicity," *Ethnicity* 1 (July 1974), p. 111.

ethnic groups ultimately "melted" into the Anglo-Saxon culture, whereas others did not. Banks, referring to the work of Milton Gordon, says that "the social goals of European immigrants, especially those from northern and western Europe, were cultural assimilation and structural inclusion; however, the goals for non-minorities and non-European immigrants were cultural assimilation and structural exclusion."[5] The Irish, for example, were able to trade their cultural heritage for full acceptance and participation in American society. In contrast, Mexican-Americans, Afro-Americans, and Native Americans were asked to assimilate culturally by giving up their own culture, and were denied participation in the institutions of mainstream American society. As a result, members of ethnic "groups of color" lost much of their culture but remained isolated and unable to benefit from the mainstream culture.[6]

Although individuals within an ethnic group share many characteristics, the degree and nature of ethnic identity will vary from one person to the next and may vary from one setting to another. The cultural content of any ethnic group in the United States today is also likely to be a complex combination of traditional elements from the original ethnic group and elements created in response to living in the United States. For example, the black, or Afro-American, culture is a combination of the cultural characteristics brought to the United States from Africa and the adaptation of that culture to slavery.

HISTORICAL OVERVIEW

Afro-Americans

There are 29.3 million Afro-Americans in the United States today. They make up 12.2 percent of the population.

Afro-Americans were first brought to this country in 1619 and had a status similar to other indentured servants. Later in the seventeenth century, however, the large plantations' need for more human labor resulted in the institution of slavery. By the middle of the eighteenth century, slavery had been legalized in every colony, and tens of thousands of slaves were brought in from West Africa. By 1776, there were over a half million blacks in slavery or indentured servitude in this country, one-sixth of the total population.

In 1783, Massachusetts abolished slavery, and other northern states soon followed suit. The South, however, was too dependent on slavery, and although slavery was banned from the Northwest Territory, Congress could not restrict the slave trade in other areas until 1808. Blacks served in the Revolutionary army, as they have in every war since that time, but their use has consistently been more

[5]Banks, *Multiethnic Education*, p. 59.
[6]Ibid.

out of a desperate need for manpower than out of any sense of equality. An early indication of black people's status in American society was that they were counted as only three-fifths of a person in determining the number of representatives of a state in Congress.

Slaves could own no property, could enter into no contract (not even a contract of marriage), and had no right to assemble in public unless a white person was present. They had no standing in courts. Without legal means of defense, slaves were susceptible to the premise that any white person could threaten their lives or take them with impunity.[7]

Free blacks fared little better, suffering from a great deal of prejudice and discrimination. By 1860, 4 million blacks were enslaved, and although an abolition-ist movement had gained strength, not all its supporters were sincere in their efforts. The Dred Scott decision in 1857 confirmed that blacks were not citizens and thus not protected by the Constitution. Blacks were initially rejected for service in the military during the Civil War, but when a shortage of men devel-oped, they were quickly admitted. With the Union victory, blacks were given their freedom, but not equality or freedom from aggression. Lynchings and other forms of violence were perpetrated on the black population until well into the twentieth century and, many would argue, up to the present day. The Thirteenth, Four-teenth, and Fifteenth Amendments gave blacks the right to vote and the promise of equality, and the Civil Rights Act of 1875 gave them the right to equal accommodations, but the act contained no effective enforcement. During the Reconstruction period, blacks served in every Southern legislature and in the House and Senate. Through the pressures of the Ku Klux Klan and a barrage of laws that followed the 1883 ruling that the Civil Rights Act of 1875 was unconstitu-tional, blacks were effectively eliminated from participation in the political process and from equality of treatment or opportunity. This culminated in the important Supreme Court case, *Plessy* v. *Ferguson* (1896), which established that "separate but equal" facilities were permissible by law.

At the beginning of the twentieth century, blacks were politically disen-franchised, economically kept at the bottom of the ladder, and subject to every form of legal and illegal discrimination.

In the early twentieth century, Booker T. Washington exemplified the posi-tion of accommodation, conciliation, and gradualism in contact between the races, whereas men such as W.E.B. Du Bois in the Niagara Movement sought equality through agitation and protest. The National Association for the Advancement of Colored People (NAACP) took many forms of legal action and carried on a nationwide propaganda effort to fight prejudice and discriminatory statutes. Marcus Garvey led a movement "back to Africa," where he hoped to liberate both African and American blacks from their oppressors. The Ku Klux Klan gained a great deal of power and influence between the wars, and during the Depression

---

[7]National Advisory Commission on Civil Disorders, *Report* (New York: Bantam Books, Inc., 1968), p. 209.

blacks suffered more severely than whites because of many forms of discrimination in aid and work opportunities. With the New Deal and the CIO's policy of nondiscrimination, the plight of American blacks slowly began to improve.

During World War II, blacks again were initially prevented from fighting but later were accepted in separate, mostly noncombat units. It was not until 1949 that the armed forces outlawed segregation. During the Depression, war, and early postwar period, the legal pressures began to build, leading in 1954 to the crucial Court decision, *Brown* v. *Board of Education,* in which the Court reversed its "separate but equal" doctrine of 1896 and declared that segregated schools give black children

> a feeling of inferiority as to their status in the community that may affect their hearts and minds in a way unlikely ever to be undone. . . . We conclude that in the field of public education the doctrine of separate but equal has no place.

With the major 1954 decision, the dam broke and a series of court decisions and civil rights acts outlawed all forms of discrimination on the basis of race or ethnicity. Without the moral leadership of Dr. Martin Luther King Jr. and the political action of such groups as the NAACP, the Southern Christian Leadership Conference, the Student Non-Violent Coordinating Committee, the Black Muslims, and a variety of black power advocates, it is unlikely that many of the laws would have been passed, much less enforced. A great deal of legal progress has been made by black America in the past thirty years, but prejudice still exists. The role of the school in alleviating and perpetuating that prejudice will be dealt with later in the chapter.

Hispanic Americans

There were 19.4 million people in the United States in 1988 who referred to themselves as Hispanic. The composition of this group of people is diverse. Mexican-Americans comprise 62 percent of this population, whereas the remaining 38 percent is made up of people whose ancestors originated in Puerto Rico, Cuba, Central America, and South America. Since 1980, the U.S. Hispanic population has grown by 34 percent, whereas the non-Hispanic population has grown 7 percent. Immigration from Mexico accounted for about half of this increase.[8]

Although a growing number of Hispanics are recent immigrants from Mexico or are children of recent immigrants, many Hispanic-Americans are descendants of Mexicans who unwillingly became part of the United States through territorial conquest and annexation.

Concentrated in the southwestern part of the United States, many Mexican-Americans can trace their ancestry for 150 or more years prior to the annexation of New Mexico in 1848, after the war with Mexico. Anglo-Americans are only the

[8]U.S. Bureau of the Census, *Current Population Reports,* Series P-23, No. 159, "Population Profile of the United States, 1989" (Washington, D.C.: U.S. Government Printing Office, 1989).

most recent of a line of conquerors, from Spain to France to Mexico, none of whom took much interest in what now comprises the states of California, Arizona, New Mexico, Texas, and Colorado.

Trade routes, set up in the 1840s, were replaced by the railroads later in the century as the Anglo-Americans set up forts and trading posts. Cattlemen moved in and claimed vast amounts of land for themselves, as did the mining and forestry interests. Indian and Hispanic systems of land ownership were invalidated and replaced by Anglo deeds and titles. By 1892, the land grab was complete, with the opening of grazing privileges to people other than the Hispanos from whom they had been taken. The traditional ties to the land were effectively broken, and the "original" citizens of the Southwest soon were forced into the mines and lumber camps, and into the bottom layer of the economy. Where once citizens of Mexican origin could be found in all levels of society, by the end of the nineteenth century most had been forced from their lands to become part of the lower working class. Millions of acres of common or group-owned land were declared to be government land and sold to Anglos throughout the last half of the nineteenth century.

The label *Spanish-American* came into social usage after the exodus from Mexico following the revolution in 1910. Hispanos of many generations' residence, not wishing to identify with the impoverished Mexican immigrants, took on the name Spanish-Americans, while labeling the others as Mexicans or Mexican-Americans. Of more recent origin is the word *Chicano*, which has rapidly replaced the other names as that preferred by the more militant groups.

Article IX of the Treaty of Guadalupe Hidalgo, bringing the Southwest into the United States, guarantees that the people in the annexed territories would have "all the rights of citizens of the United States." Most historians agree that the treaty has been more breached than honored and that the Anglo-American power structure, through land grabs, economic exploitation of migrant labor and *braceros*, numerous discriminatory laws, and outright violence has kept the Chicano in economic and political powerlessness for the past century and a quarter.

Housing discrimination against the Mexican-American was practiced throughout the Southwest, and segregated schools could be found until the Supreme Court declared them unconstitutional in a series of cases from 1948 until the famous *Brown* decision of 1954. Amazingly, however, in 1970 a U.S. District Circuit court in Houston in *Ross v. Eckels* declared that Mexican-Americans were part of "the larger American majority" and paired them with black schools, leaving the dominant Anglo schools segregated. Numerous other forms of school discrimination can be found in textbooks, IQ tests, tracking, language, and cultural training, all of which will be dealt with in greater detail later. Like other racial and ethnic minorities, the Mexican-American population has been the subject of ethnic jokes and racial slurs, with many of the forms of discrimination practiced in the South against blacks being practiced against Chicanos in the Southwest.

Elwyn Stoddard lists five recognizable periods in the struggle for equal rights. The first was the 450-year period from the Spanish Conquest until the Mexican Revolution in 1910, during which the people were kept in a subordinate position. From 1910 until World War II, Mexican-Americans, like other "hyphenated Americans," attempted to assimilate totally into the "melting pot." Separatism followed the war, when veterans discovered that they were still not accepted into the dominant society. During the larger civil rights movement, Chicano activists came to the forefront to pressure society for greater justice and to abolish discrimination. Men such as Cesar Chavez and Rudolfo "Corky" Gonzalez led the movement, which included boycotts and a variety of public confrontations. Stoddard concludes that the movement is now entering its fifth stage, in which overt actions are declining in favor of penetrating professional, political, and economic organizations at all levels.[9]

Asian-Americans and Pacific Islanders

In 1987 Asians represented 43 percent of the total immigration to the United States—making it one of the fastest-growing ethnic groups in the country. The nearly 3.5 million Asians are comprised of a variety of nationalities. Although Chinese, Filipinos, and Japanese account almost equally for 62 percent of the total, an increasing number of Vietnamese and other Southeast-Asian people enter the United States every year.

Historically, the Chinese-Americans and Japanese-Americans have been the largest Asian groups. Although they have often been singled out as the example of an ethnic minority that has succeeded, they too have suffered.

The history of maltreatment, racism, and prejudice began with the arrival of the Chinese workers for the railroad in 1850 and in the mining camps of the nineteenth century. Japanese immigrants to the plantations on Hawaii provided cheap labor; but when they came to San Francisco in the late nineteenth century, American laborers felt threatened, and cries of the "yellow peril" were heard. This led in 1907 to an informal agreement between the United States and Japan to ban further immigration. The Japanese tended to settle in rural areas rather than urban "Chinatowns." With Japanese success in small farming, the American farmers soon felt threatened and succeeded in getting the Alien Land Law passed in 1913, prohibiting "foreign" ownership of land. When that failed to stop Japanese immigration, they got a prohibition on the leasing of land passed in 1920; and with its failure, the Alien Exclusion Act of 1924 prevented further immigration to the United States by Japanese.

Many of the same forms of discrimination practiced against blacks in the South and Mexican-Americans in the Southwest could be found in the areas of urban and rural California where many Oriental-Americans settled. In addition, the stereotype of the "slant-eyed, treacherous, and subversive Oriental" pervaded the newspapers and popular thinking for the first half of the twentieth century. This led to perhaps the greatest violation of constitutional and civil rights in American history—the internment of tens of thousands of Americans of Japanese descent, including many American citizens, during World War II. The decision involved such liberal leaders as President Roosevelt and Earl Warren, who later became Chief Justice of the Supreme Court. The Japanese and Japanese-Ameri-

[9]Elwyn R. Stoddard, *Mexican-Americans* (New York: Random House, 1973), pp. 242–43.

cans were deprived of property, freedom of movement, and numerous other civil rights—further evidence of the racism so prevalent in American society.

Chinese were crowded into "Chinatowns," and the chances of their moving outside the confines of these areas or even working in other locations were extremely limited. The Chinese immigrants and their descendants were cut off from the dominant American society. Although there has been an awakening among Chinese youth, the Chinese-Americans have not been accepted nor have they attempted to enter the dominant culture in large numbers.

Of more recent origin are the Filipinos, Koreans, and Polynesians; since the end of the Indochinese war, large numbers of Vietnamese and Laotians have entered the Oriental-American community. It is too early to state with any assurance what the treatment of these newer groups will be, but it probably will not differ too greatly from the overt racism of the past or the not-so-subtle racism presently experienced by Chinese- and Japanese-Americans. Skin color and features still play a role in American society.

Native Americans

Through four centuries of conquest, cultural extermination, genocide, and coercive assimilation, the Native American has borne the brunt of the most pervasive physical, economic, political, and cultural discrimination in this country's history. That over three hundred tribes have survived is remarkable indeed.

The European explorers and the settlers who followed viewed the Indians as savages in need of conversion to Christianity. Almost all saw them as inferiors whose lands could be taken and whose rights as human beings could be violated. Alvin M. Josephy, Jr., in his *The Indian Heritage of America*, puts the destruction of Indian peoples in its starkest reality:

> The European conquest of the Americas has been termed one of the darkest chapters of human history, for the conquerors demanded and won authority over the lives, territories, religious beliefs, ways of life, and means of existence of every native group with which they came in contact. No one will ever know how many Indians or how many tribes were enslaved, tortured, debauched and killed. . . . The stain is made all the darker by the realization that the conflict was forced upon those who suffered; the aggressors were the whites, the scenes of tragedy the very homelands of the victims.[10]

Throughout the warfare and treaties that marked the colonial period and the nineteenth century, the Indians were forced to abandon their tribal lands in exchange for money, "guarantees" on other lands, hunting and fishing rights, educational programs, and a variety of other promises, all too often broken as the pressures of new settlers were brought to bear. The treaties raised questions concerning the legal status of the Indians, and the Supreme Court ruled that they had some of the attributes of sovereignty, although not to the same extent as foreign nations. This led to the federal government's role as "guardian" and regula-

[10]Alvin M. Josephy, Jr., *The Indian Heritage of America* (New York: Bantam Books, Inc., 1969), p. 277.

tor of the Indians, primarily through the Bureau of Indian Affairs (BIA). In recent days the courts have upheld the rights of Indian tribes in various parts of the country to retake lands, to be paid for lands taken illegally, and to regain traditional hunting and fishing privileges. These cases have been one factor in the continued animosity and prejudice of the dominant society toward the Native American population.

If blacks, Mexican-Americans, and Oriental-Americans were segregated in their ghettos or barrios, the Native Americans were treated even worse. Indians were placed on reservations throughout the nineteenth century in the American equivalent of South African apartheid. They were often made to move hundreds of miles from their homelands, put in inhospitable environments, prevented from practicing their traditional religion, forced to adopt private land ownership patterns, and perhaps as an ultimate indignity, had their children taken away from them and placed in white-run boarding schools. Indian political leadership was replaced by BIA bureaucrats, and Indians were forced into near-total dependency on the dominant power structure of the society.

The Indian Reorganization Act of 1934 attempted to remedy some of the worse conditions by encouraging tribal self-government and the retention of traditional cultures, in addition to placing all tribal lands in trust, to prevent their being taken over by non-Indians. Tribal religions and customs were permitted again, and medical and educational facilities were upgraded. The paternalism of the BIA, however, continues to the present day. A policy of "termination" of the reservation system throughout the 1950s and 1960s has placed additional hardships on the Indian peoples and forced many of them into urban centers. The Civil Rights Bill of 1968 included an Indian Rights Section, extending civil rights protections to Indians, subject to tribal courts, and preventing the further erosion of Indian jurisdiction on the reservations.

Equal rights for Native Americans are a product of legislation of the past ten years. Into the 1970s there were school districts that prohibited Spanish-speaking children from using their native language. Some thirty years ago, black activists were boycotting buses for the right to sit wherever they pleased, and about fifty years ago, Japanese-Americans were deprived of their civil rights and placed in detention camps. American racism has run the gamut from prejudicial beliefs and behavior to the segregation of peoples on the basis of race. Concentration camps and apartheid policy have been part of our history, as has extermination through lynchings and Indian massacres. Progress has been made through the courts and in mass media, economic opportunities, and rising political involvement, but prejudice still exists. We now turn our attention to the origins of prejudice and why it still exists.

MELTING POT: ASSIMILATION AND ACCULTURATION

In 1909, Israel Zangwill wrote a play entitled *The Melting Pot*. The title captured a popular ideal: that the diverse national and ethnic peoples who come to the United States to live would, over time, lose their distinctive qualities of national origin and become Americans. Indeed, many who came to find economic, personal, and political opportunity and freedom wanted very much to become Americans and to have their children succeed in America. The schools were important institutions for Americanizing the children of these immigrants.

America represented hope and a better future. Zangwill's play reflects this optimism and joy.

> There she lies, the great Melting pot — listen! Can't you hear the roaring and the bubbling? There gapes her mouth — the harbour where a thousand mammoth feeders come from the end of the world to pour in their human freight. Ah, what a stirring and a seething! Celt and Latin, Slav and Teuton, Greek and Syrian — black and yellow — . . . East and West, and North and South . . . the crescent and the cross . . . how the great Alchemist melts and fuses them . . . what is the glory of Rome and Jerusalem, where all nations and races come to worship and look back, compared with the glory of America, where all races and nations come to labour and look forward?[11]

The glory of America, however, was denied to many who lived here. Those whose appearance and cultural traits set them apart found that they were excluded from the benefits of being American. There were, for example, Native Americans and some Spanish-speaking citizens who had been conquered people and, unlike the immigrants, had no wish to become American.

The process by which immigrants and others became part of the melting pot has been variously labeled by sociologists and anthropologists as *socialization, acculturation,* or *assimilation.* Although each of these terms has a distinct definition, it is sufficient to say here that they all describe a process by which persons become a part of a group by adopting a set of attributes: common language, appearance, behaviors, and values.

The degree to which each ethnic or culturally distinct group was absorbed into the American culture varied considerably from one group to another. Although many western and northern Europeans maintained symbolic and culinary elements of their homeland, their assimilation was almost complete. Japanese-Americans, however, adopted an outward conformity while never being fully assimilated.

PREJUDICE ✳

People in all societies tend to view others from an ethnocentric frame of reference. This is as true of the United States as it is of other countries. Because of the multiplicity of subcultures and social groups in this country, Americans have in-groups and out-groups, with judgments being passed on how closely others conform to "our" standards.

Ranking and generalizing are two characteristics of ethnocentric thinking,

[11]Israel Zangwill, *The Melting Pot* (New York: The Jewish Publication Society of America, 1909), pp. 198–99.

and the greater the differences, the more likely gross overgeneralizations will occur, such as "lazy, shiftless Negroes," "hot and passionate Latins," or "penny-pinching Scots." Ethnocentrism lays the groundwork for prejudice. A lack of strong feelings about one's own group makes it difficult for prejudicial feelings to arise toward other groups. Gordon Allport defines ethnic prejudice as "an antipathy based upon a faulty and inflexible generalization. It may be felt or expressed. It may be directed toward a group as a whole, or toward an individual because he is a member of that group.[12] Prejudices may be positive or negative, but because of the consequences of the latter, most research deals only with the negative. Prejudice contains not only intellectual and affective components but also a predisposition to act in a certain manner.When prejudice enters the realm of behavior, its effects are visible.

By the age of four, most children have developed "distinct in-group/out-group orientations (incipient race attitudes)."[13] All studies indicate that awareness of the physical characteristics of race comes at an early age. Although studies vary on the percentage of young children who are "clearly prejudiced," evidence indicates that by the age of seven children have formed a variety of concepts and feelings about race, much of it negatively prejudicial in nature.

From what does racial prejudice spring? During much of human history up to the present day, in many parts of the world, the answer has been "innate racial differences." It is falsely claimed that evolutionary processes have made the white race the leaders and the "colored" races the followers or servants. This invalid position served racist colonialists well in Asia, Africa, and Latin America and justified the subjugation of the conquered peoples.

Prejudice is too widespread to be explained as strictly a matter of psychological deviancy, and one is reluctant to attribute its ubiquitousness to an innate human trait. Prejudice seems to be the result of learned social behavior and attitudes. Attitudes internalized by children as part of their socialization become solidly implanted and resistant to change. A number of studies report that gaining positive cognitive information about a group toward which one is negatively prejudiced does not necessarily result in a more positive attitude.[14] Other studies indicate that racial prejudice is strongest among those whose economic and social position is under the greatest direct threat.

John Dollard and Clyde Kluckhohn explain prejudice using the following thesis:

> One goes through life seeking gratification for felt needs, and, while many such needs have their origin in the organic structure of the individual, there are others which are culturally determined. These are learned early in life and are canalized and directed toward certain goals. When goal-directed behavior is blocked, hostile impulses are

[12]Gordon W. Allport, *The Nature of Prejudice* (Reading, Mass.: Addison-Wesley Publishing Company, Inc., 1954), p. 10.

[13]Mary Ellen Goodman, *Race Awareness in Young Children* (London: Collier-Macmillan, Ltd., 1964), p. 253.

[14]Glenn S. Pate, "Research on Prejudice Reduction." *Educational Leadership* (Jan. 1981), p. 288.

frequently created in the individual, who, unable to determine the real source of his frustration and in an attempt to overcome it, manifests "free-floating aggression."[15]

Scapegoating is the name given to a psychological mechanism used to deal with this "free-floating aggression." The treatment of the Jews in Nazi Germany is the prime example of the mechanism at work.

Discrimination and Segregation

Stereotyping provides the rationalization for prejudice, and together they provide both the motive and the defense for discrimination against racial and ethnic groups. At one level, discrimination may simply mean avoidance, but it can also be escalated to the level of denial or deprivation. In U.S. history, Orientals were denied their right to come to this country; blacks were denied the right to vote or sit wherever they pleased on buses; and Native Americans and Mexican-Americans were deprived of their land. Not until the 1960s, with that decade's series of civil rights laws and civil liberties court cases, did most of the legal bases for denial and deprivation disappear from this country.

Segregation, the institutionalized form of discrimination, restricts contact between groups or individuals. Throughout most of U.S. history, various forms of de jure (legal) discrimination have been practiced in housing, hospitals, schools, and churches. To be sure, there have been forms of de facto (in fact) segregation that are completely voluntary in nature, but given the complexity of our society and economy, there have been many examples of de facto segregation with overtones of ethnic discrimination, which led to many of the northern court orders on busing to effect school desegregation.

Most segregation laws in this country have limited contact in certain situations but permitted it in others. For example, blacks in the South, although not permitted to sit next to whites, could work in their homes or fields and shop in their stores. More extreme forms of segregation are South Africa's apartheid system and concentration camps, used to a certain degree in South Africa today and in America during World War II for Americans of Japanese descent. Expulsion, exile, or total removal from the society is an even more extreme form of segregation. Its practice has been somewhat limited in U.S. history, although a few "undesirables" have been so treated, and one can still hear people say, "Why don't we send them back where they came from?" when speaking of blacks or Mexican-Americans. The speakers are rarely cognizant of the absurdity of the statement, as only the Native Americans and some Mexican-Americans have any "right" to be here under such a position.

Discrimination can become violent and, in its ultimate form, can lead to extermination or genocide. Violence may not be as "American as apple pie," but there is no denying its role in our history. The massacres of the American Indians

---

[15]Peter I. Rose, *They and We: Racial and Ethnical Relations in the United States* (New York: Random House, 1968).

can only be called genocide, and the hundreds of lynchings of blacks in the late nineteenth and early twentieth centuries are examples of extermination in a society that guarantees the "right to life." Although some militants would point to Attica and Kent State as evidence that extermination of those who differ from the societal norms is still practiced, "ultimate solutions" are no longer condoned by the power structure or society in general.

Reactions to Discrimination

Minority groups have reacted to their status in a variety of ways. The psychiatrist Robert Coles, in his study of black and white children in the South during the 1960s, demonstrated the effects of discrimination on the black children and how it led to self-hatred. Numerous schools have been founded in the black community to counteract this self-hatred and to instill a pride in race. The outward evidences can be seen in the slogans that arose in the 1960s: "Black is beautiful" and "Black Power." This move on the part of blacks has been followed by other groups, whose slogans are "Brown Power," "La Raza Unida," "Yellow Power," and "Gray Panthers," in addition to such historically related themes as "Custer died for your sins."

If the 1960s and 1970s saw an upsurge in self- and group pride, these were not the traditional reactions to discrimination. Perhaps the dominant reaction has been one of submission; it didn't take a black slave long to know who had the power, nor for the Japanese-Americans to see the hopelessness of fighting the whole U.S. government when they were caught up in a xenophobic hatred of the "Japs." Within every minority can be found those who attempt to withdraw from their group and assimilate into the dominant society. Success in this venture often depends on how closely the individual resembles the majority in racial, social class, or other characteristics. Examples of this type of withdrawal are hair straightening by blacks and the taking of new names by Jews and Mexican-Americans.

The various "power" movements and pride in race and ethnic heritage in recent American history have led to a rise in the avoidance mechanism as a reaction to discrimination or minority status. With their newfound pride, many individuals within the minority communities, and some large groups such as the Black Muslims, have rejected the inferior image of themselves and have segregated themselves from the society at large. Voluntary separation from the society at large is a difficult position to maintain, and the pressure to "give" California to the blacks, or New Mexico and Arizona to the Mexican-Americans is called for only by a small percentage of those minority communities. The new militancy among Native Americans, however, has led to greater autonomy on the reservations and attempts to preserve their cultural heritage in a segregated setting. But the dominant trend in American society is integration, one very important aspect of which is school integration, the focus of many of the legal battles in recent years.

True integration presupposes the inherent equality of opportunity for all groups, and for this reason, it would appear to be some time in the future before minority citizens will participate fully in all aspects of American culture and society.

THE SCHOOLS

The almost universal American faith in education as the vehicle for success has made the schools a hotbed of racial and ethnic controversy. The period beginning with the *Brown* decision in 1954 to the present day has been filled with legal, moral, and educational controversy regarding the school's role in bringing about equity in American society.

Since 1954, the issues have become more complicated and more difficult. As James Farmer explained, "Now we have moved into a more difficult period. We are dealing with nationwide problems rather than largely Southern problems; more complex issues than the front seat of the bus. We are dealing with how to close gaps between the haves and have-nots when the have-nots have been deprived through the interaction of poverty and racism."[16] It was a coalition of blacks, liberals, Catholics, Jews, and others that brought about the passage of the Civil Rights Act of 1964. The coalition was united by a common belief in the fundamental principle that everyone should be considered an individual without regard to social origin. But today's issues, such as "racial balancing," "busing," "affirmative action," and "quotas," do not enjoy the same consensus.

Desegregation

The 1954 Supreme Court decision in *Brown* v. *Board of Education* declared that it was unconstitutional for states to assign children to schools on the basis of race. In 1964 the *Brown* position was strengthened by the passage of the Civil Rights Act, which stated that "desegregation means the assignment of students to public schools and within such schools without regard to their race, color, religion or national origin but desegregation shall not mean the assignment to public schools in order to overcome racial imbalance."

It has now been over thirty years since the *Brown* decision. That decision, which was to eliminate segregation, now appears to have created ambiguities that have impeded progress toward equal opportunity. Some unresolved questions raised by the decision are: "Was it segregation itself that constituted the wrong, or segregation mandated by law? Was segregation wrong because it distinguished on the basis of race or because it limited the educational futures of black children?"[17] Was the constitutional wrong to blacks the denial of liberty or the denial of integration? Was the intent of the *Brown* decision to be color-conscious or color-blind?[18] What began as an attack on separate black schools in the South became a move actively to desegregate schools everywhere, even in the face of segregated residential patterns.

The courts not only determined whether or not schools were unlawfully

[16]James Farmer, *Human Rights: A National Perspective*; reprinted in *Annual Editions: Education 83/84* (Guilford, Conn.: Dushkin Publishing Group, Inc., 1984), p. 150.

[17]David L. Kirp, "The Bounded Politics of School Desegregation Litigation," *Harvard Educational Review*, 51, no. 3 (Aug. 1981), pp. 395–405.

[18]Diane Ravitch, "Color Blind or Color-Conscious?" *The New Republic*, May 5, 1979; reprinted in *Annual Editions: Education 83/84* (Guilford, Conn.: Dushkin Publishing Group, Inc., 1984), p. 160.

segregated but also decided what the remedy must be to rectify the wrong. It appears that the courts took on this added burden in order to overcome the unwillingness of school districts to remedy their own segregated schools with "all deliberate speed." The courts' remedies became more and more specific. In *Jefferson County* (*U.S. v. Jefferson County Board of Education*, 1372 F.2d 836 [5th Cir. 1966]), the Fifth Circuit Court specified not only the timing but also the nature of the equalization efforts, the remedial programs to be offered, the location of the new schools, and the reassignment of the faculty.[19]

Since the mid-1960s the courts have moved away from the "color-blind" intent of the *Brown* decision. Court-mandated integration measures required students to be assigned to schools and programs in a fashion designed to bring about racial balance, a practice that demanded identifying students by race and assigning them accordingly.

In the late 1970s and 1980s, observers of the Supreme Court report that it has retreated from making decisions about equal rights for minorities.[20] The Court has been subject to considerable criticism for its lack of consistency. David Kirp claims that it is "increasingly difficult to detect the thread of principle running through equal protection case law and hence harder to justify any court decision, whether rights-expanding or rights-contracting in its effect."[21]

Integration

"Color-blind" desegregation as defined by the *Brown* decision in 1954 and restated in the Civil Rights Act of 1964 did not result in a marked increase in the achievement of minorities either in education or in economic progress. Erasing the color line had not produced the desired result. The explanation for this failure lay first in the resistance of school boards and other institutions to integration efforts, and second in the realization by some that minorities had been severely damaged by years of discrimination and isolation. As President Lyndon B. Johnson said, "it is not enough to open the gates of opportunity. All our citizens must have the ability to walk through those gates."[22] This policy shift by the Johnson administration represented a departure from the original concepts of equality and affirmative action. Affirmative action no longer meant that tests for employment or educational qualification had to be free of racial bias. It now meant that businesses, schools, and public employment had to demonstrate not only that they had made every effort to attract minority applicants but also that quotas for minority employees or minority students had been met to achieve racial balance.

Given the high degree of resistance to antidiscrimination policies and court decisions, it is no surprise to find that the more aggressive integration steps were

[19]Kirp, "The Bounded Politics," p. 397.

[20]Ibid.

[21]Ibid.

[22]Terry Eastland and William J. Bennett, *Counting by Race* (New York: Basic Books, Inc., Publishers, 1979), p. 6.

TABLE 8-1   Black and Hispanic School Enrollment, 1984

RANK	BLACK PERCENTAGE OF TOTAL ENROLLMENT	PERCENTAGE OF BLACK STUDENTS IN 90–100% MINORITY SCHOOLS	HISPANIC PERCENTAGE OF TOTAL ENROLLMENT	PERCENTAGE OF HISPANIC STUDENTS IN 90–100% MINORITY SCHOOLS
1	Washington, D.C. (92.5)	Washington, D.C. (95.2)	New Mexico (43.4)	Washington, D.C. (65.3)
2	Mississippi (50.4)	Illnois (69.0)	California (29.2)	New York (59.1)
3	Louisiana (42.5)	New York (56.7)	Texas (27.9)	Illinois (41.2)
4	South Carolina (40.6)	Michigan (56.3)	Arizona (21.5)	Texas (40.0)
5	Maryland (37.2)	New Jersey (48.8)	Colorado (15.7)	New Jersey (37.1)
6	Georgia (35.8)	Missouri (44.6)	New York (13.6)	Connecticut (29.4)
7	Alabama (34.5)	Pennsylvania (41.6)	New Jersey (8.8)	Pennsylvania (29.4)
8	North Carolina (30.0)	Mississippi (38.7)	Florida (8.1)	California (26.8)
9	Delaware (25.8)	Maryland (38.3)	Illinois (8.0)	Florida (25.6)
10	Arkansas (25.3)	Tennesses (36.2)	Connecticut (6.8)	Mississippi (25.2)
11	Illinois (24.8)	California (35.4)	Nevada (6.6)	Arizona (18.0)
12	Virginia (23.8)	Alabama (34.8)	Wyoming (6.4)	New Mexico (17.5)
13	Florida (23.1)	Connecticut (33.0)	Massachusetts (5.0)	Indiana (16.8)
14	Tennessee (20.9)	Georgia (31.7)	Washington (4.3)	Hawaii (12.2)
15	New Jersey (18.8)	Texas (31.4)	Idaho (3.8)	Louisana (7.6)
16	New York (18.7)	Louisiana (30.4)	Rhode Island (3.8)	Rhode Island (5.0)
17	Michigan (16.7)	Indiana (24.8)	Oregon (3.5)	Georgia (4.1)
18	Missouri (16.2)	Arizona (23.8)	Utah (3.3)	South Carolina (3.5)
19	Ohio (14.4)	Wisconsin (19.5)	Kansas (2.9)	Michigan (3.4)
20	Texas (13.9)	Florida (19.4)	Washington, D.C. (2.9)	Maryland (2.5)
21	Pennsylvania (12.6)	South Carolina (15.7)	Delaware (2.1)	Wisconsin (2.3)
22	Indiana (10.7)	Ohio (13.3)	Hawaii (2.1)	Massachusetts (2.1)
23	Kentucky (10.6)	Arkansas (11.3)	Nebraska (2.0)	Arkansas (1.5)
24	Connecticut (10.3)	Virginia (8.4)	Oklahoma (2.1)	Montana (1.4)
25	California (10.1)	Oklahoma (7.3)	Michigan (1.9)	Missouri (1.2)
26	Nevada (9.9)	Hawaii (7.3)	Indiana (1.7)	Tennessee (1.1)
27	Oklahoma (9.9)	North Carolina (6.3)	Wisconsin (1.7)	North Carolina (1.0)
28	Wisconsin (7.7)	New Mexico (5.2)	Pennsylvania (1.6)	Alabama (.8)
29	Kansas (6.8)	Kansas (5.3)	Maryland (1.5)	Alaska (.4)
30	Massachusetts (6.3)	Nevada (3.0)	Alaska (1.4)	Ohio (.4)
31	Rhode Island (5.5)	Massachusetts (1.7)	Ohio (1.1)	Utah (.4)
32	Colorado (5.1)	North Dakota (1.4)	Virginia (1.1)	North Dakota (.3)
33		Rhode Island (1.3)	Iowa (1.0)	Nevada (.2)
34			Montana (1.0)	Colorado (.1)
35			Minnesota (.9)	Idaho (.1)
36			Louisiana (.8)	Kansas (.1)
37			Missouri (.8)	Minnesota (.1)
38			Georgia (.4)	Oklahoma (.1)
39			Arkansas (.3)	Virginia (.1)
40			North Carolina (.3)	
41			South Carolina (.2)	
42			Tennessee (.1)	

Source: National School Desegregation Project, University of Chicago.

not met with enthusiasm. It is a thesis of Diane Ravitch that one could be opposed to discriminatory practices, in favor of equal opportunity for everyone, and still oppose race-conscious policies such as busing and affirmative action quotas.[23]

In 1978, the inevitable happened: a case was brought before the Supreme Court that challenged the constitutionality of a quota system established by the University of California Medical School at Davis. Bakke, a white male, was denied admission to the school although he was more qualified than minority students who were admitted. Bakke was challenging a system which, he claimed, denied him his rights on the basis of his race. Terry Eastland, in *Counting by Race*, holds the position that the Bakke case is "supremely a case about the nature of equality in American life . . . a conflict between the idea of numerical equality and moral equality."[24] Does equality mean forbidding discrimination or affirming help to minorities?

Justice Blackmun said that in the opinion of the Court, the only way to achieve a society that is not race-conscious, a society where persons are regarded as persons, it must first take race into account. "In order to get beyond racism . . . we must first take account of race. . . . In order to treat persons equally we must treat them differently."[25] The Court held that race can be taken into consideration but that the quota system established by the University of California Medical School at Davis was not valid. The Court left open the use of race as a category but did not specify how it may be used. The decision also did not abolish the philosophy behind the goal of achieving racial balance.[26]

The Bakke case also raised the unfortunate label of "reverse discrimination," which raises this question: Do affirmative action programs requiring preferential treatment for minorities constitute the same issues as the discrimination experienced by minorities in the past because of racism? The issues are not simple. How do we in a society guided by the ideal of equality of treatment for every individual create policies that will counteract decades of prejudice and discrimination against identifiable groups without violating individual rights?

While the debates and litigation regarding the proper meaning of equality and how it may be achieved go on in the courts and literature, there are some who are pointing out that even now, more than thirty years after the *Brown* decision, the promise of desegregation goes unrealized. These critics argue that although data show improvement, more subtle forms of segregation are substituted to maintain a dual educational system. Also, evidence points to the continued discrepancy in the economic achievements between minorities and the mainstream white population. For example, in July 1980 the jobless rate was 7.8 percent, but the rate for blacks was 15.2 percent, and the rate for black teenagers was 40.3 percent. The median income for blacks was about 59 percent that of whites.[27]

[23]Ravitch, "Color Blind," p. 163.

[24]Eastland and Bennett, *Counting by Race*, pp. 15–19.

[25]Ibid., p. 181.

[26]William R. Hazard, "The *Bakke* Decision: Mixed Signals from the Court," *Phi Delta Kappan*, 60, no. 1 (Sept. 1978), p. 16.

[27]Farmer, *Human Rights*, p. 143.

It is also charged that in many school districts, boundaries are drawn to contain minorities in segregated schools. A 1977 study shows that two out of every three black and Hispanic students still attend schools where they constitute more than 50 percent of the student body. Even in desegregated schools, studies indicate that minority students are often resegregated by being channeled into compensatory and remedial programs. In a national survey it was discovered that although minority students comprise 25 percent of the nation's student population, they account for 40 percent of all suspensions and expulsions.[28]

The desegregation picture does have some pluses. The figures indicate that larger numbers of minorities are attending and graduating from school. For example, high school enrollment for whites increased by 3.9 percent in the 1977 census, whereas black enrollment increased by 23.1 percent. In the same period, the dropout rates for black and white students were falling and moving closer together.[29]

Coleman Report

A 1966 study describing the status of equal educational opportunity was conducted by James S. Coleman for the U.S. Office of Education. It involved over 900,000 children of all races from every section of the country. It documented that racial segregation in education was nearly absolute in the South and very high nationwide; it also concluded that achievement in school was affected most by the educational backgrounds and aspirations of other students in the school. These findings provided a rationale for active integration efforts based on the idea that black students would benefit from attending school with achievement-oriented white students.

One of the most effective and controversial tools employed by the courts to achieve racial integration has been the practice of busing students from their home neighborhood to schools in other neighborhoods. Busing became the means whereby schools could be racially mixed even when the population of a city lived in segregated communities. The opposition to busing for racial balance, however, has been strong. The battles have been waged in the courts, with school districts looking for ways to avoid busing and citizens' groups demonstrating in opposition.

Cities faced with already segregated populations have claimed that they have not drawn boundary lines nor instituted policies designed to bring about segregated schools. They have claimed that this de facto segregation is not their responsibility, and therefore forced busing should not be required to remedy that which reflects a larger social issue.

Because such claims became a shelter for districts wishing to maintain segregated schools, the courts began to eliminate *de facto segregation* as an oper-

[28]Robert L. Green, Margaret A. Parsons, and Frances Thomas, "Desegregation: The Unfinished Agenda," *Educational Leadership* (Jan. 1971), pp. 282–85.

[29]William Price-Curtis, "Black Progress Toward Educational Equity," *Educational Leadership* (Jan. 1971).

able term, claiming instead that all segregation is the result of state action and therefore can be remedied by state action, such as busing students for integration.

White flight is the popular term used to describe the movement of white families out of school districts, largely urban districts, seemingly to avoid court-directed integration. Required integration of schools has also been avoided by the wealthy who have withdrawn their children from public schools and enrolled them in segregated private schools, which are immune to court-ordered integration.

In 1982, the *Denver Post* reported that under President Reagan's administration the Justice Department would intervene to stop court-ordered busing. Naomi Bradford, a Denver school board member and long-standing foe of busing, hailed the report as a victory. The Denver segregation case began in 1967, and it has been a seesaw battle between those supporting and those opposing racial integration. A plan was presented to the courts that proposed to end busing by creating special schools that would allow for voluntary integration. In 1982, the plan was rejected because it could be used as a tool for resegregation. In the spring of 1982, a revised plan was submitted that would reduce busing but not eliminate it. Some people contend that the 1954 *Brown* decision does not require such measures as busing to achieve equal educational opportunity.

The *Brown* decision has two components:

1. Separate cannot be equal because it is damaging to the excluded group.
2. The remedy is to eliminate segregated schools, that is, to guarantee freedom of choice for all students.

The intended result was that by providing freedom of choice, integration would take place and minorities would find themselves in the mainstream of American life. It did not happen, and "freedom of choice" was used by segregationists to continue segregated schools.

Racial Attitudes

Not only have schools been major battlegrounds over the segregation issue, they also have been expected to institute special programs to eliminate racism.

Prejudice, like all attitudes, is learned; it is the product of experiences. Attitudes are composed of a cognitive aspect (that is, what we believe about something) and an affective aspect (that is, what one likes and dislikes). Prejudice is an interaction between these two aspects. We know little, however, about how intentionally to change attitudes such as racial prejudice. Glenn Pate has synthesized the collected research on reducing prejudice and has formulated seven generalizations.

1. Factual information about another group is not sufficient to change attitudes. ... Facts do not speak for themselves; rather they are interpreted through the experiences and biases of those hearing them.
2. Class prejudice can be stronger than racial or religious prejudice.

3. An individual who has a high degree of self-acceptance will likely have a low degree of prejudice.
4. Students who work in interracial learning teams develop positive attitudes and cross-ethnic friendships.
5. The cognitive, affective, and behavioral components of prejudice are not necessarily related.
6. Films and other media can improve students' attitudes.
7. Social contacts may reduce prejudice under certain circumstances.[30]

One of the hopes of those supporting integration is that contact among races will improve interracial relationships. However, the research seems to indicate that whether or not contact reduces prejudice depends on other factors. Contact alone may have either positive or negative outcomes.

Some conditions that create problems in desegregated schools are these:

1. Low expectations of minority students by teachers
2. The use of inappropriate materials that are biased or fail to represent minorities in illustrations or content
3. Poor relationships between teachers and minority students
4. Failure to value and acknowledge contributions of minorities
5. The grouping of children for instruction
6. Biased counseling, which channels minority students into vocational programs
7. Biased institutional practices, which may include
   failure to acknowledge holidays
   failure to provide minority models
   failure to accommodate bus schedules in planning extracurricular programs
8. Biased discipline[31]

The conditions that seem to be necessary for interracial contact in school to create favorable changes in attitude are these:

1. Students should be given an opportunity to know one another as individuals.
2. The individuals of both races must have equal status.
3. The students who are put together should have common interests and similar characteristics such as age or occupation.
4. The social norms should be favorable to association between the races.
5. The circumstances should favor cooperation or at least not introduce competition or conflict.
6. The presence of persons of both races should be seen as beneficial in the achievement of the individual goals or at least as not presenting obstacles to them.[32]

[30]Pate, "Research on Prejudice Reduction," pp. 288–90.
[31]Barbara J. Love, "Desegregation in Your School: Behavior Patterns that Get in the Way," *Phi Delta Kappan*, 59, no. 2 (Nov. 1977), pp. 168–70.
[32]Pate, "Research on Prejudice Reduction," p. 290.

Whether schools can be effective tools for eliminating prejudice, it is clear that "if we are serious about developing the . . . society we claim we want, we must begin to apply what we know."[33]

In spite of laws, the courts, and programs designed to redress injustices, the U.S. educational system is failing a large number of ethnic minority students. Thirty-five percent of the black students and 25 percent of Hispanic students between the ages of eighteen and twenty did not finish high school in 1988. In some urban areas, more than 50 percent of the minority students do not finish high school. The average math and verbal scores for blacks and Hispanics on the Scholastic Aptitude Test (SAT) were one hundred points lower than those of white students. SAT test scores of blacks, Hispanics, and Native Americans fall well below those of whites.[34]

Because education is a sequential process, the gap in academic achievement between white students and ethnic minorities continues to widen. For blacks, the situation has worsened since the mid-1970s. Even though more black students are graduating from high school, black college enrollment has declined by 11 percent. The figures for Hispanic students are even more discouraging. High school graduation for Hispanics increased by 38 percent from 1975 to 1982, but college enrollment dropped 16 percent.[35]

To the extent that teachers and administrators serve as role models for ethnic minorities of color in education, the future looks bleak. Between 1976 and 1983 the percentage of bachelors degrees in education awarded to blacks declined by 52 percent; the percentage of such degrees to Hispanics rose by only a fraction of a percent.[36] The decreasing participation of the largest racial and ethnic groups in American education is represented in Figure 8-1. What becomes of those students who do not graduate from high school? Where do those students go who enter but do not complete college? At best they fill the lowest-skilled, lowest-paid jobs in our economy, jobs with the lowest job security. At worst, they become a part of what is becoming the permanent underclass in our society.

How to explain the conditions described above has been and will continue to be the subject of hot debate and the subject of public policy decisions. The way the problem is framed determines the answers that are proposed. For example, William Julius Wilson, author of *The Truly Disadvantaged*, believes that "many of the current problems of race, particularly those that plague the minority poor, derive from broader processes of societal organizations and therefore may have no direct or indirect connection with race." He believes that the problems should be addressed at a national level with a combination of economic and social policies. He proposes economic policies that will improve the job market so that the disadvan

[33]Ibid.

[34]Education Week, "At Risk: Pupils and Their Teachers," *Here They Come, Ready or Not,* Education Week Special Supplement (May 14, 1986), pp. 28–29.

[35]Dennis Williams, et al., "Is the Dream Over?" *Newsweek on Campus: Missing Persons* (Feb. 1987), pp. 10–14.

[36]American Association of Colleges for Teacher Education, *Teaching Teachers: Facts and Figures* (Washington, D.C.: AACTE, 1987), pp. 26–27.

taged can have jobs. He proposes a social policy that will allow people to have a healthy family life and work. He contends that "unless it is possible for adults to manage their work and family lives without undue strain on themselves and their

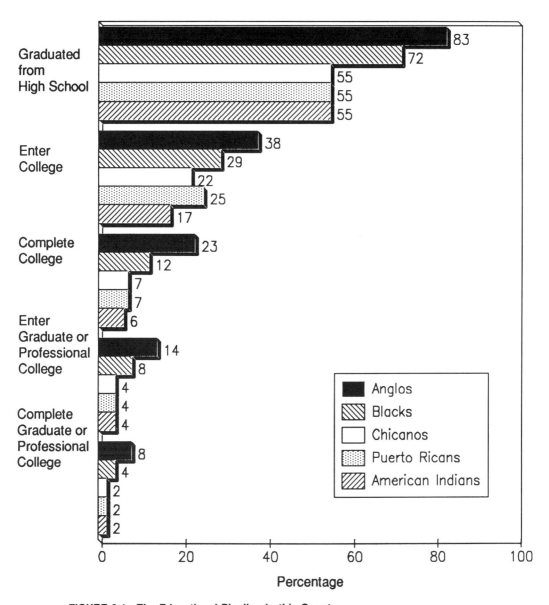

FIGURE 8-1   The Educational Pipeline in this Country

Source: Alexander Astin. *Minorities in American Higher Education* (San Francisco: Jossey-Bass, Inc., Publishers, 1982).

children, society will suffer a significant loss in productivity and an even more significant loss in the quantity and quality of future generations."[37]

Multicultural / Multiethnic Education

Multiethnic or multicultural education is one approach to addressing the problems that ethnic groups have had with schools. If one assumes that the very organization of the schools as white Anglo-Saxon institutions creates problems for some ethnic groups, then changing the way schools function may improve the chance that ethnic minority students will succeed.

Allan Ornstein and Daniel Levine define multicultural education as education that advocates "differential instructional approaches to teaching students with different ethnic and racial backgrounds."[38] Educators, Ornstein and Levine explain, need to be aware of different learning styles, dialect differences, and bilingual education. James Banks adds that multicultural education, in contrast with multiethnic education, encompasses a broader concern for the educational problems of cultural groups such as women and religious groups.[39]

Multiethnic education, according to Banks, is a reform movement in education based on the assumption that "many school practices related to race and ethnicity are harmful to students and reinforce many ethnic stereotypes and discriminatory practices in Western societies." The goals of multiethnic education include:

1. Helping individuals gain greater self-understanding by seeing themselves in their own culture as others might see them.
2. Providing students of each ethnic group with information about the unique cultures of other ethnic groups, and helping them see that those cultures also are meaningful.
3. Providing students with cultural and ethnic alternatives. (Teaching Anglo-American children only about their own culture denies them the richness of the music, literature, values, lifestyles and perspectives that exist in other cultures.)
4. Reducing the pain and discrimination that members of some ethnic and racial groups experience in schools.
5. Helping students master essential reading, writing, and computational skills.[40]

Multicultural education carries some risks. Too much emphasis placed upon differences and the separation of cultures can be a divisive force. And calling a program multicultural to sanction a second-rate education for ethnically different students corrupts the concept and is a disservice to its participants.[41]

---

[37]William Julius Wilson, "The Hidden Agenda," *University of Chicago Magazine* (Fall 1987), pp. 2–11.

[38]Allan C. Ornstein and Daniel U. Levine, "Multicultural Education: Trends and Issues," *Childhood Education* (Mar./Apr. 1982), p. 241.

[39]Banks, *Multiethnic Education*, p. 31.

[40]Ibid., p. 33.

[41]Ornstein and Levine, "Multicultural Education: Trends and Issues," p. 216.

CULTURAL PLURALISM

There is now a movement in the United States away from assimilation of minorities toward cultural or ethnic pluralism. In an important ethnographic study of integration in a Portland, Oregon, elementary school, Ray Rist states: "Day after day, the . . . black students came off the bus to a setting where the goal was to render them invisible. And the more invisible they became, the greater the satisfaction of the school personnel that the integration plan was succeeding."[42] Rist's study uncovers at least one school integration plan in which the goal it to make black students more and more like white students: "To educate Blacks to the point where their unfortunate stigma of blackness fades away. This will occur as a result of exposing black students to the majority values so that they may . . . eventually be absorbed into a culture based upon white middle class values and biases."[43]

Rist documents the failure of this attempt at color-blind assimilation and in its place advocates racial pluralism because "children are to be acknowledged and respected for what they are, not for what others say they must become."[44] This call to pluralism by Rist in 1978 was an echo of a provocative article by William Greenbaum on the rise of pluralism, in which he claims that the "Protestant Anglo American ideal of assimilation has failed in important ways and cannot guide the policies of our social institutions. The result in education has been movements for . . . community control, vouchers, ethnic studies and bilingual programs." The antidote for the future is building "pluralistic institutions."[45]

Against this rising interest in pluralism are its critics who claim that it will simply become another front for those who wish to discriminate against minorities. Tied to this belief is the fear that pluralism will result in a fragmentation of our society into hostile factions.

Stephen Steinberg, in *The Ethnic Myth*, states that "there is a fundamental tension between pluralism and democracy. That is to say, our society in principle sanctions the rights of ethnic groups to maintain their separate cultures and communities, but it also guarantees individual freedoms and specifically proscribes various forms of discrimination."[46]

Diane Ravitch offers this summary:

> As a people we are still far from that sense of common humanity to which the civil rights movement appealed. . . . Whether it is possible to treat people as individuals rather than as group members is as uncertain today as it was in 1954. And, whether it is possible to achieve an integrated society without distributing jobs and school places on the basis of group identity is equally uncertain.[47]

[42]Ray Rist, *The Invisible Children: School Integration in American Society* (Cambridge, Mass.: Harvard University Press, 1978), p. 244.

[43]Robert Green, "Book Review of *The Invisible Children: School Integration in American Society* by Ray Rist," *Harvard Educational Review*, 48, no. 3 (Aug. 1978), p. 411.

[44]Rist, *Invisible Children*, pp. 245–46.

[45]William Greenbaum, "America in Search of a New Ideal: An Essay on the Rise of Pluralism," *Harvard Educational Review*, 44, no. 3 (Aug. 1974), p. 439.

[46]Stephen Steinberg, *The Ethnic Myth* (New York: Atheneum Publishers, 1981), p. 258.

[47]Ravitch, "Color Blind," p. 163.

As long as there is widespread racial prejudice, the problems of discrimination and segregation will continue to create dilemmas for a democratic society.

Case Study: The Newly Integrated School System

Just before the beginning of the fall term, the federal district court mandated that the school system in which you teach must integrate its schools. In addition to the general mandate, the court is requiring a massive busing program to bring about racial balance in all the elementary and secondary schools in the district. The school board has been fighting the issue in the courts for many years to prevent integration, and the climate in the community is tense. The night of the ruling fifty buses were blown up by opponents of the decision. Parents have begun to put their homes up for sale, and teachers in some of the formerly all-white schools are seeking to move to the suburbs.

The previously all-white school in which you teach soon will have 50 percent of its children from black and Mexican-American homes. From remarks in the teacher's lounge in past years, you know that many of your colleagues are prejudiced against minorities and generally believe them to be incapable of high-quality academic work. Your principal has been opposed to integration in the past, but with the court order, is now desperately trying to prepare the school, teachers, parents, and children in the community for the change.

What feelings do you have about teaching in an integrated setting for the first time? What actions can you take in conjunction with parents, principal, and fellow teachers to facilitate a smooth transition to a new type of school? What can you do to make the "new" children feel welcome in your school and to prevent resentment among the other children, many of whose friends are being bused elsewhere? What curricular and extracurricular changes do you think might be necessary, given the new makeup of your student body?

Thought Questions

1. What evidence can you cite to prove that racism and prejudice are not strictly a thing of the historical past but are still to be found in the United States today?
2. Has any group to which you belong ever suffered discrimination in this country or abroad?
3. For what historical and other reasons have blacks, Mexican-Americans, Native Americans, and Oriental-Americans suffered comparatively greater degrees of discrimination than other ethnic groups in American society?
4. Differentiate between the concepts of cultural pluralism and the melting pot. Bring evidence to bear on which seems to be the dominant theme in American culture today.
5. In *Brown v. Board of Education* (1954), the Supreme Court stated that "separate

but equal" schools were inherently unequal. What impact has that Court case, and subsequent ones based on it, had on American society since 1954?

6. What mechanisms can be used to provide a truly multicultural education for children in the overwhelmingly white-Anglo suburbs?

7. Why do you agree or disagree with the thesis that the racial dilemma facing this country is basically a "white problem?"

8. Martin Luther King Jr. and other civil rights advocates have demonstrated the effectiveness of "civil disobedience" in bringing about social and legal change. Do you agree or disagree with using it, and why? Is violence ever justified to bring about change?

9. "Cultural pluralism" has become the new popular position to take in American race relations. What do you see as the advantages and potential dangers of such a posture for the schools?

Practical Activities

1. Visit a bilingual program in a nearby school district and compare the activities, textbooks, teaching materials, and overall program with regular classroom situations.

2. Analyze the textbooks being used in your school for evidence of racial bias. Look for the omission of certain events and individuals, in addition to bias in statements, interpretations, pictures, and illustrations.

3. Visit a school in your district that has a significant number of children or young people of minority descent. What do you observe about the treatment of children of various racial groups? How much segregation and integration do you observe in the classrooms, lunchrooms, and on the playground?

4. Interview a colleague who is a member of a racial minority. Ask questions about where he or she was raised, whether he or she experienced discrimination and what forms it took.

5. Survey the course listings of a school district, and list all the courses offered from kindergarten through twelfth grade that deal either directly or indirectly with minority groups in the United States.

6. Examine the racial makeup of the staff of a local school district. What do the employment patterns tell you about the status and treatment of minorities?

7. From your own past, detail examples of bias or prejudice that you have experienced or observed, and tell how you felt in the situation.

8. Design a lesson plan, appropriate for the grade level you hope to teach, that deals with personal and societal prejudice.

9. Obtain a copy of a simulation game that deals with prejudice, e.g., Star Power. Play the game with a group of friends or with a class of students. Briefly describe what occurred in the game and give your analysis of what can be learned from such simulations.

10. Interview a personnel manager of a school, college, or business. Ask the individual questions about affirmative action plans, employment practices, and problems he or she has encountered. Write your conclusions about the status of minority employment in the institution.

Bibliography

ALLPORT, GORDON W., *The Nature of Prejudice*. Reading, Mass.: Addison-Wesley Publishing Company, Inc., 1954.

DeLORIA, VINE, *Custer Died for Your Sins*. New York: Macmillan, 1969.

EASTLAND, TERRY, and WILLIAM J. BENNETT, *Counting by Race*. New York: Basic Books, Inc., Publishers, 1979.

GREEN, ROBERT L., MARGARET A. PARSONS, and FRANCES THOMAS, "Desegregation: The Unfinished Agenda." *Educational Leadership*, Jan. 1981, pp. 282–85.

GREENBAUM, WILLIAM, "America in Search of a new Ideal: An Essay on the Rise of Pluralism." *Harvard Educational Review*, 44, no. 3 (Aug. 1974), pp. 411–40.

HAZARD, WILLIAM R., "The *Bakke* Decision: Mixed Signals from the Court." *Phi Delta Kappan*, 60, no. 1 (Sept. 1978), pp. 16–29.

ITZKOFF, SEYMOUR, *Cultural Pluralism and American Education*. Scranton, Pa.: International Textbook Company, 1969.

MONTAGUE, ASHLEY, *Man's Most Dangerous Myth: The Fallacy of Race*, 5th ed. New York: Oxford University Press, 1974.

MYRDAL, GUNNAR, *An American Dilemma: The Negro Problem and Modern Democracy*, 2nd ed. New York: Harper & Row, Publishers, Inc., 1962.

OTHEGUY, RICARDO, "Thinking About Bilingual Education: A Critical Appraisal." *Harvard Educational Review*, 52, no. 3 (Aug. 1983), pp. 301–14.

PATE, GLENN S., "Research on Prejudice Reduction." *Educational Leadership*, Jan. 1981, pp. 288–91.

RAVITCH, DIANE, "Color Blind or Color-Conscious?" *The New Republic*, May 5, 1979. Reprinted in *Annual Editions: Education 83/84*. Guilford, Conn.: Dushkin Publishing Group, Inc., 1984.

RIST, RAY, *The Invisible Children: School Integration in American Society*. Cambridge, Mass.: Harvard University Press, 1978.

SANTIAGO, RAMON L., and ROSA CASTRO FEINBERG, "The Status of Education for Hispanics," *Educational Leadership*, Jan. 1981.

STEINBERG, STEPHEN, *The Ethnic Myth*. New York: Atheneum Publishers, 1981.

9

Gender and Education

What if "maternal thinking" and sensitivity to others were treated as philosophical virtues and curricular goals rather than taken for granted as exploitable female traits.[1]

Social organization of gender is, just as a society's dominant mode of production, a fundamental determining and constituting element of that society, socially constructed, subject to historical change and development, and organized in such a way that it is systematically reproduced.[2]

SOCIALIZATION AND GENDER IDENTITY

Every society is organized by a gender system that provides a systematic way to deal with sex, gender, and roles. In other words, every culture has processes by which people are socialized into sex roles. Nancy Romer, in *The Sex Role Cycle,* observes that every society trains its young people to function within its own view of the world and according to the rules and regulations that control that world. People are not just victims; people "eagerly participate" in the process of socialization because they want to fit in, to be like other people in their world. It is this process that prepares children to play the roles that society expects or requires of them as adults. Societal rules are the "set of expected behaviors and responsibilities" that vary according to sex, race, ethnicity, and social class.[3] Of these, sex is almost universally the most basic social category. Technically, sex is a biological category, which when it is discussed as a social category, is often referred to as *gender.*

The success of the socialization process is indicated by the studies that show that gender identity as an "unchanging core of personality formation is with rare

[1]Frances Maher and Charles H. Rathbone, "Teacher Education and Feminist Theory: Some Implications for Practice," *American Journal of Education* (Feb. 1986), p. 221.

[2]Nancy Chodorow, *The Reproduction of Mothering* (Berkeley: University of California Press, 1978), p. 8.

[3]Nancy Romer, *The Sex Role Cycle* (Old Westbury, N.Y.: Feminist Press, 1981), p. xvi.

exception firmly and irreversibly established for both sexes by the time a child is three."[4]

Although Romer pegs the age at six rather than three, she too is convinced that "by the time children enter elementary school, they most likely think of themselves as members of their own sex, behave in sex-typical ways, want to be like members of their own sex, and feel emotionally committed to this point of view."[5] There is strong evidence that every society assigns roles according to sex, yet there is amazing variability among cultures in the roles that are assigned, their extent, and their rigidity.[6]

Biological differences between men and women are universal throughout human history. Across cultures, those differences have been used to create categories and assign social roles. Some roles, such as those connected with childbirth and breast-feeding, are intimately tied to the obvious biological characteristics of women. However, role assignments according to sex have gone well beyond those connected with reproduction. A division of labor along lines of gender has prescribed that most of the caretaking tasks in the society are assigned to women and most of the external, public, and production-related tasks are given to men.

Nancy Chodorow claims that the sexual division of labor is inseparable from sexual inequality. She says that "the sexual division of labor and women's responsibility for child care are linked to and generate male dominance. They [anthropologists] show that women's continued relegation to the domestic, 'natural' sphere, as an extension of their mothering functions, has ensured that they remain less social, less cultural, and less powerful than men." These conditions, she says, are the result of men's dealing with the "extra domestic distribution networks that gave them control over the means of production."[7] Chodorow's thesis is that even the mothering role need not be limited to women, that it could be performed by men, and that in this change of roles there would be a change in the power structure in society.

Other writers have suggested that the differences between the sexes, such as the division of labor, go back to the days when people lived a hunter-gathering existence and that the division of labor then was essential to survival. The theory is extended to say that these characteristics are built into the physiology of the two sexes and are genetically determined.[8]

The evidence concerning which characteristics are genetically determined and which socially determined is not conclusive. Certain physical, structural, and hormonal differences can be observed, but whether or not they also imply emotional, intellectual, personality, and social differences, and the extent of those differences if they exist, is simply not known.

Whether or not there are differences is only one issue. Two other issues, although separate, are related to this topic. If there are no differences between

[4]Carol Gilligan, *In a Different Voice* (Cambridge, Mass.: Harvard University Press, 1982), p. 7.

[5]Romer, *The Sex Role Cycle*, p. 50.

[6]Casey Miller and Kate Swift, *Words and Women* (New York: Anchor Books, 1977), p. 51; Romer, *The Sex Role Cycle*, p. xvii.

[7]Chodorow, *The Reproduction of Mothering*, p. 214.

[8]Ibid., pp. 18–19.

men and women except that women can conceive and give birth to children and nurse them and that men can provide the sperm for fertilizing the egg, are all other sex-assigned roles or expectations arbitrary? If, however, differences go beyond these basic biological functions, two issues still must be resolved. First, are there differences of quality between the characteristics of the two sexes? That is, are the qualities of one sex more valuable, more essential, more important than the qualities of the other sex? Second, if there are other differences, to what extent do those differences warrant differential treatment of the two sexes? The issues are not simple, nor can they be readily resolved.

In one sense it does not matter how many differences observed between men and women are genetically determined. If the differences were largely social, we would be able to alter the social structures in such a way that changes in roles would occur. There is evidence to suggest that this is a real possibility. For example, the number of women who hold managerial positions in business and in government has increased.

The nature or nurture argument is not likely to be resolved in time to help this generation make policies about education, work, insurance, and pay. It is more important to understand how our society contributes to a rigid separation of characteristics, jobs, and behaviors into masculine and feminine.

SEX DISCRIMINATION, SEX STEREOTYPING, SEX BIAS, SEXISM

It is a short step from a discussion of sex roles and socialization to that of stereotyping and discrimination. Assigning social roles based on sex is not in itself a problem. However, when role assignments come to be seen as unreasonable limitations or unjust burdens, those who feel oppressed by the conditions will work for changes. The 1963 publication of Betty Friedan's *The Feminine Mystique* gave public voice to a feeling of alienation and discrimination that had been felt by many women and some men who were dissatisfied with the limitations they felt from narrow, rigidly defined sex roles.

Although discrimination, stereotyping, bias, and sexism each have their separate meanings, they are all part of the same larger construct of attitudes, behaviors, rules, laws, customs, language, and expectations that restrict women's lives. These terms underline the injustice of a society dominated by men and male institutions that perpetuates the subordinate position of women by (1) preventing them from gaining the tools of power by limiting their access to training, education, and jobs, and (2) creating the conditions in which male characteristics are considered superior to female characteristics, that is, "actions or practices carried out by members of dominant groups, or their representatives which have a differential and negative impact on members of subordinate groups."[9] Examples of discrimination are paying women less than men for the same job, keeping women out of jobs, and prohibiting women from pursuing educational opportunities because of their sex.

[9]Joe R. Feagin and Clairece Booker Feagin, *Discrimination American Style* (Englewood Cliffs, N.J.: Prentice-Hall, Inc., 1978), p. 20.

Discriminatory practices such as these seem to have their roots in stereotyping, which is here defined to mean a standardized mental picture held in common by members of a group and representing an oversimplified opinion, affective attitude, or judgment.

Discrimination, according to Joe and Clairece Feagin, originates with prejudice. They adopt Gunnar Myrdal's definition of prejudice as "the whole complex of valuations and beliefs which are behind discriminatory behavior."[10] The Feagins cite three different modes of discrimination: (1) the "Interest Theory," in which discrimination arises as a mechanism for protecting one's own interests, privileges, or power; (2) "Internal Colonialism" in which the institutional arrangements that are established by a colonizing power guarantee certain inequalities; and (3) "Institutional Racism," in which all the prejudices that cause individual discrimination become a part of the policies and practices of the institutions to the extent that individuals no longer need to take the full responsibility for discriminatory conditions.[11]

Sexism is used as an easy catchall term for a large and diverse collection of feelings, beliefs, and attitudes about the status of women in the United States. It is a new word that bears some examination. A liberal reworking of the dictionary definition of *racism* makes it apply to gender: the assumption that psychocultural traits and capacities are determined by sex and that the sexes differ decisively from one another, usually coupled with the belief in the inherent superiority of a particular sex and its right to domination over the other. One student of the subject was more concise when she wrote that sexism is a "pervasive ideology that sees females as inferior beings."[12]

Rita Bornstein provided a description of what she calls the "circle of sexism" (Figure 9-1). This scheme helps to illuminate the connection between what is perceived and what is actual.[13]

The variability in sex roles across cultures suggests that much of what is thought of as feminine or masculine is culturally determined. Because the elements of socialization are buried deep within a culture, they are difficult to see and even more difficult to analyze in an objective fashion.

To confound the situation further, many elements of socialization are very personal and close to home. Parents, grandparents, friends, teachers, and church officials are agents of socialization who carry out their tasks with the best of intentions.

Many people feel that learning the appropriate masculine and feminine behavior helps one to be happy and to succeed in the social and economic world. People often fear that unusual behavior or choices make an individual unhappy; unhappiness and

[10]Ibid., p. 2.

[11]Ibid., pp. 9–12.

[12]Miller and Swift, *Words and Women*, p. 128.

[13]Rita Bornstein, "Sexism in Education," in *Sex Equity Handbook for Schools*, Myra Pollack Sadker and David Miller Sadker, eds., (New York: Longman, Inc., 1982).

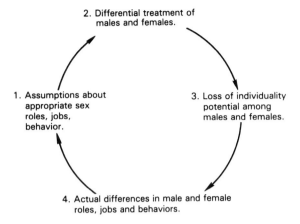

2. Differential treatment of
males and females.

1. Assumptions about
appropriate sex
roles, jobs,
behavior.

3. Loss of individuality
potential among
males and females.

4. Actual differences in male and female
roles, jobs and behaviors.

FIGURE 9-1 Circle of Sexism

nonconformity are equated. This is particularly true in relation to issues surrounding sex roles: sexuality, marriage, having children, masculine and feminine appearance.[14]

HISTORY OF PATRIARCHY

Patriarchal systems go back at least as far as Old Testament times, the Genesis account of creation stating,

> And the rib, which the Lord God had taken from man, made he a woman, and brought her unto the man. . . . Unto the woman [God] said, I will greatly multiply thy sorrow and thy conception, in sorrow thou shalt bring forth children; and thy desire shall be to thy husband, and he shall rule over thee.

The apostle Paul helped to institutionalize this view into the Christian church. In 1 Corinthians 11, he states:

> The head of the woman is the man . . . the woman is the glory of the man . . . neither was the man created for the woman; but the woman for the man.

and again in 1 Timothy 2:

> Let the woman learn in silence with all subjection. But I suffer not a woman to teach, nor to usurp authority over the man, but to be in silence.

Christianity was not the only religion to insist on male superiority. An Orthodox Jewish prayer states, "Blessed art Thou, O Lord our God, King of the Universe, that I was not born a woman."

[14]Romer, *The Sex Role Cycle,* p. xix.

Although Plato, in *The Republic,* appears to advocate equality of the sexes, Aristotle places women in an inferior role in *Politics.* Using Aristotle's writings as a basis for much of his own work, St. Thomas Aquinas, the Roman Catholic theologian of the Middle Ages, set the basis for centuries of discrimination against women in the church and society at large. The Reformation did little to help matters, as the Protestant churches and new nation-states did not emancipate women. This was as true in Puritan New England as it was in Great Britain, France, and Russia.

Patriarchies, built around the supremacy of the male head of the household and the inferior status of women, are not unique to religions but can be found in social, political, and economic systems throughout history. Property, titles, king-ships, and a host of other privileges were passed on through the male line, and women were barred from owning property or participating in any meaningful way in the political life of the community. Not until the 1920s were women given the right to vote in the United States, long after former male slaves had been given the franchise.

SEX DISCRIMINATION IN SCHOOLS AND THE LAW

> The promise of equal opportunity in the United States implies access to education. Underlying this promise is the belief that educational achievement can be translated into occupational success. Belief in this ideal of equal opportunity and the value of education, coupled with a changing sociopolitical climate, prompted the challenges made to the educational status quo in the 1960s and 1970s. During those turbulent years women activists once again found their political voice to lobby for educational and occupational reforms. The success of [their] lobbying efforts resulted in landmark legislation prohibiting sex discrimination in school and at work.[15]

The 1961 formation of the first Presidential Commission on the Status of Women set the stage for women's legislative advances in the United States. Shortly thereafter, the Equal Pay Act of 1963 was passed, establishing the first statutory prohibition against sex discrimination. Title VII of the Civil Rights Act of 1964 was extended to include gender. In 1972 it was further extended to take in employment in educational institutions. In 1967 an Executive Order further protected women in employment. In the 1970s the first congressional hearings were held on women and education. These hearings stimulated the passage of Title IX of the Education Amendments of 1972 (Public Law 92-318).

Equal Rights Amendment (ERA)

In 1982, the major hope of eliminating sex discrimination with a single, clean blow—the ERA—faltered when this proposed amendment to the Constitution was defeated. The wording of the amendment was simple and direct: "Equality of

---

[15]Paul Thurston, "Judicial Dismemberment of Title IX," *Phi Delta Kappan* 60, no. 8 (Apr. 1979), p. 189.

rights under the law shall not be abridged by the United States or by any state on account of sex."

The struggle for adopting the amendment to the Constitution began in the 1970s, when Congress passed the measure and the process of ratification by state legislatures began. By 1973, thirty of the necessary thirty-eight states had ratified the amendment. During the new conservative atmosphere of the late 1970s and 1980s, however, opposition to the measure grew. Legislatures in the remaining states began defeating the amendment.

The supporters of the amendment then turned their efforts to other political realms. Believing that it is necessary to change the political membership of the state legislatures and other political officers before basic changes will be made in the laws, the ERA backers began raising money and creating political organizations to put women into political office.

Title IX

With the defeat of the ERA, the next most powerful tool for eliminating sex discrimination is Title IX of the Education Amendments of 1972 and the regulations passed in 1975 to implement its provisions. The act states that

> No person in the United States shall, on the basis of sex, be excluded from participation in, be denied the benefits of, or be subject to discrimination under any education program receiving federal financial assistance.

In effect, the act applies to virtually every aspect of schooling. In the area of admissions, schools may not discriminate, except in the case of all-male or all-female institutions and those church-related colleges where beliefs prohibit participation of both sexes in certain activities. All students must be permitted to take any course in the curriculum, and home economics courses or shop courses may not be required unless they are required of both sexes. Guidance testing and other mechanisms used to track males or females into certain programs or occupations are prohibited, as are job employment opportunities that differentiate between boys and girls.

The weakness of the legislation is that it does not have the force of the Constitution behind it. Because it prohibits those educational institutions receiving federal money from discriminating on the basis of sex, its enforcement rests in the ability of the federal government to withdraw federal funds for noncompliance.

Because virtually all public school systems receive some form of federal aid, there was a flurry of excitement and opposition to the law when it was passed. In subsequent years the courts have had the task of interpreting the application of the law and the constitutionality of its provisions. In an analysis of the judicial treatment of Title IX, Paul Thurston concludes that "the courts have more consistently dismembered Title IX than enforced it."[16] He points out that the result of the court decisions has left a "confusing picture" for school districts. The two areas in

[16]Ibid., p. 594.

which the courts have had the greatest effect are in the constitutionality of the athletics section and in the enforceability of the provisions of subpart E, which prohibits sex discrimination against employees.[17] Thurston charges that "taken as a whole . . . the changes envisioned in public education as a result of Title IX have not been made voluntarily by school districts."[18] A major hindrance to enforcement of Title IX lies in the fact that federal dollars can only be withheld for noncompliance on a program-specific basis. It is often difficult, especially in the realm of discrimination in employment, to determine which programs are affected. The result is that enforcement is largely a matter of negotiating with school districts found to be in noncompliance.

Among the provisions of Title IX, none has been as controversial as the athletics section, Section D. Few things are as close to the American people as athletics, and in few other aspects of our culture are the American people as supportive of distinct sex roles as they are in sports. Title IX affects school athletics in two ways: first, by who may be a participant, and second, by the offerings of athletic programs. The law allows schools to limit participation in a contact sport exclusively to members of one sex. For noncontact sports, schools may choose between providing two separate teams (a girls' team and a boys' team) or providing only one team in which admission is open to either sex, depending solely on one's ability. The challenges to these provisions have been frequent, and the resulting litigation has created confusion. For example, even though the law seems to be saying that schools may limit participation in a contact sport exclusively to members of one sex, the Pennsylvania Supreme Court held that a state athletic association rule prohibiting both sexes from participating in contact sports was unconstitutional.[19]

SCHOOLS AND SEX ROLE SOCIALIZATION

If, as James Jones has suggested, we in the United States along with the rest of the Western world suffer the consequences of cultural sexism, the way to change conditions is to change the processes of socialization so that new assumptions are created and new expectations are built into the belief systems of young people.[20] To some, this smacks of indoctrination, but indoctrination is the intent of all socialization. It is not a matter of whether or not there will be indoctrination; what is at stake is what values will be passed along.

The school, next to the family, is one of the most effective instruments of socialization. So it is no surprise to find that the women's movement has sought the cooperation of teachers, administrators, and textbook publishers in their cam-

[17]Ibid.
[18]Ibid., p. 596.
[19]Ibid., p. 594.
[20]Feagin and Feagin, *Discrimination American Style*, pp. 36–37.

paign to change the subtle elements of schooling that promote attitudes, behaviors, and practices that create sex roles. Frank Zepenzauer noted that feminists have been exceedingly successful in winning over the educational establishment. In an informal survey of the major education journals from 1970 to 1979, he was surprised to find that there was very little evidence of any debate of feminist issues. He observed that there has been debate in other publications but was disturbed by the degree to which education journals seemed simply to adopt the "feminist ideology."[21] On the other hand, some people believe that even with antidiscrimination laws, many elements in schools promote a sexist society.

Whether the schools are the handmaidens of the women's movement or not, they do have a variety of media available to them through which messages about sex roles can be communicated. The selection of curriculum is only one of the most obvious. The language that is used in the classroom is a subtle but critical element of socialization, and the hiring practices in schools and admissions policies in universities can also reflect sex biases. The management of the schedule so that sex-specific classes are offered at the same time discourages male students from taking traditionally female courses and vice versa. The counseling program, which helps students make choices not only in curriculum but also in careers and higher education, can also have an impact on sex roles. The decision to include or exclude information about women in history, literature, science, and other fields is said to convey subtle messages about women. And finally, teachers' nonverbal behavior can reflect sex roles.

Textbooks

Public school textbooks have been studied by David and Myra Sadker. The results indicate that the characteristics of males portrayed therein are ingenuity, creativity, bravery, perseverance, achievement, adventurousness, curiosity, sportsmanship, helpfulness, acquisition of skills, competitiveness, use of power, autonomy, self-respect, friendship, and the avoidance of anything feminine. The characteristics that they found attributed to girls were dependency, passivity, incompetence, fearfulness, concern about physical appearance, obedience, and domesticity. They also found that the books were dominated by males. In their sample they discovered the following ratios[22]

Boy-centered to girl-centered stories	5:2
Adult male to adult female main characters	3:1
Male to female biographies	6:1
Males to female animal stories	2:1
Male to female fantasy stories	4:1

[21]Frank Zepenzauer, "Threading Through the Feminist Minefield," *Phi Delta Kappan* 63, no. 4 (Dec. 1981), pp. 268–73.
[22]Ibid., p. 268.

Language

Language is a powerful tool in establishing the meaning of our experience. It enables us to interpret and organize the world we experience through our senses, and in that way provides structure and meaning to what would otherwise be a jumble of impressions. Conversely, a language largely limits the thinking of its speakers to ideas that can be expressed in that language. But language, like society, can and does change over time. Those who argue for changes in language point out that there are conventions of language that exclude women. For example, phrases such as "the history of mankind" may not be ambiguous to those who know that it is intended to include women as well as men, but such usage does limit our understanding. Those who want to see the language changed argue that the situation can be easily corrected by the use of terms such as *people* or *citizens* rather than *men* or *mankind* and that we can say *ancestors* rather than *forefathers*. A number of professional organizations have supported the movement to rid themselves of gender-related terminology. For example, the Council of the American Library Association stated in 1975 that "consistent and exclusive use of the masculine gender perpetuates the traditional language of the society which discriminates against women" and resolved that all future publications of the association would "avoid terminology which perpetuates sex stereotypes."[23]

A strong case for change can be made by noticing that our language excludes the female gender by using *men* or *man* as generic terms meant to convey *humanity*. For example, we may not always assume that the "man of the street" means only males, or that the discovery of Java "man" means only a race of men. The proponents of change claim that avoiding ambiguity is a sufficient reason for using terms such as *ancestors* rather than *forefathers*. Some linguists, however, have objected to the campaign to do away with gender-specific language, claiming that the changes, such as replacing *chairwoman* with *chairperson*, corrupt our language. What these people tend to forget is that language, like the society it reflects, is changeable.

Language is not only significant as a communicator and teacher of our culture and its values, but it also communicates information about the person using it. For example, the way people speak often reveals their educational background or social class. In our society, as in others, language in all its subtle dimensions is used differently by men and women and communicates differences in their status and their role in social settings.

Roberta Hall discovered that although men and women speak the same language, their manner of speech differs. Men's speech patterns, according to Hall, are assertive, impersonal, abstract, and tend to be competitive exchanges, whereas women's speech is often characterized by hesitation, false starts, high pitch, questioning intonation, excessive use of qualifiers, and is accompanied by inappropriate smiling and averting of the speaker's eyes.[24]

[23]Sadker and Sadker, *Sex Equity Handbook for Schools*, p. 15.
[24]Roberta M. Hall and Bernice R. Sandler, *The Classroom Climate: A Chilly One for Women?* (Washington, D.C.: Association of American Colleges, 1982), pp. 1–20.

Teachers' Behavior

Certain observable discriminatory practices in schools have been banned by federal legislation under Title IX of the 1972 Education Amendments. In spite of this legislation, however, there are subtle ways in which teachers' behavior can result in "women's educational experiences . . . differing . . . considerably from those of men even when they attend the same institutions, share the same classrooms, and work with the same teachers."[25]

The differential treatment of girls that hinders their education begins in preschool and continues through graduate education. A study completed by Lisa Serbin and K. Daniel O'Leary revealed that even in preschool, teachers gave more attention to boys than girls and were more likely to carry on extended conversations with boys than with girls.[26] The nearly automatic and unconscious discounting of girls that is reflected in this study is characteristic of the findings from many such studies at every level of education.

The discrimination that girls experience in school is all the more devastating for its subtlety and its invisibility. The Sadkers report the results of a remarkable study in which teachers were shown a videotape of students and teachers in a normal classroom setting. The teachers viewing the tape were then asked to decide whether girls or boys had verbally dominated the interactions. All the viewers believed that the girls had dominated the classroom. They were all wrong. When the actual speaking time for girls and boys was computed, it was revealed that boys out-talked the girls 3 to 1. The study is a startling demonstration that our assumptions about the sexes are so powerful that they distort our direct observation.[27]

The persistence of male domination of educational and social settings was also found in a study of over one hundred fourth-, sixth-, and eighth-grade classes where they found that boys were eight times more likely than girls to "grab" attention. The same study revealed that even when girls were spoken to by the teacher, they did not get the same kind of feedback as the boys. The reaction to boys was often dynamic, precise, and effective, whereas the reaction to girls was often bland and diffuse.[28] The result is that many girls go through their education surrounded by a puzzling, unresponsive silence about what effect, if any, their actions or contributions are having. Consequently, girls grow up without sufficient information about the quality of their work and without confirmation that their presence is felt.

An unresponsive environment is not conducive to continued engagement or learning. To live in an environment where one's words or actions seem not to matter is likely to result in withdrawal or damaged self-esteem. In light of these findings, it is not surprising that although girls start school intellectually ahead of boys, by graduation they have lower SAT scores than boys. By the time they begin

[25]Elizabeth Moen, "Sexism Grows from the Seeds." *Boulder Daily Camera* (Aug. 1, 1983), p. 8B.
[26]Myra Sadker and David Sadker, "Sexism in the Schoolroom of the 80's," *Psychology Today* (Mar. 1985), p. 55.
[27]Ibid., p. 54.
[28]Ibid., p. 56.

high school, girls also are less interested in careers than are boys, even when their achievement scores are as high, and girls are less likely than boys to participate in gifted programs.[29]

Other, seemingly innocent, behaviors in schools promote distinctions. Dividing the class according to gender for purposes of organization, such as seating or "lining-up," heightens distinctions of sex roles. Selecting classroom helpers by asking the girl to water the flowers and the boy to run the projector, when done as a consistent pattern, communicates expectations regarding gender and acceptable roles.

One study that attempted to ascertain the attitudes of junior high school teachers toward appropriate sex-related characteristics indicated that the teachers expected good female students to exhibit the following characteristics:

appreciative	sensitive
calm	dependable
conscientious	efficient
considerate	mature
cooperative	obliging
mannerly	thorough
poised	

The same teachers expected good male students to exhibit the following characteristics:[30]

active	energetic
adventurous	enterprising
aggressive	frank
assertive	independent
curious	inventive

These conditions result in women being low in self-esteem; ambivalent about success, power, and achievement; intellectually underdeveloped; unassertive; over-educated for their jobs; underprepared for traditionally male career opportunities; and at the bottom of the ladder in employment, status, pay, and opportunities for advancement.

Athletics

The public schools have made progress in recent years in equalizing athletic opportunity in intramural and interscholastic sports, but the thornier issues of equal expenditures and facilities are a long way from being resolved. Progress has generally been made under pressure from the courts. Studies indicate, however,

---

[29]Ibid., p. 57.
[30]Hall and Sandler, *The Classroom Climate*, p. 20.

that most school districts do not provide an equal number of sports for girls and boys.

Sex discrimination takes other forms as well. Sex-role stereotyping of the sports themselves often occurs, with girls being encouraged to go into gymnastics, figure skating, swimming, and such "noncontact sports" as golf and tennis, whereas the team sports such as baseball, football, soccer, and basketball are left to the boys. When girls are allowed in team sports, they find them to be gender-separated, so that only in rare instances are girls permitted to compete on the same team with boys.

Title IX has begun to reverse discrimination against women in athletics and physical education, but parity has yet to be achieved. Girls' gymnasiums have traditionally been smaller and more poorly equipped, with inadequate locker rooms and other facilities. Until recently, one was hard put to find women coaches being paid for extra coaching duties, although it has been traditional to pay men for the same services. Men have been thought to be capable of coaching women's sports, but even today, few women can be found coaching male or even coeducational teams. Refereeing is a male bastion, even in interscholastic female sports, and the few female officials are generally paid on a lower scale than their male counterparts.

Interscholastic and intercollegiate interest in women's athletics, however, is increasing. A number of scholarships for female athletes have become available; travel money is set aside for girls' teams; girls' uniforms are bought by the schools; and girls' games are no longer played only as an adjunct to the "real" contest, the boys' games. Changes have begun, but in most cases it has taken state or federal court suits to bring about equal treatment.

The society at large is slowly beginning to accept changes in the stereotypes of appropriate behavior for each of the sexes, resulting in a rise in female teams in most sports, and even coeducational teams in such sports as soccer. Males are learning to dance, figure skate, jump rope, and express emotions other than the aggressiveness and competitiveness the "macho" image forced on them. Females run marathons, lift weights, and enter body-building contests; they now are permitted to express aggressiveness and to escape programmed passivity. As girls have been able to express their athletic ability, the male ego has not suffered the predicted shattering, nor has the quality of male sports declined.

Scholastic Aptitude Test (SAT)

Not only are girls treated differently from boys in school but something is affecting their performance on some measures of scholastic ability. Phyllis Rosser reports that since 1972, when boys began to outscore girls on the verbal portion of the SAT test, the gap between boys' and girls' scores has been increasing. Boys' average verbal score in 1989 was 434 compared with 421 for girls. In math the gap widened to 46 points, with boys having an average score of 500 and girls 454.

Why is it that girls, who have higher average grades than boys in both high school and college and score about the same on achievement tests, score much lower than boys on the SAT? The question is not just academic. Girls' lower scores on this important test keep many of them out of the best universities and colleges and exclude them from millions of dollars in scholarships.

Various explanations have been offered by authorities to explain the gap in scores. For example, one official of the Educational Testing Service (ETS) suggests that the difference results from variations in the population of the boys and the girls who take the test. He explains that among the girls who take the test there is a larger proportion of students from lower-income families; therefore, the average for girls is lower.

Critics of this ETS position explain that a more fundamental reason for girls' low scores is that they approach learning and problem solving differently from boys. The SAT, they argue, is a male-biased construct that favors boys in its style and its content. Rosser points out that standardized tests of any kind exemplify the masculine way of learning. Standardized tests, she adds, are "value free, require a choice of one 'right answer' with no chance to explain choices, emphasize quantitative subject matter rather than the arts and humanities, test understanding of small bits of knowledge in isolation rather than large chunks of related information and are given in a hurried, competitive environment that girls may find more stressful than boys do."[31]

Some remarkable inconsistencies support those who believe that the primary fault lies with the SAT test instrument itself. For example, although boys are now outscoring girls on the verbal portion of the SAT, girls continue to outscore boys on the Test of Standard Written English, a part of the SAT that is reported to colleges but not included in the overall score. The results of a New York State Education Department study found that girls and boys had virtually identical math scores on the Regents Exams, yet there is a large difference between girls' and boys' SAT math scores. The controversy about SAT scores for boys and girls indicates that we should take such examinations much more lightly. They are not measures of intelligence; rather, they are hurdles to be jumped. Carol Gilligan says that boys don't take the test as a measure of their intelligence but as a game to be won. If students, parents, and teachers accept this practical view of the test, then those who want what high scores on the test can give should prepare for them as they would for any other game. On the other hand, the lower grades "earned" by boys suggests a reverse-bias favoring girls. Girls tend to be more cooperative, obedient and punctual in the classroom than boys. Given the subjective dimension of grading, these are behaviors that favor girls at report card time.

WOMEN IN HIGHER EDUCATION

There is considerable evidence to indicate that women's access to higher education has increased in the last twenty years. Some of the statistics reported indicate a dramatic increase, which may be misleading as an indicator of true parity. For example, the statistic that women made up 50.9 percent of those enrolled in higher

[31]Phyllis Rosser, "Girls, Boys, and the SAT: Can We Even the Score?" *NEA Journal* (Jan. 1988), p. 48–49.

education in 1979 is statistically accurate, but it does not tell us that more women were part-time students or that more women than men were enrolled in two-year institutions.[32]

Statistics for degrees earned follow a similar pattern. Although it is true that the percentage of women earning degrees is increasing and the number of men earning degrees is declining, the numbers do not reveal the lack of parity. For example, women's degrees are still concentrated in the traditionally female fields such as education, fine arts, foreign languages, health professions, home economics, and library science. Although women are making inroads into traditionally male fields such as engineering, their progress there is slower. Although more women than ever are earning advanced degrees, there is an inverse relationship between the level of degree earned and the percentage of women earning that degree.[33]

Women, however, are making solid progress in higher education. Since 1975, the number of female college presidents in the United States has doubled and the number of women with Ph.D.s in full-time academic jobs has grown to over 50,000, or about 20 percent of the total.[34] Still, some telling disparities indicate continued discrimination. At the bottom of the academic hierarchy is a class of nontenured instructors who have little chance of moving into the upper echelons of the profession. According to the statistics compiled by the American Association of University Professors, more than eight thousand of these positions are held by women. Even in the humanities, where women have traditionally been the strongest, only 9.5 percent of these nontenured positions were held by men, whereas 24.1 percent were held by women.[35]

Comparisons of salaries for men and women in each of the academic ranks indicate that women are still being paid less than men for the same position. Because women have only recently begun to catch up with men in academia, the difference in salaries at the professor rank might be explained by differences in the number of years of service. Table 9-1, however, illustrates that discrepancies also exist at the entry-level ranks.

As might be expected, the number of women who pursue advanced degrees in education is greater than in most other disciplines. Although 70 percent of the education professors are white males, there are a growing number of women in all academic ranks. Table 9-2 indicates that although men make up 84 percent of the full professors, women comprise a majority of the assistant professor rank and a third of the associate rank.[36] If these figures represent a trend, the number of women professors in education schools eventually will exceed the number of male professors.

[32]MaryLou Randour, Georgia L. Strasburg, Jean Lipman-Blumen, "Women in Higher Education: Trends in Enrollments and Degrees Earned," *Harvard Educational Review* 52, no. 2 (May 1982), pp. 191–93.

[33]Ibid., p. 199.

[34]Larry Rohter, "Women Gain Degrees, But Not Tenure," *New York Times*, Jan. 4, 1987.

[35]Ibid.

[36]"Teaching Teachers: Facts and Figures," (Washington, D.C.: American Association of Colleges for Teacher Education, 1987), p. 26.

TABLE 9-1   Average Salary for Faculty at Institutions with Doctoral-Level Programs (1985–86)

ACADEMIC RANK	SALARY	
	MEN	WOMEN
Professor	$47,660	$42,470
Associate	34,480	32,320
Assistant	29,330	26,650
Instructor	22,130	20,050
Lecturer	26,140	22,650

Source· American Association of University Professors; National Research Council.

TABLE 9-2   Education Professoriate by Rank and Gender

	PROFESSOR	ASSOCIATE PROFESSOR	ASSISTANT PROFESSOR
Male	84%	68%	46%
Female	16%	32%	54%

Source: RATE Project Institutional Survey.

Research and Women

The growth in women's studies programs and an increase in the number of women receiving advanced degrees have resulted in an increasing number of research studies about women and the status of women in society. These studies, especially those by women, have raised a new issue: that the old social science research begins from a biased set of assumptions, resulting in conclusions that women are lacking or are inferior. For example, one author describes a study by Inge Brouerman, who asked clinical psychologists, psychiatrists, and social workers to identify traits of clinically mentally healthy adults, males and females. The results were that the list of traits for males and the list of traits for adults were identical, but they were different from the list of traits for females.[37]

The same bias from a different perspective is described by Gilligan, who identifies sex biases in the theories of Freud, Piaget, Kohlberg, and Erickson. They create world views that say that male social, intellectual, moral, and physical development is coequal with normal development and that female development, when it differs from that standard, is deviant.[38]

Jane Rowland Martin, in an article for the *Harvard Educational Review*, makes a convincing case that the academic disciplines have excluded women from their subject matter, distorted their image according to the "male image of her," and have denied the "feminine" by forcing women into a masculine mold.[39]

[37]Pauline Gough, *Sexism: New Issue in American Education* (Bloomington, Ind.: Phi Delta Kappa Educational Foundation, 1976), p. 14.

[38]Carol Gilligan, *In a Different Voice* (Cambridge, Mass.: Harvard University Press, 1982).

[39]Jane Rowland Martin, "Excluding Women from the Educational Realm," *Harvard Educational Review* 52, no. 2 (May 1981), p. 133.

Martin, like many of her contemporaries, believes that a part of the problem is in defining everything from a masculine point of view. For example, she believes that women have been excluded from the philosophical and theoretical writing about education, in part because of the widespread acceptance of an unnecessarily narrow definition of education, which is virtually coextensive with schooling, related in turn to the masculine-oriented productive aspects of society, which excludes the feminine "reproductive" elements.[40]

In 1968, Matina Horner completed her research into a phenomenon known as "fear of success." Women had been largely excluded from the early research on "achievement motivation" conducted by David McClelland and John Atkinson, and Horner attempted to fill the gap. She hypothesized that women would be more likely to exhibit a fear of success than men, when that phenomenon was measured with the Thematic Apperception Test. Indeed, she found that women were more likely than men to show evidence of anxiety and uncertainty. Whereas 65 percent of the women demonstrated these traits, only 10 percent of the boys in the study showed the same traits. Boys were more likely than girls to thrive on a competitive situation.[41] Subsequent studies have not been consistent in replicating Horner's results, which may lead some people to doubt the validity of the original study.

The time is long past when it can be assumed that feminist scholarship can be considered a single body of thought. As more women are engaged in research and writing, the issues raised will become more finely honed, and an atmosphere of scholarly controversy and enlightenment will bring new insights to all the disciplines, including education.

● ━━ ●

Case Study: The Nonsexist Classroom

It is your second year as a teacher in a medium-sized family community in the Midwest. You observed in your first year that traditional sex roles and stereotypes were evident in the behavior of the students, and these were reinforced by the way teachers and administrators treated the children.

In an enlightened condition you decided to counteract the trend by introducing materials that show women doing traditionally male jobs. You make it a point to discuss sex roles with your students and to eliminate sex bias in the conduct of your class.

Some parents have become upset that you are disrupting the "natural order" of things and take their complaint to the principal. The principal, who has no personal objections to your activities, is sympathetic with the parents because he believes that they represent the general feeling of the community. He asked that

[40]Ibid., pp. 130–40.

[41]Matina Horner, "A Bright Woman Is Caught in a Double Bind in Achievement Oriented Situations: She Worries Not Only About Failure But About Success," *Psychology Today* 3, no. 6 (Nov. 1969), pp. 36–38.

you revert to a more traditional curriculum and teaching style. Short of quitting, what would you do?

Thought Questions

1. Some of the literature suggests that gender identity is not only established early but also is a basic reference point for who we are. To what behaviors, characteristics, or traits is your sense of maleness or femaleness attached?
2. Regardless of whether the behavioral differences between men and women in our society are genetically or socially determined, there is evidence that in traditional male spheres women are often treated as inferior. What are some of the ways that this message of inferiority is communicated to children?
3. The subject of sex roles and discrimination is complex. The answers are neither simple nor obvious. What are the issues on which you believe there can be honest disagreement among well-informed persons?
4. What physiological differences are there between males and females, and what effects, if any, should or do these differences have in the emotional and psychological makeup of people and in the roles they play in society?
5. As more schools strive to establish equal funding for girls' athletics, what effects is this policy having on secondary and higher educational institutions?
6. What are the basic presuppositions of traditional groups such as Fascinating Womanhood and Total Woman about women's role and place in the home and in society? What are the presuppositions of radical feminists?
7. What are the societal reasons for discrimination against women in the economy?
8. How have the roles of men and women changed since your grandparents' time? Deal with such things as child rearing, jobs, relationships with spouses and others of the same or opposite sex, and any other differences. In what ways have things remained the same?
9. List, from memory, women who have made a major contribution to our history. Why have women been so ignored by historians?
10. Which characteristics and behaviors are male and which are female as defined by today's standards? What effects on society would there be if they were reversed?

Practical Activities

1. Make a thorough evaluation of a textbook currently in use in an elementary or secondary school. Look for examples of sexism in the illustrations, use of language, end-of-chapter questions, sex of the authors, sex of main characters (if it is a reading or literature book), sexism through omission, roles of men and women, and anything else you can find.
2. Conduct a study of the curricular offerings in a school district. Look for places where the role of women might properly be included in the curriculum. Document places where the school district has attempted or is attempting to change, along with places where women and their role in American society are being ignored.

3. Attend a meeting of NOW, Fascinating Womanhood, Total Woman, a women's political caucus, League of Women Voters, a church women's group, or any other organization made up predominantly of women. Deal with the issues discussed at the meeting and your reaction to the issues and the participants.

4. Make a study of the number of male and female teachers and administrators at each level of schooling in a school district. Calculate the percentages of male to female in each type of position: teacher, principal, assistant principal, coordinators, central administrators, and so on. Do the percentages indicate any sexism at work in the school district?

5. Spend an afternoon or an evening watching television, both the advertisements and the regular programming. What roles do you see portrayed by men and by women? What overt and covert forms of sexism are evident? How closely does what is portrayed on television parallel society in general?

6. List the words you use or hear regularly that are gender related, for example, *mankind* or *he* (when referring to both male and female). What words could be substituted for them? Which do you feel are nonsexist and should be left alone?

7. Spend some time in the school library. Count the number of biographies and autobiographies of women and estimate the number about men. Why the big difference? Compare the sex of the authors of the biographies.

8. Ask several children, boys and girls, what they would like to be when they grow up. Ask them if they would still want to be in that type of job if they were a member of the opposite sex. Did you find any examples of sex-role stereotyping among the children? If so, where do they get the messages from?

9. Make a collage or draw a picture of the "ideal man" and the "ideal woman"; then explain that ideal, including descriptions of the physical, emotional, and psychological aspects that make such a person your ideal. With the exception of obvious physiological differences, how do your ideal male and female differ from each other?

10. List all the ways that you have benefited from or have been negatively affected by the fact that you are male or female.

Bibliography

ANDELIN, HELEN B., *Fascinating Womanhood.* Santa Barbara, Calif.: Pacific Press, 1970.

BELENKY, MARY FIELD, et al., *Women's Ways of Knowing: The Development of Self, Voice, and Mind.* New York: Basic Books, Inc., Publishers, 1986.

CHODOROW, NANCY, *The Reproduction of Mothering.* Berkeley: University of California Press, 1978.

FEAGIN, JOE R., and CLAIRECE BOOKER FEAGIN, *Discrimination American Style.* Englewood Cliffs, N.J.: Prentice-Hall, Inc., 1978.

FRIEDAN, BETTY, *The Feminine Mystique.* New York: W.W. Norton & Company, Inc., 1963.

GILLIGAN, CAROL, *In a Different Voice.* Cambridge, Mass.: Harvard University Press, 1982.

HALL, ROBERTA M., and BERNICE R. SANDLER, *The Classroom Climate: A Chilly One for Women?* Washington, D.C.: Association of American Colleges, 1982.

MILLER, CASEY, and KATE SWIFT, *Words and Women.* New York: Anchor Books, 1977.

MILLETT, KATE, *Sexual Politics.* Garden City, N.Y.: Doubleday & Company, Inc., 1970.

MORGAN, ROBIN, ed., *Sisterhood Is Powerful: An Anthology of Writings from the Women's Liberation Movement.* New York: Random House, 1970.

ROMER, NANCY, *The Sex Role Cycle.* Old Westbury, N.Y.: Feminist Press, 1981.

SADKER, MYRA POLLACK, and DAVID MILLER SADKER, *Sex Equity Handbook for Schools.* New York: Longman, Inc., 1982.

SIMONE, ANGELA, *Academic Women: Working Towards Equality.* Boston: Bergin & Garvey Publishers, Inc., 1987.

STACEY, JUDITH, SUSAN BEREAUD, and JOAN DANIELS, eds., *And Jill Came Tumbling After: Sexism in American Education.* New York: Dell Publishing Company, Inc., 1974.

10

Alternative Schooling

The argument, therefore, is simple and, hopefully, cogent: students vary significantly, learning is of diverse sorts. No type of teacher, method, or climate is inherently superior. Thus a range of teachers, methods, and climates will better respond to the varied needs of students in mastering different types of learning.[1]

In the past two decades alternative schooling has spread from a handful to thousands of schools and programs enrolling millions of students in virtually every school district in the country. From being nearly invisible in the late 1960s, it became the subject of hundreds of articles, books, and special issues of various journals in the 1970s, nearly disappeared from the literature in the early 1980s, and has reappeared as we enter the 1990s. In the same period it stopped being associated with free schools and became a catchall term of hundreds of different experiments, ranging from Summerhill-like to extremely conservative schools. From being considered a liberal panacea, it has become a tool of even the most conservative educators for trying new ideas or returning to old ideas without jeopardizing an entire school system.

Alternative schooling does not refer to any particular, definable, identifiable form of schooling. It is one of those unfortunate terms that is laden with emotion and devoid of specific content. To say that one teaches in an alternative school tells the listener almost nothing about the school's philosophy, goals, organizations, curriculum, or pedagogy. At best it communicates a belief that the school is somehow different from what one might expect to encounter.

The host of programs and schools that have been called "alternative" includes, but has not been limited to, free schools, fundamental schools, open education, open classrooms, vocational programs, dropout programs, unwed mother programs, back to basics, career education, special schools or programs for handicapped students, magnet schools, gifted programs, school within a school, voucher schools, and "schools of choice."

The emotional load that *alternative schooling* carries can be attributed to the

---

[1]Allan A. Glatthorn, *Alternatives in Education: Schools and Programs* (New York: Dodd, Mead & Company, 1975), p. 7.

fervor with which its early promoters believed in the beneficial effects of their proposals and the equally strong feelings expressed by detractors who claim that "alternatives" of any sort are damaging to the democratic ideal of free public education.

A PERSPECTIVE ON ALTERNATIVE SCHOOLS

Alternative schooling often is associated with some version of the "free school" movement of the late 1960s and 1970s, which has been characterized as a desire "to humanize education, to restore joy to the process of learning; to shape new kinds of relationships for children and adults; and to create liberating environments where people might become free, caring happy human beings." Such a view is based on a "faith in the innate goodness and curiosity of children."[2]

Lawrence Cremin notes that the free school movement was rooted in the progressive movement of the 1920s and 1930s and in the writings of John Dewey. As recently as 1978, alternative schools were still being characterized in terms of the progressive movement as places where

1. Individual needs of students are the beginning point for education.
2. Teachers are advisors.
3. School is acknowledged to be a social community.
4. There is active versus passive learning.
5. There are a variety of learning resources, especially in the community.
6. Skills are a means, not an end.
7. Students participate in decision making.
8. Individuality of teachers and students is recognized and valued.

Those in favor of free schools believed that their particular version of schooling was the best and that it should become the wave of the future. In this belief they joined the reformers before them who thought that "team teaching," "modular teaching," "new math," or any one of a dozen innovations would usher in a new day for schools.

However, as studies began to produce information about the effectiveness of various innovations, it was discovered that they produced no significant difference and it was likely that "we shall never find the ideal teacher, method, or climate for learning," that there is great diversity in students and in learning, and that no single method of teaching is necessarily superior to another.[3]

Another version of the free school movement was that presented by Jonathan Kozol in his book *Free Schools*. His title refers to urban schools that place a high premium on learning as a way to "free" children from racism and indoctrination of

---

[2]David Thornton Moore, "Social Order in an Alternative School," *Teachers College Record* 79, no. 3 (Feb. 1978), p. 436.

[3]Glatthorn, *Alternatives in Education*, p. 6.

the white culture.[4] Although Kozol's alternative was not a "do your own thing" kind of school, the urban alternative and the middle-class free schools showed the same critical view of schools and society of the 1960s, accompanied by an optimism that a better method of education could be realized. However, the Ford Foundation's evaluation of the programs that it had sponsored revealed that "we really don't know how to improve schools."[5]

It was in this context that *alternative schooling* came to mean "choice." Belief that there was one best answer was waning, and in its place reformers of many different beliefs united in promoting a variety of alternatives from which students and parent could choose the schooling best suited for them. David Tyack's *The One Best System* and Mario Fantini's *Public Schools of Choice* provided the historical and theoretical rationalizations for many alternatives in education.

Alternative choices proliferated throughout the 1970s and 1980s. Greater numbers of educators began to see "alternatives" as a way to solve their own problems. Setting up a small program or school in a temporary building became a means of serving a definable group of students, whether they were dropouts or pregnant teenagers. The alternative could be designed to meet the particular needs of a specific population by adjusting any of the variables, such as content, structure, climate, and teaching style.

Unfortunately, alternatives also could become dumping grounds; some alternatives are little more than grim detention centers.[6] In 1981 there was a class action suit brought against the state of Florida by blacks who charged that, as a result of Florida's "Alternative School Law," black children were being labeled disruptive and forced into inferior programs. The Florida law charges school districts "to offer alternatives to conventional education which will meet the needs and interests of students." The law goes on to say that when the conventional school program does not meet the needs of certain students it may cause them to become "disruptive or disinterested in school."[7]

Robert Barr speculates that over 150 different kinds of schools and programs have been labeled as alternative schooling. Some programs now falling under the alternative umbrella, such as vocational programs, predate the alternative movement, whereas others, such as the Jefferson County Fundamental School in Colorado, represent a return to an earlier view of basic education and standards of behavior.

Although the expanding number of alternatives is logically explainable, it is curious that this should occur during a period of fiscal and philosophical conservatism in American education. Vernon Smith, a knowledgeable observer of alternative schooling, believes there are several explanations:

[4]Jonathan Kozol, *Free Schools* (Boston: Houghton Mifflin Company, 1972), pp. 7–12.

[5]Mary Ann Raywid, "The First Decade of Public School Alternatives," *Phi Delta Kappan* 62, no. 8 (Apr. 1981), p. 6.

[6]Robert Barr, "Alternatives for the Eighties: A Second Decade of Development," *Phi Delta Kappan* 62, no. 8 (Apr. 1981), p. 571.

[7]Rita Thrasher, "Florida's Alternative Education Law Stresses Positive, Not Punitive Schooling," *Phi Delta Kappan* 62, no. 8 (Apr. 1981), p. 547.

1. The optional nature of alternatives creates new structures without forcing students, parents, and teachers into something they don't want. In short, alternatives are there only for those who want them.
2. There are choices among significantly different alternatives, making choice available to everyone, not just those who could afford private schools.
3. The atmosphere in alternatives, regardless of their type, tends to be one in which teachers and students feel better about going to a school they have chosen. The results indicate that there are less violence and vandalism in alternative schools.
4. The "most powerful" reason for the growing popularity of alternatives is that they provide local control for parents, students, teachers, and administrators when outside control of schools from legislatures and courts is on the rise.[8]

Frameworks for Alternatives

In attempts to bring some analytic order to the plethora of choices, several authors have offered systems for organizing and categorizing alternatives.

Allan Glatthorn begins with simple categories along a continuum of autonomy:

1. Alternative schools: Autonomous, usually small instructional units that have their own territory, leadership, rules, and budget.
2. Alternative programs: Units within a conventional school that are dependent on the school for budget, resources, and authority but offer a program of study significantly different from the host school.
3. Alternative paths wherein individual students may make arrangements to create their own program, such as apprenticeships or correspondence study.[9]

Glatthorn presents a three-dimensional model, developed by Ralph Hansen, which, although it produces forty-eight permutations, is still inadequate for describing all the alternatives available (Figure 10-1). Glatthorn proposes twenty factors that he claims are the most common characteristics of alternative schools (Table 10-1). To this taxonomy he adds a typology into which most alternative schools would fit.

Student-Centered Alternatives

1. Schools for students who would otherwise be out of school, such as pregnant students or teenage mothers
2. Schools for disruptive students
3. Schools for special ethnic groups
4. Schools for the gifted and talented

[8]Vernon H. Smith, "Alternative Education Is Here to Stay," *Phi Delta Kappan* 62, no. 8 (Apr. 1981), p. 546.
[9]Glatthorn, *Alternatives in Education*, p. 11.

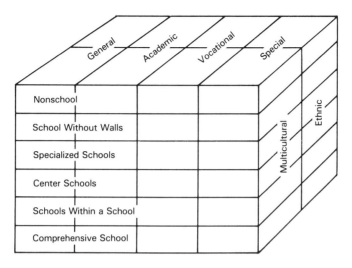

FIGURE 10-1 Alternative Schools

Source: Glatthorn, Allan A., *Alternatives in Education* (New York: Dodd, Mead & Company, 1975), p. 19.

Program-Centered Alternatives

1. Career schools
2. Performing-arts schools
3. Skills-training schools in which there is emphasis on learning basic skills
4. Open-learning schools (the option that is the most common) stressing community-based learning

Place-Centered Alternatives

1. Schools without walls
2. Community schools, most often associated with an ethnically cohesive neighborhood
3. Multidistrict schools
4. Wilderness schools, such as Outward Bound[10]

Another conceptual scheme for alternative schools, presented by Terrence Deal and Robert Nolan, is based on differences among educational ideologies. Deal and Nolan describe two kinds of schools:

1. The "traditional" school, which is dedicated to transmitting traditional cultural values and norms and in which decisions are made by hierarchical superiors.

[10]Ibid., pp. 27–32.

TABLE 10-1 A Taxonomy for Alternatives

FACTORS	OPTION 1	OPTION 2	OPTION 3
1. Funding	Public tax funds	Federal, state, foundations	Tuition and contributions
2. Control	Public school system	Church, university, or other institution	Parents, community
3. Students	Heterogeneous	Basically homogeneous by virtue of interest	Intentionally homogeneous on basis of predetermined criteria
4. Board	Inactive board	Moderately active board	Dominating board
5. Daily governance	Teachers	Teachers and students	Students
6. Leadership	Single strong leader	Single democratic leader or team of leaders	No single leader, decision by consensus
7. Relationships with conventional school	Housed in same building	Annex	Completely separate
8. Facilities	School building	Nonschool facility	No single building
9. Full-time or part-time program	Part of day or part of year	Chiefly full-time, with some movement back to main school	All education in alternative
10. Staff	Certificated	Chiefly certificated, with some noncertificated	Noncertificated
11. Staff organization	Differentiated	Some differentiation	No differentiation or specialization
12. Student selection	"Forced" assignment	Lottery from among applicants	Open admissions
13. Exclusion	Pupils excluded if they break rules	Only a few pupils excluded for very serious infractions	No one ever asked to leave
14. Program evaluation	Comprehensive	Minimal	None
15. Degree of structure	Highly structured and controlled	Students and staff develop minimal structure	Openly permissive
16. Nature of program	Conventional school offerings	Mixture of conventional and esoteric	Chiefly esoteric offerings
17. Grade organization	Graded	Nongraded within limits	Wide range of ages intentionally mixed
18. Schedule	College schedule	College schedule with variations	No schedule
19. Pupil grading	Letter grades with options	Noncompetitive evaluation	No evaluation at all
20. Crediting	Carnegie unit	Carnegie unit with variations	No credit

Source: Allan A. Glatthorn, *Alternatives in Education* (New York: Dodd, Mead & Company, 1975), pp. 28–29.

2. The "do your own thing" school, which is dedicated to removing barriers to the natural acquisition of knowledge and in which decisions are made according to the nature of the problem.[11]

[11]Terrence E. Deal and Robert R. Nolan, eds., *Alternative Schools: Ideologies, Realities, Guidelines* (Chicago: Nelson-Hall Publishers, 1978), pp. 12–14.

As the number and variety of alternative schools and programs continue to grow, the schemes for classifying them also will proliferate. Although typologies, categories, and taxonomies are helpful in bringing order out of the confusing array of choices springing up, they do not provide generalizations about alternatives. Gerald Smith, after studying the effects of nineteen different alternatives, concluded that the one thing they all had in common was free choice: The students and teachers had freely chosen to work and study in these schools. Others found what they believe to be the common or unifying elements, for example, their small size, which allows for more personal contact. Mary Ann Raywid, in her summary of ten years of alternative schools, observed that whatever the common characteristics may be, a common result is the "commitment that these schools engender from all within them, students and staff alike."[12]

OPEN SCHOOLS

Open schools based on the British "infant school" have been and continue to be the most common kind of elementary school alternative. Because of their popularity and because of the misuse of the term *open school,* it will be discussed here in greater detail than the other alternatives mentioned.

A variety of terms are used to describe or identify open schools: *informal education,* the *free day,* the *integrated day, integrated curriculum,* and *informal education,* which is the most descriptive of all.[13]

The British infant school approach to learning was widespread in England and expanded rapidly after World War II. During the war, because it was necessary to keep children in schools for more hours during the day and more days in the week, informal teaching became not just popular but also essential. In 1967 the so-called Plowden Committee called attention to this approach and urged its adoption in the primary schools. As might be surmised from the labels *informal* and *open,* the classroom atmosphere was casual: Students work simultaneously in small groups or individually and on different material, students are integrated across grades, and different subjects are integrated.

Charles Silberman explains that informal education is less an approach or method than a set of shared attitudes and convictions about the nature of childhood, learning, and schooling. Teachers in informal schools begin with the notion of childhood as something to be cherished and are concerned with the quality of a child's school experience in its own right, not merely as preparation for later schooling or for later life. They also believe that learning is likely to be more effective if it grows out of what interests the learner, rather than what interests the teacher. Silberman hastens to add that what chiefly distinguishes the contempor-

[12]Raywid, "The First Decade of Public School Alternatives," p. 552.

[13]There are several excellent books that describe the philosophy and practice of the English primary schools. These include John Blackie's *Inside the Primary School* (New York: Schocken Books, Inc., 1971); Mary Brown and Normal Precious, *The Integrated Day in the Primary School* (London: Wardlock Educational Publishers, 1968); and Alvin Hertzberg and Edward Stone, *Schools Are for Children! An American Approach to the Open Classroom* (New York: Schocken Books, Inc., 1971).

ary English informal schools from the American child-centered progressive schools of the 1920s and 1930s, as well as the education advocated by romantic critics like John Holt, George Dennison, and Herbert Kohl, is the clear understanding of and insistence on the teacher's central role. Teachers are more than just sympathetic, intelligent, even creative adults in the classroom who permit children to discover what they may. As Silberman puts it, they are there to teach.[14]

The concept of British informal learning appears to have been introduced to Americans by Joseph Featherstone through a three-part series on the English schools in *The New Republic* in August and September 1967. Since then, Featherstone and a few other writers and educators, such as [David Hawkins, Vito Perrone, Roland Barth, Vincent Rogers, and Silberman,] have articulated the theory and practice of the informal classroom to Americans.

Although open or informal primary education developed in a very practical, intuitive manner in the classrooms of many teachers, the concept is supported by a substantial body of theory on the way children learn, the nature of knowledge, and the aims of education. The theoretical foundations for this concept can be found in the work of Jean J. Rousseau, Friedrich Froebel, Maria Montessori, and Susan Isaacs, but of most importance is Jean Piaget's research on the mental development of children and John Dewey's philosophic treatment of instruction and learning. Both Piaget and Dewey hold that it is crucial for the child to act on his or her world. Actively manipulating, creating, and reinventing, according to both Piaget and Dewey, are imperative to the child's understanding. Genuine understanding occurs in the act of doing, not in telling children, nor even in demonstrating to them.

According to Piaget, children proceed through stages of development in learning, each stage reflecting a higher level of abstraction; but each child will develop in a particular learning area at the individual's own rate. In turn, the child must work on a learning task at his or her own speed. Teachers must first decide what learning is important to the growth of a child and then arrange the classroom to permit each child to learn at an individual's own pace and in his or her own way. Dewey said that if intellectual growth is to take place, the teacher must take objects (and later ideas) from the material or external surroundings and bring them together with the experiences and interests of the child's (internal) world. Both Piaget and Dewey stressed that not only does the individual child act on material things but also each child does so with other children in a communicative or group fashion. This is important not only for social development but also for intellectual development.[15]

---

[14]Charles E. Silberman, *Crisis in the Classroom* (New York: Random House, 1970), chap. 6.

[15]There are numerous publications by both Piaget and Dewey that are useful for further understanding of these ideas. We recommend to the reader Jean Piaget and Barbel Inhelder, *The Psychology of the Child* (New York: Basic Books, Inc., Publishers, 1969), as well as Frank G. Jennings, "Jean Piaget: Notes on Learning," *Saturday Review* (May 20, 1967), and Jerome Bruner's treatment in *The Process of Education* (Cambridge, Mass.: Harvard University Press, 1961), chap. 3. As for John Dewey, we suggest three of his major works: *The Child and Curriculum* (Chicago: University of Chicago Press, 1902); *Democracy and Education* (New York: Macmillan, 1916); *Experience and Education* (New York: Macmillan, 1938).

Although the idea of an open classroom or school has been embraced largely by people from the liberal, in some cases radical progressive, tradition in education, the concept itself is essentially pedagogical and apolitical. As described, its practice is anchored in the substructure of educational psychology and philosophy. In contrast to the fashionable American open-space schools, architecture is irrelevant. Open, informal classrooms have been created with equal effectiveness in new structures, ancient schools, church basements, and warehouses; in classrooms, auditoriums, and corridors.

Figure 10-2 illustrates a historical relationship among experimental or alternative schools and open, informal schools. The informal schools in this country are descendants of early public school experiments, many of which emerged during the progressive era, roughly extending from the 1910s to the early 1940s. Notable examples of progressive public school systems include Quincy, Massachusetts, under Francis W. Parker in the 1870s; Winnetka, Illinois, under Carleton Washburne in the 1920s; and Bronxville, New York, under Willard Beatty, and Shaker

FIGURE 10-2 The Development of Experimental and Alternative Schools

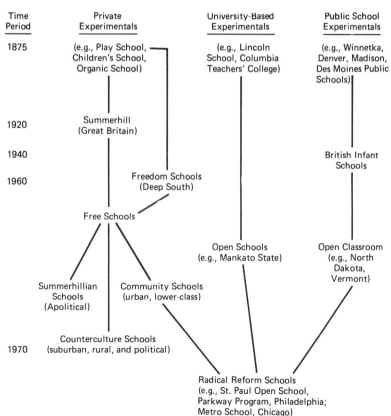

Heights, Ohio, under Arthur K. Loomis during the 1930s.[16] The historic Eight-Year Study (1932–1940), conducted by the Commission on the Relation of School and College of the Progressive Education Association (PEA), was a major catalyst to public school experiments. As a result, progressive informal programs and classroom approaches were developed in Denver, Colorado; Madison, Wisconsin; Des Moines, Iowa; Grand Rapids, Michigan; and several other communities. With only slight differences, the aims, theory, and practices of the earlier American progressive experiments and the informal schools in England (and America, notably in North Dakota and Vermont) have been the same. The writing and work of John Dewey are the strongest links that bind the two forms. Although often misinterpreted and misconstructed, Dewey's teachings provide the basis for the early progressive schools.

Today there are entire schools built on the informal concept of learning, as well as classrooms within schools. The approach has been more successful and extensive in elementary schools, but there also has been development at the secondary level.

MAGNET SCHOOLS: A PEDAGOGICAL ALTERNATIVE

In the 1980s there was strong movement towards "magnet schools," particularly in urban settings, where there was sufficient enrollment to attract students to specialized settings, or in districts with high dropout rates and attendance problems. In the latter half of the decade magnet schools became part of the broader debate on public schools of choice. There has been considerable debate about whether such schools facilitate desegregation or lead to greater "skimming" of the best and the brightest, leaving the rest of the public schools for the poor, minorities, or those without special talent or interest. The research on the effects of "magnetizing" the public schools is mixed, with generally positive reports on attendance, graduation rates, student and parental interest and commitment, achievement test scores, and a range of other indicators. Some observers suggest that it is important for all schools to become magnets, or schools of choice, to avoid the stigma of remaining in the "regular" schools and to avoid further segregation by ability, race, social class, or economic status.

Magnets in the late 1980s consisted of both open and fundamental schools; Montessori schools; central theme schools such as science, mathematics, computers, social studies, or humanities; dual-language schools in French, Spanish, German, Russian, Chinese, and Japanese; International Baccalaureate schools; public ROTC/military-type schools; schools with a career/vocational theme; a wide range of performing-arts institutions; and many special-needs schools.[17]

[16]Lawrence A. Cremin, *The Transformation of the School: Progressivism in American Education 1876–1957* (New York: Alfred A. Knopf, Inc., 1962), pp. 128–35, 276–77.

[17]William Snider, "The Call for Choice," *Education Week*, 7, no. 34 (June 24, 1987), pp. C1–C23.

DECENTRALIZATION: A POLITICAL ALTERNATIVE

Decentralization or community control is most appropriate for urban settings, where turgid, monolithic bureaucracies operate the schools. This plan places control of neighborhood schools with the local citizens, who have the power to form their own school boards. Those neighborhood school boards in turn can effect important policies and decisions concerning school organization, staff, and curriculum. Although many cities have discussed plans for decentralization and community control, New York City initiated several experimental local-control areas in 1968. The most publicized was the Ocean Hill-Brownsville community. Much controversy still surrounds the wisdom of community control within a large city, in part because of resulting political struggles.[18]

Decentralization is not intended to foster a range of alternative schools. Its purpose is to create a smaller, more responsive school system covering a relatively homogeneous population (for example, black, Mexican-American, Puerto Rican, lower-class white, middle-class white, or other ethnic groups) in a much larger heterogeneous city or school district. As in the present traditional system, children still attend their neighborhood school. But it is reasoned that this school is the proper "choice" for a child because the children of the community share common educational and cultural needs and the school is operated by adults in the community who are attuned to these needs.

In the late 1980s the decentralization movement took the form of "site-based management" and individual school accountability committees. This movement resulted from the many national reports indicating that the top-down reforms of the previous decades had not substantively changed the classroom or the schools. Although the results included longer school days and years, teacher and student testing, and salary increases and career ladders for teachers, the classroom pedagogy, curriculum, and environment of the school remained substantially unchanged throughout much of this century. In frustration, the business community began to take an active interest in schooling, suggesting that successful businesses were characterized by flat organizational charts, little middle management, a high degree of collegiality, and professionals with great responsibility and accountability for the end product.[19]

Colorado, like many states, has attempted to promote the decentralization of schooling through the passage of accountability laws that mandate local building committees made up of parents, teachers, students, citizens, and administrators who function much like a local school board. It is still too early to know whether these latest attempts at decentralization will have any more success than previous

[18]*Challenges to Education* (New York: Dodd, Mead & Company, 1972), a book of readings edited by Emanual Hurwitz, Jr., and Charles A. Tesconi, Jr., contains several excellent articles on community control and decentralization of schools, particularly as they relate to the Ocean Hill-Brownsville experiment. See especially chap. 3.

[19]D.T. Kearns and D. P. Doyle. *Winning the Brain Race: A Bold Plan to Make Our Schools Competitive* (San Francisco: Institute for Contemporary Studies, 1988), p. 116.

ones at breaking up the current school bureaucratic power structures. With the support of the business and political communities, there is perhaps a greater chance of success than in the past.

EDUCATIONAL VOUCHERS: AN ECONOMIC ALTERNATIVE

The idea of vouchers for schooling dates at least to the economist Adam Smith's recommendation in the eighteenth century that public monies be given to private families to pay for educational needs. Smith, laissez-faire in economic matters, is often credited as being the father of capitalism. It is no surprise, then, that like Adam Smith many contemporary classical economists, notably Milton Friedman of the University of Chicago, enthusiastically support proposals to reduce, even eliminate, government control in financing education. When it comes to support for educational vouchers, conservatives are joined by many liberal educators, including Christopher Jencks and James Coleman. Vouchers have a wide appeal in educational circles because they afford people the purchasing power (in the case of most liberal proposals, *equal* purchasing power) to select the school, and therefore the kind of education, they desire. In addition, voucher plans allow schools to free themselves from the restrictions of their traditional monopolistic position; that is, a school is able to establish goals and programs of its choosing, within the framework of basic requirements applicable to all schools.

Several objections are raised to voucher plans. For one, opponents argue that the more affluent families would supplement the vouchers in acquiring a "better" education; on the contrary, a poor child, even with a voucher, still could not afford a suburban-type education. Second, opponents reason that ethnically, racially, and religiously segregated schools would be encouraged. Third, they believe that private business persuasion and "hucksterism" would prevail, preying on parents and children who don't have an informative consumer's report on education. Finally, they argue that because vouchers would be available to private schools, including those affiliated with churches, they would violate the First Amendment's prohibition against the "establishment of religion."

Conservative advocates of vouchers, such as Milton Friedman, would have the EVA impose few if any restrictions on the participating schools and parents. Liberal supporters, especially Christopher Jencks, carefully build in provisions to ensure equality of purchasing power and to prevent discriminatory selection of students.[20]

In 1972, the Office of Economic Opportunity (OEO) funded an experiment in vouchers with the Alum Rock School District in San Jose, California. Parents in this pilot project received vouchers worth $680 for children in elementary school and $970 for those in seventh and eighth grades. However, only one-third of the

---

[20]See Friedman's article, "Voucher Idea," in the September 23 and October 21, 1972, issues of the *New York Times* Magazine.

school district was involved, or just six schools and about four thousand students; only public school programs participated; the Alum Rock Board of Education retained control, although it was advised by a voucher committee (composed of parents); and the plan offered a choice of programs within a school, not among competing schools. Alum Rock officials found that close to 40 percent of the parents selected nontraditional programs. In other words, 60 percent of the students were enrolled in the familiar standard program. The Alum Rock plan was something less than a "real" voucher plan, but the results were generally favorable.[21]

PUBLIC SCHOOLS OF CHOICE

The voucher plan, public or private, never took off and was supplanted in the late 1980s by the concept of public schools of choice. Although the words *public schools of choice* have been used for almost two decades, they took on new meaning, and a new educational and political coalition was formed. The concept of public schools of choice embraced the old alternative school movement, with its advocates for small, decentralized, humane schools. It added advocates from the right of the political spectrum seeking schools that would return to the basics and offer a fundamental curriculum. Perhaps of most importance, the political and business communities, spurred on by economic fears of competing with the Japanese in the world market and the indications of rising dropout rates and lower test scores, joined the cry to "decontrol" the educational marketplace and let schools compete for students. The new coalition crossed almost all traditional lines, with Democrats and Republicans, liberals and conservatives, parents, teachers, and administrators on both sides of the issue.

Among the leading advocates for empowering teachers and decontrolling many aspects of the educational system are such unlikely allies as President Bush, Minnesota Democratic Governor Rudy Perpich, Al Shanker, president of the American Federation of Teachers, the National Governor's Association, numerous business groups, with David Kearns, chief executive of the Xerox Corporation leading the way, and many parents, teachers, and administrators. Opposition has tended to come primarily from within the educational establishment, from many members of the two teachers' unions (the AFT and NEA), school board and administrator associations, and even some parent groups. Minnesota has led the nation with several choice bills: permitting students to attend any school in the state, regardless of where they live; having the school district pay the tuition of students who are admitted to an institution of higher education; and providing special state funding to promote alternatives.

East Harlem, with a successful middle-school choice program in place for over fifteen years, has become the prototype of intradistrict choice programs. All

[21]James Mecklenberger, "Vouchers at Alum Rock," *Phi Delta Kappan* 52, no. 7 (Mar. 1971), pp. 23–25.

middle-school students and their parents must choose from among an array of theme-based schools. The district, which is almost 95 percent poor, black, and Hispanic, improved its test scores from the bottom of the city's thirty-two districts to sixteenth, and dramatically improved attendance and dropout rates. Other states and districts around the United States have also experimented with various forms of student and parental choice that include magnet schools, children attending school in the area where their parents work, and early attendance in higher education.

Opposition to choice centers around the possibility of additional costs, transportation problems, athletic recruitment, shift of power and decision making from boards to parents and teachers, skimming of the best students, and resegregation. Proponents believe that a carefully designed choice program can overcome these obstacles, but until there is a broader track record throughout the country, the debate will continue to be heated. With over half of the states considering some form of choice bill in 1988 and 1989 and with strong political and business support, it appears likely that school choice in many varieties will be a part of the educational landscape throughout the 1990s.[22]

EVALUATION OF ALTERNATIVES

Evaluation of alternatives suffers as a result of the confusion about their definition. In a review of the literature Daniel Duke and Irene Muzio criticize the quality of evaluations of specific alternatives, noting several important weaknesses that they believe must be rectified before useful data can be collected:

1. Lack of control-group data with which to compare the performance of students in alternative programs
2. Notoriously bad record keeping (of attendance, grades, and so on) in alternative schools, resulting in low-quality data
3. Lack of clearly stated purposes for the evaluations, suggesting that many of the evaluations were made to defend funding
4. A tendency to apologize for or offer impressionistic explanations for negative findings
5. Failure to randomize when sampling
6. A tendency to eliminate data on program dropouts from the aggregate statistics
7. An absence of data about per-pupil costs
8. A scarcity of studies that follow students after they leave the programs

These weaknesses have resulted in a body of information so uneven and contradictory that there are no supportable generalizations regarding the effectiveness of alternative schools in academic achievement, affective achievement, work

---

[22]Richard J. Kraft and Paul Deering, "Public Schools of Choice," *The State Board Connection* 9, no. 1 (Jan. 1989), pp. 1–10.

habits, responsibility, social behavior, or postgraduate achievement.[23] Another review of the literature is more optimistic, saying that the most recent research indicates that students in alternatives do "as well, if not better than in the comprehensive school available to them."[24]

Gerald Smith and his colleagues conducted a study of nineteen alternatives that varied not only from the traditional school but also from one another to discover how well these schools met the needs of students as defined by and judged by students and teachers. They found that teachers and students in alternative schools reported more belief that school was meeting their needs for security, social interaction, self-actualization, and self-esteem than students in conventional schools. The alternatives differed from one another in content, size, degree of formality, but they all differed from the conventional school in that students and teachers were in the school by choice.[25]

Another way to evaluate alternative schools is to examine their survival. Barbara Case identified five factors that appear to account for the survival of alternative schools. These schools

1. Continue to be attractive to students and teachers.
2. Have a clear goal, mainly because they have to explain programs to school boards and have to avoid managerial and discipline problems that plague traditional schools.
3. Gained legitimacy with the educational establishment by attracting respected staff and solving problems.
4. Have achieved reliable funding, often as a result of gaining legitimacy.
5. Have created positive school climates that help attract participants and solve problems.[26]

Assumptions

The philosophy and policy that support and promote the creation of options, alternatives, or choices are grounded in a set of assumptions that should be examined.

Assumption: The singular, monolithic, traditional school has not served all students' needs effectively. This assessment is supported by the deteriorating dropout rate and average daily attendance as well as achievement scores, particularly of low-income groups.

Assumption: Choice for students and parents is desirable. This is usually argued on the ground that choice of schooling is an individual right. However,

[23]Daniel Linden Duke and Irene Muzio, "How Effective Are Alternative Schools? A Review of Recent Evaluations and Reports," *Teachers College Record* 79, no. 3 (Feb. 1978), pp. 461–83.

[24]Barr, "Alternatives for the Eighties," p. 573.

[25]Gerald R. Smith, Thomas B. Gregory, Richard C. Pugn, "Meeting Students' Needs: Evidence for the Superiority of Alternative Schools," *Phi Delta Kappan* 62, no. 8 (Apr. 1981), pp. 561–64.

[26]Barbara J. Case, "Lasting Alternatives: A Lesson in Survival," *Phi Delta Kappan*, 62, no. 8 (Apr. 1971), pp. 554–57.

Harry Broudy raises a serious question about this right in regard to education. He argues that education is a *public* good and not merely a *private* one. The individual student and family are not the only benefactors of a sound education (or the victims of an inadequate education); society has a stake in the schooling of each child.[27] Broudy adds that if the argument is not based on individual right, it is based on the assertion that the public good can be satisfied by whatever alternative parents choose. In other words, one form of educational experience is potentially as good as another, or, nothing we do in education makes any difference. This claim, he states, overlooks historical evidence to the contrary.[28]

Assumption: Alternatives promote freedom for parents and children. Generally this freedom is in the form of freedom *from* the control of school authorities and *from* the constraints of the established school structure and curriculum. Broudy argues that some educational constraints cannot be avoided and, in fact, are desirable. Contrary to the view that learning should be fun, joyous, and ecstatic, some things one must learn in school, Broudy explains, do not come naturally or easily—namely, an understanding of the intellectual resources of a culture. In addition, our culture imposes certain other demands on the individual as a condition for coping with it: occupational, civic, and personal adequacy. The first is needed to earn a living; the second, to plan one's role in a social order; and the third, to live as a fully developed, authentic human individual. It is unrealistic and irresponsible, Broudy states, for any school to ignore these constraints. To be sure, some alternative schools do. Yet many advocates of alternatives, including Fantini, insist that they all meet a common set of educational objectives, including career development, political socialization, and talent development, as well as basic skills.

Assumption: Given a choice among competing alternatives, parents and children can make intelligent selections. But intelligent choice presupposes that they can identify the best or most appropriate instruction. Because of lack of experience, the young student selects largely according to what "feels right," which may be a useful guide but no guarantee of an intelligent decision. Many parents also lack the necessary knowledge, interest, and wisdom to make this choice. As a group, teachers and other educators should be more informed than parents about what is an appropriate education and how to achieve it in the classroom. That there exist widely different viewpoints within the educational community tends to confuse the public.

When placed in the position of deciding what school to choose, parents often are at a loss and rely on the immediate and transitory interest of young students. Many appear to be asking for more than information about the alternatives; they want the experts to make the decisions.

Sound educative experiences, in John Dewey's terms, are not easily achieved. An educator who is a professional should be able to distinguish between "educa-

---

[27]Harry S. Broudy, "Educational Alternatives, Why Not? Why Not," *Phi Delta Kappan*, 54, no. 7 (Mar. 1973), p. 438.
[28]Ibid., p. 439.

tive" and "miseducative" experiences. Interest and enjoyability are no guarantee that an experience will be educative. In assessing the potential of a learning experience, a teacher, unlike a parent, always considers (or ought to) whether or not a child is prepared to make the most of an experience and where the experience is leading developmentally. The first consideration requires that educational resources be adapted to the needs and abilities of the learner; the second requires that no matter what stage of learning is involved, the teacher should keep an eye on future stages as well as the present. These are simply what Dewey described as the principles of interaction and continuity.[29]

CLARIFYING THE RATIONALE

Alternative schooling is built on two major premises:

1. Students have different dispositions toward learning and different learning styles. Therefore, they require different learning environments and teaching methods.
2. The list of competing objectives in education is endless and really a matter of taste; therefore, options should be available.

The first premise has considerable support, but still demands the continued attention of researchers and practitioners. The second is much more suspect. Philip Jackson and others take the position that educators who operate from this belief are retreating behind the relativist, and culturally sanctioned, democratic principle. In doing so they are abdicating their responsibility as educators. Jackson argues that professional educators, teachers, and administrators must keep at the forefront of their thinking the idea that education should be a "purposeful" activity and should entail "life-enhancing experiences." Such a discussion takes us back to the ideas of Dewey on the nature of educative experiences. Teachers can and must plan such learning into a child's experiences.[30]

There are several central questions in considering the validity of educational alternatives:

Are all learning environments and teaching methods equally useful in providing educative experiences? In other words, if sound education in any school demands in some form a command of basic reading, writing, and computing skills, as well as problem solving and inquiry skills, will any of a number of different types of schools function equally well?

Are educators abandoning their responsibility in advocating alternatives?

Are parents and pupils competent judges of the education that is best for them, or are they equally as competent judges as the professionals?

Different types of alternative schools will surely have to compromise on their

[29]John Dewey's entire book, *Experience and Education* (New York: Collier Books, 1938), originally a series of lectures, is devoted to an examination of this idea.

[30]Philip Jackson, in "After Apple-Picking," *Harvard Educational Review* 43, no. 1 (Feb. 1973), pp. 51–60, lucidly discusses this position.

basic styles to accomplish these objectives. The free-school types probably will have to make special efforts toward building skills, whereas the traditional and fundamental schools will have to make appropriate changes to develop problem-solving and inquiry abilities. But educators will not be irresponsible nor parents and students incapable if timely and competent guidance is provided.

Another concept of alternative education is to use the natural educative capacities of community organizations and institutions—museums, studios, parks, businesses, churches, professional and social organizations—otherwise called "configurations" or an "ecology of education." These agencies in the past have played an important part in "informal" education. School, until the twentieth century, was considered only one environment where learning took place, and a minor one for most children. As the enrollment and time spent in formal education increased, learning became associated with the activities of schools. What took place informally, outside schools, was falsely considered to be quite different, namely, work, play, hobbies, and amusements.

During the early history of this country, informal or incidental learning was the dominant form of education. For both children and adults, the influence of the informal agencies declined as industrialization, urbanization, and automation replaced the shopkeeper, craftsperson, and rural, small-town way of life. With the urbanization and more recently the suburbanization of life, the natural surroundings of the young have become less utilitarian and educative. In an earlier era, adults during their daily living and working were naturally teachers; valuable learning experiences were to be found everywhere—on farms, in homes, in shops, and on the streets of every community. The call to include organizations, professionals, and other working people in the education network recognizes that these agencies can play a critical role in education and that children gradually have been cut off from the natural, incidental learning of life and society.

Over time, schools have assumed greater and greater responsibility—with considerable success, considering the difficulty, perhaps impossibility, of the total task. Schools may be providing services and educational experiences that never existed in the past, but there are important experiences that schools cannot provide, or only provide artificially. The schoolhouse is only one of numerous educational agencies in a community.

HOME STUDY

It has not been widely publicized, but the number of children being educated at home has been increasing in recent years. The home-study issue raises some difficult questions regarding the constitutionality of compulsory education. Parental decisions to keep their children home put parental rights and duties into conflict with the state's responsibilities as expressed by compulsory education laws.

Thirty-nine states have statutory provisions for home instruction. In virtually all cases, the law requires that the education the children receive must be equivalent to the education they would have received had they attended school. The laws specify equivalency by stating various requirements. Some states require the teacher to be certified, whereas others specify courses or subjects that must be included.

Court cases concerning home study have recognized the parent's rights to educate but have also acknowledged the right of the states to regulate education. However, compulsory education laws, especially as they apply to secondary schools, are being reexamined. For example, a recommendation of the National Commission on the Reform of Secondary Education states,

> If high school is to not be a custodial institution, the state must not force adolescents to attend. Earlier maturity, physical, sexual and intellectual, requires an option of early departure from the restraints of formal schools.[31]

Although the number and variety of school alternatives has grown immensely in the past decade, David Moberly charged that "compulsory schooling has not created an incentive to provide alternative programs for American youth." He adds that an institutional response is needed and suggests three options:

1. That more alternatives be created by the public schools.
2. That schools or other government agencies create consortiums of educative agencies.
3. That a national public service program be created as an alternative to schooling.[32]

THE FUTURE OF ALTERNATIVES

The case for alternatives rests on the argument that schools can increase their capacity to individualize student programs. A student's learning style and educational needs can be matched with the methods and goals of a particular school. In the process, parents and pupils, as well as teachers, are permitted to select the learning environment that they judge most suitable. Ultimately, the privilege and also the responsibility of selection rests with the client. Although schools and their personnel will be forced to meet the client's needs or "go out of business," offering alternatives reduces institutional political conflict. If constituents don't like one option, they can try another; the schools collectively adapt to the learner, not the reverse.

It may happen that choice in education will become such a common practice that the subject of "alternatives" will become passé. It may also be true that "the development of alternative schools could be the last best chance for reforming public education."[33]

[31]David L. Moberly, "Compulsory Attendance: A Second Look," *High School Journal* 63, no. 5 (Feb. 1980), pp. 195–99.
[32]Ibid., p. 198.
[33]Raywid, "The First Decade of Public School Alternatives," p. 553.

● ——— ●

Case Study: Alternative Schools

The school administrators for the community in which you teach submitted a plan for the development of several alternative schools. The board of education recently approved the plan, which will go into effect this coming year. The plan calls for several different elementary schools, including two traditional schools, two continuous progress schools (open space), an open school, a Montessori school, and a free school. The free school will be kindergarten through grade 12; all others will be kindergarten through grade 6. The school district is small enough to allow parents and students anywhere in the district to choose any one of the schools. Transportation will be provided for students who live farther than one mile from the school they wish to attend.

The parents and students of the community will also be offered a choice of three junior high schools: a standard school with traditional course offerings; an open-space school based in large part on student contracts and programmed learning; an open, informal school with combined teacher-student decision making in the curriculum. Junior high and senior high students wanting a free school environment can attend the kindergarten through grade 12 free school in the district.

The single high school in the community has four wings, which now in effect will become four-schools-in-one-school, with a different curriculum for each wing. Students may select any one of these four curricula. One wing, or school, will be the traditional comprehensive school, emphasizing basic skills in both academic and vocational studies; a second will be traditional but with a heavy academic or college-prep orientation; a third will be largely vocational, with the minimum required general education courses and a heavy emphasis on work-study courses; the last school will be an informal program made of an array of academic courses (for example, history and literature), special interest courses (pottery, black studies, wilderness ecology), and vocational courses (welding, typing, mechanics), in the form of either a regular semester or minicourses.

The school administration is offering the teachers of the community a choice of school. A major effort will be made to ensure a proper mix of teacher with school; it is guaranteed that no teacher in the system will be placed in a school that is incompatible with his or her teaching philosophy and methods. Considering the school level at which you teach, elementary, junior high, or senior high, which would you choose? Why would this be the best setting for you? Why do you consider this school a desirable option of the district's alternative plan? What problems might occur in implementing the overall plan? How would you and other faculty members handle the problems in your school?

Thought Questions

1. Do you favor the elimination of compulsory school attendance laws? Defend your answer. What could be the possible outcome of such a decision over a ten-year period?

2. If you had the opportunity to choose an alternative program or school during your public school years,
   a. What would be its main goal?
   b. How would decisions be made regarding the policies and philosophy and who would make them?
   c. What would be the content of courses?
   d. How would it be funded?

3. A number of advocates of the open classroom argue that this concept has the most solid empirical learning base and should be the learning environment of most, if not all, students. What support is there for this position and what objections?

4. Considering that the free school is a politically oriented, countercultural concept, does it have a legitimate position among public school options? Consider carefully arguments on all sides of this question and support a decision.

5. Assessments of the experiments on educational vouchers are just now becoming available. What does the evidence to date suggest about the success, strengths, and weaknesses of the idea? Should the voucher plans be modified to fit more closely the liberal proposals of Christopher Jencks and others or the conservative proposals of Milton Friedman, or should the idea be scuttled?

6. Are parents and pupils the best judges of an appropriate education? Are educators abdicating their professional responsibility if they leave the decision of what school students should attend to the family?

7. Harry Broudy questions whether or not alternatives really promote freedom for the public. What is the distinction between "freedom from" controls or constraints and "freedom to" behave in an intelligent fashion? Of the legitimate constraints demanded as a condition of living in a society, are there any that all schools must be held accountable for? Would you add to or subtract from Broudy's list?

8. Given the increased concern for education in basic skills, can this objective be achieved in all types of alternatives? Explain. What about the other educational objectives?

9. Discuss the strong points of a community-based educational program. Should the school remain as the primary place of learning in such a program, or should it merely be one of many relatively equal learning centers in the community?

10. How are outdoor wilderness experiences justified as an integral part of a public education program? How can they augment the academic education of a student? The total education of a student?

Practical Activities

1. Visit an alternative school or program (a free, community, or open school). Write a description of the physical structure, curriculum, and administrative organization, as well as treatment of students, teachers' roles, and teaching methods. Comment on how the school compares with the one you are working in or with those with which you are familiar.

2. Visit an open-space school in your area. Discuss the physical structure, curriculum, administrative organization, treatment of students, teachers' roles, and teaching

methods. If possible, do so by comparing and contrasting this school with a traditional school and other alternative schools.

3. Assume you are teaching in a high school. Set up a plan for a school-within-a-school in your building. Consider the number of students and teachers, teaching fields, faculty organization, courses offered, space needed, and grading system.

4. Design a comprehensive alternative school plan for the district in which you will be teaching. Use either the elementary, middle, junior high, or senior high school level to illustrate. What types of schools would you include? Describe them briefly. How would students and teachers be selected for the different schools? Which school would you want to teach in? Why?

5. Design an educational system for your community in which the school is only one center of learning. What businesses, clubs, organizations, and public facilities could be tapped? How would these agencies fit in? What businesspeople, entrepreneurs, craftspeople, and other professionals would you enlist as teachers?

6. Take the subject you will be teaching (if you are an elementary teacher, select one subject area) and outline a curriculum, learning resources, and room arrangement for "opening," or informalizing, your classroom, Explain your rationale for this arrangement. (For example, how does it help students to learn and you to teach?)

7. Participate in an outdoor or wilderness program offered at your college or in the community. Of what value was the program to you? What place should such experiences have in the public schools?

8. Design a wilderness program for your school. What would the setting be? How long would the program be and how many students would participate? Write five or six major objectives (knowledge, attitudes, and skills) for the program.

Bibliography

BARR, ROBERT, "Alternatives for the Eighties: A Second Decade of Development." *Phi Delta Kappan,* 62, no. 8 (Apr. 1981), pp. 570–73.

BARTH, ROLAND S., *Open Education and the American School.* New York: Agathon Press, 1973.

BLACKIE, JOHN, *Inside the Primary School.* New York: Schocken Books, Inc., 1971.

BLANK, R.K., "Magnet Schools Offer Diversity and Quality," *Educational Leadership,* 41, no. 7 (1984).

BREMMER, JOHN, and ANNE BREMMER, *Open Education: A Beginning.* New York: Holt, Rinehart & Winston, 1972.

CASE, BARBARA J., "Lasting Alternatives: A Lesson in Survival." *Phi Delta Kappan,* 62, no. 8 (Apr. 1981), pp. 554–57.

COLEMAN, JAMES S., and THOMAS HOFFER, *Public and Private High Schools: The Impact of Communities.* New York: Basic Books, Inc., 1987.

CREMIN, LAWRENCE A., "The Free School Maneuver: A Perspective." In *Alternative Schools: Realities, Ideologies, Guidelines,* eds. Terrence E. Deal and Robert R. Nolan. Chicago: Nelson-Hall Publishers, 1978.

DEAL, TERRENCE E., and ROBERT R. NOLAN, eds., *Alternative Schools: Ideologies, Realities, Guidelines.* Chicago: Nelson-Hall, Publishers, 1978.

DUKE, DANIEL LINDEN, and IRENE MUZIO, "How Effective Are Alternative Schools? A

Review of Recent Evaluations and Reports." *Teacher College Record,* 79, no. 3 (Feb. 1978), pp. 461–83.

FANTINI, MARIO D., *Public Schools of Choice: Alternatives in Education.* New York: Simon & Schuster, Inc., 1974.

FEATHERSTONE, JOSEPH, *Schools Where Children Learn.* New York: Liveright Publishing Corporation, 1971.

GARDNER, HOWARD, *Frames of Mind: The Theory of Multiple Intelligences.* New York: Basic Books, Inc., Publishers, 1985.

GLATTHORN, ALLAN A., *Alternatives in Education: Schools and Programs.* New York: Dodd, Mead & Company, 1975.

GLENN, CHARLES L., *The Myth of the Common School.* Amherst: The University of Massachusetts Press, 1988.

GRAUBARD, ALLEN, *Free the Children: Radical Reform and Free School Movement.* New York: Pantheon Books, Inc., 1972.

HAZARD, WILLIAM R., "Flight from the Public Schools." *Compact,* 14, no. 4 (Winter 1981), pp. 22–23.

HOLT, JOHN, *Freedom and Beyond.* New York: E.P. Dutton, 1972.

KOHL, HERBERT, *The Open Classroom.* New York: Random House, 1970.

KOZOL, JONATHAN, *Free Schools.* Boston: Houghton Mifflin Company, 1972.

KRAFT, RICHARD J., and PAUL DEERING, "Public Schools of Choice." *The State Board Connection: Issues in Brief,* 9, no. 1 (Jan. 1989), pp. 1–10.

MOBERLY, DAVID L., "Compulsory Attendance: A Second Look." *High School Journal,* 63, no. 5 (Feb. 1980), pp. 195–99.

NATHAN, JOE, *Free to Teach: Achieving Equity and Excellence in Schools.* New York: The Pilgrim Press, 1983.

NEIL, A.S., *Summerhill: A Radical Approach to Child Rearing.* New York: Hart Publishing Company, 1960.

Phi Delta Kappan, Mar. 1973 and Apr. 1981. (Special issues on alternative schools.)

RAVITCH, DIANE, *The Schools We Deserve.* New York: Basic Books, Inc., Publishers, 1985.

RAYWID, MARY ANN, "The First Decade of Public School Alternatives." *Phi Delta Kappan,* 62, no. 8 (Apr. 1981), p. 6.

———, "Public Choice, Yes: Vouchers, No!" *Phi Delta Kappan,* 68, no. 10 (June 1987), pp. 762–69.

RUST, VAL DEAN, *Alternatives in Education: Theoretical and Historical Perspectives.* Beverly Hills, Calif.: Sage Publications, 1977.

SILBERMAN, CHARLES E., *Crisis in the Classroom.* New York: Random House, 1970.

SNIDER, WILLIAM, "The Call for Choice: Competition in the Educational Marketplace." *Education Week,* 7, no. 34 (June 24, 1987), pp. C1–C23.

11

The History of
American Education

The ideal of equal opportunity for education open to all has led to the development of a single and common public system of education, extending downward to the earliest age levels and upward to include secondary and higher education. . . . Free schooling is not distinctively American, but the idea of equal opportunity from the lowest to the highest levels of education has nowhere else been so explicitly stated or so effectively achieved.[1]

Both popular thought and political rhetoric have measured the moral worth of American society by equality of opportunity not equality of condition. The test has been the degree to which the individual has remained free to rise as far as his talents could take him.

Aside from its consequences for individuals, a preoccupation with individual equality of opportunity engenders frustration. When each new cycle of reformers learns that schools cannot alter the structure of inequality, it leaves the scene of action, cynical and defeated, and without the reformer's harassment the system's biases flourish more easily. These biases—discrimination based on class, race, and gender; inequality of resources, access, and achievement—remain critical because they represent a contradiction between political values and social institutions.[2]

The architects of American public schooling had visions of a bold experiment in education. The public school would be the forum to spread the values of a young republic and to unify politically disparate social and cultural groups. Public education was designed to foster equality of opportunity, social mobility, and economic justice.

The route to these aims was not always smooth or consistent. Some scholars question how genuine these goals have been, how vigorously they were pursued, and to what extent they were achieved. The traditional view of education holds

[1]R. Freeman Butts and Lawrence A. Cremin, *The History of Education in American Culture* (New York: Holt, Rinehart & Winston, 1953), pp. 564–65.

[2]Michael B. Katz, *Reconstructing American Education* (Cambridge, Mass.: Harvard University Press, 1987), pp. 117–18.

that our quest for these democratic goals has been successful. However, revisionists question both the sincerity and the effectiveness of this quest. Public education has been and still is laden with promises, myths, and realities.

EDUCATION OF THE YOUNG IN COLONIAL AMERICA

Harshness and intolerance, not patience and understanding, characterize the social and religious atmosphere of the colonial period. Discipline was severe in the schools, and physical punishment common. People generally were viewed as sinful sorts who needed strong punitive rule. A typical passage from the *New England Primer* reads, "Foolishness is bound up in the heart of the child; but the rod of correction shall drive it from him." The *Primer* was the most distinctive of the colonial schoolbooks, whose ostensible purpose was to teach the children to read, but which served other, wider functions, particularly religious indoctrination. The *Primer* was the only textbook many students knew. Teaching methods also were hardly imaginative, memorization and drill being the dominant techniques of the colonial classroom. As Lawrence Cremin and Merle Borrowman relate, pupils as a rule were taught one by one. If the student did well there were words of praise and a new assignment; if the performance was poor, reprimand (sometimes physical) and ridicule followed.[3] Today's dominant learning theory, based on reward or the lack of it, with punishment frowned on, would have been thought quite silly then.

It may have been fortunate that so few children had the dubious advantage of attending the early schools; their number was probably no more than 10 percent of the school-age population. Even though some influential colonists viewed the school as potentially performing very important functions for the society, most children received only a limited amount of education in school. Many never saw the interior of a schoolhouse, and few if any received all their education in school. Most often, the distinction between those attending and not attending school was along class lines. Children of the poor and lower-class families had no formal schooling and learned trades early in life. Children of the upper class received as much education as was available, in many cases through college. In addition, colonial schools were quite small, normally one-room structures, and in session for much shorter periods of the year than they are now. Schooling, by necessity, played a limited and minor role in colonial life, but this ought not be construed as a disadvantage to the education of colonial children and adults.

The family and the community, including the shops, workplaces, social gatherings, news media, and particularly churches were major educative institutions. When one of these agencies weakened in effectiveness, it was fortified with new laws (such as those requiring master craftsmen to provide apprenticeship training) or alternative mechanisms were developed (such as training schools or

---

[3]Lawrence A. Cremin and Merle L. Borrowman, *Public Schools in Our Democracy* (New York: Macmillan, 1956), p. 64.

private academies). Cremin, in *American Education: The Colonial Experience,* finds that the colonial family was the most flexible and instrumental educating agency in transmitting new functional and practical ideas for managing and establishing change. In Cremin's assessment, not only the number of deliberate educative institutions but also the diversity of education is impressive and is a distinct strength of this period.[4] This is a strength that was neglected and permitted to vanish as educational policy unfolded over the next two centuries.

Signs of change were evident as early as 1642, when the colonial legislature of Massachusetts passed a general education law requiring all parents to see that their children were taught to read, to understand the major laws of the colony, to know the catechism, and to learn a trade. Five years later, in 1647, the Massachusetts legislature mandated a second educational law requiring all towns of at least fifty families to appoint an elementary teacher for the express purpose of teaching reading and writing, who would be paid from municipal taxes. This law also required any town of a hundred or more families to appoint a teacher of Latin grammar, in modern terms, a secondary teacher. The wealthy families' exclusive access to formal education was beginning to erode.

Elementary schools rapidly increased in the Massachusetts Bay Colony, and with them the sale of the *New England Primer.* This trend gradually extended to the other colonies along the East Coast, but with less government persuasion the impact was not as great. Latin grammar schools, not much different in structure and kind from the elementary schools, also began to flourish. Latin, not surprisingly, was the heart of the curriculum; the schools' main purpose was to prepare young men for entrance into college.

Harvard was the first college to be established (1636). All students studied a set curriculum based on Greek, Hebrew, logic, rhetoric, arithmetic, and, of course, theology, because many were educated for the clergy. It was several decades before the next colleges, William and Mary (1693) and Yale (1701), were started. One goal of these first colleges was to train students for civic leadership so as to bring a coherence and sense of unity to the nation as they took their positions in business and the professions.

The *New England Primer* also was an instrument of religious instruction. It contained pieces of biblical information, prayers to be recited, questions and answers on religious matters (a catechism), and an alphabet complete with complementary moral lessons. The type of religion coincided with that established in the colony. In New England, this was Puritanism, or Congregational Calvinism. In the southern colonies, the Church of England was established by law, and orthodox Anglicanism was taught in the schools. Religion in the middle colonies was heterogeneous: such minority groups as Quakers, Dutch Protestants, Presbyterians, Baptists, Lutherans, Methodists, and Mennonites developed distinctive schools.

[4]Lawrence A. Cremin, *American Education: The Colonial Experience, 1607–1783* (New York: Harper & Row, Publishers, Inc., 1970), pp. 123–37, 243–48.

FIGURE 11-1   Hornbook of the Seventeenth Century

Schools had become an institution designed to serve the larger community by assisting in the socialization of the young to the dominant cultural values. At this time, these values were largely religious.

In retrospect, education in the colonial period was not intended to mobilize individual potentials. Most people, it was believed, didn't need schooling, or at best, needed schooling only for basic reading, writing, and computation. A liberal education, or schooling in secondary schools and colleges, a requisite to educational freedom, was fitting only for the few, not for the many. Yet Freeman Butts explains that education designed to enable each individual to develop oneself to the utmost was emerging as a desired goal. In his words, "Building schools for a colonial society prior to the Revolutionary War was a dress rehearsal for freedom, not the main performance."[5]

IN QUEST OF A NATION OF LITERATE AND EDUCATED CITIZENS

The founders of the new nation took very seriously the question of what type of educational institution was appropriate for a republican government. James Madison wrote, "A popular Government without popular information, or the means of acquiring it, is but a Prologue to a Farce or Tragedy, or perhaps both." The task of

[5]R. Freeman Butts, "Search for Freedom: The Story of American Education," *NEA Journal* 49, no. 3 (Mar. 1960), p. 37.

building an educational system with remnants from the colonial period would be messy. Not only were the schools divided along different religious lines, but also they were attended by "Americans" who spoke different languages and practiced a variety of ethnic customs originating in western Europe. The answer was a *common* school, taught in English without religious messages and attended by children from families of all backgrounds, regardless of spoken language, religious beliefs, and economic status. Furthermore, schooling was "free" in the sense that it was funded by taxes collected from everyone. This was imperative to the existence of a representative government. Yet there was a sharp limit to the amount of education considered necessary and tolerable. As Butts concluded, the *republican* ideal was to provide *some* education for all and *much* education for a few.[6]

Franklin, Jefferson, and the Republican Ideal

Many of the political leaders of the revolutionary period also were educational leaders; most notable among these were Benjamin Franklin and Thomas Jefferson. Franklin's ideas on education were set forth in a pamphlet entitled *Proposals Relating to the Education of Youth in Pennsylvania* (1749). In a striking break from tradition, Franklin proposed a new kind of secondary school—an academy—designed to prepare youth for the practical affairs of life, namely, business, vocation, and leisure. The colonial secondary school, aptly named Latin grammar school because the primary curriculum was Latin, existed to serve only the few who would enter college and later go on to professional careers. Franklin antedated later practice by suggesting that the emerging nation needed secondary schools that were useful and practical and that would serve a much larger segment of the populace. English was to replace Latin and Greek, and the general curriculum was to include such heretofore pedestrian subjects as history, science, and agriculture.

If the inscription on his tombstone is accurate testimony, Thomas Jefferson wished to be remembered more for his work in education than as the third president of the country. Jefferson's most significant ideas for education were set forth in a piece of legislation he proposed while a member of the Virginia Assembly, entitled *Bill for the More General Diffusion of Knowledge* (1779). On the surface, Jefferson's entrance into education did not appear successful. Although the bill was defeated, it had a significant influence on the future course of educational policy. His plan was no less than a blueprint for the education of all children in Virginia. He proposed that all free children of the state receive three years of free elementary schooling in reading, writing, arithmetic, and history. The bill carefully spelled out the location and requirements of the elementary schools. He also proposed that grammar schools be constructed in distinct areas of the state to accommodate a select group of the best male students from the elementary

[6]Ibid., p. 42.

schools for further studies. The brightest graduates of these secondary schools were then to be granted scholarships for university study at William and Mary College. The bill clearly was the work of a person who valued the role of education in the new society. It was awesome in its comprehensiveness, fascinating in its detail, and unique in its structure.[7]

Jefferson conceived his plan to provide a broad base of intelligent citizens, who could judge important issues as well as combat tyrannical leadership, and to develop enlightened leaders predisposed to democratic leadership. The plan, ideologically, pedagogically, and economically, was radical for the times. Jefferson, later, saw tangible effects of his labors in education when the University of Virginia, which he conceived, was established in 1819 after years of oral and written persuasion.

Although Jefferson had only modest success with his educational inspirations, the idea of the common school was planted, and the drive toward universal elementary schooling was underway. The establishment of public schooling took strong and dedicated leadership, and the movement in the 1800s produced some capable educators: Horace Mann and James Carter in Massachusetts, Henry Barnard in Connecticut, Gideon Hawley in New York, Calvin Wiley in North Carolina, Samuel Lewis in Ohio, Caleb Mills in Indiana, Ninian Edwards in Illinois, and John Swett in California. Lecturing, writing, organizing, and at times offering their personal finances, these leaders worked unselfishly for the cause of common public schooling.

Horace Mann and the Common School

Perhaps the most dedicated of this group was Horace Mann (1796–1859). Although he had much in common with Thomas Jefferson, Mann, in contrast, was an uncompromising champion of equality in education. Like Jefferson, he argued for the general diffusion of basic skills and knowledge, but he was rather unconcerned with the advanced liberal education of an enlightened leadership. In his words, "The scientific or literary well-being of a community is to be estimated not so much by its possessing a few men of great knowledge as having many men of competent knowledge." Mann's ideas were the initial break from the republican ideal that guided the nation's schooling through the first century.

Mann sacrificed a promising law career to become the first secretary of the Massachusetts State Board of Education in 1837. His presence was felt from the start, and he traveled and labored tirelessly to promote free schooling in the state. During his twelve years as head of the board, Mann produced annual reports on timely aspects of education. His travails brought changes and occasional praise, but they also resulted in failures, criticism, and even attacks. The best known of his

[7]Gordon C. Lee, ed., *Crusade Against Ignorance: Thomas Jefferson on Education* (New York: Teachers College, Columbia University, 1961), pp. 83–97.

annual reports was the seventh, which followed his travels to Europe. Mann was particularly impressed with the Prussian schools that had adopted the teaching methods of Johann Pestalozzi. Pestalozzi emphasized love and patience for the young and used real objects in teaching. Mann's praise for the civility and progressive techniques of the Prussian teachers aroused considerable anger and protest among educators in Boston.[8]

More important for the future role of schooling in the larger society, Mann perceived the school as potentially an omnipotent and omniscient force. In his Twelfth Annual Report (1848) he made a financial plea to business and property owners, arguing that a schooled populace was safe and tame. It would offer more effective protection than any police force. He also wrote that schooling was the best way to eliminate poverty and ignorance, thereby promoting equality in the state. Mann also viewed the school as an instrument of moral education. Quoting the Bible, he wrote, "Train up a child in the way he should go, and when he is old he will not depart from it."[9] The decline of established religion in nineteenth-century America and the rise of the public school were not merely coincidental. Public schools assumed the function of character development, and with this, the door had been opened to their expanding role.

The Changing School

The development of public schools was not an isolated movement during the first half of the nineteenth century. William Ellery Channing referred to the 1830s as "an age of great movements." Several forces or movements including immigration, urbanization, industrialization, and organized labor, significantly influenced the course of education.

By 1850, 12 percent of the citizens were foreign born, most of these immigrants from Ireland, Germany, and Italy. Their numbers, including groups from southern and eastern Europe, grew precipitously for the next hundred years. In large part, character development in the schools functioned to assimilate immigrants into the dominant American culture. Along with learning accepted forms of behavior, children from diverse native lands were taught to speak a common language and to study the heroics of courageous leaders, the blessings of a benevolent government, and the establishment of an extraordinary nation. In addition, these children were taught accepted standards of hygiene and nutrition. A large number of the immigrants came to live in the burgeoning cities, hoping to find work in the industrial developments of the new nation.

Urban life, influenced by the rapid growth of factories, spawned social and economic problems. Poverty and crime were side effects of economic change in a young industrial nation. Despite the environment factors, blame for social deviance, as Michael Katz points out, fell on the lower class—considered to be a

---

[8]Lawrence A. Cremin, ed., *The Republic and the School: Horace Mann on the Education of Free Men* (New York: Teachers College, Columbia University, 1957), pp. 54–56.

[9]Ibid., p. 100.

breeding place for criminals and paupers. Exposure to public education, advocates of schooling argued, would provide a healthy environment that could alter the still pliable personalities of young people.[10]

Character development in schools also served the interests of industrialists who were dependent on the labor of the working class. Capitalism fostered the creation of public institutions, including school systems, to help shape both the work skills and behaviors of wage-earning laborers. "Institutions," Katz explains, "reflected the drive toward order, rationality, discipline, and specialization inherent in capitalism." The design and organization of emerging public schools helped industry to transform "casual, episodic, and flexible work patterns into steady, punctual, and predictable labor." Efficiency and the productive use of time were critical for a business to reduce costs and maximize profits; schools were one institution that promoted order and shaped industrious behavior.[11]

Education was an area in which industrial management and labor organizations could agree: both supported more and "better" schooling for the working class. Labor saw education as the primary means of increasing the economic welfare of the industrial employee. To better one's position in the system, the worker had to learn new and technological skills. Just as important, the individual was obliged to develop compatible work behaviors, such as obedience, industriousness, reliability, neatness, modesty, and loyalty.

By 1900, the public schools not only were securely established but also had come to serve various economic, social, and pedagogical functions. When industry needed skilled workers, schools initiated manual training courses and vocational programs. When specific values, beliefs, and behaviors were required for a smoothly functioning society, the schools were the most accessible and effective agency to carry out such teachings. If the needs of the community were for home care, health, or recreation, the schools were responsive in developing appropriate programs. Schools, in effect, became implements for economic growth, social reform, and community harmony. As expectations grew, the schools took on jobs once performed by families, churches, local businesses, settlement houses, and other community agencies. This they did with admirable success in the short run but with dubious consequences over the long haul.

The Emerging Bureaucratic Structure

Revisionist historians, including Katz, point out that industrialization during the nineteenth century dictated the development of school organization. The structure of an organization, in turn, creates its purposes and effects. The kind of school organization that emerged during the nineteenth century was what Katz labels "incipient bureaucracy." School bureaucracies were an answer to the heterogeneity of urban schools and the requirements of industrialization. By 1880 the basic structure of American education was fixed and has not been altered funda-

[10]Katz, *Reconstructing American Education*, p. 17.
[11]Ibid., pp. 14, 15.

mentally since. Educators during the first half of that century, however, had alternative models from which to choose, states Katz, namely, paternalistic voluntarism, democratic localism, and corporate voluntarism.[12] Examples of each existed plentifully, but the bureaucratic model was clearly the choice of early reformist educators.

Reformers such as Horace Mann and Henry Barnard worked to create a rational system out of what they saw as chaos. They were dismayed, even appalled, at the inadequacies of the typical public school. As David Tyack describes, the rapidly increasing number of students were attending schools in which teachers were inexperienced, untrained, and lacking any semblance of professionalism; where curricula were haphazard, and textbooks miscellaneous; where students varied widely in age and ability, attended irregularly, and behaved intractably; where school buildings were rough and messy, often serving as community centers for virtually all the town or neighborhood's social, political, and religious activities.[13] Ironically, reform led to standardization and stereotyping, as school personnel graded classes, prescribed uniform curricula and texts, trained teachers in particular methods, and appointed proper supervising officials. Incipient bureaucracy prevailed essentially because of the functions, and the privileged people, that it served.

Katz believes there is sufficient evidence indicating that the poor and the working classes, threatened by industrialization, supported democratic localism during times of technological change. The middle class, however, sought to obtain advantages for their children as technology increased the importance of formal schooling; they therefore supported an elaborate, business-oriented, graded school system. In Katz's analysis this system was *bureaucratic* in organization and *class biased* in function: two characteristics that are interrelated and mutually suppor-

---

[12]Michael B. Katz, *Class, Bureaucracy, and Schools: The Illusion of Educational Change in America* (New York: Praeger Publishers, Inc., 1975), chap. 1.

In Katz's model, examples of *paternalistic voluntarism* were early schools administered by distinguished and capable, but largely disinterested, men who gave rudimentary training in literacy and morals to lower-class children. Voluntarism in effect was a form of *noblesse oblige*, of one class helping to civilize another. The New York Free School Society operated an extensive network of these schools for several decades in the early 1800s.

The *democratic localism* model consisted of neighborhood or community schools run by elected boards that valued variety, local autonomy from city supervision, and symbiotic school and community relations, while disdaining any professionalization of schoolteaching and administration. Democratic localists had an uphill struggle from the start, for their conception was essentially a rural viewpoint incompatible with what educators saw as the needs of urban education.

Corporate voluntarism schools were single institutions operated by self-perpetuating boards of trustees, financed through endowment and tuition. Academies and colleges for secondary and higher education were widely used examples of this model at the time. These schools in effect were extensions of private and public business organizations, with general political support from the middle class. In the late eighteenth and early nineteenth centuries, the states did offer financial assistance to these schools; extending such aid downward to elementary schools would have made it possible to operate universal, common, and free schools on the corporate model.

For a detailed analysis and comparison of these three school models, see Chapter 2 of Katz's *Reconstructing American Education*.

[13]David Tyack, "Bureaucracy and the Common School: The Example of Portland, Oregon, 1851–1913," in *Education in American History: Readings on the Social Issues*, ed. Michael B. Katz (New York: Praeger Publishers, Inc., 1973), p. 165.

tive. Modern bureaucracy is a bourgeois invention, representing a crystallization of bourgeois social attitudes.[14] The irony, Katz adds, is that school reformers thought they were promoting value-free and classless schools, but the structure under-mined them. The character traits promulgated in the schools represented a chau-vinistic, Protestant position appropriate for proper urban living as portrayed by Victorian middle-class values. Unable to perceive the cultural bias and lack of social mobility, school reformers were persuaded that such a system fostered equality of opportunity. The results were precisely the opposite of the reformers' intent. Bureaucracy, it turns out, simply reinforced the notion that education is some-thing that the better part of the community does to others, so that they are orderly, moral, and tractable.[15]

EXTENDING UNIVERSAL SCHOOLING UPWARD AND OUTWARD

For most of the nineteenth century, the efforts of public school advocates and educational reformers focused on the early school years, and by the late 1800s universal elementary schooling had been established. By 1900 a substantial major-ity of children ages six to thirteen were in elementary schools; today virtually every child is enrolled in some form of elementary school. Most attend the modern version of public-supported common school, and some (about 12 percent) choose parochial or other private schools. The Protestant bias of public schools led, particularly Catholics, but also Lutherans, to develop their own schools. Only about 10 percent of young people aged fourteen to seventeen were in school at the turn of this century. During the next fifty to sixty years there was a remarkable increase in secondary school enrollment. By 1930 more than 50 percent of this age-group were in schools, and by 1960 enrollment had climbed to about 90 percent, where it has stabilized.

Butts described this period from roughly the 1870s to the 1970s as a century of *democratic* education. In the republican era (the century from the 1770s to 1870s) the ideal had been to provide *some* education for all and *much* education for a few; the democratic ideal, in contrast, was to provide *as much education as possible for all*. The conventional view of educational history teaches that the underlying goal during this democratic era was *more education for more people*.[16]

What reasons account for this phenomenal growth in secondary schooling? The quest for democratic ideas is not a sufficient explanation; the major force was a shift in the economic or productive base of our society. The economic landscape changed dramatically during the late 1800s from an agrarian society to an emerging industrial society. A republican education, explains Butts, was sufficient for a society with a relatively small population scattered over large areas of richly

[14]Katz, *Class, Bureaucracy, and Schools*, p. xxi.
[15]Ibid., pp. 32–39.
[16]Butts, "Search for Freedom," p. 42.

endowed land, with most of the workers engaged in agriculture and agriculture-related occupations. In a society that was industrialized; that was based on steam, electric, or nuclear power; and that relied on science and technology, the demands were quite different. Business required greater literacy, certain industrial skills, and basic work habits. Because this society also had the alarming potential to be controlled and managed by an elite few, more schooling, it was argued, was required to prevent autocratic use of political and economic power.[17]

Shaping the High School

The term *high school* has a familiar ring today, but this was not so only a little more than a century ago. The high school, which was to become a distinctively American institution in ways never imagined by its early supporters, superseded the Latin grammar school and the academy during the 1880s. A series of court decisions in the 1870s concerning the legality of publicly supported high schools led to this development. The most important was the *Kalamazoo* (Michigan) case of 1874, in which the courts established the principle that people of the states could start and support public high schools with tax funds. High schools, along with public elementary schools and public universities, were part of a total formal educational scheme established in the state and the Republic. Thereupon the public high school movement gained momentum.

Few high schools existed in the late 1800s, and those in existence had haphazard curricula. High schools were the "gap" between elementary schools and colleges. In 1892 the Committee of Ten on Secondary Studies of the National Education Association (NEA) was formed to standardize the high school curriculum and to secure uniform college entrance requirements. The committee, chaired by Charles Elliot, then president of Harvard University, also set out to "broaden the channel" from high school to college. At that time, the prevailing standard for college preparation was the classical course, with four years of Latin and two or three years of Greek. An English course was accepted for terminal high school students. President Elliot and a few other committee members sought to make the English course acceptable for college entrance.

The result was a compromise outlining four courses of study: (1) classical (including Greek and Latin), (2) Latin scientific (with no Greek required), (3) modern language (requiring neither Latin nor Greek), and (4) English (requiring only one foreign language). More important than the details of this plan was the committee's position that secondary schools existed primarily to prepare for life, and secondarily for college. The plan also established English, one foreign language (either modern or ancient), history, mathematics, and to a lesser extent, science as the core high school curriculum. In addition, the committee recommended that high school consist of grades seven through twelve, that students should be permitted few electives, and that the Carnegie Unit (one course taken daily for one year) be established as the standard of measurement. To Elliot's

[17]Ibid., pp. 42–43.

TABLE 11-1   The Growth of the American High School

YEAR	HIGH SCHOOL ENROLLMENTS (IN THOUSANDS)	14- TO 17-YEAR-OLDS IN SCHOOL %	HIGH SCHOOL GRADUATES AGE 25-29 %	MEDIAN YEARS OF SCHOOLING IN THE U.S.
1890	359	6.7	3.5	—
1900	699	11.4	6.3	—
1910	1,115	15.4	8.6	8.1
1920	2,500	32.3	16.3	8.2
1930	4,804	51.4	28.8	8.4
1940	7,123	73.3	38.1	8.6
1950	6,453	76.8	52.7	9.3
1960	9,600	86.1	60.7	10.5
1970	14,643	92.0	75.4	12.2
1976	15,653	91.4	83.1	12.3
1980	14,652	90.8	85.4	12.5
1986	13,734	92.8	86.1	12.6

Source: Adapted from *Digest of Education Statistics 1988* (Washington, D.C.: U.S. Government Printing Office, 1988), pp. 15, 60.

delight, the committee recommended that colleges accept students who had completed any one of the four courses. Latin and Greek were no longer the foundation for college preparation.[18]

Elliot and others who designed the new high school curriculum wanted to reach as many of the talented young as possible and prepare them for college. What was good for Harvard and other elite colleges was good for the country.

Around the turn of the century, high school enrollments increased substantially. Suddenly a majority of the students now were not continuing on to college, and preparation for further schooling was not a high priority for many. The NEA appointed another committee, the Commission on the Reorganization of Secondary Education. In 1918, the commission published a thirty-two page pamphlet called the *Cardinal Principles of Secondary Education,* an unimpressive-looking little publication that ironically shaped the dimensions of the discussion on secondary education for the next several decades. The authors of *Cardinal Principles,* unlike most of those who wrote the Committee of Ten report, were mostly members of the newly emerging professional education field. In recommending that all "normal boys and girls" be encouraged to attend school full time until age seventeen or eighteen, this 1918 report offered the first call for universal secondary education. It also called for *comprehensive* high schools that include a variety of programs guided by the seven aims of education: health, command of fundamental processes, worthy home membership, vocation, citizenship, worthy use of leisure time, and ethical character.

The report was received favorably, and the "Seven Cardinal Principles," as they were popularly called, inspired educators. It established the pattern of Ameri-

[18]Edward A. Krug, *Salient Dates in American Education, 1635-1964* (New York: Harper & Row, Publishers, Inc., 1966), pp. 95-99.

can education to the present.[19] *Cardinal Principles* reflected the confidence of professional educators and others who shared the spirit of progressivism, that schooling could ameliorate social ills. It was a classic statement of the possibility of social engineering through education.[20]

THE PROGRESSIVE MOOD IN EDUCATION

The 1890s were a time of progressive reform in America, and reformist thought critically viewed the squalor of urban slums, the harsh conditions of industrial workplaces, the corruption of local and state governments, and eventually the dullness of public schools. This was a period when muckrakers such as Jacob Riis wrote about poverty in the cities, Lincoln Steffens exposed the alliance between corrupt government and corrupt business, and Ida Tarbell detailed the power-accruing practices of Standard Oil. Muckraker journalism reached the schools initially as a result of a series of articles during 1892 in an unobtrusive New York monthly *The Forum.*

Joseph Rice, a young pediatrician with deep interest in the methods used in treating and teaching children, prepared a first-hand appraisal of American schools for *The Forum.* Rice visited 1,200 classrooms in 36 cities, and in a vividly documented report, charged that schools and teachers "dehumanized, immobilized, and automized the children." The results of his investigations, however, were not uniformly bleak; Rice found examples of humane, resourceful, imaginative, or progressive teaching in a scattering of schools. The most noteworthy was the Cook County Normal School in metropolitan Chicago, run by the then-venerable educator Francis Parker. In his final article for *The Forum,* Rice called on the people of local communities to demand "progressive schools" for their children. He argued that the educational spirit of the country was progressive and that the stimulation and warmth of these schools were within the reach of all citizens.[21]

Cremin pointed out in *The Transformation of the School* (1961) that progressive education began as part of a broader social and political progressive reform movement. In his words, "The Progressive mind was ultimately an educator's mind, and . . . its characteristic contribution was that of a socially responsible reformist pedagogue." For all their sense of rage, Cremin pointed out that progressives were diligent, thoughtful, and patient moderates.[22] About this time the young philosopher John Dewey began to make his incomparable mark on educational thought and American schools.

[19]Ibid., pp. 117–20.

[20]Thomas James and David Tyack, "Learning from Past Efforts to Reform the High School," *Phi Delta Kappan,* 64, no. 6 (Feb. 1983), pp. 402–403.

[21]Lawrence A. Cremin, *The Transformation of the School* (New York: Random House, 1961), pp. 3–6.

[22]Ibid., pp. 88–89.

John Dewey and the Liberal Transformation of Schools

As a village schoolteacher in his native Vermont, John Dewey saw the sterility, inactivity, and numbness of the traditional classroom. In 1894, when he arrived at the University of Chicago as head of the department of philosophy, psychology, and pedagogy, Dewey began working out new ideas for America's schools. Two years later he started the Laboratory School in order to test his ideas in practice and refine his theory on learning experiences, teaching methods, and school organization. Dewey wanted to demonstrate that individuals learned best by "doing," be it learning to walk, talk, swim, play a musical instrument, or solve problems and conceptualize. For the best results, he hypothesized, learning should involve using not only books but also tools and related materials. And it should involve interaction with people as much as possible in a community—work and social settings. Dewey explained this theory in *The School and Society* (1899), where he added that the occupations and associations in life that serve human social needs should be the basic context of education, and that the most reliable measure of learning is the ability of the individual to act intelligently in new social situations.

Dewey took great pains in many subsequent writings to elaborate on this theme of learning through real-life experiences. The teacher, he wrote, must know the individual character of the learner (implying a knowledge of the pupil's background, experiences, and abilities), understand the present moment in learning, and have a sense of what is to follow. Likewise, the teacher must have the intellectual ability to know both what information is needed in a learning situation and where to retrieve and how to organize this subject matter, so that the learner may gain new insights and knowledge as the material is presented. These two interrelated processes Dewey labeled the *continuity* and *interaction* effects, respectively.

Dewey took the relationship between the school and larger society a step further, however, with his idea of education as an "embryonic community." In practice the school would offer many new learning environments for the student, including libraries, gymnasiums, working areas, art and music rooms, science laboratories, gardens, and playgrounds. Beyond the "classroom walls," he envisioned the school as a dynamic center of the community.

In addition, the school was to be a lever for social change and reform in the immediate community and society at large. Dewey believed that experimental, investigative, and intelligent behavior is essentially progressive in that it tends to improve the conditions of life for people. Educators such as George Counts and Harold Ruggs extended the work of Dewey by redefining the purpose of schooling to promote the values of liberal democracy. Recognizing that schools were not value free, these *reconstructionists* focused on schooling for citizenship development. The curriculum would be designed to liberate students to understand the cultural controls and confront the political and economic struggles of society.

Social reconstructionism had a major impact on the curriculum, particularly the social studies during the late 1920s and 1930s. If education and schools were to advance the aims of democracy, they must be more than just agencies of cultural transmission, which essentially served the dominant capitalist interests. Counts, Ruggs, Theodore Bramfeld, and others promulgated many of their ideas in *The Social Frontier*, a journal for the reconstructionist. Their aim was to work through schools to build a "just" and "good society." Dewey cautioned, however, that schools could not effect this reform alone, for the school was only one institution among many that have an educational impact on the community and society.

Dewey's distinction between education in schools and education in the community, particularly in *Democracy and Education* (1916), is relevant to the problems of education today. Although, as Dewey pointed out, schools are only one agency among many for transmitting culture, they are the only means adults really have for systematically and deliberately educating the young. Although education in its broadest sense is continuous, ubiquitous, pervasive, and powerful, there is a difference between the education one receives from actively living life and that offered in school. As Cremin states, "In the ordinary course of living, education is *incidental*; in schooling, education is *intentional*."[23] Dewey acknowledged this distinction but ignored its implications in restricting his analysis of education to the role of schooling. The paradox is that Dewey increased the scope and impact of schools while tacitly recognizing their limitations. In short, schools are simultaneously crucial but limited. This is a dualism that ironically Dewey never resolved and a dilemma that today still underlies much educational discontent. Over time, this polarity in Dewey's analysis has led to an overreliance on schooling while creating flurries of disenchantment with the schools.

In practice most "progressive" educators emphasized student freedom and development but neglected the systematic organization of subject matter and the central role of the teacher. This direction, fostered by the Progressive Education Association (formed in 1919), was a source of much frustration for Dewey. One of his last works, *Experience and Education* (1938), was an effort to set the record straight on precisely what progressive education *is* and *isn't*. Both the so-called old and new education, he explained, are miseducative. Traditionalists neglected to develop a theory of experience, whereas progressive educators exalted the learner's experiences, impulses, and desires at the expense of the orderly development of subject matter built on these experiences. Both interest and content are essential, but neither is a sufficient condition for *educative* experiences.[24]

The Withering of the Progressive Education Movement

Progressive education reached its peak in the late 1930s; then declined in the 1940s. During its surge, few schools in the country completely escaped its influence. Among the reason for the collapse of this movement were the inordinate

[23]Lawrence A. Cremin, *Public Education* (New York: Basic Books, Inc., Publishers, 1976), pp. 4–8.

[24]John Dewey, *Experience and Education* (New York: Collier Books, 1963), pp. 70–75.

demands that progressive learning placed on the teacher. Perhaps more telling was the mood of the nation, which had shifted to an uneasy conservatism with the advent of World War II and the postwar years. The wave of literature on education and the schools announced in harsh and no uncertain terms that the schools were too soft and intellectually bankrupt.[25]

The nation was changing in another crucial way. The educative (and, frequently, miseducative) role of the mass media—including radio, television, expanded journalism, film, and eventually recording industry—was increasing vastly. Society as a whole had always been a source of education; but with profound changes in the agencies of communication and in the shape of community life generally, nonschool education had never been so pervasive.

THE ILLUSION OF EDUCATIONAL REFORM

The 1940s and 1950s were a period of retrenchment and return to a concentration on traditional American values and basic skills. In 1957, with the launching of the Sputnik and the publicized advances in Soviet technology, the traditionalists' hand was strengthened in science as well as in education. By 1960, school methods and curricular programs had been tightened. The clincher was a report of a study financed by the Carnegie Corporation (through the Educational Testing Service) and conducted by James Conant, an internationally respected chemist, past president of Harvard University, and a former U.S. Ambassador to the Federal Republic of Germany. Conant reported his findings in his widely read *The American High School Today* (1959).

Reshaping the High School

Conant was not in total agreement with essentialist critics who argued that American schools needed to be geared foremostly to intellectual and academic study. He argued that in a nation as diverse as the United States, schools must be "comprehensive" if they are to meet the needs of all students. "Comprehensive" implies a general education for all students, a sound nonacademic elective program for those who will join the work force after graduation, and a solid academic program for those whose vocations require study in college.[26] The focus of Conant's study was the "comprehensive" high school—a uniquely American phenomenon.

Conant has been placed in the line of famous educational reformers, extending back to Jefferson through Dewey, Elliot, and Mann, who struggled for popular,

[25]Some of this antiprogressive literature was reactionary to the point of irrationality and paranoia. Other criticism was thoughtful and responsive. The more popular works from these writings include Idding Bell's *Crisis in Education* (1949), Arthur Bestor's *Educational Wastelands* (1953), and two books by Mortimer Smith, *And Madly Teach* (1949) and *The Diminished Mind* (1953).

[26]James B. Conant, *The American High School Today* (New York: McGraw-Hill Book Company, Inc., 1959), p. 26.

universal common schooling.[27] He, nevertheless, was most interested in those whom he labeled the "academically talented" (the top 15 to 20 percent with the most promising intellectual potential), who, not sufficiently challenged, do not work hard enough. He documented shortcomings in the programs for the academically talented in the schools he investigated, and he specified the number of full-year courses these students should have in mathematics and science, foreign language, English, and social studies. The general educational recommendations required of all students were not so rigorous.[28]

The Conant study reinforced the essential disciplines, traditional subject matter, and traditional teaching methods. Conant had no radical recommendations for the basic pattern of American education, except one—to reduce drastically the number of small high schools (those with fewer than a hundred students in the graduating class), a size he judged inadequate to offer or maintain solid academic programs.[29]

Conant's critics point out that his agenda, and that of the fifties reformers in general, is flawed because of this selective excellence. He makes a strong case for excellence, but only for a few students, while advocating mediocrity for the rest.[30]

Institutional Rigidity

Despite the efforts of progressive reformers such as John Dewey, or more traditional reformers like James Conant, the structure of American schooling has changed little over the past century. Critics of public education, whatever their persuasion, need to look first to the traditions that American schools institutionalized in the 1890s. As Theodore Sizer explains, American are caught in a *web of assumptions* about the operation and management of schools that retard imaginative steps to act on "rising pedagogical expectations." These assumptions, including those that are blatantly false, go unchallenged by all but the most radical or utopian critics, and they constitute a set of institutional verities.[31]

The first and key "verity" assumes a *national consensus on the general purposes of education*; the only questions are those of execution. One does not have to sit in on too many meetings of school administrators to see this pattern emerging: Few people ask what purpose is to be served, or what education is for. Education is simply what goes on in schools. Charles Silberman labeled this syndrome "mindlessness." Other assumptions in this web include the importance of *formal* education and the goodness bequeathed with degrees, diplomas, and academic symbols,

---

[27]Merle Borrowman, "Conant, the Man," *Saturday Review* (Sept. 21, 1963), pp. 58–60.

[28]Conant, *American High School Today*, pp. 53–56, 62–63.

[29]Ibid., pp. 44–45. Interestingly, by the late 1970s even this one major change is being questioned. A growing number of educators, observing the impersonalization and vastness of many modern high schools, argue that we should return to smaller decentralized schools.

[30]Arthur G. Powell, Eleanor Farrar, and David K. Cohen, *The Shopping Mall High School: Winners and Losers in the Educational Marketplace* (Boston: Houghton Mifflin Company, 1985), p. 299.

[31]Theodore R. Sizer, *Places for Learning, Places for Joy: Speculations on American School Reform* (Cambridge, Mass.: Harvard University Press, 1973), pp. 17, 30.

in contrast to the triviality of incidental education; the necessity of *compulsory attendance* through a certain age; and an allegiance to *local control.* As a result, students are still grouped by ages; children are taught in clusters of twenty to forty; schools were and are organized around an autonomous teacher responsible for a group of students; the principal assignments involve texts, tests, reading, some memorization, and workbook exercises; and the time allotment to the basic subjects is about the same.[32]

A MIRROR FOR SOCIETY

For all the criticism given public schools, educators have done a credible job in providing what the public demands. And it has demanded a great deal, more than has been educationally prudent. Schools have taught democracy, free enterprise, and patriotism, and the virtues of hard work, obedience, cleanliness, and competitive sport; they have acculturated the immigrant, socialized the native born, tooled up the future worker, taught boys industrial skills, girls clerical and homemaking skills, and everybody how to drive the automobile. It is virtually heresy to suggest that none of this is truly educational and therefore ought not to be the function of schools.

Schools serve not as a distinct social agency but as an agent for the society. Schools have succeeded in teaching the young to adjust to the society, but have not provided them (despite earlier efforts of the social reconstructionists) with the intellectual skills and knowledge that would enable them to adjust the society. In part, our message is that schools cannot, and should not, do all that we expect of them. Ironically, John Dewey, however, never envisioned the school as extending so far. The school, he explained, should educate the *whole child,* but it would be sheer folly for it to try to provide the *whole education* for the child.

Radical Attempts to Restructure Schools

The humanistic reform writers of the 1960s and early 1970s (including John Holt, Jonathan Kozol, James Herndon, Herbert Kohl, and many others) focused on making the schools more decent, civil, liberating, individualized places for young people. In this respect, they were very much like Dewey and the host of earlier reformers, who saw progressive schools as the means to improve education. Dewey understood the educational potential in the rest of society, as did the later reformers, particularly John Holt in *Freedom and Beyond* (1972) and later *Teach Your Own* (1983). But in the view of another group of educators, these reformers were moderates. According to Ivan Illich and Everett Reimer, as well as Carl Bereiter and Paul Goodman, the fatal flaw of educators, even those who take a critical view of school operations, is that they envision only a "schooled society."

The similarities between Reimer's *School Is Dead* and Illich's *Deschooling*

[32]Ibid., pp. 17–24.

Society, both published in 1971, are immense. Whether in the developed or developing parts of the world, they say, schools serve, or self-serve, several functions.[33] Schools rest much of their case on the claim of teaching cognitive skills — particularly language and mathematics; this they do mostly with intermittent success, the lack of success falling largely on the poor of a nation. Cognitive teaching, however, is not the schools' most important function. Their crucial services to the larger society stem from their unrecognized functions of child care, social screening or sorting, and teaching values or state indoctrination.[34] Reimer and Illich label this dimension the "hidden curriculum." Its purpose is to propagate the social myths of society, such as equality of opportunity, freedom, progress, and efficiency.

Social myths, Reimer adds, are not totally deleterious in their effects (nor necessarily untrue), for they do distinguish one society from another, and they help to build a society. The distortion and injustice occur when they serve to sustain beliefs that increasingly cease to represent the reality of a society and when they function to segregate and favor one or more groups of people over others.[35] The effect of present schooling systems and of the "hidden curriculum" is, first, a failure to educate, in a basic literate sense, most of the students of the society's lower class; and second, a failure to truly educate the more privileged students — to nurture their authentic talents and their lifetime capacity and desire to learn.[36]

Schools are not the only modern institution that intentionally educates, or as Illich observes, "has as its primary purpose the shaping of man's vision of reality." There are hidden curricula in family life, health care, social services, the legal structure, and the media, serving essentially the same purpose as that of the school. The school, however, is the most powerful of these agents, for only it is granted the *official* sanction to shape the beliefs, attitudes, perceptions, and critical judgments of individuals. The school is able to do this in a way that maintains the dependency of the learner on the institution.[37]

To replace schooling, a "manipulative" agency, Illich and Reimer would substitute "convivial" learning agencies called *learning webs*: networks of people, places, and things. These networks would be designed to provide people with convenient and economical access to deliberate learning in such traditional places as libraries, laboratories, museums, theaters, hospitals, factories, farms, and shops; economical use of and instruction in such educational objects as books, records, films, tools, machines, computers, games, and natural preserves; informal and

[33]Illich and Reimer actually met during 1956 in Puerto Rico while doing unrelated educational work. By 1960 both had left for other parts of Latin America, where they studied the problems of Third World school systems and maintained close intellectual contact.

[34]Everett Reimer, *School Is Dead: Alternatives in Education* (New York: Doubleday & Company, Inc., 1971), pp. 13–23.

[35]Ibid., p. 39.

[36]Ibid., pp. 4–10. Reimer also draws what he calls an inescapable conclusion that no country in the world can afford the school systems they want, and only a few of the richer nations can afford accepted means of formal education at the current unit costs. We examine the attempts of some Third and Fourth World countries to emulate the U.S. educational system in Chapter 12.

[37]Ivan Illich, *Deschooling Society* (New York: Harper & Row, Publishers, Inc., 1971), p. 47.

convenient means of gathering in small groups to share ideas or discuss books; and access to professionals, paraprofessionals, consultants, and free-lancers prepared to teach particular skills.[38] This arrangement would acknowledge both the potential educative nature of other socially pertinent institutions and the teaching dimensions inherent in all skilled work.

Carl Bereiter, who subscribes to the convivial education model, would institutionalize personal choice, reduce extensively the role of schooling in education, and render cultural resources much more accessible to the learner. Bereiter observes that schools serve three universal functions: *child care, skill training,* and *education* (the last meaning teaching of values, socialization, or indoctrination). The efforts toward humanistic educational reform fail because to develop a sufficient number of teachers who are masters of all three functions is an impossible task.[39] We would be wiser on practical and moral grounds (because values education rightly belongs within the domain of the family and other institutions) to reduce the scope of schooling to child care and training. Furthermore, these two functions should be separated. One cadre of teachers would be charged with child care and another with skill training. "Good training and good child care," Bereiter explains, have almost nothing in common. "Training is authoritarian by its very nature.... Child care on the other hand allows maximum reasonable freedom. Training has definite goals and aims to reach them; child care flows along indefinitely like life itself."[40]

Paul Goodman, like Bereiter, places substantial emphasis on the early years of schooling, requests greater educational opportunities for adults, and calls for freeing adolescents from the chains of compulsory high school. In the final work before his death, *New Reformation: Notes of a Neolithic Conservative* (1969), Goodman outlines his thoughts on making *incidental education* the chief means of learning and teaching; eliminating most high schools, with various youth communities assuming their social functions; having college education generally follow, rather than precede, entry into the professions; and designing elementary pedagogy in such a way as to delay socialization and protect the child's free growth.[41]

These four radical educators are linked to Dewey in their pursuit of a theory of education founded on quality of experiences selected to enhance the individual's life. Furthermore, the dilemma inadvertently posed by Dewey several decades back assumes new importance with the deschooling ideology. If we consider the construct of Reimer and Illich alone, the predicament is not substantially relieved. Whereas Dewey was left precariously perched on one horn of the dilemma (the potential of the school), Illich and Reimer are perched on the other horn (the potential of the community). Goodman and Bereiter offer strategies for resolving the dilemma.

---

[38]See Reimer, *School Is Dead,* chaps. 8 and 9; and Illich, *Deschooling Society,* chap. 6.

[39]Carl Bereiter, *Must We Educate?* (Englewood Cliffs, N.J.: Prentice-Hall, Inc., 1973), chap. 6.

[40]Ibid., p. 93.

[41]Paul Goodman, *New Reformation: Notes of a Neolithic Conservative* (New York: Random House, 1969), pp. 85–86.

A RETURN TO TRADITIONAL VALUES

Policy makers and reformers have done little to resolve the basic issues in American education. In liberal times—the progressive eras: 1910s, 1930s, 1960s and early 1970s—reformers focused on broadening the curriculum, helping the "disadvantaged," and humanizing the schools. In conservative times—1890s, 1950s, and 1970s—the reforms emphasized the basics and coherence in the curriculum, the "talented," and discipline. As James and Tyack point out, "Calls for change in both kinds of periods reflect the anxieties and the aspirations of the time and an image of a preferred future . . . reformers seem to wear blinders, to see only part of what constitutes a healthy education system—a system in which the persisting reality is that such values as equity, excellence, and liberty are always in tension."[42]

The 1960s and early 1970s was a period of more calls for radical change in education. As we described in Chapter 2, the Elementary and Secondary Education Act (ESEA) served the underprivileged and furthered the goal of *equity*. Funds and programs were provided to help those who came from culturally different environments, as well as youngsters with physical, emotional, and intellectual learning disabilities. Curriculum specialists also embarked on bold attempts to reformulate the content and processes of learning in math, science, social studies, and English. These, in large part, were designed to foster higher levels of thinking and make the curriculum more relevant to the social and physical environment.

By the mid-1980s, the pendulum had swung back to a traditional perspective. Movements in educational reform tend to mirror those in the political arena. After a decade or more of public action and idealism, people, as historian Arthur Schlesinger explains, tend to be "exhausted by the process and disenchanted with the results." In education, the public did not understand the rationale of the "new" curricula, and schools too often were unable to execute effectively the ambitious learning objectives. When achievement levels dropped for many of the middle-class students with middle-range learning abilities and the dropout rate of these average students increased, the public turned its attention from compensatory education and intellectual ideals to testing and accountability. In the larger perspective, the nation was challenged scientifically by the Russians and outperformed technologically by the Japanese. By 1980 the national focus was clearly on *excellence* in education.

There were various reasons for the decline in learning of the average student with modest intellectual inclinations—not the least of which were persuasions of an increasingly entertaining and distracting culture. Nevertheless, changes within schools, also, were a catalyst to the academic drift of these students. Disproportionate attention was given to those on both sides of the "majority" student. At one extreme were special programs for slow learners and other handicapped students; at the other, the gifted and academically talented were treated to accelerated programs in smaller classes often with the most capable teachers. Many students and families also never adapted to the consolidation of smaller schools into larger

---

[42]James and Tyack, "Learning from Past Efforts," p. 406.

districts, nor embraced the racial integration within districts. Many tiny high schools (100 to 200 students) were eliminated as a result of consolidation, but the giants (1,500 and more) that resulted had few if any educational advantages over smaller schools (500 to 1,000 students) and several disadvantages—particularly for the middle-range student. The sprawling urbanization of metropolitan areas contributed as much to the bureaucratic impersonalization of schools as did consolidation. And the mixed results of racial integration illustrated the difficulty of effecting social change through school reform. Until neighborhoods and communities are culturally and ethnically mixed, most school integration attempts will be artificial and strained.

The Shift from Citizen to Patriot

The 1980s-style swing to traditional goals contains far-reaching implications for the role of schools in society. As Henry Giroux points out, this shift calls for an ideological restructuring of the concept of *citizenship*. The message was explicitly announced in such reform documents as *A Nation at Risk*, in pronouncements from the executive branch of the federal government, and from spokespersons in business, such as Xerox's David Kearns (*Winning the Brain Race*). Underlying the new conservative agenda, explains Henry Giroux, is a shift from the issues of equity and justice accompanied by "little concern with how public education will serve the interests of diverse groups of students so they will be better able to understand and gain some control over the sociopolitical forces that influence their destinies." The goal of citizenship, he adds, is barely mentioned in the new reform proposals. "In its place, there is a preoccupation with patriotism, which in this case is made synonymous with the tenets of economic productivity and national defense." In this latest drive toward "excellence," education for self- and social understanding gives way to the "imperatives of corporate self-interest, industrial psychology, and cultural uniformity."[43]

The emphasis on values education, which we examined in Chapter 4, further defines the shift from the development of citizens. In character education, teachers are asked to convey a clear sense of right and wrong and promote the skills of achievement through the values of "hard work," "respect for authority," "loyalty," and "obedience." This discourse, Giroux says, avoids conflict and mention of "messy" topics such as racism and class discrimination and says little about equity and social justice.[44]

Public education has been asked to do much: to increase its custodial function, to be an agency for civil rights, to expand the curriculum to meet a host of social urgencies, to serve as a scapegoat for the extravagances and tangle policies of the economic society. Faith in public schools and respect for teachers has dwindled during the past two decades. Until schools clearly define their purpose

[43]Henry A. Giroux, *Schooling and the Struggle for Public Life: Critical Pedagogy in the Modern Age* (Minneapolis: University of Minnesota Press, 1988), pp. 17–18.
[44]Ibid., p. 19.

and limit the scope of services, either public opinion will control the schools or the lack of support will destroy them.

PROSPECTS FOR INSTITUTIONALIZED PLURALISM

Our nineteenth-century forebears struggled to forge an omnipotent public school system. The American common and comprehensive school was meant to enculturate, socialize, politicize, and assimilate the disparate many, as well as eliminate illiteracy and nurture talent.

Schools do have functions they perform better than other social institutions. They are the most appropriate institution for teaching literacy, rational inquiry, and citizenship development. Ironically, schools have not performed well enough in these areas. Nevertheless, public schools have been providing the "education" demanded by the larger society—vocational education, career education, sex education, drug education, economic education, driver education, and so forth. Although these may be important to the survival of society, schools are merely the most convenient, not necessarily the best, agency to provide this learning. The *essential* function of our schools has been diluted and its effectiveness reduced.

Illich, Reimer, Bereiter, Goodman, and others provide a wholistic vision toward an educational pluralism. They would revise the role of the schools, reduce their scope, and increase the functions of other community agencies. This calls for nothing less than a redefinition of the conventional meanings of education and schooling. Schooling and education never have been synonymous, though we've come to associate the one with the other. With a new vision and blueprint, education would become a total community responsibility, and the function of *the school* would be more specific. There would be many "schools" (a multiplicity of institutions), where people of all ages intentionally are educated.

In his *Public Education* (1976), Cremin speaks of an *ecology of education* in which this "multiplicity of institutions" and individuals educate. These, Cremin explains, include parents, peers, siblings, and friends, as well as families, churches, synagogues, museums, summer camps, agricultural fairs, settlement houses, factories, television networks, and the like. They also include writers, journalists, doctors, dentists, lawyers, social workers, mechanics, computer programmers, farmers, builders, and many others. Together, these agencies and people interact with one another and with the larger society to form a "configuration of education."[45] In the eighteenth-century version of this configuration, these agencies interacted in an incidental, and largely educative, way. Today their effects are hardly coordinated and too often miseducative, so as to foster helplessness, dependency, and confusion in the learner (who is more commonly referred to as client, customer, patron, patient, and student). The new configurations of education would be a systematic, deliberate, community-based arrangement to bring out the potentially educative qualities of all the institutions and people who affect all learners today, young and old.

---

[45]Cremin, *Public Education*, pp. 85–86. We elaborated on this concept in Chapter 5.

Paradoxically, we are back where we were two hundred years ago, when education was relevant, communal, and lifelong. And with this, Dewey's school-community dilemma is resolved. The difference between then and now is that yesterday's learning was spontaneous and incidental; today's must be systematic and intentional. The intervening years of industrialization, technological development, specialization, and urbanization have turned the basic manipulative character of society upside down. Once it was the things and institutions that were manipulated by the people; in modern times it is the people who are manipulated by things and institutions. This prescription for a new pluralism, configuration, ecology, and conviviality would fundamentally restructure education.

Case Study: Home Schooling

The "League of Parents of School Students" has written a "model law" that would lower the compulsory attendance laws in your state from sixteen to twelve. The establishment of compulsory attendance laws is a state function, and the proposed bill that was introduced in the current session is under discussion now by the state legislature's education committee. The bill has attracted interest throughout the state, but the discussions have been particularly intense in your community as a result of an incident with parents who decided to educate their children without assistance from the schools.

The incident involved a local newspaper editor who had four children in the public schools, the youngest in first grade and the oldest in eleventh grade. Last year the parents pulled all four children out of school and began their own education program. The children now are home in the morning completing math, spelling, literature, and history lessons under the mother's tutorage. They spend afternoons at the newspaper office reading, writing (sometimes for the paper), and generally helping with the publication of the weekly newspaper. The father's work takes him to many businesses, shops, and farms in the area. Often the older children will remain for several afternoons at an establishment where there are skills or knowledge to be learned. Evenings are spent reading and discussing local, state, and national events (social studies). Basic course plans had been obtained through the community college, and the parents were preparing to begin instruction in Spanish and the physical sciences.

The family's home- and work-study program was progressing this year, but not without considerable excitement in the community. Some people strongly supported the family, arguing that the schools were inadequately staffed and equipped. In fact, a group had been trying to convince the "League of Parents of School Students" to work for elimination, not just reduction, of compulsory school laws. Other citizens condemned the editor and his wife as lawbreakers and irresponsible parents.

Last month the superintendent of schools brought charges against the parents. In their hearing they were charged with breaking a state law and put on bail. The parents are now under legal pressure for their children to return to school. What should they do and why? Where do you stand on the compulsory education bill in the state legislature? Should the bill be withdrawn or defeated? Should it be revised to abolish compulsory attendance?

Thought Questions

1. How do you explain the harsh, dictatorial, punitive, drill-oriented character of early American schools, when there were examples of more thoughtful and humane ideas on schooling available from current and earlier European sources?

2. What similarities and differences do you see in "modern" elementary schools and those of colonial times? In answering this question, consider school architecture, curriculum, teaching methods, teachers' training, and student-teacher relations.

3. Using Michael Katz's models (see footnote 12), describe what education, and schools, would be like today if the "democratic localism" rather than the "incipient bureaucracy" form of school organization had prevailed. How might the effects of such a form differ from what Katz describes as the effects of bureaucracy?

4. Ralph Tyler, an eminent educator, identified six basic functions of public schools: individual self-realization, literacy, social mobility, preparation for the world of work, wise choices of nonmaterial services, and learning how to learn. Place these in their order of importance as you view them. Defend your first choice. Do you agree that all six should be functions of the schools? If so, which should not be, and why?

5. "What kind of education will best develop the free citizen and the free person?" According to R. Freeman Butts, this question runs through the history of American education and has been answered in different ways at different times. Briefly explain how this question was answered during the colonial, republican, and democratic phases of American education. Has a new response to this question developed in very recent years? If so, what is it?

6. Explain how the secondary schools in this century have served the goals of the "Seven Cardinal Principles" set forth in 1918. Are these goals appropriate for the end of the twentieth century? If they need revising, what would you eliminate, add, or change?

7. If Dewey's theories of progressive education had been properly practiced in early decades, what would schooling have been like in classroom arrangements, curriculum organization, and teaching methods? Was it reasonable to expect that schools and teachers could fully implement these progressive principles? What characteristics of society and schools made the philosophy difficult to implement? What changes in community attitudes, school organization, and teachers' training would have been necessary?

8. Do you agree with George Counts that our schools should have as their central aim the reconstruction of society? Why is this necessary or unnecessary? A wise or unwise course of action? Is Counts's goal any more or less pertinent today? Explain.

9. Describe the present mood in education. Is it traditional, progressive, or some combination of the two? Cite characteristics of schools that reflect one view or the other.

10. How realistic do you think it is to expect schools to assume a reduced educational role in the future, and subsequently, to expect community institutions to take a more active part in educating citizens? Do you see any indicators that this is developing? What problems might exist? How could the goal of excellence be used to support this change?

Practical Activities

1. Put together a pictorial or photographic essay showing the changes in school architecture and classroom organization over the past hundred years in your state. Comment on the relationship between these arrangements and the nature of education over time. Prepare your work for display.

2. Interview a grandparent or another older relative or friend and report what schooling was like in the past. Find out about the curriculum, methods, class size, school size, students' role, discipline procedures, and administrative personnel. Relate any anecdotes that would provide today's students with a picture of yesterday's schools.

3. From school records, news clippings, interviews, or any other source, write a brief history of one school. Select a school you attended, one in your college or university community, or any public or private school that significantly interests you.

4. Interview an older public school teacher, active or retired, who taught during the 1930s or 1940s. Inquire specifically about the effects of progressive education on the schools in those days: What changes took place? What debates went on about the nature of schooling? How did this teacher's school and colleagues respond to progressivism? Ask also about changes in the school curriculum and organization during the latter 1940s and 1950s. Write up the results, highlighting the effects of both progressive and traditional ideas about schools during this era.

5. Devise a questionnaire assessing people's reaction to a comprehensive community education program, and administer it to students, teachers, administrators, and parents. Areas to survey include shifting to community agencies such curricula as industrial arts, business education, and home economics; using the community to develop theater groups, orchestra, band, art, photography, film-making, and related programs; conducting all competitive athletic programs for various age-groups with total community support; actively engaging businesses, organizations, institutions, and members of the professions in the formal educational configuration of the community. Tabulate the results and write a summary of your findings.

6. Design an "ecological system of education" for a community with which you are familiar. The schools should be only one of many learning centers. What businesses, organizations, associations, and other institutions would you include? How would these agencies operate, and what would their responsibilities be? What businesspersons, entrepreneurs, artisans, and professionals would you enlist in the system and how would they function? How would you organize and administer this system?

7. Examine the selected bibliography at the end of this chapter, and choose one book by an author who offers a particular historical interpretation of education. Write

an analysis and critique or summary exploring educational implications of this work in educational policy and practices today.

Bibliography

Books

BESTOR, ARTHUR E., *Educational Wastelands: The Retreat from Learning in Our Public Schools*. Urbana: University of Illinois Press, 1953.

BRUNER, JEROME S., *The Process of Education*. New York: Random House, 1960.

BUTTS, R. FREEMAN, and LAWRENCE A. CREMIN, *A History of Education in American Culture*. New York: Holt, Rinehart & Winston, 1953.

CONANT, JAMES B., *The American High School Today*. New York: McGraw-Hill Book Company, Inc., 1959.

CREMIN, LAWRENCE A., *American Education: The Colonial Experience, 1607–1783*. New York: Harper & Row, Publishers, Inc., 1970.

———, *Public Education*. New York: Basic Books, Inc., Publishers, 1976.

———, ed., *The Republic and the School: Horace Mann on the Education of Free Men*. New York: Bureau of Publications, Teachers College, Columbia University, 1962.

DEWEY, JOHN, *Democracy and Education*. New York: Macmillan, 1916.

———, *Experience and Education*. New York: Macmillan, 1938.

GIROUX, HENRY A., *Schooling and the Struggle for Public Life: Critical Pedagogy in the Modern Age*. Minneapolis: University of Minnesota Press, 1988.

GOODMAN, PAUL, *Compulsory Mid-education*. New York: Random House, 1962.

HAMPEL, ROBERT L., *The Last Little Citadel: American High Schools Since 1940*. Boston: Houghton Mifflin Company, 1986.

HUTCHINS, ROBERT M., *The Conflict in Education*. New York: Harper & Row, Publishers, Inc., 1953.

ILLICH, IVAN, *Deschooling Society*. New York: Harper & Row, Publishers, Inc., 1971.

KATZ, MICHAEL B., *The Irony of Early School Reform*. Cambridge, Mass.: Harvard University Press, 1966.

———, *Reconstructing American Education*. Cambridge, Mass.: Harvard University Press, 1987.

KRUG, EDWARD A., *Salient Dates in American Education, 1635–1964*. New York: Harper & Row, Publishers, Inc., 1966.

———, *The Shaping of the American High School*. New York: Harper & Row, Publishers, Inc., 1970.

LEE, GORDON C., ed., *Crusade Against Ignorance: Thomas Jefferson on Education*. New York: Bureau of Publications, Teachers College, Columbia University, 1961.

REIMER, EVERETT, *School Is Dead: Alternatives in Education*. New York: Doubleday & Company, Inc., 1971.

SILBERMAN, CHARLES E., *Crisis in the Classroom: The Remaking of American Education*. New York: Random House, 1970.

SIZER, THEODORE R., *Horace's Compromise: The Dilemma of the American High School*. Boston: Houghton Mifflin Company, 1985.

———, *Places for Learning, Places for Joy: Speculations on American School Reform*. Cambridge, Mass.: Harvard University Press, 1973.

Periodicals

BUTTS, R. FREEMAN, "Search for Freedom: The Story of American Education." *National Education Association Journal,* 49, no. 3 (Mar. 1960), pp. 33–48.

COMMAGER, HENRY STEELE, *The People and Their Schools* (Fastback 79). Bloomington, Ind.: Phi Delta Kappa Educational Foundation, 1976.

———, *Harvard Educational Review,* 46, no. 3 (Aug. 1976). A special issue on history and education.

JAMES, THOMAS, and DAVID TYACK, "Learning from Past Efforts to Reform the High School." *Phi Delta Kappan,* 64, no. 6 (Feb. 1983), pp. 400–406.

LAUDERDALE, WILLIAM BURT, *Educational Reform: The Forgotten Half* (Fastback 252). Bloomington, Ind.: Phi Delta Kappa Educational Foundation, 1987.

12

Education from an International Perspective

We cannot wander at pleasure among the educational systems of the world, like a child strolling through a garden, and pick off a flower from one bush and some leaves from another, and then expect that if we stick what we have gathered into the soil at home, we shall have a living plant. A national system of education is a living thing, the outcome of forgotten struggles and difficulties and "of battles long ago."[1]

The goal of the campaign was always greater than to teach poor people how to read. The dream was to enable those two portions of the population that had been most instrumental in the process of the revolution from the first, to find a common bond, a common spirit, and a common goal. The peasants discovered the word. The students discovered the poor. Together, they all discovered their own patria.[2]

DIMENSIONS OF THE PROBLEM

Although great strides have been made in educating the world's 5 billion people, there are a growing number of illiterates in many countries. In spite of massive efforts at population control, the world's population continues to explode, with resultant problems in jobs, housing, food, and health care. In the 1980s the poor nations faced a precipitous fall in prices for their basic commodities, massive inflation, and an actual decline in living standards for most of their people. Although many industrial nations faced growing unemployment lines, the poor countries faced the real possibility of starvation.

War and internal violence continue to plague the nations and people of this

[1]M.E. Sadler, *How Far Can We Learn Anything of Practical Value from the Study of Foreign Systems of Education?* 1900.

[2]Mier Febles, Cuban educator in Havana, 1976.

world, in spite of efforts by the United Nations and proclamations of peaceful intentions by superpowers and small nations alike. Military expenditures on a worldwide scale are in the hundreds of billions of dollars annually, while millions of persons face starvation, inadequate health care, poor housing, and often a life of illiteracy.

Education is often looked on as a way out of these seemingly intractable problems. In its early history, the United States borrowed educational ideas from Europe. During the late nineteenth and throughout much of the twentieth century, however, many European nations and some of their colonies (or former colonies) borrowed from the United States. In the late twentieth century the pendulum has once again swung back, as it did following Sputnik, so that politicians, citizens, and educators alike are looking to Japan and Germany to help the United States solve the educational problems it now faces.

The National Commission on Excellence in Education in 1983 claimed that "if an unfriendly foreign power had attempted to impose on America the mediocre educational performance that exists today, we might well have viewed it as an act of war."[3] The commission asserted that in a comparison study with other nations, American students never ranked first or second and were last seven times. Other reports have pointed to deficiencies in American education when compared with schools in the Soviet Union or western Europe, where students take considerably more science, mathematics, and foreign languages throughout their formal schooling. Still other critics have pointed to the fact that most American young people attend school for only 180 days each year, whereas students in Japan and certain other nations attend from 200 to 220 days.

Following Sputnik in 1957, Americans felt the need to catch up to the Russians militarily. The political rhetoric of the past decade has exhorted Americans to catch up with the Japanese economically. Political and educational leaders are again looking to other nations for educational models and successful practices.

EDUCATION AND ECONOMIC DEVELOPMENT

In any comparison of nations, it is important to point out that there are often profound differences among their educational, cultural, religious, political, and economic institutions. Economists and development experts differentiate among countries on the basis of economic and social indicators. Many factors go into making up the quality of life, but the following are some of the most important indicators of the development for a nation (see Table 12-1).

Economists from the World Bank look at these and many other indicators of the quality of life and economic growth or decline in over 120 nations around the world. With the exception of eastern Europe, the Soviet Union, and a few other Marxist regimes throughout the world, most nations participate in the Interna-

[3]National Commission on Excellence in Education, *A Nation at Risk* (Washington, D.C.: U.S. Department of Education, 1983), p. 5.

TABLE 12-1   **Quality-of-Life Indicators**

Per capita GNP
Per capita GNP growth or decline over previous years
Birthrate per 1,000 persons
Life expectancy at birth
Infant mortality per 1,000 live births
Mortality rates under age 5
Literacy rate
Per capita public education expenditures
Per capita medical expenditures
Per capita doctors and hospital beds
Distribution of wealth
Total exports and imports
International reserves or debt
Per capita calorie consumption
Agriculture for local consumption or export
Percent of population with potable water
Percent of population with electricity
Percent of population with adequate housing

tional Monetary Fund, the World Bank, and other international economic agencies. With the dramatic changes in the Soviet Union, Hungary, and Poland in 1989, and General Secretary Gorbachev's request to become an active participant in the international economic system, it is likely that only a few renegade countries such as Albania, North Korea, and possibly Cuba will remain outside the world economy by the year 2000. The development of the European Economic Community in 1992, with its 5-trillion-dollar economy and over 350 million people, along with the economic power of Japan and the newly industrialized countries of Singapore, Korea, Hong Kong, and Taiwan in Asia, has put tremendous economic pressure on both the Soviet Union and its allies in eastern Europe, and also on the United States. As both superpowers have recognized the erosion of their economic, political, and military leadership in the face of a united Europe and the threat of the "Asian Century," changes thought impossible in the late 1980s are becoming commonplace in the 1990s.

The *World Development Report 1988* from the World Bank contains an array of information that can help to place in perspective the vast differences that exist between the predominantly poor countries of the Southern Hemisphere and the generally wealthier nations of the Northern. Although there are some "developed" nations in Africa, South America, and Asia, those continents contain the major centers of poverty and famine. Table 12-2 gives some indication of the differences among some of the rich and poor nations of the world.

Economists have differentiated among First, Second, Third, and Fourth Worlds. The United States and Europe make up most of the First World; the Soviet bloc countries, the Second World; countries making some economic progress are the Third World; and the Fourth World includes those in a state of near perpetual economic and political collapse, described by a former U.S. secretary of state as the "international basket cases."

TABLE 12-2   Basic Indicators—1986

COUNTRY	GNP PER CAPITA	ANNUAL GROWTH RATE	LIFE EXPECTANCY	BIRTHRATE PER 1000
1965–86				
Ethiopia	120	0.0	46	47
Kenya	300	1.9	57	52
China	300	5.1	69	19
Haiti	290	0.6	54	35
Philippines	560	1.9	63	35
Nicaragua	790	−2.2	61	42
Congo	990	3.6	58	46
Jordan	1540	5.5	65	39
Mexico	1860	2.6	68	29
Hungary	2020	3.9	71	12
Venezuela	2920	0.4	70	30
Singapore	7410	7.6	73	16
U.K.	8870	1.7	75	13
Japan	12840	4.3	78	12
Kuwait	13890	−0.6	73	32
U.S.	17480	1.6	75	16

Another similar categorization lists countries as "developed" or "developing." Some futurists have categorized countries as preindustrial, industrial, and postindustrial. Whatever system one uses, there are obvious and extreme differences among nations on the whole range of political, economic, educational, health, military, religious, and cultural factors.

A country such as Kenya, with a birthrate of 52 per 1,000, has a considerably more difficult time keeping up with the problems of feeding, housing, and educating its people than does the United Kingdom, with a birthrate of only 13 per 1,000. With a per capita income of only $120, Ethiopia must struggle just to keep its people alive; whereas Kuwait, with a per capita income of $13,890, can concentrate on the whole range of social and economic benefits. It is much harder to educate one's people in such countries as Guinea or Malawi, where only 5 percent of the people are literate, than in the Soviet Union or Japan, where literacy rates exceed 98 percent. Upper Volta can afford to spend only $2 per capita on education, whereas Canada spends $486. These are some mitigating factors that need to be considered when looking at the similarities and differences among nations.[4]

POLITICAL AND ANTHROPOLOGICAL MODELS

Even as economists and developmental experts have differentiated among countries on a range of variables related to economic growth and development, political scientists have pointed up the differences in how power is distributed and deci-

[4]The World Bank, *World Development Report 1988* (Oxford: Oxford University Press, 1988).

sions are made, using a host of terms or phrases like capitalism, communism, the free world, iron curtain countries, parliamentary democracies, socialist democracies, and kingdoms.

R. Murray Thomas argues that schools influence a nation's political system in seven basic ways:

1. Political socialization or citizenship training
2. Political legitimation
3. Manpower production
4. The sorting of persons for the hierarchy
5. Social assessment
6. Social control
7. The stimulation of change

Conversely, the political system controls the schools through its provision of support for and access to education, its influences over curricular content and teaching procedures, and the latitude of social and political action it permits in the schools.[5] Interactions between the schools and the political system occur in all societies, but the individual national responses vary greatly. It is possible to categorize schools by the ways in which interactions between the political and educational systems occur.

Many people, for example, assume that the Communist nations have the most centralized and controlled educational systems, whereas democratic nations have a more decentralized system. This, however, is not always necessarily the case. In the People's Republic of China during the Cultural Revolution from 1966 to 1976, the regime practiced many forms of extreme decentralization, whereas in France there is a highly centralized and administered educational system. Other observers have suggested that the free world is more deeply committed to education than the Communist world, but the extremely high literacy rates in many eastern European countries and in the Soviet Union, and the commitment of China and Cuba to literacy and education suggest that educational development can occur under a variety of political structures.

Anthropologist Anthony Wallace has given us a model for looking at the basic functions of the school from an anthropological and political perspective, while getting away from the stereotypical categories of Communist, free world, or Third World. He defines *schooling* as the learning that occurs in a school, whereas *education* is all learning, including but not confined to schooling. *Enculturation* is learning enjoined on the person with a particular status in a particular culture.

Learning, according to Wallace, can be classified into three basic categories. *Technic* is the stimulus-response-reinforcement type of learning described by behavioral psychologists. *Morality*, the second type, deals not with the "how-to" but with the "what" of learning. Moral learning focuses on a particular set of socially approved values that promote the welfare of the total community. The final form

---

[5]R. Murray Thomas, ed., *Politics and Education* (Oxford: Pergamon Press, 1983), p. 19.

of learning, *intellect*, involves a particular cognitive way of looking at the world.[6] Wallace's model emphasizes that what one needs to learn in a particular society may or may not be useful in another. Cultural tradition, political structure, social class, historical tradition, and other factors influence the type of learning emphasized in a society and the subject matter taught in its schools.

Although there are innumerable "learnings" that a society might wish to pass on to its young, there are at least three contrasting value orientations: (1) the revolutionary, or utopian; (2) the conservative, or ideological; and (3) the reactionary. These value orientations control not only what a person will learn but also where, how, and from whom it will be learned. Further, the types of learning discussed (that is, technic, morality, and intellect) receive different relative emphases in the three value orientations:

1. Revolutionary — morality, intellect, technic
2. Conservative — technic, intellect, morality
3. Reactionary — morality, technic, intellect

A contemporary example of revolutionary society is Cuba, which has a Marxist/Socialist orientation. China and Nicaragua also were prime examples — China until 1976, and Nicaragua until 1990. Within revolutionary societies, morality is paramount in schooling, which becomes the key institution in constructing a "new society." Intellect is next in importance, because a morally reliable and intellectually resourceful cadre of individuals is needed to carry on the revolution. Technic takes a back seat to the other two in such societies, as the schools become the moral battleground for transforming the society.

Conservative societies such as the United States and most of Europe have technic as their primary educational mission. The transformation of society is basically complete, and intellectual codes or ways of looking at the world are basically in place. Those who do not accept the dominant morality are dealt with by police, counselors, the medical profession, or other control mechanisms.

Reactionary societies such as South Africa (and Chile until the fall of Pinochet) place morality at the heart of their educational systems, but the morality emphasizes religiosity, political ritualism, laws, police, and other control agents. Technical activity is of secondary importance, and the role of intellect is downgraded as being dangerous to the controlled social and political order.

In the United States today there are critiques and recommended reforms for each of the three learning orientations. Critics have decried the denigration of the intellect in contemporary American society, while citing the example of the Europeans and the Soviet Union as societies that give great time and effort to matters of the intellect in their schools. The Governors' Task Force on Economic Development has criticized the lack of technic, or technical skills, on the part of American youth. The Gallup Polls on Education have found that lack of discipline

---

[6]Anthony F.C. Wallace, "School in Revolutionary and Conservative Societies," in Francis A.J. Ianni, ed., *Conflict and Change in Education* (Glenview, Ill.: Scott, Foresman & Company, 1975), pp. 15–28.

in schools, morality, has been the major concern of Americans for the past fifteen years. The Moral Majority continues to raise the issue of lack of morality in our society.

Some observers claim that the growth in the Moral Majority, the Reagan era, and the election of President George Bush all indicate that we are already in a reactionary era in American politics and education. Others, pointing to the growing numbers of the poor and unemployed, suggest that we might well be moving into a new revolutionary period. The evidence indicates, however, that the United States, with most of the First and Second Worlds, fits within Wallace's framework of conservative societies. Most Third and Fourth World nations are in a reactionary stage, and only a few, such as Cuba, are revolutionary.

COMPARING THE INCOMPARABLE

Torsten Husen, the Swedish director of the International Assessment for the Evaluation of Educational Achievement (IEA), writes of the difficulties in making valid comparisons among countries on something as complex as educational achievement. Earlier in this chapter we detailed some of the differences in economic development, political systems, and other factors that impinge on education in a nation. Critics, however, point to the IEA studies that appear to place the United States last in many categories of educational achievement, compared with "similar" countries in western Europe. These countries are industrialized democracies like the United States, and yet their students appear to do better on standardized examinations in mathematics, science, foreign languages, and other subjects.

The major reason for the apparent differences is the nature of secondary education in the United States and Europe. The Europeans traditionally have had an elitist secondary system, supported by their national governments and enrolling as few as 9 percent of the age-group. The United States, however, has a long tradition of attempting to educate *all* students up through the secondary school. When the upper 5 to 10 percent of the student populations were compared, Husen concludes that the "elite among U.S. high school seniors did not differ considerably in their performance from their age-mates in France, England or Germany." He goes on to point out that in comprehensive systems such as the United States, a much wider net is cast, resulting in a bigger "talent catch."[7]

Most industrialized nations also have clearly stated national educational objectives and national curricula, whereas in the United States educational objectives and programs are locally controlled. Time spent in class on particular subjects is one critical variable not often given sufficient attention by critics of education. In a study of achievement in the French language, for example, it is not surprising that the U.S. sample did worse, with only two years in the subject, than Romanian

[7]Torsten Husen, "Are Standards in U.S. Schools Really Lagging Behind Those in Other Countries?" *Phi Delta Kappan*, 64, no. 7 (Mar. 1983), pp. 455–61.

students who had studied French for six years. Significant differences in emphasis given to creativity and problem solving, as opposed to memorizing for standardized examinations, also exist.

Cultural and historical differences among countries are neglected: The fact that many nations have one ethnic, racial, linguistic, and cultural group, compared with the extreme heterogeneity found in the United States, has seldom been adequately considered in the attacks on the U.S. educational system. Educational achievement is the result of a complex interaction of many factors, and education and schooling are ill served by political rhetoric that does not consider the important differences among societies.

EDUCATIONAL MODELS

Clark Kerr described five educational models that can be found in practice in the countries of the world today:[8]

1. Elite-oriented education
2. Production-oriented education
3. Universal-access education
4. Horizontal education
5. Atomistic education

Elite-oriented Education

In this type of educational system, schools serve only a small group of students who are chosen either because of birth into the aristocracy or through demonstrated talent, as in a meritocracy. Until the nineteenth century, most educational systems were elitist, and this remains true for many Third World countries today. Almost all school systems have some aspects of elitism still at work, but the egalitarian nature of education pervades most developed countries. The following figure portrays the three major elitist approaches:[9]

FIGURE 12-1 Elitist Models

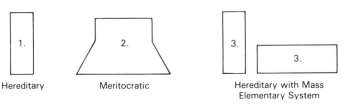

Hereditary   Meritocratic   Hereditary with Mass
                                           Elementary System

[8]Clark Kerr, "Five Strategies for Education and Their Major Variants," *Comparative Education Review*, 23, no. 2 (June 1979), pp. 171–82.
[9]Ibid., p. 173.

Nicaragua.   Prior to its revolution in 1979, Nicaragua was a prime example of an *elitist* educational system, containing elements of all three diagrams found in Figure 12-1. Nicaragua has been inextricably bound to the United States ever since soldier-of-fortune William Walker declared himself president of the country in the mid-1850s. For the next 130 years, relationships consisted of a near-unending series of U.S.-backed coups and countercoups, with our Marines occupying the country off and on from 1912 through 1933. In 1936, with the help of the U.S. government, the Somoza family took over the country and retained control until the revolution of 1979.

Prerevolutionary education in Nicaragua resembled that of many Third World countries and was characterized by massive illiteracy, estimated nationwide at 60 percent and in some rural areas at over 90 percent. High birthrates wiped out gains in literacy, so that there were a growing number of illiterates at the same time that numerous schools were being built. The rich sent their children to private, predominantly Catholic schools or out of the country. The masses of students tended to stay in school for only a short period of time, so that in many parts of the country less than 10 percent of the school-age population was still enrolled by sixth grade. By the end of secondary school, only a handful of students were still enrolled, and these came primarily from the economic and political elite.

Nicaragua under Somoza had a tiny ruling oligarchy, a small middle class of perhaps 10 percent, and a massive unemployed and underemployed class of workers and peasants. Rural areas not only lacked schools but also had no infrastructure of medical care, roads, electricity, potable water, or other basic necessities. USAID estimated that over half the population of Nicaragua survived on an annual per capita income of only $75. Although the Nicaraguan constitution guaranteed all children an education up through the sixth grade, the government was unable or unwilling to provide it for most of the rural poor.

The example of Nicaragua is not atypical of the 141 other developing nations. The historical context for much of Asia and Africa dictated that British, French, German, Belgian, Portuguese, or Spanish elitist models of education were set up. Even after thirty years of independence, most former colonies still continue in the traditions set up by their colonial masters in the nineteenth and early twentieth centuries. Children throughout the Third World continue to be denied the basics of education and literacy, even though inexpensive methodologies and technologies are readily available. Most countries have had at least to make an attempt to set up a *mass elementary system,* but the elite private schools, boarding schools, and intensive examination systems assure that only a small minority will rise up from poverty.

France.   The French *baccalaureate,* or examination for secondary graduation and university admission, has been copied throughout much of the Third World, although it has been the center of controversy in France itself. The French secondary schools, called *lycées,* have traditionally been an elitist system, with the best students from the best *lycées* doing well enough on the *"Bac"* to go into the technical schools and universities and from there into the French power structure.

With the student rebellions of the 1960s and 1970s, and the election of the Socialist party in France, attempts have been made to deemphasize the role of a single examination for the future of students and to provide greater access for the working class to higher education.

Many more examples of elitist education could be drawn from the First, Second, and Third Worlds. Despite the near universal demand for education throughout the world, most systems continue to be elitist in nature and serve as a major sorting device for their societies.

Production-oriented Education

In this model, young people from throughout the population are brought into a technically and vocationally oriented school system and trained for a wider variety of occupations and professions than in the elitist model. Whereas most elitist systems train large numbers of lawyers, economists, and liberal arts graduates, the production-oriented systems emphasize engineering, agriculture, and a wide range of technical skills. The pyramid in Figure 12-2 represents a production-oriented system, which has a very large base, with meritocratic judgments made at various levels, and a large portion of the adolescents in technical schools and colleges rather than liberal arts programs.

The Soviet Union.   Before 1917 the Soviet Union had an elitist system, but since the Bolshevik Revolution of that year it has become, along with post–World War II Japan, the prime example of a production-oriented educational system. The Soviet Union has a population of over 279 million people in fifteen sovereign union republics. Although half of the Soviet citizens speak Russian as their native language, over 180 languages are spoken in the Soviet Union. Considerable linguistic and cultural nationalism can be found in many of the republics. Bilingual education is not something unique to the United States, because over 100 native languages are used in the early elementary grades in the Soviet Union, and secondary education is conducted in over 50 different languages. Political nationalism, however, has not been permitted until recently, and the Communist party has been the dominant force in both Soviet society and in education. Although 70 percent of the Soviet people live in European Russia and are European in orientation, the vast country includes millions of persons of Oriental heritage, ethnicity, language, and culture.

FIGURE 12-2   Meritocratic Pyramid in a Production-Oriented Educational System[10]

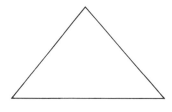

[10]Ibid., p. 175.

Prerevolutionary Russian had a long tradition in science and the arts, but it was an elitist tradition. Over 60 percent of the population still was illiterate in 1917. The revolution set the educational system back, and World War II, with 20 million dead, caused extensive damage to the economic infrastructure and the schools. Despite these cataclysms, the Soviet Union has made dramatic educational strides over the past sixty years and today has a literacy rate of 95 to 99 percent, one of the highest in the world. Its production of engineers and scientists is at a rate from three to ten times higher than most other industrialized nations, and it continues its strong tradition in the arts. Under the control of authoritarian Marxist leadership, however, the social sciences and humanities have tended to suffer.

The formal Soviet educational system, as with most Communist countries, begins shortly after birth. Children attend the *crèche* from the age of two or three months. The reasons for beginning education at such an early age are both economic and ideological. Most mothers work outside the home, and the party begins the process of teaching cooperative behavior and ideological concerns in the extensive preschool and nursery system that most children attend. Researchers and teachers in the Soviet Union have perhaps done more work on early childhood education than any other country in the world.

The regular schooling process begins at age seven and lasts for eleven or twelve years; by 1980, 97 percent were completing a three- or four-year secondary program.

Soviet educational policy has fluctuated over the years, from attempts to get all eight-year graduates into some type of work-study or technical or vocational program, to efforts to have most, if not all, students complete the ten-year general secondary program. During the Khrushchev reforms of 1957, the emphasis was strongly toward work and vocational training. Attempts were made to have all students spend two years in the labor force, following their full ten-year schooling process. In more recent years, the Soviet goal has been to have 100 percent of school-age children complete the regular secondary program and to select some for higher education through an analysis of their cumulative records (not just test scores).

Under the leadership of General Secretary Gorbachev, the late 1980s have proven to be another period of dramatic educational and societal reform. In his book on *perestroika*, Gorbachev writes that "perestroika is a revolution . . . which involves radical changes." Among the educationally related goals of *perestroika* are such things as the fostering of democratic processes, the development of nontraditional attitudes and values, and a generation willing to take risks and innovate. Gorbachev seeks an educational system that will help young people be open to new ideas and comfortable with competition — ideas in radical opposition to more traditional Marxist-Leninist goals. *Glasnost* (openness) has led to a great deal of public criticism of the educational system, and the 1990s will no doubt continue to be an era of major educational reform in the Soviet Union.[11]

[11]Gerald Howard Read, "Education in the Soviet Union: Has Perestroika Met Its Match?" *Phi Delta Kappan*, 70, no. 8 (Apr. 1989), pp. 606–13.

The curriculum in Soviet schools tends to be more academic than what is typically found in the United States. It has a strong emphasis on the sciences, mathematics, physical education, Russian, and foreign languages, but much less emphasis on the humanities and social sciences. History, from a Marxist perspective, plays a critical role in the Soviet curriculum. Although children attend school six days a week, each school day tends to be a bit shorter than found in most Western nations. Because most parents work, however, the school year is among the longest in the world, averaging from 210 to 230 days, compared with 175 to 180 in most Western industrialized countries.

Soviet youth organizations, such as the Young Pioneers (ages nine to fifteen) and the Komsomol (ages fifteen and up), help prepare youngsters for adult life. These organizations also are connected to Children's Palaces, after-school centers where special instruction is given in the arts, sports, and technical and vocational skills.

Education in the Soviet Union is quite formal, with generally austere classrooms, strict discipline, and up to three hours of homework a night for older students. Individual students have no choice in the curriculum, and most decisions on what is to be taught and how it is to be taught are made at a national level. As might be expected in a Marxist or Communist state, there are no private schools and no religious education. Marxist dogma affects the way not only history is taught but also science and other subjects. Moral or character education is an important part of the curriculum at all levels. In keeping with the Marxist emphasis on an egalitarian society, there is no homogeneous grouping throughout the basic eight years of schooling, although students can be held back if they do not keep up with their class. Education has been free at all levels since World War II, although there are hidden costs of supplies and uniforms. The system is basically meritocratic, with some exceptions made for the children of party officials. Tests are given at the end of the eighth and eleventh years, but the cumulative record of students has as much impact on further education as do the examinations.

Like many other nations, the Soviet Union has more secondary graduates wishing to enter institutions of higher education than it has room for; thus some of the more prestigious institutions require students to take a special entrance examination. The Soviet Union has close to 5 million students in higher education. Some attend universities located in each of the republics, often with instruction in the language of that region, and many attend institutes that emphasize a range of specialties from science to technology to pedagogy. Unlike the traditional full-time student to be found in most other countries, a large portion of students in higher education in the Soviet Union combine part-time study with part-time work and take an extra year or two beyond the full-time four or five to complete their degrees. Given the reward structure in the Soviet Union, university professors, researchers, and senior teachers are paid more than medical doctors and only slightly less than engineers.

In many ways *the Soviet educational system is more like that of the United States than of other European countries.* The near-universal nature of its eleven-year schooling and the meritocratic emphasis more closely parallel the U.S. system

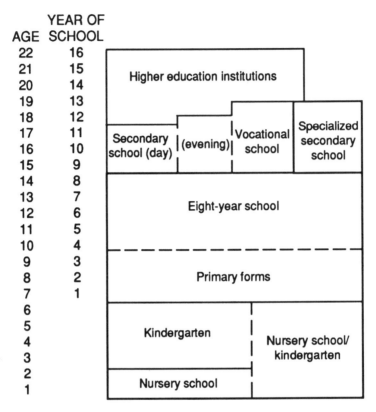

YEAR OF
AGE SCHOOL

FIGURE 12-3   Educational Options Available to Soviet Children and Youth

than the traditionally more elitist western European models. Although the United States has a separation of church and state in schooling, moral training and character building are emphasized in many schools, much as one can observe in many Soviet classrooms. Coeducation is widespread in both societies, but because of the massive number of deaths of men during World War II and other historical and ideological factors, the Soviet Union has made greater strides in the placement of women in nontraditional careers. Both systems have extensive vocational programs, although the Soviet work-study model, during both secondary and higher education, appears to be more extensive and more closely related to the actual needs of the society. The formality of most of the instructional process and emphasis on memorization rather than critical thinking have led to boredom and some evidence of delinquency by alienated Soviet youth. Because of the control mechanisms of the society, Soviet schools do not suffer the large dropout rates faced by many U.S. school systems. The lack of academic freedom and the controls on what can be taught, read, and seen, however, have led to some disaffection by Soviet youths.

With the dramatic changes in Soviet society under General Secretary Gorbachev and the renewed emphasis on an open society, it is impossible to predict how the educational system might change during the final decade of the twentieth century. If Gorbachev succeeds in his reform efforts and continues along the same path, the Soviet Union will likely develop more along the lines of the United States and Europe. If, however, the conservative forces regain power, a period of repression will bring a return to traditional Marxist-Leninist thought.

Japan. The other major production-oriented educational system is Japan. In the past decade, the United States and much of the rest of the world have looked to Japan and its educational system for insight into the economic miracle that has occurred in that country since World War II. On the surface, the Japanese educational system looks remarkably like that of the United States, as well it should, having been designed and implemented in the days following World War II by General MacArthur and his American educational consultants. The system, however, is a highly meritocratic one, with testing at the youngest ages to select students for elite kindergartens and similar screening throughout the system up to the elite Tokyo University.

The extreme pressure on children and young people to pass examinations has led to a high suicide rate, personality disorders, and societal cleavages. There can be no denying, however, that the economic success of the Japanese has been aided by the educational system. General qualities of Japanese culture, though, may have been more crucial. The drive for success built into the Japanese character, child-rearing patterns, respect for authority, cooperative behaviors, and deference to the group make the Japanese a unique culture and people. Japan's homogeneous society, its geographical and geopolitical situation, and many other critical factors are undoubtedly related to its success as a nation. Whether other nations can "copy" Japan remains to be seen.

The Chinese, Koreans, and Germans are three other contemporary examples of societies that have made dramatic educational and economic advances.

Universal-access Education

Kerr's third model is best exemplified by the United States, with some minor examples in other industrialized nations. Universal primary and secondary education is followed by open-access institutions of higher education. This model is based on the presupposition that education is a lifelong task for all people and for whatever purpose. The curriculum under the open-access model is designed to meet the needs and interests of the individual in daily living—not the development of a political leadership, as in the elite model, or the needs of the labor market, as in the production-oriented educational systems.

Figure 12-4 represents open or universal access, in contrast to elite or production-oriented pyramids, which strictly limit students from moving up through the system.[12]

[12]Clark, "Five Strategies for Education," p. 177.

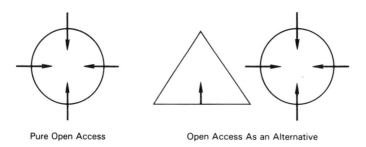

Pure Open Access   Open Access As an Alternative

FIGURE 12-4   Universal-access Education Models

United States.   Universal primary education was achieved in this country in the late nineteenth and early twentieth centuries. Secondary education is now universally available, primarily in that uniquely American invention, the comprehensive high school. Approximately 25 percent of adolescents in the United States do not complete secondary school, but they are not screened out for elitist or meritocratic reasons. The vast majority of American citizens now live within commuting distance of an open-access institution of higher education. Hundreds of community colleges have been founded in the years since World War II, and countless other institutions of higher education admit any candidate possessing a high school diploma. Although these institutions are not free, most are comparatively inexpensive, so that the United States can truly be said to have developed the first universal open access to higher education.

Universal or open-access systems are obviously dependent on society's willingness to spend vast sums of money on education. Most Third World countries could not afford universal secondary or higher education, even if they so desired. Second World Communist nations prefer a meritocratic production-oriented system. In Europe and the rest of the Western industrialized world, a tradition of elitism and social class differences offset pressures to democratize secondary and higher education and move toward an American model.

Other countries.   Because of the pressures to democratize, the British have built many universities in the past forty years, including an Open University that uses television and other media to channel higher education to the masses. Many other countries have started adult or continuing-education programs to provide educational opportunity for those unable to pass special examinations or attend college for economic reasons. Under Julius Nyerere, Tanzania has made dramatic strides in providing basic literacy and elementary education for his people, but the nation cannot afford universal secondary and higher education.

China, during its cultural revolution from 1966 to 1976, attempted to make its total society a school and to move away from centuries of elitism in schooling. All children were guaranteed elementary and middle school education, and students for the universities were selected for political reasons and work habits rather than ability to pass traditional examinations. Since Mao's death, however, the

Chinese have returned once again to a meritocratic model to select the one percent of its students who go on to the university.

Two other democratic types of institutions that fit well into the universal or open-access model are the *Danish folk high schools* and the *British infant schools*. The folk high schools are residential secondary schools, which have educated and trained the rural Danish farm children since 1840 in both vocational skills and more traditional academic and religious subjects. In addition to excellence in academics, these schools emphasize cooperative behavior and modern farming techniques. The spiritual and physical aspects of life are critical parts of every student's training. The folk schools continue to be austere environments, but are filled with an almost evangelistic fervor in passing on a unique blend of academics, vocational skills, physical fitness, and religious and moral values.

The United States traditionally has looked to Great Britain for much of its inspiration in education, from the first Pilgrims and the "dame schools" to the contemporary infant schools, which are models of humane, quality education for young children. The British infant and primary schools are characterized by a high degree of informality in the classroom. The role of the teacher is that of a facilitator of individual learning rather than a disseminator of knowledge through lecture and recitation. Students have a great deal of choice in what is learned, and the teaching method is primarily one of inquiry.

Equally admired by other nations are Britain's elitist, wealthy, private "public" schools, and the highly traditional, academically rigorous "grammar" schools. When the Labour party is in power, the infant schools, comprehensive secondary schools, red brick universities, and the Open University tend to be favored. When the Conservative party is in power, attempts usually are made to restore a strict testing system, return to the "basics," and continue the meritocratic traditions of Eton, Harrow, Oxford, and Cambridge.

Horizontal Education

Horizontal education has only been tried within revolutionary Marxist settings: during the Cultural Revolution in China, in Castro's Cuba, and most recently in postrevolutionary Nicaragua. Equality and the lack of trained experts with authority and control are major characteristics. Figure 12-5 portrays the purely egalitarian version, one generally found in even the most revolutionary

FIGURE 12-5   Horizontal Education Models

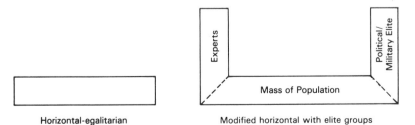

Horizontal-egalitarian   Modified horizontal with elite groups

societies, where the need to train experts in certain fields is paramount. After the revolution, Castro is reported to have said that if he had it to do over, he would have had a trained cadre of experts ready to counteract the massive defection of the educated class in the early years of the revolution.

China.   As stated earlier, the Chinese experimented with perhaps the most extreme form of a horizontal-egalitarian system during its Cultural Revolution from 1966 to 1976. During that ten-year period, teachers and professors were attacked emotionally and even physically by revolutionary students, who came to be known as the Red Guards. Schools were closed for months or years, as students spent their time memorizing and chanting passages from Mao's *Little Red Book.* Experts of all varieties were sent to new institutions called the May 7 Cadre Schools. There professors, teachers, scientists, politicians, and any other members of the society who were seen to be "above" the peasants, workers, and soldiers were forced to do manual labor for long periods of time. Factories were declared to be universities, and learning was to occur in the workplace. Admission to the few universities allowed to remain open was based on political considerations and votes by fellow workers, not the traditional family ties or meritocratic tests. Affirmative action was taken to extremes, so that children of the educated, bureaucratic, former capitalist classes were denied admission to educational institutions, and children of peasants, workers, and soldiers were given preference.

Following Mao's death in 1976, the educational system, along with the rest of Chinese society, returned to more traditional Chinese ways. Although China attempts to educate all its children up through the middle school or secondary education, it has reinstituted a number of "elitist" practices. *Key Schools* have been set up to educate gifted children in most urban areas, and admission tests to the small university system are among the most difficult in the world. The outstanding young scientists and mathematicians are sent overseas to the United States and Europe for graduate training, and countless incentive systems are being put into place in the classrooms, factories, and rural communes. The Chinese educational system in the 1980s could be characterized as a broad-based pyramid up through middle or secondary school with an extremely small pyramid on top.

Cuba.   Like China, Cuba went through an extreme egalitarian phase and reduced illiteracy to one of the lowest levels in the world. It also recognized the need to develop expertise to keep a modern Marxist state functioning. As a result, the Cuban system provides mass education for all students up through secondary school, and it has developed an extensive system of higher education to educate its elite. Like China, however, it has attempted to keep salaries for the educated elite from getting too far out of line with those of the regular working population.

Nicaragua.   Nicaragua was the latest experiment in horizontal-egalitarian education, even as prerevolutionary Nicaragua exemplified elite-oriented education. The Sandinista revolution of 1979 led the country to restructure its school system almost totally. Private Catholic parochial schools remained, but they were government controlled. The university system was dramatically expanded to provide education for a much broader spectrum of Nicaraguan youths.

Following the revolution of 1979, the new Sandinista government (named after the revolutionary hero who fought against the Americans in the 1920s and 1930s) announced the National Literacy Crusade, modeled after the successful Cuban crusade of 1960 and based on the radical educational theories of Brazilian educator Paulo Freire. In one of the most dramatic programs in educational history, the crusade in Nicaragua cut illiteracy in the country from 60 percent to 23 percent in five months and down to 15 percent in nine months. Large amounts of aid in the form of funds, materials, and personnel came from all over the world, but particularly from Scandinavia and Cuba.

Liberation, mass or popular participation, transformation, commitment to community, education for and within socialism, and dialogue were among the many themes that came out of the National Literacy Crusade and continue to dominate the educational system. The crusade used Freire's concept of *generative themes*, ideas that come from the people rather than those imposed from above. The primers developed for use in the crusade contained stories about the heroes of the revolution; the contributions of the new government in such critical areas as democracy, land reform, economic development, and unionization; the integration of the East Coast into the broader society; and the role that the new Nicaragua was to play on the international scene in support of justice and progressive regimes.

Nicaragua took to heart Castro's dictum that "education and revolution are one and the same." It also revered Chè Guevara's statement that "society as a whole must become a huge school." In addition to the literacy crusade, the Nicaraguans rapidly expanded their elementary, secondary, and higher education systems and opened them to children of all social classes.

Schools in revolutionary societies are not isolated institutions. With the education of the urban poor and rural peasants, the new government moved rapidly in land reform, minimum wages, banking controls, nationalization of some businesses and industries, and major health programs. These programs of health care for all citizens virtually eliminated the diseases that had given Nicaragua one of the highest infant mortality rates and shortest life spans in the Western Hemisphere.

The actions of the new government were an attempt to liberate the people through an understanding of the past and their present reality. The combination of Marxism from many of the Sandinista leaders, with the liberation theology of many within the Catholic Church, proved to be powerful in bringing about radical change within the society. Most Latin American revolutions, with the exceptions of Cuba and Nicaragua, have tended to be a shifting of oligarchies and have brought little real change to the lives of common citizens. Unlike Cuba, Nicaragua sought to maintain a mixed socialist-capitalist economic system as well as a strong Catholic religious tradition.

The Nicaraguan revolution in politics, economics, education, and religion became a major threat to many traditional power structures. The U.S. government covertly and overtly began attempting to overthrow the regime. The Catholic

Church was split, both within Nicaragua and throughout the world, on the role it should play in "liberating" the poor. The international banking community cut off almost all aid to Nicaragua, forcing it to rely on the Soviet Union and Cuba to survive. External pressures and internal strife brought down the Sandinista regime in 1990. The effects on education are still to be seen.

Although the horizontal and universal-access models both have democratic themes, they differ significantly. The universal-access model provides freedom for the individual to pursue a wide variety of types of education, at any time, and at any level. The horizontal approach, in contrast, tends to limit strictly the amount and type of education the individual can pursue. In horizontal systems the emphasis is on basic skills rather than higher levels of academic or scientific achievement. Also, universal-access systems tend to promote academic freedom, whereas the horizontal systems limit it.

Atomistic Education

This form of education is both the oldest and the newest. It has been described as education of the individual as a by-product of some other activity, or learning on one's own. Informal and nonformal education have gone on since time immemorial, but recent calls by deschooling anarchists such as Ivan Illich have brought it once again to public attention. Kerr represents atomistic education as a series of random dots.

Atomistic education takes such forms as apprenticeships, experiential learning in a variety of settings, learning from television and other mass media, and informal education in nonschool agencies such as churches, businesses, and bureaucracies. This type of education has neither formal curricula nor explicit arrangements with other educating agencies. It is random and individualistic; nevertheless, much of what everyone knows has been learned in this idiosyncratic manner.

There are obviously no national examples of atomistic education because no society has seen fit to leave the education of its young up to chance. Both Communist and capitalist regimes seek to pass on their values to the next generation. Kingdoms, democracies, and dictatorships alike have formed school systems to deal with technic, intellect, and morality. Formal educational systems, although attempting to change the next generation in some manner or another, are by definition conservators of the heritage of the society, regardless of its political, economic, social, or religious nature.

A CRITIQUE OF WORLD EDUCATION

The model of education chosen by countries who must contend with overpopulation, illiteracy, malnutrition, and starvation has life-and-death implications for its people. The amount of money, or percentage of the gross national product, that a society spends on education has a profound effect on the economic and political development of that society for generations to come, and has an immediate effect by taking money from other sectors.

With a GNP over two trillion dollars, the United States can afford expenditures on education in excess of $200 billion annually. Except for the newly rich oil nations, the Third and Fourth World countries must carefully shepherd their scarce resources, spending them only on education that benefits all members of the society and not just the elite. In a poor country, each dollar spent on an educational system that tends to perpetuate elites is one less dollar that can be spent on health care and basic food production. Too many poor nations have rapidly expanded their educational systems, only to be unable to provide jobs for the graduates of the secondary and higher institutions. In the absence of a democratic and egalitarian ideology, education tends to secure the positions and power of the elite.

In spite of two to three decades of independence, most former colonies retain the elite educational systems left by Great Britain, France, and the other colonial powers. More recently, Third and Fourth World nations looked to the United States and the Soviet Union for teachers, textbooks, and instructional technology. None of the models from the developed world have met the needs of most poor nations. Critics have suggested that knowledge itself has been colonized and curricularized and that only knowledge in the Western mode has been considered true and appropriate. Nations such as Cuba and Nicaragua have discovered the danger of breaking away from the traditional models of education, economics, and politics. The Third and Fourth Worlds, however, are now looking to their own educational experiments, not to Europe, Japan, the United States, or the Soviet Union.

THE INTERDEPENDENCE OF PEOPLE AND NATIONS

The problems of population growth, energy usage, pollution, war, and the distribution of wealth indicate the increasing interrelatedness of all nations. Marshall McLuhan heralded the new age in the title of his book *War and Peace in the Global Village*. No longer are people separated in time or in space, but we now live in a world of "all at onceness," in which we are not just observers of other nations' tragedies and wars but also participants. The same theme was struck by Kenneth Boulding, who said that humankind no longer lives on an "illimitable plane," where there is always somewhere to go over the horizon, where neither humanity's ignorance nor armies could be considered fatal flaws. Instead, we now find ourselves on a crowded and precarious spaceship. It is imperative that people and nations recognize the nature of the global village and spaceship earth and the demands put on societies in general and the schools in particular. At one time it was possible for humanity to exist in small, separate, isolated cultures or nations. The development of modern methods of warfare, our interdependence for raw materials and manufactured goods, and new forms of transportation and instantaneous communication have brought people from far-flung lands closer together.

Traditionally the schools have emphasized the nation-state and the geographical and cultural differences among nations. Within the United States we have placed the emphasis on the melting pot. Only recently has our society moved toward cultural pluralism and an acceptance of diversity on a worldwide scale. Humanity must learn to value differences in religion, race, language, culture, economic systems, and forms of government. In that process the role of the schools can assume great importance.

Case Study: Equity and Excellence

One of the most difficult issues nations must face is that of equity and excellence in education. A former U.S. secretary of education stated it in the form of a question: Can we be equal and excellent too? More recently, the President's Task Force on Excellence in Education stated that our nation is "at risk" because of its overemphasis on equality and lack of attention to excellence. Political parties and ideologies generally emphasize one end of the equity-excellence continuum more than the other, and the educational models discussed in this chapter also come down on one side or the other.

Discuss which educational model you believe to be most appropriate for the United States today and the reasons for your choice. Which model is most applicable to the needs of a poor Third or Fourth World country?

Using what you have learned about the U.S. educational system in this chapter and the rest of the text, respond to the following. What are the school characteristics that promote *equity*; that promote *excellence?* Can our schools provide both equality and excellence?

Thought Questions

1. What reasons can you give for the dramatic disparities found in Table 12-2? What political, economic, religious, social, and historical reasons might lead to such dramatic differences among countries?

2. Give examples of ways in which the political and educational systems interrelate in the United States.

3. Is the United States at basically a revolutionary, conservative, or reactionary stage in its development? Defend your choice with concrete examples.

4. What qualitative and statistical reasons can you give for the American students doing poorly when compared with those of other developed nations? In your opinion, are students in this country receiving an inferior education, when compared with those in the Soviet Union, western Europe, and Japan?

5. What historical reasons can you give for why such a vast majority of the Third and Fourth World countries still maintain an elite-oriented educational system?

6. Why have Marxist revolutions been more successful in moving away from elite systems to other models than have revolutions of the right?

7. What aspects of the Soviet educational system might be applicable in the American setting, and which are not at all appropriate?

8. Japan is well known for the pressure it puts on its students of all ages through its examination system. What advantages and disadvantages can you see if the United States adopted such a system?

9. Does the universal-access model found in the United States hinder the drive for excellence in education?

10. The Chinese, during the decade from 1966 to 1976, attempted the most extreme forms of equal education. Why do you think they rejected the horizontal model following Mao's death?

11. With the vast amounts of wealth in the world and the unequal distribution among rich and poor individuals and nations, what can be done to bring about a greater balance? What values support the superiority of the rich over the poor? Can and should the schools attempt to change those values?

Practical Activities

1. Design an educational system for a Third or Fourth World nation that takes into consideration the following realities: a high adult illiteracy rate, a dictatorial government of the right, extreme poverty for most of the people, a poorly trained and uneducated teaching staff, a dependence on agriculture in the nation's economy, a lack of communication facilities, and a host of other governmental priorities.

2. Using UNESCO sources, comparative education textbooks, and other library materials, compare the U.S. educational system with that of another developed country. Deal with such topics as how the schools are financed, the curriculum, the organized structure, who teaches, and the percentage of the age-group still in school at each level.

3. Study the curriculum of a local school district for evidence of internationalization. Look at course titles, units, textbooks, and any other aspects of the system that might show evidence of international or global perspectives. In particular, concentrate on the social studies courses and textbooks, and see how other nations are treated. Make a chart showing how much time is spent on the United States and its history and how much is spent on other nations.

4. From your observations of the community in which you live, your own background, an analysis of the media (radio, television, advertising, newspapers, and magazines), and any other relevant materials, what appear to be the dominant values of American society? Are these values compatible with the ecological, military, and social realities facing the world today?

5. Describe a day in the life of a school child in another nation. Information can be obtained through your own visits to a school in another country; through interviews with a former Peace Corps volunteer, missionary, businessperson, military person, or others who have lived overseas; or perhaps through discussions with a foreign student on your campus. How might such a day be similar to or different from that experienced by an American child of the same age?

Bibliography

ALTBACH, PHILIP G., ROBERT F. ARNOVE, and GAIL P. KELLEY, eds., *Comparative Education*. New York: Macmillan, 1982.

BERGER, PETER L., *Pyramids of Sacrifice*. Garden City, N.Y.: Anchor Books, 1976.

BOWLES, SAMUEL, and HERBERT GINTIS, *Schooling in Capitalist America*. New York: Basic Books, Inc., Publishers, 1976.

BROWN, LESTER, *State of the World: 1988*. New York: W.W. Norton & Company, Inc., 1988.

CARNOY, MARTIN, *Education as Cultural Imperialism* New York: David McKay Company, Inc., 1974.

COOMBS, PHILIP H., *The World Crisis in Education: The View from the Eighties*. New York: Oxford University Press, 1985.

FREIRE, PAULO, *Pedagogy of the Oppressed*. New York: Seabury Press, 1970.

HOROWITZ, IRVING LOUIS, *Three Worlds of Development*. New York: Oxford University Press, 1972.

ILLICH, IVAN, *Deschooling Society*. New York: Harper & Row, Publishers, Inc., 1971.

KING, EDMUND J., *Other Schools and Ours*, 5th ed. New York: Holt, Rinehart & Winston, 1979.

OVERSEAS DEVELOPMENT COUNCIL, *The United States and World Development: Agenda 1979*. New York: Praeger Publishers, Inc., 1979.

POSTLETHWAITE, T. NEVILLE., *The Encyclopedia of Comparative Education and National Systems of Education*. Oxford, Pergamon Press, 1988.

THE WORLD BANK, *World Development Report 1988*. Oxford: Oxford University Press, 1988.

THOMAS, R. MURRAY, ed., *Politics and Education*. Oxford: Pergamon Press, 1983.

TOMIAK, J.J., ed., *Soviet Education in the 1980s*. London: Croom Helm, 1983.

U.S. DEPARTMENT OF EDUCATION, *Japanese Education Today*. Washington, D.C.: U.S. Government Printing Office, 1987.

WRIGGINS, W. HOWARD, and GUNNAR ADLER-KARLSSON, *Reducing Global Inequities*. New York: McGraw-Hill Book Company, Inc., 1978.

13

Futures: Societal and Educational

Now there is one outstanding important fact regarding Spaceship Earth, and that is that no instruction book came with it. . . . Thus, because the instruction manual was missing we are learning how we safely can anticipate the consequence of an increasing number of alternative ways of extending our satisfaction, survival and growth—both physical and metaphysical.[1]

Time, said St. Augustine, is a three-fold present: the present as we experience it, the past as a present memory, and the future as a present expectation.[2]

As a species, humankind is unique in several respects, one of which is the ability to transport itself mentally from present to past to future. To understand fully oneself and one's world requires that perspectives from the past and future both converge on the present. Conjectures of the future are partly factual and partly imaginative, a combination of extrapolation and intuition.

Education also is influenced by concepts of time—as in the use of instructional and learning objectives, the administrative emphasis on planning and policy studies, the tradition of relying on "olders" to be the teachers of "youngers," and the custom of grouping students by age for instruction. Most of all, education is cumulative and antientropic. It is cumulative both in the residue retained by the individual and in the collective value to society of diversely educated individuals; it is antientropic in that the knowledge created in the process is an energy source (actual and metaphorical) equal to if not greater than the energy expended to create it.

Knowledge seekers are time travelers in the sense that learning is a process, a "continuous reconstruction of experience," to use John Dewey's phrase. Learning

---

[1]R. Buckminster Fuller, *Operating Manual for Spaceship Earth* (New York: Pocket Books, 1970), pp. 47–48.

[2]Daniel Bell, "The Year 2000—The Trajectory of an Idea," *Daedalus* 95, no. 3 (Summer 1957), p. 639.

is an integration of past experience with one's present condition, together with the potential for future applications. For the teachers of children and adolescents, the future is the broad realm in which their clients will spend 80 or 90 percent of their lives. The students of the young teacher in the 1990s will probably experience more than half of the twenty-first century.

The twenty-first century will require a crucial attitude for the survivors aboard earth—to view the human condition from a global perspective. More and more, one's immediate local needs and concerns are inextricably entwined with those of other human beings in many other places on the planet.

ORIENTATIONS TO THE FUTURE

There are many attitudes toward and points of view about the future. Futurists are a curious blend of colors and shades: of cautious and starry-eyed optimists; of fatalistic and realistic pessimists; of eschatologists (religionists who prophesy or study world endings); of cornucopians (optimists who see a horn of plenty for all) and catastrophists (pessimists who see crisis upon crisis); of utopians and their opposite, dystopians; and of extrapolationists (who view the future as a continuation of past-to-present trends), transitionists (who anticipate slow, significant change over generations or centuries), and transformationists (who forecast rapid, dramatic, traumatic, revolutionary change).

Futurists prefer to call their work *forecasting* rather than prediction (which implies too much precision) or prophesying (which bears too much of a religious connotation). Although they do forecast single events (for example, when a space colony will be created), they prefer to describe a combination of related events in the form of a scenario. Even more desirable are multiple scenarios, because these allow leaders, citizens, and others to choose from alternatives. Further, they allow people not only to decide on a preferred scenario but also to decide which scenarios they don't want to occur. Finally, the presentation of multiple alternative scenarios makes it possible for persons to determine degrees of possibility and probability for any scenario in comparison with the others.

In presenting scenarios, futurists often simplify the alternatives by use of graph drawings, as in Figure 13-1.

THREE TYPES OF FUTURISTS

As noted, one way of classifying futurists is by how they view continuity and change. We offer three ideal types: extrapolationist, transitionist, and transformationist. They can be arrayed on a continuum extending from *continuity*, or minimal change at one end, to *perpetual*, rapid, revolutionary change at the opposite extreme (Figure 13-2).

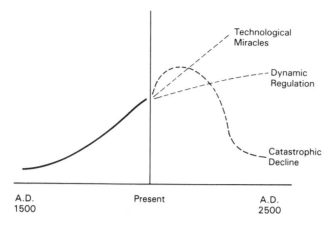

FIGURE 13-1 Three Future Scenarios

Extrapolationist

In one sense, all futurists are extrapolationists because to *extrapolate* means to estimate an unknown based on known facts and data. We, however, are using the term to describe those futurists who view the future as a continuation of past-to-present dominant trends. For this group, the past-to-present time frame varies from five hundred years (since 1500 — the end of the Middle Ages in Europe) to one hundred years (since about 1880 — the Industrial Revolution era in the United States) to the post–World War II period in Europe, Japan, and North America.

The prototype nation or society for the extrapolationist is one that is highly industrialized, urbanized, and technology driven, such as Japan, West Germany, or the United States. By "trickle down" or "exportation," the rest of the world's nations will follow the lead of these "advanced" examples of modernization. For the extrapolationist, talk of "limits" is a defeatist attitude, and sustained economic growth is the ideal and is synonymous with progress.

The extrapolationist is an optimist and a cornucopian, one who believes in Western civilization and its cultural and material benefits, especially the standard of living provided by capitalism, industrialism, and scientific and technological developments. A flavor of this viewpoint comes through the following quotation from a special issue of *U.S. News and World Report* on the future:

FIGURE 13-2 Futurists and Change

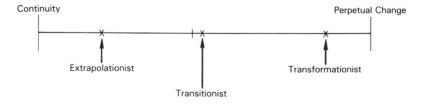

What lies ahead could well be a renaissance for the U.S. in political prestige and technological power. People will live to a healthy old age of 100 or more, as superdrugs cure diseases such as cancer and senility. Genetic techniques will expand food production and curb pollution. Space colonies will orbit the earth, and the moon will be mined for its wealth. Robots will do household and factory chores, and cars will be programmed to avoid accidents. . . . With home computers and other electronic marvels, families will tap into enormous sources of data and entertainment. As the revolution in high technology gains momentum, an economic boom will give tomorrow's citizens the highest standard of living ever known.[3]

Given the extrapolationists' near-absolute faith in the fruits of science and technology, the following projected developments would certainly be welcome to them:

1. There will be improvements in the type and use of contraceptives for fertility control. Oral and male contraceptives will be perfected. National and international fertility control programs will be implemented.

2. Continuing progress in medical science (for example, prosthetic devices, surgical procedures, and vaccines), will allow U.S. citizens to expect an average hundred-year life span. Improvements in cryogenics could make possible longer, interrupted life spans.

3. Pharmacology will develop a number of nonnarcotic and nonaddictive personality modification and control drugs. Also, there will be drugs to enhance intelligence and learning.

4. Weapons research will grow apace with the more benign technologies, producing *both* lethal and incapacitating biochemical weapons. (A weapon on the drawing board even in the late 1980s is the neutron bomb, which kills human beings but doesn't destroy buildings.)

5. New generations of computers and new computer applications will be developed, including home computer terminals and new versions of computer-assisted instruction.

6. Artificial forms of life will be created as outcomes of research on self-replicating molecules, recombinant DNA, and procedures for cloning.

7. Genetic control products and procedures will be developed that will eliminate many hereditary defects and allow for "choices" by prospective parents of a range of hereditary human characteristics for their planned offspring. Also, ovum banks and sperm banks will be established.

8. Household robots will be created, first, to do just a few simple tasks and then to do many complex chores.

9. Space exploration of our galaxy and solar system will continue, with a manned landing on Mars and a space colony established, equidistant from earth and its moon, to collect solar energy and transmit it to earth.

10. There will be improvements in and increased use of nuclear energy—both fission and fusion reactors. Other energy sources will be investigated for availability and economic feasibility: sources such as geothermal and solar energy, wind, and evaporation.

[3]Bartrand de Jouvenal, *The Art of Conjecture* (New York: Basic Books, Inc., Publishers, 1967), p. 10.

Two futurists who appear to fit the extrapolationist mold are the late Herman Kahn (*The Year 2000,* with A.J. Wiener, 1967; *The Next 200 years,* with others, 1976; *World Economic Development,* 1979; *The Coming Boom,* 1982); and Gerard K. O'Neill (*The High Frontier: Human Colonies in Space,* 1977; *2081: A Hopeful View of the Human Future,* 1981).

Herman Kahn is probably best known as the director of the Hudson Institute (Croton-on-Hudson, N.Y.), a futures "shop" he founded after leaving the Rand Corporation (Santa Monica, Calif.). As a futurist, he propounded a continuity scheme he called "The Basic Long-Term Multifold Trend of Western Culture," a pattern or complex of interrelated trends that began about 1500 and is characterized by the concept of progress. Kahn argued that the Multifold Trend

> is best thought of as a single entity whose every aspect is both a cause and an effect — a driving force and a consequence. [The elements] should be thought of as aspects or parts of a whole. The Multifold Trend affects every aspect and part of society: fine arts, truth systems, family relationships, government, performing arts, architecture, ethics and morality, music, law, economics, civic relationships, literature, and education.[4]

The Trend is further explained in Table 13-1. Note that item 13 suggests that the basic twelve trends will spread to the less-developed nations, thus making the Trend a global phenomenon, and that item 14 anticipates that the tempo at which each preceding trend occurs will accelerate until a peak is reached.

Gerard K. O'Neill, a Princeton physics professor, has been most associated with the idea and feasibility of space colonies. For him the new frontier is space exploration and colonization, what he refers to as "the high frontier."[5] He reveals his viewpoint in this quotation from his popular book *2081:*

> But in every type of futuristic writing, from the impersonal to the subjective, I found the same pattern: most prophets overestimated how much the world would be transformed by social and political change and underestimated the forces of technological change.[6]

In a major section of *2081,* O'Neill identifies five of what he calls "drivers of change." These are "developments that [he] believes will determine, alone and in combination, the course of the next hundred years." The five are (1) computers, (2) automation, (3) space colonies, (4) energy, and (5) communications.[7]

[4]Herman Kahn, *World Economic Development* (New York: William Morrow & Company, Inc., 1979), pp. 27–30.

[5]Gerard K. O'Neill, *The High Frontier: Human Colonies in Space* (New York: William Morrow & Company, Inc., 1977).

[6]Gerard K. O'Neill, *2081: A Hopeful View of the Human Future* (New York: Simon & Schuster, Inc., 1981), p. 20.

[7]Ibid., pp. 15, 39–102.

TABLE 13-1   The Basic Long-Term Multifold Trend[8]

Some aspects of this trend go back a thousand years; except as noted, most go back several centuries. This trend is toward:

1. Increasingly Sensate Culture (empirical, this-worldly, secular, humanistic, pragmatic, manipulative, explicitly rational, utlitarian, contractual, epicurean, hedonistic, etc.) — recently, an almost complete decline of the sacred and of "irrational" taboos, charismas, and authority structures

2. Accumulation of Scientific and Technological Knowledge — recently, an emergence of a genuine theoretical framework for the biological sciences; but social sciences are still in an early, largely empirical, and idealistic state

3. Institutionalization of Technological Change, especially research, development, innovation, and diffusion — recently a conscious emphasis on finding and creating synergisms and serendipities

4. Increasing Role of Bourgeois, Bureaucratic, "Meritocratic" Elites — recently, an emergence of intellectual and technocratic elites as a class; increasing literacy and education for everyone; the "knowledge industry" and "triumph" of theoretical knowledge

5. Increasing Military Capability of Western Cultures — recently, the issues of mass destruction, terrorism, and diffusion of advanced military technologies (both nuclear and conventional) to non-Western cultures

6. Increasing Area of World Dominated or Greatly Influenced by Western Culture — but recently, the West is becoming more reticent; a consequent emphasis on synthesis with indigenous cultures and various "ethnic" revivals

7. Increasing Affluence — and recently, more stress on egalitarianism

8. Increasing Rate of World Population Growth — until recently, this rate has probably passed its zenith, or soon will

9. Urbanization — and recently, suburbanization and "urban sprawl," soon the growth of megalopoli, "sunbelts," and rural areas with urban infrastructure and amenities

10. Increasing Recent Attention to Macroenvironmental Issues (e.g., constraints set by finiteness of earth and limited capacity of various local and global reservoirs to accept pollution)

11. Decreasing Importance of Primary and, Recently, Secondary Occupations — soon a similar decline in tertiary occupations and an increasing emphasis on advanced, honorific, or desirable quaternary occupations and activities

12. Emphasis on "Progress" and Future-Oriented Thinking, Discussion, and Planning — recently, some retrogression in the technical quality of such activities; conscious and planned innovation and manipulative rationality (e.g., social engineering) increasingly applied to social, political, cultural, and economic worlds, as well as to shaping and exploiting the material world; increasing role of ritualistic, incomplete or pseudo-rationality

13. Increasing Universality of the Multifold Trend

14. Increasing Tempo of Change in All the Above (which may, however, soon peak in many areas)

O'Neill expects the microcomputer to be able to store more in less space and to manipulate data faster:

> Long before 2081, perhaps even in this century, it will be possible to store in a machine the size of a business card all the information in a good-sized library. That will help to bring about a reduction in the scale of institutions — what one might call "social miniaturization."[9]

[8]Kahn, *World Economic Development.*
[9]O'Neill, *2081*, p. 42.

For automation, he has in mind the expanded uses of computers in industrial applications such as the computer-controlled welding machines used today in most automobile factories. Beyond the single automated machine is the totally auto- mated factory, and then comes the self-replicating machine that is capable of reproducing itself.[10]

O'Neill's favorite solution for most current problems is the space colony, which will free earth's population from the many forms of troublesome limits and scarcities: territory, energy, food, clean air and water, and size of population. He sees space colonies as a means of moving from "an economics of scarcity . . . to an economics of abundance. . . . Once we break out from the confines of the planet, we can begin building new lands from the limitless resources of our solar system." When can we build such colonies as human-made Earth satellites? O'Neill con- cludes that the knowledge and technology to build a hundred square mile colony is now "within the limits of known engineering practice."[11] The price tag, however, would place such a project only within the realm of a many-nation effort.

The fourth driver of change is energy, and O'Neill expects that progress on many fronts simultaneously—nuclear (fusion and breeder reactors), improved, energy-efficient modes of transportation, liquid hydrogen, earth-based solar en- ergy, and conservation—will solve the short-term problem. But for the twenty-first century, his preference is Satellite Solar Power, solar energy captured on a space satellite and relayed as low-density microwaves to earth.[12]

Finally, O'Neill argues that global communication needs can be met by larger satellites with larger antennas and more powerful transmitters, which in turn will allow for smaller, cheaper ground equipment on earth. For education, shopping, and business, communication technologies will obviate the need to do much travel from home. What will make this feasible are computers, communication satellites, fiber optic cables, and crisscrossing networks.[13]

Transitionist

The transitionist perspective is one of gradual change over a time period of centuries or even millennia. The change, however, unlike change for the extrapola- tionist, is qualitative and pervasive, a demarcation between two differing ways of life rather than a blending of events in an inexorable flow. Thus, a transitionist talks about transitional change: "from X to Y" or "from Epoch (or era) A to Epoch B" or "from the industrial society to postindustrial society."

Jonas Salk illustrates the "from/to" evolutionary change that exemplifies the

---

[10]Ibid., pp. 50–61.
[11]Ibid., pp. 62–63.
[12]Ibid., pp. 75–94.
[13]Ibid., pp. 94–102.

transitionist orientation. He argues that today we are at a transition point, a watershed, between two societal patterns. We are moving from Epoch A (past-to-present) to Epoch B (present-to-future). A is characterized by exponential growth; whereas B is captured in the concept of dynamic stability. The two types, A and B, are juxtaposed, as in Figure 13-3.[14] Salk describes this double curve (where B is the reverse of A) as a sigmoid, or S-like curve.

Epochs A and B, according to Salk, differ in several dimensions:

Epoch A	Epoch B
1. Strong ego—dominance of intellect and will	1. Integration of being and ego
2. Antideath	2. Prolife
3. Antidisease	3. Prohealth
4. Death control	4. Birth control
5. Self-repression	5. Self-expression
6. External restraints	6. Self-restraint
7. Human-over-nature ethic	7. Ecological ethic

Along with Kenneth Boulding, Daniel Bell has popularized the term and concept *postindustrial society*. Bell posits three forms of society: preindustrial, industrial, and postindustrial. Each has origins, a peak time, and a period of decline. As can be seen in Figure 13-4, the preindustrial societies began at the earliest about 10,000 B.C. The origins of industrial society occur when preindustrial societies are the dominant mode. The invention of the horse collar might be considered a beginning of industrial society, and the period between World Wars I and II in the United States might mark its peak. Although nations in Eurasia and North America have achieved the fullest development of industrial society, many nations of Africa and Asia have not yet made the transition from the preindustrial to the industrial stage.

FIGURE 13-3 Salk's Two Epochs

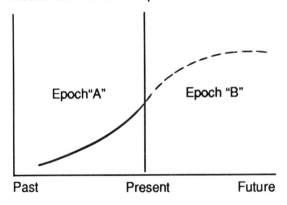

[14]Jonas Salk, *The Survival of the Wisest* (New York: Harper & Row, Publishers, Inc., 1973).

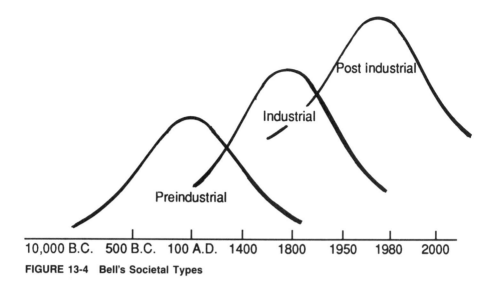

FIGURE 13-4   Bell's Societal Types

During the nineteenth century, crude forms of linotype, typewriters, and mechanical calculators appeared, and these signal the origins of postindustrial society. Today, the transition to postindustrial society has been made by the United States, the Soviet Union, eastern and western European nations, Canada, and Japan.

What are the chief characteristics of each of the three societal types? Bell summarizes these in Table 13-2, by reference to four categories: resource, mode, technology, and design. The main resources used by humans in *preindustrial societies* are such raw materials as berries, nuts, grubs, minerals, roots, wild grains, and numerous varieties of animals. The major "industries" are agriculture, mining, fishing, and forestry, all powered by raw human or animal energy. The design is a game against relentless natural forces—how merely to survive.[15]

In *industrial society,* the major resource is cheap, plentiful energy—water power and fossil fuels. The main occupational mode is the fabrication of goods—manufacture, machinery, factories. The technology grows out of science and

TABLE 13-2   Characteristics of Bell's Three Societal Types[16]

	PREINDUSTRIAL	INDUSTRIAL	POSTINDUSTRIAL
Resource	Raw materials	Energy	Information
Mode	Extraction	Fabrication	Processing
Technology	Labor-intensive	Capital-intensive	Knowledge-intensive
Design	Game against nature	Game against fabricated nature	Game between persons

[15]Daniel Bell, *The Coming of Post-Industrial Society* (New York: Basic Books, Inc., Publishers, 1973), pp. 115–19.

[16]Daniel Bell, *The Cultural Contradictions of Capitalism* (New York: Basic Books, Inc., Publishers, 1976), p. 198.

invention, yielding new machines for mass production and requiring large sums of capital to initiate the manufacturing process. Here the design is to improve on nature, to take natural raw materials and turn them into new products—steel, textiles, automobiles, airplanes, appliances—or even to create new materials such as nylon, dacron, polyester, and plastic. Efficiency is the goal, to be achieved through technical means, by rationalizing the production process (through specialization of function) and the work of the labor force (through division of labor).[17]

With the transition to *postindustrial society* comes a reliance on information as the major resource base. Information technologies emerge alongside industrial machine technologies: research and development becomes as important as production. The new technologies are designed to process information, first mechanically and then electronically. The symbol of postindustrial society is the electronic computer, whose applications impinge on every aspect of personal and social life. The computer stores, retrieves, and manipulates facts and data. It is the ultimate tool for the ultimate resource—the human being. Programs—knowledge—run computers. The design is one of person-to-person and person-to-computer. Education and the production of knowledge are the paramount industries.[18]

Another way of comparing the three forms of society is by analyzing the types of occupation that predominate in each societal form. In preindustrial societies the primary occupations are the dominant ones: agriculture, fishing, and mining. In industrial societies, there is still a need for a part of the labor force to be engaged in *primary occupations*, but the majority of workers participate in *secondary occupations* such as manufacturing, construction, transportation, and engineering. Also, in industrial societies the *tertiary occupations* come into existence: utilities, banking and commerce, insurance, and education. As the transition to postindustrial society occurs, the *quaternary occupations*, including computer science, robotics, and advanced communications, appear. Combined with the tertiary types, they tend to dominate, although here too some of the work force still practices primary and secondary occupations. At this stage, as little as 4 percent of the labor force is engaged in agriculture.

In John Naisbitt's *Megatrends*, a major national bestseller, he pointed to ten new "from/to" directions in American society.[19] These are listed in Table 13-3.

Naisbitt claims that "caught between eras, we experience turbulence. Yet, amid the sometimes painful and uncertain present, the restructuring of America proceeds unrelentingly." The interpretations of the ten new structurings follow:

> Direction 1. The United States has made the shift from industrial to postindustrial society, which Naisbitt calls the "information society: an economy based on the creation and distribution of information."
>
> Direction 2. "High tech/high touch is a formula—to describe the way we have responded to technology.... Whenever new technology is introduced into society, there must be a counterbalancing human response—that is, *high touch*—or the

[17]Ibid., pp. 115–16.
[18]Ibid., pp. 14, 115–19.
[19]John Naisbitt, *Megatrends* (New York: Warner Books, 1982).

TABLE 13-3 Naisbitt's New Directions[20]

FROM	→	TO
1. Industrial society		Information society
2. Forced technology		High tech/high touch
3. National economy		World economy
4. Short term		Long term
5. Centralization		Decentralization
6. Institutional help		Self-help
7. Representative democracy		Participatory democracy
8. Hierarchies		Networking
9. North		South
10. Either/or		Multiple option

technology is rejected." The high tech of the intensive care units in hospitals is counterbalanced by the hospice movement and the concern for the quality of death.

Direction 3. Interdependence of national economies has been on the increase since 1945. "No longer do we have the luxury of operating within an isolated, self-sufficient, national economic system."

Direction 4. Corporations under pressure from boards of directors and stockholders, and government officials under pressure from periodic elections, pursue short-term goals. American leaders, however, are learning from Japan and other nations the value of long-term, cooperatively developed economic plans.

Direction 5. Disenchanted with federal government initiatives to solve social problems and with large, bureaucratic, impersonal corporations and institutions, Americans are feeling greater efficacy and success with grassroots efforts at state and local levels and at the plant and work-group levels in industry.

Direction 6. Faith in government, schools, hospitals, and businesses is on the wane, and people are relying more on self and friends than on established institutions. Examples of this are food cooperatives, women's networks, holistic health, home schooling, and people's clinics.

Direction 7. In an era of instantaneous communication via the electronic media, representative government has become cumbersome and inconvenient. A new "ethic of participation is spreading bottom up across America and radically altering the way we think people in institutions should be governed. Citizens, workers, and consumers are demanding and getting a greater voice in government, business, and the marketplace."

Direction 8. Government and industry are organized in top-down hierarchies. "The failure of hierarchies to solve society's problems forced people to talk to one another—and that was the beginning of networks." These are informal clusters of persons with similar interests, who are held together by conferences, phone calls, books (common readings), travel, newsletters, workshops, grapevines, coalitions, radio, computers, and audio/video tapes.

Direction 9. "More Americans are living in the South and West, leaving behind the old industrial cities of the North." In the 1980 census, "for the first time in

[20]Ibid., p. 1.

American history the South and West had more people than the North and East." The shift of population reflects the same shift of wealth and economic activity.

Direction 10. "From a narrow either/or society with a limited range of personal choices, we are exploding into a free-wheeling, multiple-option society." "In a relatively short time, the unified mass society has fractionalized into many diverse groups of people with a wide array of differing tastes and values, what advertisers call a market-segmented, market-decentralized society."[21]

Transformationist

The last of our trio of future perspectives is that of the transformationist. On the continuum from continuity to change, the transformationist stands near the extreme change end. Here is a futurist who views past and future history as a series of discontinuities, of disjunctions and revolutions, all involving crisis, disorientation, and trauma. This chronicler of revolutions sees that dissatisfaction and disaffection must reach near-universal proportions before a cataclysmic change, which shakes the foundations (culture and values) of a society, can occur.

Like the transitionist, the transformationist also talks about shifts *from* one condition *to* a different one. The difference between the two positions lies in the speed and extent of change. Whereas the transitionist expects change over a period of centuries, the transformationist looks for the dramatic dislocations that happen in a few years or decades, even though the seeds of revolution had been incubating for a much longer time. Although the transitionist anticipates significant changes within a society, he or she doesn't expect the entire infrastructure, the culture, ideology, and values, of the society to be eroded and replaced. The transformationist does expect such deep-rooted and far-reaching changes—a true revolution.

In oversimplified terms, the transformationist believes that things have to get worse before they get better. The society is healthy and prosperous for a time; then contradictions surface; they lead to a complex of unsolved problems; a crisis occurs, alerting the members of the society to its flaws; crisis upon crisis occurs in quick succession, bringing on revolution. But when the clues to the fatal flaws first appear, a significant *minority* of society members, as individuals or in groups, begins to innovate, invent, and experiment, creating the potential building blocks for a new society. With the revolution also come the rudimentary structures of the new society. These structures are the new means for personal and social fulfillment in the new society.

As futurist, the transformationist looks for two types of indicators: (1) sources of contradiction, alienation, and potential crises, and (2) types of personal and social experiments that have the potential to overcome the flaws in the present social fabric. For example, in our own society indicators of contradiction and possible breakdown include critical excesses of poverty, crime, racism, sexism, pollution, inflation, unemployment, substance abuse, child abuse, famine and

[21]Ibid.

hunger, nuclear threat, overdevelopment, and overconsumption. Or in another vein, one can point to the malaise created by three historical disconnections: (1) of humans from nature, (2) of person from person, and (2) of self (outer) from self (inner). Or one could observe the failures of Western industrialized societies to provide (1) opportunities for feeling efficacious, (2) equitable distribution of wealth and power, (3) responsible management of new technologies, (4) compelling visions of desirable futures, and (5) balance between material and spiritual needs.

Examples of the second type of indicator—new, potentially promising personal and social experiments—might include these recent developments or movements: advocacy of appropriate or intermediate technology (as opposed to "high tech"); the "small is beautiful" movement (as expounded by the late E.F. Schumacher); self-restraint (in buying) and self-reliance (in fixing and creating); the voluntary simplicity movement; intentional, experimental communities (for example, Arcosanti in Arizona and Findhorn in Scotland); the reruralization movement (from center to periphery); the study of paranormal phenomena (for example, telepathy, remote viewing, precognition, telekinesis, thought photography, and involuntary processes); and the study and practice of such psychotechnologies as psychotherapy, meditation techniques (for example, TM and yoga), est, Gestalt therapy, biofeedback, logotherapy, and dream analysis.

Two transformationist futurists are Theodore Roszak (*The Making of a Counter Culture*, 1969; *Where the Wasteland Ends*, 1972; *Unfinished Animal*, 1975; *Person/Planet*, 1978) and Willis W. Harman (*An Incomplete Guide to the Future*, 1976).

Since the 1960s, Theodore Roszak has been an outspoken, articulate critic of American establishment, mainstream society, and at the same time has been a spokesman for countercultural groups and movements. As the cover of one of his books illustrates—by use of a mirror—each of us is an "Unfinished Animal," a member of a species that is continuously evolving. Roszak has faith that what is emerging is "an Aquarian Age filled with wonders and well-being, a transformation of human personality . . . which is of evolutionary proportions, a shift of consciousness fully as epoch-making as the appearance of speech or of the tool-making talents in our cultural repertory." What is bringing on this evolutionary transformation are "the new ecological awareness . . . with its sense of allegiance to the planet as a whole . . . [and] the rapid convergence of age-old spiritual disciplines and contemporary psychotherapy.[22]

On the "Aquarian Frontier" Roszak sees twelve major "points of entry." These are:

1. Judeo-Christian Revivals—e.g., new Pentecostalism, charismatic congregations, Jewish Havurot movement.
2. Eastern Religions—e.g., Zen and Tibetan Buddhism, Taoism, Yoga, Sufism.
3. Esoteric Studies—e.g., comparative religion, theosophy, anthroposophy, Kabbalism (Jewish).

[22]Theodore Roszak, *Unfinished Animal* (New York: Harper Colophon Books, 1975), pp. 3–4.

4. Eupsychian Therapies—e.g., Jungian psychiatry, psychosynthesis, Arica, transpersonal psychology.

5. Etherealized Healing—e.g., integral healing, homeopathy, acupuncture, hypnotherapy.

6. Body Therapies—e.g., Rolfing, bioenergetics, massage, aikido, sensory awareness.

7. Neo-Primitivism and Paganism—e.g., philosophical mythology, sorcery, shamanism, voluntary primitive lifestyles.

8. Organicism—e.g., ecological mysticism, macrobiotics, natural foods cults, biorhythms.

9. Wild Science—e.g., altered states of consciousness, ESP, split-brain research, synergistics.

10. Psychics, Spirtualists, Occult Groups—e.g., Edgar Cayce, Eckankar, Stele Group.

11. Psychotronics—e.g., neural cybernetics, media mysticism, mind-altering drugs.

12. Pop Culture—e.g., science fiction, metaphysical fantasy, acid rock, laser light shows.[23]

Roszak summarizes the import of this potpourri:

> But perhaps the most wisely appealing quality of the Aquarian sign is the hope it offers as water-bearer to a parched and dying culture. Aquarius, the bringer of water, an emblem of life in the midst of a wasteland. Or such is the promise of the frontier before us, though we must bear in mind that, where fertility is not matched by careful cultivation, it yields no livable human habitat, but instead the deadly luxuriance of swamp or jungle.[24]

This is the cry of the transformationist: Transform or die! And if transformation is chosen, expect "the traumas of rebirth."[25]

In a later book, Roszak transcends national frontiers by linking the transformation of the individual to the fate of the planet. *Person/Planet* continues the theme of "creative disintegration," of the new emerging from the ashes of the old. But not only in one or a few societies, for "the needs of the planet and the needs of the person have become one. . . . At the same time that our sense of personality deepens, our sense of ecological responsibility increases. Just as we grow more acutely concerned for the sanctity of the person, so we grow more anxious for the well-being of the planetary environment."[26]

Finding a "personal scale of life" means focusing on environments where one can act and make a difference. These contexts are home, school, work, and the city. Comfort and concern in these milieus prepare one to accept the world's diversity and to act as steward of the planet's ecosystem.[27]

---

[23]Ibid., pp. 25–29.

[24]Ibid., p. 31.

[25]Ibid., p. 37.

[26]Theodore Roszak, *Person/Planet* (New York: Anchor Press/Doubleday & Company, Inc., 1978), pp. xix, 32.

[27]Ibid., pp. 129–282.

From his bases in the San Francisco area—Stanford University, SRI International, and the Institute for Noetic Sciences—Willis Harman combines an academic background in physics, engineering, and economics with an experiential background in the human potential movement and the study of ways of knowing and social policy futures. He ranges broadly across fields of knowledge but avoids superficiality and oversimplification.

In his one slender volume on social futures, Harman first argues that "the industrial-era paradigm" is flawed and too limiting. Next, he analyzes four industrial-era dilemmas (i.e., growth, work roles, world distribution, and control). Finally, he presents a new image of humanity, a scenario of "the transindustrial era," and a set of change strategies.[28]

The industrial era, Harman asserts, suffers from its successes and excesses. For example, the health sciences have succeeded in reducing infant mortality, which has led to burgeoning populations. Such "problems of technological success" keep increasing and then tend to interact in complexes creating a crisis of crises.[29]

One of these success/problem paradoxes is "the growth dilemma." In this case, the industrialized world has enjoyed the benefits of plentiful consumer goods, but growth at the levels of the period 1945–1975 cannot be sustained because of the new scarcities of fossil fuels, minerals, water, arable land, and the capacity of environments to absorb wastes. Yet, "the industrialized countries of the world are structured in such a way that their economics demand growth."[30]

A second problem is "the work-roles dilemma," which is the reverse side of the growth dilemma. "If . . . economic growth slows down for any reason, a whole group of work-related problems will be exacerbated, including unemployment and the threat of unemployment, the economic and social costs of vast welfare systems, poverty and malnutrition and affluence, widespread underemployment and attendant work dissatisfaction, and discontent among the young [kept out of the economy] and the aging [pushed out]."[31]

A third paradox is "the world distribution dilemma":

> We cannot risk the international instability that results from the vast disparities between the rich and poor nations, yet neither of the obvious solutions—making the poor nations richer or the rich nations poorer—seems feasible. The world probably cannot afford to have the gap closed through making the poor nations as productive, consuming, and polluting as the rich nations; at the same time, the rich nations are not likely to choose voluntarily to become less materialistic and more frugal.[32]

The fourth dilemma concerns who is in the saddle—technology or humanity? "How can we exercise needed societal control over technology without sacrific-

[28]Willis W. Harman. *An Incomplete Guide to the Future.* (San Francisco: San Francisco Book Co., 1976).

[29]Ibid., p. 25.
[30]Ibid., p. 39.
[31]Ibid., p. 51.
[32]Ibid., p. 67.

ing individual liberty?"[33] To gain control over technological development and use, will we lose the fundamentals of free enterprise and democracy?

Dealing with the dilemmas, argues Harman, requires an alternative to "the industrial-era paradigm"—not modification but a new paradigm. The new paradigm will be rooted in new conceptions of human nature.

EDUCATIONAL FUTURES

As one of several societal institutions, education and schooling change in response to both external and internal pressures. That is, the society in general exerts external pressures on education, as for example when the public expresses dissatisfaction with results of achievement tests and SATs. On the other hand, educational leaders often initiate ideas and programs from within the school structure.

Curiously, when comparing social futures with educational futures, one is struck by the relative lack of bold, imaginative educational futures. This lack is probably caused by two crucial considerations: (1) reluctance to experiment with the lives of children and adolescents and (2) constraints on schools imposed by the necessity of performing social functions. Because virtually all adults are wary of subjecting children to any experiences other than conventional, traditional, conservative ones, educators are reluctant to attempt departures from the norms of the past, especially controversial programs.

As we discussed in Chapter 5, schools have both educational and social functions. It is mainly the social functions that constrain innovations in the public schools. The schools are asked to provide a variety of community activities (sports, music, drama, and so on); to provide custodial care during regular daily school hours (supervision, discipline, meals, recreation); to establish screening processes for social roles (grades, promotion, cumulative records, graduation requirements); and to ensure socialization or indoctrination in the values, norms, and mores of community and society (respect, punctuality, docility, competitiveness).

Despite such formidable obstacles to imaginative future visions of education, the American public still, in 1982, considered "developing the best educational system in the world" as "very important" to "America's strength 25 years from now" (84 percent). And this choice is in comparison to "the most efficient industrial production system" (66 percent) and "the strongest military force" (47 percent).[34]

THREE PERSPECTIVES ON EDUCATIONAL FUTURES

There are at least three ways of deriving images of educational futures. One is seeking implications for education from general social indicators (for example, demographic data and projections). A second approach is to determine the proba-

[33]Ibid., p. 79–80.
[34]"Fourteenth Annual Gallup Poll on the Public's Attitudes Toward Public Schools," *Phi Delta Kappan*, 64, no. 1 (Sept. 1982), p. 46.

bility that certain discrete developments or events will occur and when they may occur. A third way is to present a single scenario or a number of alternative educational scenarios.

Education and Social Indicators

All levels of government, especially the U.S. Bureau of the Census, compile statistics on various aspects of American life. This profusion of data on the past-to-present status of social variables can also be extrapolated into present-to-future projections, many of which bear directly on education in the nation and in each of the fifty states. Several trends can be seen in these projections: (1) Total kindergarten to twelfth grade enrollment peaked in 1970 and then began to decline. This trend reversed in 1984 when elementary school enrollments increased. (2) Public enrollment for the same grades will closely parallel the total pattern. (3) Private enrollment in these grades gradually declined between 1967 and 1973, when it became relatively stable. After 1984 it increased somewhat to 1989. (4) Private high school (ninth to twelfth grade) enrollment remains relatively stable.

Another example of identifying trends by data extrapolations concerns the supply of and demand for teachers. There are two major trends: (1) Supply exceeds demand for all periods but is most seriously out of synchrony in 1971 to 1975. (2) Both supply and demand decline from 1975 to 1985, after which both rise in 1986 to 1990.

Possible and/or Probable Future Developments in Education

Leaders and experts in education frequently develop descriptions and lists of discrete events or developments that they consider possible and/or probable education futuribles (small pieces of the future). Sometimes these are proffered by individual futurists; in other cases they are derived by surveying appropriate knowledgeable groups through interviews or questionnaires.

From a survey of graduate students studying educational futures, we suggest the following:

Anticipated Developments in American Education
by the Year 2000

1. Greater emphasis on global and future studies
2. Reform of state school finance formulas
3. Continuing expansion of alternative schools—both public and private and both "open" and "fundamentals" types
4. Continuing expansion of unionization of teachers and administrators
5. Expansion of adult continuing education by schools, colleges, universities, corporations, unions, and professional associations
6. Alternative paths to high school graduation (for example, "testing out," evening school, home study)

7. Expansion of early childhood education (ages two to five) in prekindergarten, nursery and prenursery schools, and day-care centers
8. Very few dramatic, system-altering changes in public education
9. Expansion of year-round school schedules
10. Greater early retirement options for schoolteachers and college professors
11. Increasing attacks on and modifications of tenure laws and policies
12. Continued exploitation of schools as scapegoats for social ills
13. Greater centralization (state level) of control of kindergarten through twelfth grade
14. Increased use of computers for myriad instructional and school management functions
15. More flexible learning environments (for example, multiple-use classrooms and out-of-school programs)
16. Expansion of leisure and recreation education
17. Increased availability of educational program software for use on home microcomputers
18. Expansion of education for elderly and retired persons
19. Decreased concern for specialization in school and work contexts, accompanied by greater emphasis on general education skills and comprehensive thinking
20. Greater parent and student control of educational choices and directions

A Single Educational Scenario

Education 2015

In the past quarter century a number of developments in American society in general and a few changes in public education in particular have had their impact on American education. Specifically, there were four major societal trends already evident in the 1990s that by the turn of the century had become dominant modes with major implications for public education.

First, the growing trend toward smaller families stabilized the U.S. population at about 300 million, and today in 2015 a "minus-ZPG" condition exists. For a decade the student enrollment in the schools has remained constant but is now showing a slight decline in the primary grades.

Second, 80 percent of the married couples in the United States between the ages of nineteen and thirty-nine find it economically necessary or personally preferable for both partners to work. For those couples with young children, this presents a problem of child care. Over the past twenty-five years, numerous private and public day-care centers, preschools, and specialized prevocational schools have come into existence to serve this burgeoning child population. Some of these services are free, some are cooperative requiring parental participation, and others charge fees ranging from moderate to expensive.

Third, because of dwindling supplies and escalating costs of oil, gasoline-powered forms of transportation have become too expensive for all but the rich to afford. Thus, less time is spent in commuting or travel, and workers and families now spend more time at home and in the immediate neighborhood. The travel that does occur is by foot or bicycle, by moving sidewalks or small people-mover electric cars on elevated fixed-route ramps, and by electric (photovoltaic batteries for power) buses, subways, and trains. Travel over longer distances, connecting major domestic cities, is by underground speed tubes powered by mass drivers; international travel is by partly orbital rockets. These developments have made it necessary to limit home-to-school-to-home travel by school students, which in turn has led to greater reliance on electronic communications media by the schools for major portions of the curriculum—a kind of partial technological deschooling.

Fourth, the communications revolution pushed America into a post-industrial society, so that by the turn of the century, what manufacturing and industrial production remained inside the nation's borders was almost totally automated, and all other businesses had fully incorporated the increased productivity potential of computers. It is now common for places of business, plants, warehouses, government offices, and homes and educational institutions to have their own computers as central controllers of an array of other electronic media. These electronic systems are called communications centers and are interconnected by cable or telephone line in vast national and international networks. This worldwide grid makes it possible to connect anyone to anyone else, anywhere, at almost any time.

In addition to these four societal trends, public education in the United States has also undergone some significant changes in the past twenty-five years. Because it became obvious that all agencies in a modern society "educate" in some manner and that the communications revolution made it possible to deliver educational services anywhere at any time, the need to require the young to "go to school" became absurd and anachronistic. Thus, by the late 1990s each state had abolished its compulsory attendance law and had enacted in its place a statute requiring the mastery of a general curriculum by all youth sometime between the ages of twelve and eighteen. This had left the nation with more than a million classrooms designed for the now obsolete mode of group instruction. Many schools were sold or rented, but most were redesigned and renovated to accommodate new modes of creating curriculum and providing instruction—most in the electronic media mode and mostly off campus. For certain special types of group-based learning, central gathering places were still needed: drama/theater productions, recreational and competitive team sports, band, orchestral and choral music performances, some rare vocational pursuits (though almost all are now conducted in the field via apprenticeships and internships—paid for by the student), and a variety of small-group activities designed to hone interpersonal/human relations skills.

At the same time, recognizing the social, economic, political, and humanistic values of education, the U.S. Congress enacted in the year 2000 the farsighted Universal Educational Opportunity Act, which provided each newborn citizen with a lifetime educational voucher or credit card worth $500,000—in 1990 U.S. dollars. This stroke of wisdom promised that a learning society would become a reality in the twenty-first century. The UEO Act also provided that one could purchase learning materials, media, and experiences from a variety of sources in both the public and private domains.

In reaction to the pressing needs for child care, baby-sitting, and away-from-home supervision of adolescents, the public schools converted some existing facilities and built some new ones to provide these services free or at a low fee. These new centers offered supervised play and recreation, and some individual computer-controlled instruction.

Gradually, new modes of learning emerged in the twenty-first century. The new norm for a kindergarten-to-grade twelve public education is now entry at age four and exit at age thirteen or fourteen, although this pattern appeals today to only about 40 percent of all families with school-age children. The remaining 60 percent are divided in their preferences among a spectrum of "Schools of Choice": Roman Catholic and Protestant Day Schools (both types partly supported by public state funds), Proprietary Specialized Technical Schools (privately owned, profit making, and vocationally oriented), Private and Public Automated Learning Centers (individualized learning for those requiring minimal help and supervision; located in neighborhoods, office complexes, and shopping malls), Special Purpose Private and Public Academies (for such broad specialties as the performing arts, engineering, computer science, and athletics; and including such nontraditional learning experiences as learning-on-tour, worldwide travel learning, global education, and futures education), and many other school systems such as Buddhist Schools of America, Waldorf Schools (originally founded by Rudolph Steiner in Europe), and Academic Excellence Schools, Inc.

The curriculum has also changed since 1990. It was at first difficult to change perceptions of the traditional subject areas because of their prevalence in schools, libraries, universities, and in the minds of the older generations. But leaders in business, industry, and government (and some in education) argued forcefully that what a citizen of the future needed was unified sets of learnings rather than knowledge in discrete bundles called subjects. This was a reaffirmation of what some farsighted educators in the early decades of the twentieth century had proposed, but under such rubrics as "correlated curriculum," "integrated studies," "multidisciplinary learning," and "interdisciplinary fields."

The areas of the new curriculum (i.e., the general education core and not specialized or vocational education) were given different names and titles depending on the nature of the various schools, but the following list is representative of the scope of learning that emerged by 2015:

Analysis and synthesis
Career planning
Communications (including foreign languages)
Computer literacy
Creativity
Critical thinking
Decision making
Evaluation

Problem solving
Orientations in time and space
Scientific method

Some of the above categories, when further subdivided, yield more specific skills, such as the following sampling:

Identify a problem
Interpret a personality inventory
Brainstorm possible solutions
Separate fact from opinion
Adapt to ambiguity and uncertainty
Accomplish a work assignment in limited time
Write a memo
Brief an employer on a work task
Interpret tables and graphs

One might wonder what ever happened to the huge, impersonal, bureaucratic, urban and suburban schools and school districts of the 1990s? It appears that four concepts that were barely visible in 1990 emerged into prominence in the 1990s and doomed the old education colossus. These were communication, decentralization, diversity, and "small is beautiful." Complex systems of electronic communication media obviated the need to assemble people in central places and also made it feasible to decentralize all large societal institutions that previously had been largely responsible for alienation and impersonality. The pluralistic nature of American society finally became accepted and valued, leading to demands for diversity in the provision and delivery of all goods and services. Finally, the previous three ideas made it possible for people to work and live in the intimacy and support of small groups, where individuality and cohesiveness could flourish side by side. In the new learning society, education prospered because it responded to the multitude of learning needs and styles, in a rainbow profusion of varied landscapes.

Multiple Alternative Educational Scenarios

Futurists generally agree that the presentation of alternative scenarios of the future is preferable to single events or extrapolated trends or the single scenario. This choice reaffirms the value that citizens and policy makers should be able to choose from an array of options. They can then make determinations concerning possibility, probability, feasibility, and desirability, deciding which to work for and which to prevent or defeat.

Clearly, it is impossible here to develop fully an array of future educational scenarios. What is presented, therefore, are brief overviews of six future educational scenarios for the year 2000, and the mere mention of a number of variables that will have differential impacts on each of the scenarios. The titles of the scenarios and the names of the impacting factors are presented in Table 13-4.

Across the top of the matrix are the titles of six futures: (1) Contemporary Traditional, (2) Humanistic Traditional, (3) Multiple Options, (4) Partial Technological Deschooling, (5) Experimental Communal, and (6) Romantic Total Deschooling. There is a logic to the left-to-right sequence of the scenarios. It is posited that there are two continuums here: one that extends from *most* probable (on the left, that is, Contemporary Traditional) to *least* probable (on the right, that is, Romantic Total Deschooling); and a second continuum that begins on the left also with an extrapolationist perspective to a transformationist viewpoint on the right.

The eleven factors listed down the left-hand column of the matrix are those social and educational indicators or variables that are most likely to impinge on the six scenarios. Each factor, however, differs in its impact on the individual scenarios. Factor 11—Surprises, crises, or catastrophes—provides for unforeseen events, like wars or depressions, that would undoubtedly affect each scenario.

Contemporary traditional.   In education, more so than elsewhere, the more things change the more they remain the same. Tradition's heavy hand holds archaic practices in place. Schools do change, but ever so slowly, so that they inevitably are constantly behind the times. Thus, if one is looking at a short-term future, say between 1984 and 2000, the best bet is to forecast that schools in the year 2000 will be very much like those of the present. One can expect some tinkering, alignments with the economy, and updating of textbooks and equipment, but no deep structural or curricular change will be evident.

Humanistic traditional.   Beginning just before the Soviet Union launched Sputnik I (in 1957) and extending through the early 1970s, an educational reform movement, with several separate strands, attempted to change schooling in America. The several strands included efforts to change (1) school organization (differentiated staffing patterns and flexible scheduling of secondary school students), (2) classroom organization (open classrooms and team teaching), and (3) curriculum (content, materials, textbooks, and simulations). Hundreds of millions of federal and foundation dollars were spent over the twenty-year span. The results of this multidimensional enterprise were generally disappointing to all parties. A few schools, mainly in relatively wealthy suburban districts, did change by adopting or adapting one or more of the organizational innovations and/or by buying and using some of the new textbooks, curriculum materials, simulations, and audiovisual products. But overall the reformers and their sponsors were frustrated and disillusioned. To many, the public schools were seen as impenetrable bastions of rigidity that could readily deflect any and all incursions of innovation.

Against this background, some educators within the public school ranks who recognized the need for improvement, yet who also had seen the failure of frontal assaults, began in the 1970s to focus their efforts on the "climate" of individual schools. By "climate" they meant the health of the organization, the degree to

TABLE 13-4 Alternative Educational Futures

| FACTORS AFFECTING THE SIX FUTURES | CONTEMPORARY TRADITIONAL | HUMANISTIC TRADITIONAL | MULTIPLE OPTIONS | | | PARTIAL TECHNOLOGICAL DESCHOOLING | EXPERIMENTAL COMMUNAL | ROMANTIC TOTAL DESCHOOLING |
			WITHIN DISTRICT	VOUCHER PLAN	TUITION TAX CREDITS			
1. Public policy								
2. Court decisions								
3. Educational leadership								
4. Economic constraints								
5. School organization patterns								
6. Curriculum framework								
7. Educational technology								
8. Demographics								
9. Ideology and social values								
10. State of knowledge								
11. Surprises, crises, or catastrophes								

which interpersonal relations of every type contributed to group purpose, cohesiveness, amicability, and comfort. They believed that improvement in school climate would directly and indirectly contribute to improved instruction and to greater learning, both occurring within a more humanistic educational setting.

The general factors that contribute to a comfortable, satisfying, and productive school climate are trust, respect, high morale, continuous personal and social growth, cohesiveness, caring, and processes for organizational renewal. Three clusters of determinants affect the degree to which these factors are present in a school: (1) program determinants, (2) process determinants, and (3) material determinants.[35]

The program determinants include opportunities for active learning, expectations of individualized performance, varied learning environments, flexible curricular and extracurricular activities, a support structure appropriate to the learner's maturity, cooperatively determined policies, rules and recommendations, and a varied reward system. The process determinants are problem-solving ability, a method for improving school goals, identifying and managing conflicts, effective communication skills, involvement and skill in making decisions, autonomy with accountability, effective learning and teaching strategies, and skills in planning for the future. Finally, the material determinants are all those physical aspects of the school that support the human activities, such as the building, furniture, equipment, esthetic features, and learning materials.[36]

This movement—improvement of the school climate—has gained momentum in the past decade, and it may become the most promising and pervasive reform effort for the remainder of the century.

Multiple options.   Gradually over the past century American schools have become more and more alike, whereas during the same period, Americans have become more dissimilar and diverse. There are numerous causes of these two trends, but two that have been particularly significant for education are (1) new immigrant groups and (2) school laws and policies that promote uniformity. The new immigrants (the old immigrant groups were mainly from western and central Europe) come from the Caribbean area (for example, Cuba, Haiti, and Puerto Rico), from Mexico and Central America, and from Asia, especially Southeast Asia. These groups, combined with the heightened ethnic awareness of blacks and Native Americans, have created a multiracial, multicultural society. Meanwhile, in public education the following policies and practices, among others, have moved schools toward uniformity: (1) assignment of students to grade levels according to the single criterion of age, (2) compulsory attendance laws, (3) national textbook industry, (4) concept of the comprehensive high school (one type for all), (5) legal requirements for equality of treatment, (6) national testing industry, and (7) state and regional school-accrediting organizations.

---

[35]Robert Fox et al., *School Climatic Improvement* (Bloomington, Ind.: Phi Delta Kappa, 1974), pp. 7–12.

[36]Ibid., pp. 13–17.

In the last two decades, there have been many calls for the creation of alternatives to and options within the public school system. Although most of the motives of advocates for specific schemes are honest, legitimate, and benign, a few are pernicious, thinly disguised moves to perpetuate bigotry, sexism, and racism. We view three variants of the multiple-options scenario as having some potential for becoming major educational movements:

1. *Options within a school district* Many parents and students who are believers in and supporters of the public schools would like to have available to them more educational options, more involvement in key decisions, more choices from an array of alternatives. Some school districts have responded to these requests for change with various organizational and curricular innovations. One of the easiest changes school leaders can implement is to allow students (and/or their parents) to choose the school within the district that they would like to attend. Where feasible, this option could be extended to include a choice of teacher. Though easier than other possible changes, giving students choices of school and teacher creates logistical and morale problems for school administrators, especially at the elementary school level.

Another plan calls for the creation of special-purpose alternative schools — kindergarten through grade 12, kindergarten through grade 6, kindergarten through grade 8, grades 7 through 9, grades 9 through 12, or grades 10 through 12. Often this means establishing one, two, or more new schools, each with a distinct focus and milieu. For example, one large suburban school district founded two new kindergarten through grade 12 schools, one called "The Fundamentals School" and the other "Open Living School." As discussed in Chapter 10, these schools can be placed at appropriate points on a continuum extending from "free" to "open" to "modified" to "standard" — a freedom-to-prescription range. In the cases of the "Fundamentals" and "Open Living" schools, the former would be located at the "standard" point on the "prescription" end of the continuum, and the latter would be placed between "free" and "open" on the "freedom" side. In this particular school district, the attendance area for the two alternative schools is coterminous with the district boundary, whereas each of the other "regular" elementary and secondary schools has a specific, restricted attendance area encompassing one or more neighborhoods in relatively close proximity to each school.

A final model in this within-a-district category allows for open enrollment in any public school in a school district. This could amount to no choice, however, if all the elementary and secondary schools are virtually alike and interchangeable. What is called for in this model are *distinctive* schools, reflecting differing educational philosophies and different curricula and organizational patterns. Because the school district does not assign any student to a school on the basis of geographical proximity, students and their parents are forced to choose from among several options.

The number of options available at each combination of grade levels (for example, kindergarten through grade 3, grades 4 through 6, 7 through 9, or 10 through 12) is somewhere in the range of three to five. Each school (that is, set or cluster of grade levels or a "nongraded" arrangement) has a unique focus, such as any one of the following:

Open Living/Free/Freedom/Street Academy
Fundamentals/Basics/Structured Skills
Multicultural
Community
School of Science/of Performing Arts/of Commerce
Montessori/Steiner/Academic Leadership
Humanistic

2. Voucher plans   When a state wishes to allow the use of tax revenues (within state and federal legal constraints) to pay for education in public, private, and parochial schools, one scheme for making such options available is called a *voucher plan.* A voucher here is an entitlement or education stamp that can be redeemed (by students or their parents) in any school licensed by the state. The school accepting the voucher then submits it to the state for reimbursement according to a funding formula (for example, $2,000 per student).

There are many versions of voucher plans and many crucial problems and issues involved with all the plans. For example, there is the problem of undermining the public schools; the issues of racism, sexism, and elitism; the church/state issue; and the problems of propaganda and false or fraudulent advertising. But there is little doubt that the voucher plan would enhance competition and promote innovation by making education into a limited market economy.

3. Tuition tax credits   Although formulated and promoted earlier, this means of providing public support for options in schooling is most associated with the Reagan administration. Here also there are many versions of the basic idea, including both federal and state schemes, but the main elements of all tuition tax credit plans are (1) prior payments of tuition to a private or parochial school and (2) a tax credit (like solar energy credits) on state or federal tax forms, in effect, an amount subtracted from gross income or from taxable income or from taxes owed to the government. Clearly, tax deductions and credits tend to favor those taxpayers with the largest amount of disposable income—the middle and upper classes. Nevertheless, this plan would place the support of the government behind diverse approaches to public education. Among the numerous criticisms of tuition tax credit proposals, probably the most serious one is that the poor would have no effective choice other than the tuition-free public schools, which would result in resegregation.

Partial technological deschooling.   In the past twenty years three developments in what is sometimes termed the *information* or *communications revolution* may in combination cause dramatic changes in the nature of public education by as early as the 1990s. The first of these is the merger of information technology companies and publishing houses in single conglomerate corporations, for example, IBM and SRA (a publisher of mainly school curriculum materials) or Xerox and Ginn, or CBS and Holt, Rinehart & Winston. This occurrence effectively links the communications industry with trade and textbook publishers. The second development is the emergence of powerful television, motion picture, newspaper, publishing conglomerates such as Warner Communications. The third is the beginning of the widespread use of two technologies—cable television systems and the microcomputer. Taken as a whole these three developments have the power and potential to alter almost every element of schooling in the United States.

We term the potential application of multiple communications media to public education as *partial technological deschooling*. What could happen in this scenario is that *some* public school functions might be decentralized to a number of places in the community, away from the schools. The "new" locations would be businesses, public agencies, students' homes, and school annexes. At the local businesses and public agencies, students would spent part of the school day in the communications center, where a master console would integrate several media technologies: over-the-air educational television, selected cable television channels, videotape (or videodisc) recordings, and computer tapes and diskettes—all under control of a microcomputer. The home communications center would handle the teaching of specific knowledge and cognitive skills as called for in individual learning modules prescribed by teachers at the school's home-learning curriculum communications center.

School annexes, located in neighborhood education cottages or storefront education arcades, would provide consoles for students without home communications centers and would also handle remediation programs. These annexes would coordinate with other social service agencies in the neighborhood and in the community at large.

School buildings similar to those of today would still exist to serve *some* of the group-oriented educational and social functions. These would probably include limited custodial care, including breakfasts, lunches, and recreation; community-oriented activities such as plays, musicals, interscholastic athletic events, and science-technology fairs; "real-world" simulations for learning interpersonal and group process skills; and a lengthy sequence of one-student-to-one-counselor career guidance and planning sessions. A major activity in the school would involve teachers in the library-media-communications center preparing new curricula and prescribing and collating individual learning modules for students' home learning.

Experimental communal. It isn't too probable that this type of educational future will become a widespread phenomenon. What is more likely is that it will be an alternative for some students and their parents to other future types. As its name implies, there are two variants of this type of future: experimental schools and communal education.

Over the years there have been many instances of educational and religious idealists founding schools, some of which remain vigorous institutions for decades and others that collapse in a year or two. We call these "experimental schools" in that they generally are experimenting with the application of one or a few ideas or theories. In its early years, for example, the federal Head Start program provided funds to establish at the local level new schools (that is, preschools) for the children of poor households. The basic ideas behind Head Start schools, then (the late 1960s) and still today, are community and parental involvement; care and concern for the growth of the whole child—physical, psychological, social, experiential, and intellectual, including regular medical and dental checkups; experiences through walks and fieldtrips that expose the child to all facets of the local community; parenting education at the Head Start center and in the homes of participating families; and inclusion of special persons and programs such as bilingual-bicultural teachers and aides or teachers and equipment for the handicapped.

In today's educational climate, the focus of many relatively new schools is on the education of gifted and academically talented youths. These are usually private schools with substantial tuitions, which tend to emphasize intellectual development or skills in the visual and performing arts, or both.

It is difficult to forecast what ideas will undergird the experimental schools of the future. Some possible organizing themes are travel or extended trips (weeks or months); multicultural and cross-cultural living and learning; high technology-based schools and camps; multiple psychotechnologies (like meditation, psychosynthesis, and ESP); and nonschools based on integrated networks of home microcomputer users.

Communal education is an old idea that was revitalized by Vietnam era dropouts and creative urban planners. The motivation to create "intentional communities" (communities founded on exclusive religious or secular ideologies) grows out of dissatisfaction with modern societies, especially the impersonality and lack of group cohesiveness in cities and their suburbs. Thus, communal social experiments attempt to reestablish a "sense of community," by which is usually meant the cohesive character of small, closely knit, extended-family-like urban or rural communes. The German language has two contrasting words that describe two different types of communities: *gesellschaft* and *gemeinschaft*. A typical small suburb of any large American city manifests *gesellschaft*, whereas an Amish community in Pennsylvania would embody *gemeinschaft*. The following lists characterize these two concepts:

Gemeinschaft	Gesellschaft
Private life	Public life
Exclusive membership	Arbitrary, unplanned membership
Face-to-face interactions	Very loose cohesiveness
Natural, unforced association	Emphasis on contracts and rights
"Family" attitude	Lack of communal atmosphere
Intentional collective	Relatively impersonal interactions
Group ends and means inextricable	Carefully specified means and ends
"Small" number of members	"Large" membership
Sympathetic identification of member with member	Interactions based on rationality

Resistant to change	Change valued; sign of progress
General knowledge of members and skills (nonspecialization)	Specialization of work
Differential status for members	Equality of treatment with statuses

Those who seek *gemeinschaft* in community life also generally have in mind definite ideas about communal education. For one thing, advocates of communal education place greater reliance on the community-as-educator rather than the school-as-educator, and on the community meeting as instructor rather than the teacher in the classroom. This is similar to life in an Israeli kibbutz, where lines distinguishing school and community, teacher and student, work and play, and age cohorts are blurred in the unity of organic existence. In communal education everyone, regardless of age or status, is sometimes teacher and sometimes learner.

In the future, there will continue to be new, planned, intentional communities, each possessing its own version of communal education, and some even substituting educational networks for what today we call schools. The prototypes of these "new towns" and rural communities already exist in such places as Auroville, a cross-cultural agrarian community in India; Columbia, a planned urban "new town" in Maryland; Findhorn, a religious agrarian community on the North Sea of Scotland; and Arcosanti, a high-density, urban-rural town being constructed in the desert seventy miles north of Phoenix, Arizona.

Romantic total deschooling.   This highly improbable educational scenario calls for the complete elimination of schools from postindustrial societies like the United States, Japan, and western European nations. It's a romantic proposal because of its naive and excessive idealism. Most forcefully advocated by Ivan Illich in *Deschooling Society*, this position draws heavily on anarchist and Marxist traditions and exemplifies the extreme of the transformationist future perspective.[37]

Illich develops his argument along the same lines as the transformationists, namely, a critique of modern society (and its schools) followed by proposed radical changes. The modern society, the United States for example, has created social institutions that are evil to the core and that cannot be adequately modified or reformed. The evils are bureaucracy, specialization and division of labor, professionalization of occupations (for example, doctors and teachers), technification of work, and alienation of workers from their work and from each other.[38]

Like every institution in these "sick" societies, schools manifest the same array of "diseases." Schools are highly bureaucratized institutions in which specialization has led to over one hundred new job classifications over the past thirty years. Yet as Illich points out, costs continue to rise while enrollments and overall student achievement decline. Schools also perpetuate the false meritocracy, where

[37]Ivan Illich, *Deschooling Society* (New York: Harper & Row, Publishers, Inc., 1970).
[38]Ibid., pp. 1–24.

job-entry levels are geared to levels of school completed, regardless of skills needed for the job or skills possessed by applicants.[39]

Illich considers schools to be an unwarranted public monopoly. Schooling is an age-specific, teacher-related process requiring full-time attendance to an obligatory curriculum. And students are subject to a hidden curriculum that socializes them to conventional norms and values and to their assigned roles and occupations. Schools also teach the young to confuse process and substance, teaching and learning, grades and education, and diplomas and competence. Finally, because membership in this institution is mandatory, schools are "nonconvivial" institutions.[40]

The solutions to these problems, says Illich, are to eliminate schools and to establish in their place four kinds of convivial networks, or "learning webs."[41]

1. Reference services to educational objects This is a directory (a special version of the Yellow Pages) that provides learners "access to things or processes used for formal learning. Some of these things can be reserved for this purpose, stored in libraries, rental agencies, laboratories, and showrooms like museums and theaters; others can be in daily use in factories, airports, or on farms, but made available to students as apprentices or on off-hours."[42]

2. Skill exchanges These are like classified advertising sections of newspapers "which permit persons to list their skills, the conditions under which they are willing to serve as models for others who want to learn these skills, and the addresses at which they can be reached."[43] Presumably, this exchange of "valuables" would occur in a barter economy.

3. Peer-matching This process requires an extensive "communications network which permits persons to describe the learning activity in which they wish to engage, in the hope of finding a partner for the inquiry.[44] Here the goal is to assemble a miniclass of learners who can then use the group's bargaining power to secure appropriate instruction.

4. Reference services to educators-at-large This is another form of Yellow Pages where self-appointed experts "can be listed in a directory giving the addresses and self-descriptions of professionals, paraprofessionals, and free-lancers, along with conditions of access to their services."[45]

[39]Ibid.
[40]Ibid.
[41]Ibid., pp. 72–77.
[42]Ibid., p. 78.
[43]Ibid., p. 79.
[44]Ibid.
[45]Ibid.

Conclusion

Although there is every reason to expect that either Scenario 1 (Contemporary Traditional) or Scenario 2 (Humanistic Traditional) will be the prevailing mode in the next century, some surprising events along the way could enhance the likelihood of one of the other four scenarios becoming more probable. For example, if more funds were to be available to public education and more and better educational software for personal computers were also available, then Scenario 4 (Partial Technological Deschooling) might come into existence in a decade or so. Or, if some alternative to state and local funding of only public schools were to gain public endorsement, along with acceptance of the concept of "alternative schools," then Scenario 3 (in some form) would have a chance to emerge.

Scenario 5 (Experimental Communal Schools) may become the case here and there, in one small community or another, but its widespread adoption is highly improbable. As for Scenario 6, short of social and cultural revolution, it will remain the romantic dream of an idealist.

●————————————————————————————●

Case Study: A Problem in Space Travel

Imagine that you are a first-class passenger on a huge spaceship traveling through space at the speed of 66,000 mph. You discover that the craft's environmental system is faulty. Passengers in some sections are actually dying because of the discharge of poisonous gases into their oxygen supply. Furthermore, you learn that food supplies are rapidly diminishing and that the water supply, previously thought to be more than adequate, is rapidly becoming polluted because of fouling from breakdowns in the craft's waste and propulsion systems.

To complicate matters, in the economy sections, where passengers are crowded together under the most difficult of situations, many are seriously ill. The ship's medical officers are able to help only a fraction of the sick, and medicines are in short supply.

Mutinies have been reported, and although some of the crew and passengers are engaged in serious conflict in one of the compartments, it is hoped that this conflict is being contained successfully. However, there is widespread fear about what may happen if it cannot be contained or resolved within that compartment.

The spacecraft has been designed with an overall destruct system, the controls of which have been carefully guarded. Unfortunately, the number of technologists who have gained access to the destruct system have increased, and all the crew and passengers have become uneasy at the evidence of instability in some of those gaining this access.

What can or should be done to save the spaceship and its inhabitants?

Thought Questions

1. For each of the following potential developments, decide if you think it will occur or won't occur by the year 2020. Also, regardless of whether you think it will or won't occur, decide if you think the development would be desirable or undesirable.

POTENTIAL DEVELOPMENT	WILL OCCUR	WON'T OCCUR	DESIRABLE	UNDESIRABLE
A cure for cancer				
Extensive use of home computers				
Existence of space colonies as satellites of moon and/or earth				
World government or world federation				
A life expectancy in U.S. of over 100 years				
Production of test-tube babies				
Nuclear war				
The three-day work week in U.S.				
Elimination of use of individually owned and operated automobiles in U.S.				
Almost total reliance on nuclear and solar energy				
Zero population growth in U.S.				
The death of capitalism				
Continued urban growth				
Farming and mining of the seas				
Genetic manipulation and control of DNA (e.g., cloning, elimination of birth defects)				

2. Which one of the following four metaphors comes closest to your conception of the future? If none seems appropriate, create one of your own. Explain.

   A. The future is a great *roller coaster* on a moonless night. It exists, twisting ahead of us in the dark, although we can only see each part as we come to it.

   B. The future is a *mighty river*. The great force of history flows inexorably along, carrying us with it. Most of our attempts to change its course are mere pebbles thrown into the river: they cause a momentary splash and a few ripples, but they make no difference. The river's course *can* be changed, but only by natural disasters like earthquakes, or landslides, or by massive, concerted human efforts on a similar scale. On the other hand, we are free as individuals to adapt to the course of history either well or poorly.

   C. The future is a *great ocean*. There are many possible destinations, and many different paths to each destination. A good navigator takes advantage of the main currents of change, adapts his course to the capricious winds of change, keeps a sharp lookout posted, and moves carefully in fog or uncharted waters.

D. The future is entirely random, a *colossal dice game*. Every second, millions of things happen that could have happened another way and produced a different future. Because everything is chance, all we can do is play the game, pray to the gods of fortune, and enjoy what good luck comes our way.[46]

3. Supply evidence to support or refute each of the following hypotheses:

The value base of American society has remained rather stable and constant for the past 200 years, and will likely remain so for at least another 200 years.

American values have evolved over hundreds of years, but are today being challenged and will probably change considerably between now and the year 2000.

4. On the blank lines, indicate whether each of the following potential educational developments in the United States will occur by 1990, by 2020, by 2050, or never.

_____ 1. A complete environmental-education curriculum, kindergarten through twelfth grade

_____ 2. Year-round school, broken up by holidays every quarter-year

_____ 3. Abolition of compulsory attendance laws in most states

_____ 4. Abolition of public schools

_____ 5. Emphasis on global and futures education

_____ 6. Gradual decrease in public school enrollments

_____ 7. Elimination of the local property-tax base for funding public schools, with all funds deriving from state and federal governments

_____ 8. The option to "test out" of high school in all states

_____ 9. Few, if any, significant changes in public education

_____ 10. Use of computers to replace some teachers for almost half the school day

_____ 11. Extensive use of drugs to enhance students' learning and to increase students' abilities to learn

_____ 12. Special schools and programs for the elderly

_____ 13. Greater uses of educational television and computer-assisted instruction in homes

_____ 14. Free child care and prekindergarten education

_____ 15. Abolition of teachers' tenure

Practical Activities

1. With respect to the following future possibilities, ask a number of children or adolescents in what ways their lives would be affected if each possibility were to occur:

[46]Draper L. Kauffman, Jr., *Teaching the Future* (Palm Springs, Calif.: ETA Publications, 1976), pp. 64–65.

You could travel to other planets as you now can visit other cities or countries.

You were allowed to work for pay only a maximum of twenty hours per week.

You were required to retire from paid employment at age 45.

You were expected to live to age 150.

You could communicate with others by the use of extrasensory perception (ESP).

Twenty babies the exact genetic duplicate of you were artificially produced.

Automobiles were available for only rent or lease.

Gasoline for cars was priced at $5.00 per gallon.

Your occupation became obsolete every ten to fifteen years.

You and your family could dispose of only one small garbage can full of garbage each month.

You lived in a city under the ocean.

You could only obtain food in capsule form.

You were only allowed to raise artificially produced "sons" and "daughters."

Write a summary of your findings.

2. Build a futures wheel. Using Figure 13-5 as a starting point, complete the first, second, and third rings. In your projections, assume that a suburban school district

FIGURE 13-5   A Futures Wheel

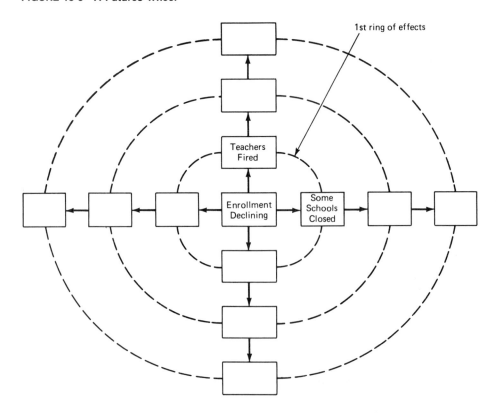

is losing its student population at the rate of 2 percent per year. In 1985, there were 120,000 students in this district, and by 1990 this number had decreased to 108,000.

3. Write a science fiction short story, drama, or scenario that describes the lives of children and adolescents in their homes and schools in the year 2000.
4. Write a unit or lesson plan on "Alternative Futures" to teach in a class.
5. Become an active member of some organization that you feel is dealing with a crucial issue involved with future world survival (peace coalitions, Planned Parenthood, ecology groups, energy groups, and so on). Describe the organization, its importance, and your involvement.

Bibliography

BAIER, KURT, and NICHOLAS RESCHER, eds., *Values and the Future*. New York: The Free Press, 1969.

BELL, DANIEL, *The Coming of Post-Industrial Society*. New York: Basic Books, Inc., Publishers, 1973.

———, *The Cultural Contradictions of Capitalism*. New York: Basic Books, Inc., Publishers, 1976.

BOTKIN, JAMES W., *No Limits to Learning*. Oxford: Pergamon Press, 1979.

BOWMAN, JIM, *The Far Side of the Future*. Washington, D.C.: World Future Society, 1978.

BROWN, LESTER R., *Building a Sustainable Society*. New York: W.W. Norton & Company, Inc., 1981.

CETRON, M., *Schools of the Future*. New York: McGraw-Hill Book Company, Inc., 1985.

CETRON, M., and T. O'TOOLE, *Encounters With the Future*. New York: McGraw-Hill Book Company, Inc., 1982.

CLARKE, A. C., *July 20, 2019: Life in the 21st Century*. New York: Macmillan, 1986.

DIDSBURY, H. F., ed., *Communications and the Future*. Washington, D.C.: World Future Society, 1982.

———, *Creating a Global Agenda*. Washington, D.C.: World Future Society, 1984.

——— *Challenges and Opportunities: From Now to 2110*. Washington, D.C.: World Future Society, 1986.

ELGIN, DUANE, *Voluntary Simplicity*. New York: Bantam Books, Inc., 1982.

FERGUSON, MARILYN, *The Aquarian Conspiracy*. New York: J.P. Tarcher/St. Martin's Press, Inc., 1980.

FULLER, R. BUCKMINSTER, *On Education*. Amherst: University of Massachusetts Press, 1979.

HARMAN, WILLIS W., *An Incomplete Guide to the Future*. New York: Simon & Schuster, Inc., 1976.

ILLICH, IVAN, *Deschooling Society*. New York: Harper & Row, Publishers, Inc., 1970.

KAHN, HERMAN, *World Economic Development*. New York: William Morrow & Company, Inc., 1979.

KIERSTEAD, FRED, ed., *Educational Futures*. Washington, D.C.: World Future Society, 1979.

MITCHELL, A., *The Nine American Lifestyles*. New York: Warner Books, 1983.

NAISBITT, JOHN, *Megatrends*. New York: Warner Books, 1982.

O'NEILL, GERARD K., *2081: A Hopeful View of the Human Future.* New York: Simon & Schuster, Inc., 1981.

OXFORD ANALYTICA, *America in Perspective.* Boston: Houghton Mifflin Company, 1986.

ROSZAK, THEODORE, *Person/Planet.* New York: Anchor Press/Doubleday & Company, Inc., 1978.

SALK, JONAS, *The Survival of the Wisest.* New York: Harper & Row, Publishers, Inc., 1973.

SCHUMACHER, E. F., *Small Is Beautiful.* New York: Harper & Row, Publishers, Inc., 1973.

SHANE, HAROLD G., *Curriculum Change Toward the 21st Century.* Washington, D.C.: National Education Association, 1977.

————, *Teaching and Learning in a Microelectronic Age.* Bloomington, Ind.: Phi Delta Kappa, 1987.

SHANE, HAROLD G., and M. BERNADINE TABLER, *Educating for a New Millennium.* Bloomington, Ind.: Phi Delta Kappa, 1981.

SULLIVAN, E. A., *The Future: Human Ecology and Education.* Palm Springs, Calif.: ETC Publications, 1975.

THEOBALD, R., *The Rapids of Change.* Indianapolis: Knowledge Systems, 1987.

TOFFLER, ALVIN, *The Third Wave.* New York: William Morrow & Company, Inc., 1980.

Index

Academic freedom, 150
Accountability, 147, 243
Accountability committees, 243
Acculturation process, 195
Adler, Mortimer, 36–37, 56–57
Administrative decisions, 147–148
Adolescents, influences on, 113–119
Affirmative action, 134, 147
AFL/CIO, 14, 158
AFT. *See* American Federation of
     Teachers
Afro-Americans, 188–190
Agriculture, decline of, 157
Aid to schools, 93
Alienation, 126
Alternative School Law (Florida), 235
Alternative schooling, 233–255
Alternatives
     assumptions, 247–249
     evaluation, 246–249
     future of, 251, 327–336
     rationale, 249–250
     taxonomy, 238
Alum Rock School District, 244–245
Amendments, constitutional, 89, 90, 92,
     140, 173, 219–220
Amendments, proposed constitutional, 93
"American Creed," 85–87
*American Education: The Colonial Experi-
     ence* (Cremin), 258
American education, history of, 256–283
American Federation of Teachers (AFT),
     12–15, 53, 141, 148, 245
American High School Today, The (Con-
     ant), 160–161, 271
Analytic process, 67
Anthropological models, 287–290
Aquinas, Thomas, 69, 70, 218
Arbitrary action, 16–17

Aristotle, 69, 98, 218
Asian Americans, 192–193
"Asian Century," 136
Assimilation process, 195, 209
Association for Supervision and Curricu-
     lum Development (ASCD), 62
"At risk" students, 139
Athletics, 219–220, 224–225
Atkinson, John, 229
Atomistic education, 302–304
Authority centered teacher, 8
Autonomy, theme of, 6
Axiology, 68

"Back-to-basics," 34, 147
Bacon, Francis, 70
Bakke case, 202
Banks, James, 187
Barnard, Henry, 143, 261, 264
Barr, Robert, 235
Beatty, Willard, 241
Bell, Daniel, 314–316
Bell, Idding, 271n
Bell, Terrell, 43
Bellow, Saul, 24, 78
Benjamin, Harold, 81
Bennett, William, 35, 200n
Bereiter, Carl, 273, 275, 278
Berg, Ivar, 169–170
Bestor, Arthur, 28, 32, 34, 39, 271n
"Big Bang" theory, 98–99
Bilingual education, 133, 149
*Bill for the More General Diffusion of
     Knowledge*, 1779 (Jefferson), 260
Blinder, Alan, 30n, 46
Bloom, Allan, 36
*Board of Education of the Hendrick Hud-
     son Central School District* v. *Rowley*,
     32

Bornstein, Rita, 216
Borrowman, Merle, 257, 272
Boulding, Kenneth, 107, 154, 168, 303,
    314
Bourgeois capitalism, tradition of, 84–85
Bowles, Samuel, 153
Bowyer, Carlton, 67
Boyer, Ernest L., 1, 24, 39, 49–50
Bradely Commission on History in
    Schools, 44–45
Brameld, Theodore, 76, 270
Brauner, Charles, 65
British infant school, 239, 299
Brodinsky, Ben, 97
Broudy, Harry, 155, 248
Brouerman, Inge, 228
Brown v. *The Board of Education,* 31, 134,
    177, 190, 191, 199–200, 204
Bruner, Jerome, 30
Bureau of the Census, U.S., 323
Bureau of Indian Affairs, U.S. (BIA), 194
Bureaucratic structure of schools, 263–265
Business and industry, 134–135, 158–159,
    162
Busing, 203–204
Butts, R. Freeman, 89n, 156, 157, 256n,
    259–260, 265

Calvinism, 85
Capital (Marx), 123
*Cardinal Principles of Secondary Educa-
    tion,* 267–268
Carnegie Council on Adolescent Develop-
    ment, 38, 53–54
Carnegie Foundation for the Advance-
    ment of Teaching, 38, 48
Carnegie High School Curriculum, 40
Carter, James, 261
Case, Barbara, 247
Channing, William Ellery, 262
Character development, 263
Character education, 95–96
Chavez, Cesar, 192
Child care. *See* Custodial care
Children, influences on, 113–119
China, 288, 298, 300
Chodorow, Nancy, 213n, 214
Choice. *See* Public schools of choice
Citizenship education, 44–46, 99–101,
    136–137, 277
Civil rights, 15–17, 187
Civil Rights Act of 1875, 189
Civil Rights Act of 1964, 187, 199, 200,
    218

Civil rights movement, 94
Class bias. *See* Social class, bias
Classroom, 10–12, 51–54, 229–230
Closing of the American Mind, The
    (Bloom), 36
Coalition of Essential Schools, 50–51
Cohen, David, 32, 38
Coleman, James, 173n, 177–178, 203–204,
    244
Coleman Report, 203–204
Coles, Robert, 198
Collective bargaining, 148
College graduates, 164–165, 166–168
Colonial America, education in, 257–259
Commager, Henry Steele, 25, 27
Committee of Ten on Secondary Studies
    of the National Education Associa-
    tion (1892), 266
Common School, 261–262
Communism, 122–123
Community activity, 112–113
Community consensus, 94
Community control, 243
Compulsory education, 250–251
Conant, James, 28, 160–161, 172, 271
Conflict in education, 30–41, 131
Conservative tradition, 72–74
Conservative value orientation, 289
Constitution, U.S., 49, 140, 175, 250
Contemporary issues, 24–60
Contemporary traditional future, 328
Content centered teacher, 9
Control of the profession, battle for,
    13–15
Convivial learning, 274, 336
Corporate voluntarism, 264n
Costs of schooling. *See* Expenditures, pub-
    lic schooling; Financing schooling
Counting by Race (Eastland), 202
Counts, George, S., 76, 270
Creationism, 98–99
Cremin, Lawrence, 119–121, 234, 256n,
    257–258, 268, 270, 278
*Crisis in the Classroom: The Remaking of
    American Education* (Silberman), 31,
    239–240
Critical thinking, 34, 66
Cuba, 300
Cultural assimilation, 187–188
Cultural literacy, 42, 147
*Cultural Literacy: What Every American
    Needs to Know* (Hirsch), 34, 41–42
Cultural pluralism, 148, 209–210. *See also*
    Ethnicity

Curriculum, 40-54, 57, 62-63, 72-75, 88, 98, 99, 148, 221, 276, 326
Custodial care, 107, 108, 112, 275

Danish folk high schools, 295
Darwin, Charles, 70-71
Deal, Terrence, 237
Decentralization, 243
Democracy and Education (Dewey), 74-75, 270
Democratic localism, 264n
Demystification, 124
Dennison, Edward, 167-168
Dennison, George, 240
Department of Education, U.S., 141
Deschooling Society (Illich), 31, 273-274, 335-336
Desegregation, 31-32, 199-200, 205
Dewey, John, 28, 62, 66, 70, 72, 74-75, 119-120, 240, 249, 269-270
Discipline, 54-55
Discrimination, 16-17, 197-198, 225
District power equalizing, 179
Dollard, John, 196
Doyle, Denis, 51
Dred Scott decision, 189
Dreeben, Robert, 115-116
Due process, 19

Eastland, Terry, 200n, 202
Eclectic agenda, 26
Ecology of education, 278
Economic competitiveness, 158
Economic development, 136, 157, 285-287
Economic growth, 157, 164, 167-168
Economics, 44, 46, 184
Economics of education, 153-185
Economy, U.S., 153, 156, 162-163
Edgewood v. *Kirby*, 174
"Education 2015," 324-327
Education and Jobs: The Great Training Robbery (Berg), 169
Education and the Rise of the Corporate State (Spring), 160
Educational foundations, 179-180
Educational futures, 307-342
Educational models, 291-304
Educational psychology, 241
Educational reference services, 336
Educational scenarios, 327
Educational Testing Service (ETS), 226
Educational Wastelands (Bestor), 35
Egerton, John, 56
Egypt, ancient, 97

Eight Year Study (1932-1940), 242
Einstein, Albert, 70
Elementary and Secondary Education Act (ESEA), 30, 32, 142, 276
Elite-oriented Education, 291-293
Elliot, Charles, 266
Emerson v. *Board of Education*, 90-91, 93
Enculturation, 288
Engle v. *Vitale*, 91
English, 42-43
English Only movement, 133, 139
Ennis, Robert, 66-67
Epistemology, 68
Equal Rights Amendment (ERA), 218-219
Equality of educational opportunity, 142, 149, 170-171, 182-183, 203
Equity, 27-30, 38-41, 276, 304
Eron, Leonard, 118
Essentialism, 28, 34, 36, 71, 72-73, 77
Establishment clause, 90-91, 92
Ethnic groups, 133-134, 139
Ethnicity, 186-212
European Economic Community (EEC), 286
Evaluative process, 67
"Evolutionary Science," 99
Evolutionism, 98-99
Excellence, 27-30, 38-41, 276, 304
Excusal, 90
Existentialism, 77-79
Expenditures, public schooling, 154, 168-169
Experience and Education (Dewey), 270
Experimental Communal future, 328, 333-335
Extrapolationist type, 309-313

Family, influence of, 113-114
Family Rights and Privacy Act (1974), 19
Fantini, Mario, 235
Feagin, Clairece, 215n, 220n
Feagin, Joe R. 215n, 220n
Featherstone, Joseph, 240
Federal government, role of, 140-142, 176
Feminine Mystique, The (Friedan), 215
Finance reform, school, 178-182
Financing schooling, 144, 153-155, 172-178
Finn, Chester, 34, 42-45
"First Curriculum," 25, 118
France, 292-293
Franklin, Benjamin, 27, 260
Free exercise clause, 91-92
Free Schools (Kozol), 234-235

Freedom, 16
Freedom and Beyond (Holt), 273
Freedom of association, 18
Freedom of the press, 18
Freedom of religion, 18
Freedom of speech, 16–17, 89–90
Freeman, Richard, 166
Friedan, Betty, 215
Friedman, Milton, 244
Futures, educational and societal, 307–342
Futurists, types, 308–322

Gagnon, Paul, 44
Galbraith, John K., 155
Gemeinschaft, 334–335
Gender, education and, 213–232
Gender identity, 213–215
General education, 108
Geography, 46
Gesellschaft, 334–335
Gintis, Herbert, 153
Giroux, Henry, 129n, 277
Glasnost, 294
Glatthorn, Allan, 233n, 236
Global education, 100–101
Globalism, 99–101, 171
Goal centered teacher, 10
Goodlad, John I., 1, 10–11, 34, 38, 45,
    49–50, 52
Goodman, Paul, 275
Goslin, David, 109, 111, 112
Grades, 226
"Great Books," 36, 74
Great Depression (1930), 75
Greece, ancient, 98
Greene, Maxine, 78
Growth of schooling, 157–159
Guardian centered teacher, 8
Guidance programs, 161

Handicapped children. *See* Mainstreaming
Harman, Willis, W., 319
Harvey, O. J., 9
Hawkins, David, 64, 240
Head Start program, 334
Heilbroner, Robert, 123
"Hidden curriculum," 88, 94, 124, 162, 274
*High School: A Report on Secondary Edu-
    cation in America* (Boyer), 39, 49–50
Higher education
    attendance, 156–157
    economic return of, 164–168
    women in, 226–229
    See also College graduates

Hirsch, E. D., 34, 41–42
Hispanic Americans, 190–192, 206
History, 43–46
Holding function, 161–162
Holt, John, 240, 273
Home study, 250–251, 279–280
Horizontal education, 299–302
Horner, Matina, 229
Households, female-headed, 172
Human capital, 164–165, 183
Human nature, 73, 78
Humanistic traditional future, 328–330
Hutchins, Robert, 28, 36, 73, 183

Idealism, 69
Ideologies, 84–97
Illich, Ivan, 31, 155, 273, 335–336
Immediacy, theme of, 6
Incidental education, 120, 270
Indian Heritage of America (Josephy), 193
Indian Reorganization Act of 1934, 194
Individualism, 75, 77–79
Individuality, theme of, 6
Indoctrination, 108
Industrial society, 315
Industrialization, 157–158
Informal education. *See* Open schools
Informality, theme of, 6
Information revolution, 332–333
Institutional racism mode, 216
Institutional rigidity, 272–273
Institutions
    economic, 162–163
    of learning, 120–121
    of society, 123
    See also Society
Integration, 200–203, 205, 210
Integrative process, 67
"Intellectual agenda," 53
Intellectual freedom, 19
Intentional education, 120, 270
Interest theory mode, 216
Internal colonialism mode, 216
International Assessment for the Evalua-
    tion of Educational Achievement
    (IEA), 290
International perspective on education,
    284–306

Jackson, Philip, 6, 249
James Madison High School (Bennett),
    35–36
Japan, 164, 285, 297
Jefferson, Thomas, 27, 89, 260–261

Jencks, Christopher, 170, 178, 244
Josephy, Alvin, Jr., 193
Judicial process, 134, 218

Kahl, Joseph, 110
Kahn, Herman, 311
Kalamazoo case (1874), 266
Karier, Clarence, 159
Katz, Michael, 256n, 262–265
Kearns, David, 51, 163, 245, 277
King, Martin Luther, Jr., 190
Kluckhohn, Clyde, 196
Kneller, George, 63–64
Knowledge, types of, 68–69, 80
Kohl, Herbert, 240
Kozol, Jonathan, 234–235

Land Ordinance of 1785, 141–142
Language, 133, 222
Lassiez-faire capitalism, 156
Lauderdale, William Burt, 28, 30
Learning, 75, 288–289, 326–327
    configurations of, 120–121
Learning webs, 336. *See also* Convivial
    learning
Lemon v. *Kurtzman*, 91, 93
Lerner, Max, 94
Levine, Daniel, 208
Levittown v. *Nyquist*, 174
Levy, Frank, 171–172
Liberal tradition, 74–75
Liberal transformation of schools, 269–270
Liberman, Myron, 2
Life in Classrooms (Jackson), 6
Lipman, Matthew, 62
Literature, 42–43
Local initiative equalizing, 178
Local school district, 144–149
Lottery, the, 180
Loyalty, 16

McClelland, David, 229
McLuhan, Marshall, 303
Madison, James, 89, 259
Magnet schools, 242
Mainstreaming, 32, 148
Mander, Jerry, 118
Mann, Horace, 27, 56, 143, 261–262, 264
Martin, Jane Rowland, 228
Marx, Karl, 122–125, 163
Maslow, Abraham, 8, 10
Masters, Nicholas A., 129
Mathematics, 46–47

Media, 25, 117–119
Megatrends (Naisbitt), 316
Melting Pot, The (Zangwill), 194–195
Mills, C. Wright, 105n
Minorities. *See* Ethnic groups
Moberly, David, 251
Montessori, Maria, 240
Montessori schools, 242
Moral education, 94–96
"Moral Majority," 97
Morrill Acts of 1862, 1890, 142
Multiethnic education, 208
Multiethnic Education: Theory and Practice
    (Banks), 187–188
Multiple domains. *See* Learning, configu-
    rations of
Multiple options future, 328, 330–332
"Murphy's Law of Economics," 46
Myrdal, Gunner, 85, 216

Naisbitt, John, 316
*Nation at Risk, A: The Imperative for Edu-
    cational Reform*, 30, 32, 34, 38, 48,
    51, 141, 144, 277
National Academy of Sciences, 47
National Assessment of Educational Pro-
    gress (NAEP), 34
National Association for the Advancement
    of Colored People (NAACP), 189–190
National Educational Association (NEA),
    12–15, 245
National Commission on Excellence in
    Education, 285
National Commission on the Reform of
    Secondary Education, 251
National Commission of the Reorganiza-
    tion of Secondary Education (1918),
    267
National Defense Education Act (1958),
    142
National School Boards Association
    (NSBA), 95
Nationalism, 99–101
Native Americans, 193–194, 206
NEA. *See* National Educational Associa-
    tion
Neo-Marxism, 123–124
Neo-realism, 70
Neo-Thomism, 70
New England Primer, 257–258
Nicaragua, 292, 300–302
Nolan, Robert, 237
Nonsexist classroom, 229–230

Norms
  achievement, 116
  changes in, 86
  independence, 116
  social, 116
  specificity, 116–117
  traditional, 85–86
  universalism, 116–117
Northwest Ordinance of 1787, 141–145

Occupations, 316
Office of Economic Opportunity, 244
One Best System, The (Tyack), 235
O'Neill, Gerald K., 311–313
Ontology, 68
Open Living School, 331
Open Schools, 239–242
Options, school districts, 331–332
Ornstein, Allan, 208

Pacific islanders, 192–193
Padiea Proposal, 36–37, 56–57
Parental choice. *See* Public schools of
  choice
Parker, Francis, 241, 268
Partial Technological Deschooling future,
  328, 332–333
Paternalistic voluntarism, 264n
Patriarchy, 217–218
Paul, Richard, 61–62, 66
Peer group, influence of, 114–115
Peer-matching, 336
Perennialism, 71, 73–74, 77
Perestroika, 294
Person/Planet (Roszak), 319–320
Personal appearance, 18–19
Personal income, 164–165, 171, 173
Pestalozzi, Johann, 261
Philosophy
  defined, 65–66
  educational, 241
  a process, 66–67
Philosophies of education, 61–83
Piaget, Jean, 240
Place Called School, A (Goodlad), 34, 38
Place-centered alternatives, 237
Plato, 69, 218
Plessy v. Ferguson, 189
Plowden Committee, 239
Political models, 287–290
Politics (Aristotle), 218
Politics
  battlegrounds in education, 146
  defined, 130–131

educational, 130–131
  educational influences on, 135–137
  political parties, 132–133
Politics of education, 129–152
Postindustrial society, 314–316
Postman, Neil, 25, 49, 55, 118
Pragmatism, 70–71
Prayer in school, 91
Preindustrial society, 315
Prejudice, 195–199
Problems in Education and Philosophy
  (Brauner), 65
Process of Education (Bruner), 30
Production-oriented education, 293–297
Productivity of schooling, 168–169
Profession, defined, 2
Professional teacher, 1–23
Program-centered alternatives, 237
Progressive Education Association, 242
Progressive movement, 28, 234, 270–271
Progressivism, 71, 74–75, 77, 268–271
*Proposals Relating to the Education of
  Youth in Pennsylvania* (Franklin), 260
Proposition 13, 179–180
Protestant bias, 265
Protestant ethic, tradition of, 84–85
Public Education (Cremin), 278
Public Law 94–142. *See* Mainstreaming
Public schools of choice, 245–246
Public Schools of Choice (Fantini), 235
Puritan temper, tradition of, 84–85

Race, education and, 186–212
Racial attitudes, 204–208
Ravitch, Diane, 34, 42–45, 202, 209
Raywid, Mary Ann, 239
Reactionary value orientation, 289
Realism, 70
Reconstructionism, 71, 75–76, 77, 269–270
Reform, 48–54, 271–273
Reimer, Everett, 31, 107, 111, 112, 273,
  278
Religious ideologies, 96–99, 134
Religious observances, 92–93
Religious schools, aid to, 93
Republic, The (Plato), 218
Restructuring, 51–54
Revenue sources, 175–176
Revisionism, 162
Revolutionary value orientation, 289
Riesman, David, 110
Rice, Joseph, 268
Rogers, Carl, 8, 10
Rogers, Vincent, 240

Romantic Total Deschooling future, 328, 335–336
Romer, Nancy, 213–214
Roszak, Theodore, 319
ROTC programs, 142
Russell, Bertrand, 64, 70
Ryans, David, 6

Saber-Tooth Curriculum (Benjamin), 81
Sadker, David, 223
Sadker, Myra, 223
Salaries, 154, 170, 228
San Antonio Independent School District v. *Rodriguez*, 174
Sarason, Seymour, 6
Scholastic Aptitude Test (SAT), 206, 225–226, 322
School boards, 137–138
School Is Dead, (Reimer), 31, 273–274
School District of Abington Township v. *Schempp*, 91
School holidays, 101–102
School and Society (Dewey), 269
School year, length, 51–52
Schooling industry. *See* Expenditures, public schooling; Financing schools; Revenue sources
Schools
  bureaucracies, 263–265
  changing, 261–263
  construction of, 154
  enrollments, 138, 156, 201
  influence of, 115–117
  organizational levels, 139, 149
  political institutions, 54
  reducing burden on, 182
  resources, 177–178
  social functions of, 108–113
Schultz, Theodore, 167–168
Science, 46–47
"Scientific Creationism," 99
Scientific movement, early, 70
Secular humanism, 97–98
Secular ideologies, 96–101
Segregation, 197–198
Self-centered teacher, 9
Serrano v. *Priest*, 144, 173, 174, 176
"Seven Cardinal Principles." *See Cardinal Principles of Secondary Education*
Sex discrimination, 215–216, 218, 225
Sex Role Cycle, The (Romer), 213–214
Sex roles, 214–215, 220–229
Sexism, 215–217
Shanker, Albert, 53–54

Shopping Mall High School, The (Powell, Farrar, Cohen), 32, 41
Silberman, Charles, 31, 56, 120, 239–240, 272
Sizer, Theodore, 50, 53–54, 272
Skill exchanges, 336
Skills, 107
Smith, Adam, 156, 244
Smith, Gerald, 239, 247
Smith-Doran Act (1917), 142
Smith-Lever Act (1914), 142
Social capital, 164
Social change, education and, 122, 137. *See also* Futures, educational and societal
Social class
  acquired characteristics, 110
  ascribed characteristics, 110
  bias, 115
  structure, 123
Social indicators, 323
Social institutions, 94
Social reconstructionism. *See* Reconstructionism
Social-role selection, 108, 109–112
Social studies, 43–46, 99
Sociological perspectives in education, 105–128
Socialization, 106–119, 136–137, 220–229
Society
  economic, 156, 163–164
  futures, 307–342
  nature of, 105–106
  postindustrial, 158
  relationship to education, 106–113, 273–276
  sex roles in, 225
Sorting Machine, The: National Educational Policy Since 1945 (Spring), 136
Soviet Union, 137, 285, 293–297
Specialized education, 108
Speculative process, 67
Spring, Joel, 136, 160, 162–163
Sputnik, 24–25, 285
State board of education, 143, 144–146
State government, role of, 142–144, 176
Steinberg, Stephen, 209
Steiner, Rudolf, 326
Stereotyping, 215. *See also* Sex roles
Structural inclusion, 187–188
Structure of education, 129–152
Student-centered alternatives, 236
Students
  achievement, 125

Students (*cont.*)
  behavior, 54–55
  legal rights of, 17–19
  role, 109–112
  status, 109–112
Superintendent of schools, 146, 147
Swann v. *Charlotte-Mecklenburg Board of Education*, 31

Tanzania, 298
Task centered teacher, 9
Teach Your Own (Holt), 272
Teachers
  attitudes, 223–224
  behavior, 8–10, 52–54, 95, 223–224
  burnout, 11
  demand, 13
  legal rights of, 15–17
  models, 7–10
  organizations for, 12–15
  supply, 13
Teaching
  art of, 3–10
  as moral activity, 64
Teaching as a Moral Craft (Tom), 62
Television, 25, 49, 117–119
Testing, sorting and, 160–161
Textbooks, 52, 221
Thermostatic view, 49
Thomism, 70
Thurow, Lester, 123, 169
Tinker v. *Des Moines School District*, 89
Title IX, Education Amendment, 219–220, 225
Tom, Alan, 62, 64
Traditional education, 28
Training, 159–160
Transformation of the School, The (Cremin), 107, 119–121, 268
Transformationist, 318–319
Transitionist type, 313–318
Trends, educational, 312
Truly Disadvantaged, The (Wilson), 206
Tucker, Jan, 44
Tuition tax credit, 181–182, 332
Twenty-first century, 49–51
Tyack, David, 235, 276

Unemployment rates, 166
Universal-access education, 297–299
Universal schooling, 265–268
"U.S. English" movement, 133

Values
  conflicts, 26–27, 84–104
  democratic orientation, 85, 95
  emergent, 87–88
  moral, 89–90
  nature of, 80
  in school, 80, 84–104
  in society, 84–104, 112
  traditional, 85–88, 276–278
Vietnam war, 94
Violence, 55
Vocational programs, 160, 161–162
Vouchers, educational, 244–245, 332

Waldorf Schools, 326
War and Peace in a Global Village (McLuhan), 303
War on Poverty, 142
Wealth of Nations (Smith), 156
Weber, Max, 85
Western philosophy, tradition of, 84–85
Western society, 78–79, 97
What Do Our 17-Year-Olds Know? (Ravitch and Finn), 34, 42–43
White flight, 204
Whitehead, Alfred North, 70
Wilson, William Julius, 206
Winning the Brain Race: A Bold Plan to Make Our Schools Competitive (Doyle and Kearns), 51
Wisconsin v. *Yoder*, 92
World Citizen Curriculum, 100
World Development Report (1988), 286
World education, 302–303

Yankelovich, Daniel, 85–87

Zangwill, Israel, 194